The Soviet Dream World of Retail Trade and
Consumption in the 1930s

Consumption and Public Life

Series Editors: Frank Trentmann and Richard Wilk

Titles include:

Mark Bevir and Frank Trentmann (*editors*)
GOVERNANCE, CITIZENS AND CONSUMERS
Agency and Resistance in Contemporary Politics

Daniel Thomas Cook (*editor*)
LIVED EXPERIENCES OF PUBLIC CONSUMPTION
Encounters with Value in Marketplaces on Five Continents

Nick Couldry, Sonia Livingstone and Tim Markham
MEDIA CONSUMPTION AND PUBLIC ENGAGEMENT
Beyond the Presumption of Attention

Amy E. Randall
THE SOVIET DREAM WORLD OF RETAIL TRADE AND CONSUMPTION
IN THE 1930S

Kate Soper and Frank Trentman (*editors*)
CITIZENSHIP AND CONSUMPTION

Harold Wilhite
CONSUMPTION AND THE TRANSFORMATION OF EVERYDAY LIFE
A View from South India

Forthcoming:

Jacqueline Botterill
CONSUMER CULTURE AND PERSONAL FINANCE
Money Goes to Market

Roberta Sassatelli
FITNESS CULTURE
Gyms and the Commercialisation of Discipline and Fun

Consumption and Public Life
Series Standing Order ISBN 978–1–4039–9983–2 Hardback 978–1–4039–9984–9
Paperback
(*outside North America only*)

You can receive future titles in this series as they are published by placing a standing order.
Please contact your bookseller or, in case of difficulty, write to us at the address below with
your name and address, the title of the series and the ISBN quoted above.

Customer Services Department, Macmillan Distribution Ltd, Houndmills, Basingstoke,
Hampshire RG21 6XS, England

The Soviet Dream World of Retail Trade and Consumption in the 1930s

Amy E. Randall
Santa Clara University, USA

First published 2008 by
PALGRAVE MACMILLAN

Palgrave Macmillan in the UK is an imprint of Macmillan Publishers Limited,
registered in England, company number 785998, of Houndmills, Basingstoke,
Hampshire RG21 6XS.

Palgrave Macmillan in the US is a division of St Martin's Press LLC,
175 Fifth Avenue, New York, NY 10010.

Palgrave Macmillan is the global academic imprint of the above companies
and has companies and representatives throughout the world.

Palgrave® and Macmillan® are registered trademarks in the United States,
the United Kingdom, Europe and other countries.

ISBN-13: 978–0–230–57396–3   hardback
ISBN-10: 0–230–57396–7   hardback

This book is printed on paper suitable for recycling and made from fully
managed and sustained forest sources. Logging, pulping and manufacturing
processes are expected to conform to the environmental regulations of the
country of origin.

A catalogue record for this book is available from the British Library.

Library of Congress Cataloging-in-Publication Data

Randall, Amy E. (Amy Elise) 1967–
    The Soviet dream world of retail trade and consumption in the 1930s /
Amy Randall.
        p. cm.—(Consumption and public life)
    Includes bibliographical references and index.
    ISBN-13: 978–0–230–57396–3 (alk. paper)
    ISBN-10: 0–230–57396–7 (alk. paper)
        1. Retail trade – Soviet Union. 2. Consumption (Economics) – Soviet
Union. 3. Soviet Union – Economic conditions – 1917–1945. I. Title.

HF5429.6.S63R36 2008
381'.1094709043—dc22   2008016320

10 9 8 7 6 5 4 3 2 1
17 16 15 14 13 12 11 10 09 08

Transferred to digital printing in 2009.

Contents

List of Illustrations   vi

Acknowledgments   vii

Russian Terms, Acronyms, and Abbreviations   xi

Introduction   1

1   A New Approach to Retailing and Consumption:
    The Campaign for Soviet Trade   17

2   The *"Perestroika"* of Retail Trade: Visionary Planning
    for Revolutionary Retailing   44

3   Legitimizing Soviet Trade: Gender and the
    Feminization of the Retail Workforce   67

4   "Revolutionary Bolshevik Work":
    Stakhanovite Retail Labor Heroes   89

5   The *Kontrol'* of Soviet Trade from Above and from Below   112

6   The Making of the New Soviet Consumer   134

7   Soviet Retailing and Consumer Culture in
    Comparative Perspective   158

Conclusion   180

Notes   184

Bibliography   231

Index   245

Illustrations

1.1 A full meal in 20 minutes! Buy food concentrates   33
1.2 Book kiosk, Fergana 1939   34
1.3 Department store, Tashkent 1936   35
1.4 New Year's Eve in *Gastronom* No. 1, Tashkent 1937   38
1.5 Mother and children's corner, store for
  cultured goods, Tashkent, 1933   39
1.6 Demand our tooth powder, tooth paste, perfume,
  face cream, powder   41

Acknowledgments

This book has been a long time in the making, and I am delighted to thank the many people and institutions that have offered encouragement and support over the years.

Santa Clara University provided financial assistance and a Junior Faculty Development Leave – both critical for making final revisions for Palgrave Macmillan. An Area Studies Fellowship from the American Council of Learned Societies, Social Science Research Council, and National Endowment for the Humanities allowed me to revise and complete much of the writing of this manuscript. Grants from the College of Liberal Arts at the University of Mississippi facilitated two summer research trips. Support for earlier stages of research and writing was provided by the Andrew Mellon Foundation and Princeton University, including the Graduate School, Department of History, Council on Regional Studies and the Center for International Studies.

This project began as a doctoral dissertation at Princeton University. I wish to thank my fellow comrades there in Russian and Soviet history: Bob Crews, Loretta Fleurs, Fran Hirsch, and Cynthia Hooper. My special thanks to Laura Bass, Wendy Chun, Rob Cronin, Anore Horton, Danna James, Steven Kantrowitz, Jennifer Kates, Felicia Kornbluh, Paul Kramer, Jessica Meyerson, Nicole Monnier, Gabriella Safran, Chuck Walton, who through their good humor, emotional support, and intellectual insights helped to make graduate school more enjoyable.

Fellow graduate students Peter Blitstein, Jonathan Bone, Nick Breyfogle, Chris Burton, Loretta Fleurs, Rebecca Friedman, Dmitry Gorenburg, Dan Healey, Yoshiko Herrera, Rebecca Balmas Neary, and Joshua Sanborn provided excellent companionship during the year of initial research for this project in Moscow. Subsequent research trips to the motherland have been improved by the camaraderie of Michael David-Fox, Mark Edele, Wendy Goldman, Mark Kramer, Thomas Lahusen, Tracy McDonald, Steven Solnick, and Lynne Viola. These trips have also been made much more interesting and pleasurable by various Russian friends and colleagues, including the Ostrovsky family, Katya Chernyak, Nikolai Khramov, Aleksei Kilin, Sasha Rubchenko, and Sergei Zhuravlev. Raya Ostrovskaya in particular has been a dear friend over the years, opening her home and heart, and cheerfully accompanying me on many Moscow adventures.

At an earlier stage this work benefited from the criticisms and suggestions of many others. Members of my dissertation committee, Laura Engelstein, Stephen Kotkin, Phil Nord, and Elizabeth Wood, deserve my special gratitude. Laura Engelstein, my advisor, set a standard for academic excellence to which I continue to aspire, and offered incisive feedback and critical support. Her important reminder to think of Soviet history in light of its imperial Russian past has left its imprint on my work. Stephen Kotkin, my other advisor, provoked my initial interest in Soviet retailing, and his approach to Stalinism has had an enormous influence on me. I have benefited from his faith in my project as well as his keen academic scrutiny and assistance. Philip Nord introduced me to the history of modern Europe, and pushed me to examine the Soviet Union in the context of European development. Elizabeth Wood read and commented on several drafts with tremendous care and enthusiasm. She inspired me to integrate gender analysis into the study of Soviet history. I am also particularly grateful to Christine Ruane and Jerry Watts, who provided generous and constructive commentary on how to think about reformulating the dissertation into a book. Jerry is additionally one of my oldest mentors and friends, and I cherish our connection.

Parts of this work have been presented at various conferences, colloquia, and workshops. Thoughtful comments and questions from the audiences and discussants, especially from Karen Fox, Ellen Furlough, Wendy Goldman, Julie Hessler, Eric Naiman, Barbara Newman, Rebecca Plant, Christine Ruane, and Jonathan Zatlin, have been much appreciated.

The ideas and suggestions of numerous colleagues and friends have shaped this project. Naomi Andrews, Angela Bonin, Thomas Ewing, David Hoffmann, Barbara Newman, and Rochelle Ruthchild read all or almost all of the manuscript. Their wise comments helped me to improve the final manuscript. Peter Blitstein, David Engerman, Paul Josephson, Stephen Kotkin, Mark Kramer, Barbara Molony, Eric Oberle, Susan Reid, Jessica Shubow, Laura Winkiel, and Elizabeth Wood read one or more chapters. I am grateful to all of these people for taking time out of their busy schedules to offer invaluable feedback and advice.

At Palgrave Macmillan I owe thanks to editor Philippa Grand, editorial assistant Olivia Middleton, Vidhya Jayaprakash and the production team, and the two reviewers, particularly Frank Trentmann.

Many archivists, librarians, and staffs have facilitated my research. I am grateful for the assistance of those at the Russian State Archive on the Economy, State Archive of the Russian Federation, Russian State Archive of Socio-Political History, Central Archive of the City of Moscow,

Central Archive of Socio-Political History of Moscow, State Archive of the Saratov *Oblast'*, Center for the Documentation of Recent History of the Saratov *Oblast'*, Tashkent City Archive, Central State Archive of Uzbekistan Republic, and Central State Archive of Uzbekistan Republic of Films, Photo and Sound Documents. Thanks also to the staffs at Firestone Library, Regenstein Library, the New York Public Library, the Library of Congress, the Russian Historical Library, and the Russian State Library. I am especially indebted to Iuliia Dvoretskaya in the Department of Printed Arts at the Russian State Library for helping me to locate relevant old posters and providing me with many cups of tea and great conversation. Additional thanks to the Russian State Library and the Central State Archive of Uzbekistan Republic of Films, Photo and Sound Documents for permission to reproduce copies of posters and photographs included in the book. I also thank Hurshida Abdurasulova for research assistance.

In addition to the individuals mentioned already, I am grateful to many others. Thanks to friends John Aney, David Belman, Julie Burkley, Mary Dakin, Mark Healey, Doug Howland, Marjorie Levine-Clark, Diana Odynets, Magda Perrera, Ronen Raz, Margaret Sena, Josh Sens, and Jed Smith. Micah Lubensky, Hannah Doress, and Jessica Shubow deserve special thanks for their unflagging affection, great wisdom, and inspiring friendship.

During my time at the University of Mississippi many individuals enriched my experience and helped me to better understand the Deep South: Kirsten Dellinger, Peter Frost, Kees Gispen, Joshua Howard, Scott Kreger, Theresa Levitt, Kevin and Marty McCarthy, Jennifer Nelson, Marie Shadle, and Joe Ward. I am particularly indebted to Nancy Bercaw, Sue Grayzel, and Brett Shadle for their friendship. I owe great thanks also to my colleagues and friends at Santa Clara University, especially Naomi Andrews, Brigitte Charaus, Jane Curry, Karen Fox, Steven Gelber, Judy Gillette, Diane Jonte-Pace, Pedro Machado, Krista Maglen, Barbara Molony, Eric Oberle, Dan Ostrov, Laurie Poe, Nancy Unger. They have provided important intellectual exchange as well as emotional and practical assistance during a time of illness, death, and birth in my family.

I wish to express deep appreciation to my family for their help and encouragement over the years. Among others, I am grateful to Brenda Mendes, and David and Sydney Reed, for providing much-needed support. Thanks to Robert Bonin, my stepfather, for years of affection, and for facilitating my pursuit of learning. I am indebted to Angela Bonin, my mother, for believing in me and my work, and for serving as a model of strength, intelligence, and generosity. Her willingness to read and provide feedback on chapter after chapter of this manuscript went far beyond the call of duty. I owe thanks to my father, Wayne Randall, for his quiet but consistent love, and for teaching me the dignity of retail work. My father was employed in the retail sector his entire life, winning numerous awards for his artistic displays in supermarkets, including a trip to Bermuda. When he competed in a national competition in the 1970s to build the largest display of Ragu products in the world, he won the East Coast award. Had he lived in the Soviet Union in the 1930s it is likely he would have been a Stakhanovite retail labor hero. My father passed away unexpectedly just as I finished final revisions of this manuscript, and I miss him terribly.

This book is dedicated to my mother and to the memory of my father. It is also dedicated to my life partner, Mathew Reed, our son Zeiler Robeson Randall-Reed, and our daughter Zaria Jordan Randall-Reed. Mathew has read and perceptively commented on countless drafts of my work. His brilliance has sharpened my thinking about the Soviet 1930s and many other things. His love and companionship sustain me, and have enabled me to complete this book. Zeiler is a source of unbelievable joy and constant learning. Mathew and Zeiler remind me of what is most important in life, and I am sure that Zaria – a quite recent addition to our family – will do so too.

*   *   *

Earlier versions of parts of two chapters have been published elsewhere: "'Revolutionary Bolshevik Work': Stakhanovism in Retail Trade," *The Russian Review* 59: 3 (2000): 425–41; and "Legitimizing Soviet Trade: Gender and the Feminization of the Retail Workforce in the Soviet 1930s," *Journal of Social History* 37: 4 (2004): 965–90. I am grateful for permission to use these materials here.

In this book I use the Library of Congress transliteration system for Russian. All translations are mine, unless othewise indicated.

Russian Terms, Acronyms, and Abbreviations

GTI	State Trade Inspectorate
FYP	Five-Year Plan
Kolkhoz	Collective farm
Komsomol	Communist Youth League
Krai	Administrative territory
Kulak	Well-to-do peasant
Kul'turnost'	Culturedness
Narkomtorg	People's Commissariat of Foreign and Domestic Trade
Narkomvnutorg	People's Commissariat of Domestic Trade
NEP	New Economic Policy
Oblast'	Province
PRGT	Trade Union of State Trade Workers
PRKGT	Trade Union of Cooperative and State Trade Workers
Rabkrin	Workers' and Peasants' Inspectorate
Tsentrosoiuz	All-Union Central Union of Consumer Cooperative Societies
TsKK	Central Control Commission
Udarnik	Shock worker
VTsSPS	All-Union Central Council of Trade Unions
Zhenotdel	Women's Department of the Communist Party

Introduction

This is a book about Soviet retailing and consumption in the 1930s. In today's post-communist Russia and the nations that once fell under the yoke of the Soviet Union, images and memories of shopping have become iconic. Whether it be surly salesclerks, mostly empty store shelves, window displays of canned sprats stacked in a pyramid, bread shortages, ill-fitting polyester suits, Lada cars, or sickly sweet champagne, the Soviet retail sector and consumer goods have come to epitomize all that was wrong with the socialist system and to explain why in the long run it could not last in the face of a capitalist West more capable of meeting the consumer needs of its citizens. As the writer Slavenka Drakulić noted about communism in Yugoslavia, as soon as people realized that quality toilet paper was a possibility and began to want better paper for themselves, "communism was doomed."[1] This was no less true throughout the Soviet Union.

Strange as it may seem today, there was once a time when retail trade and consumption were heralded as not only central to the socialist revolution but also the stage upon which the limits of capitalism would be exposed. *The Soviet Dream World of Retail Trade and Consumption in the 1930s* looks at this time, examining the Stalinist campaign to create a new "socialist" system of distribution and retailing, what political leaders called Soviet trade (*sovetskaia torgovlia*). Communist authorities launched the campaign in 1931 as a pragmatic response to a structurally untenable situation – a major distribution and consumer goods crisis largely engendered by Soviet policies. Terribly inadequate distribution and retail networks (both in terms of quality and quantity) and extreme scarcity of essential goods fueled popular outrage and social unrest, and in some cases, resulted in violence. In 1930, for example, in response to poor-quality bread and an interruption in supply, hundreds of women

1

and dock workers in Novorossisk wrecked two bread shops, demonstrated in front of the city *soviet* (elected council), and beat three local officials.[2] Retail problems and shortages also contributed to rapid labor turnover and decreased worker morale and productivity. Workers frequently left jobs in search of better living conditions, including food supplies, and wasted hours every day in line for goods.[3] Faced with a dire situation that threatened to further undermine social stability and impede rapid industrialization, the *raison d'etre* of the First Five-Year Plan (1928–1932), the Stalinist regime was forced to confront a major question: What was the place of retailing and consumption in a socialist society? Never before in history had there been an entirely state-run "socialist" economy, nor was there a blueprint of how to create one. The Stalinist regime faced the challenges of mass distribution and consumption with no clear plan.

Although the campaign was initially a pragmatic strategy for managing an economic crisis, as the campaign advanced, Communist authorities promoted a "Soviet dream world" of retailing and consumption. This Soviet dream world differed from the capitalist vision of mass consumption that had already emerged in parts of Western Europe and the United States. In the *capitalist* dream world, which Rosalind Williams and other scholars have explored, exotic department stores, flashy store windows, and new forms of credit encouraged ordinary people to "indulge temporarily in a fantasy of wealth" and material pleasure.[4] The proliferation of consumer goods and new commodity spectacles captured the imagination of consumers, meeting psychological as well as economic needs. In the *Soviet* dream world ordinary people were similarly encouraged to envision the construction of a society of greater abundance from which they would benefit. But in contrast to the capitalist dream world, the Soviet version urged citizens to imagine retailing and consumption as vehicles for fostering socialist goals. Communist authorities conjured up a vision in which the retail sector would become yet another realm of modernity, a realm that would underscore the Soviet Union's victory over backwardness and complement the technological and industrial utopia of the Moscow metro, the Magnitogorsk Metallurgical Complex, and the Moscow–Volga Canal. They imagined a retail system that would overcome its primary association with corruption and counterrevolutionary elements and become instead a site of socialist acculturation, heroic labor, and mass participation. They envisioned a new world of consumption, in which consumerism would function as a symbol of and device for cultural refinement and modernization, a new productivist consumer culture would emerge, and consumers would become cultivated and socially integrated citizens. What is more, the pursuit of this dream world contributed to the transformation of the economy, society, and socialism.

The 1930s campaign for "Soviet trade" marked a new direction for social and economic policy. As the construction of "socialist" retailing became an important party-state objective and authorities took on the task of developing a union-wide and more modern system of distribution, the retail infrastructure changed dramatically. Hundreds of thousands of new stores and stalls opened, tens of thousands of shops received renovations (e.g., heat), and many commercial venues acquired new retail tools and technologies. To meet the needs of the expanding system and "Bolshevize" the retail workforce, Soviet officials hired tens of thousands of new workers and expanded previous efforts to educate employees in the cooperative and state trade system. They also employed women en masse, promoted a retail labor hero movement, and encouraged hundreds of thousands of ordinary people to participate in the mass monitoring and regulation of retailing.[5] Although some Soviet republics (particularly the Russian and Ukrainian Republics) gained considerably more retail outlets than other republics, urban areas and state trade venues benefited more from retail reform than rural areas and cooperative trade venues, and massive problems and failures accompanied reform efforts, the trade campaign nonetheless resulted in significant changes. In conjunction with retail reform, Communist leaders and policymakers adopted new policies to increase the mass production of foodstuffs and consumer goods. Ultimately, manufacturing remained terribly insufficient given overall demand. But the subsequent increases in output in the mid-1930s were not insignificant, particularly in light of the pathetic production levels of essential and nonessential commodities during the First Five-Year Plan (FYP). Although expanded goods production never came close to satisfying people's needs, consumers had a better chance of finding many items in 1937 than in 1932. In a striking change from the 1920s, the government additionally recognized Soviet people as not only workers but also consumers. Moreover, Soviet authorities realized that consumers could be incorporated into the building of socialism, and mobilized them on behalf of retail reform. They also legitimized consumer demand, and began to endorse a seeming contradiction in terms: Soviet consumer culture. Paradoxically, Communist leaders promoted a new politics of retailing and consumption even as scarcity persisted, famine struck, and the economy continued to prioritize industrial production at the expense of basic daily necessities.

The challenges of making retail trade and consumption "socialist"

The project to remake retailing and consumption in the 1930s was complicated both practically and ideologically by their history, not only in the recent past but also in prerevolutionary Russia. Establishing a state-controlled retail system for a population of approximately 150 to 160 million would have been a formidable undertaking for any government. But the Stalinist regime faced a particular disadvantage: an extremely underdeveloped commercial infrastructure. This problem was a product of prerevolutionary structures of retailing and earlier Soviet trade policies. During the late 1800s and early 1900s Tsarist Russia witnessed considerable commercial growth. But even though the number of large urban stores, retail arcades, department stores, and small shops burgeoned, bazaars and petty trade remained central to retailing, and the formal retail network was small in comparison to those in more advanced industrialized countries. Moreover, fixed retail venues were concentrated in major urban centers, creating "enormous 'trade deserts' throughout the Russian Empire, particularly in rural and national regions."[6] After the Revolution and during the Civil War, Julie Hessler notes, the Bolsheviks promoted antitrade policies that contributed to the "degradation of trade" and devastated the already limited commercial infrastructure.[7] Even when the Bolsheviks reversed course in 1921 and officially sanctioned private retailing, the number of private large-scale stores and small shops never reached prewar levels during the 1920s.[8] When the Stalinist regime launched a major offensive against private retailing in 1928, the formal private retail trade network disintegrated even further. By 1929 the number of private shops and stalls dropped to less than 15 percent of what had existed in 1926/1927, and by 1930, almost all private shops had closed. Although the socialist sector of cooperative and state trade expanded significantly in the 1920s, its increased stock of retail venues did not compensate for the destruction of private outlets.[9] By 1931 the retail infrastructure as a whole was so decimated that it amounted to "less than one-fifth of the pre-Revolutionary average" per person, providing only "12.5 stores, shops, and stalls" for every ten thousand residents.[10] Meanwhile, the regime's drive for rapid industrialization and its forced collectivization of agriculture in the late 1920s fostered mass urbanization and a huge expansion of the wage labor force, which intensified and created significant new consumer demand just as there were greatly reduced official mechanisms for the manufacture and distribution of goods. Between 1928 and 1932, approximately 12.5 million individuals entered the urban workforce, with 8.5 million from rural areas.[11] This demographic shift increased both the number and proportion of individuals who did not produce the bulk of food and material goods they needed on a daily basis, and resulted in considerably greater concentrations of people who needed to rely on a commercial sector for access to basic foodstuffs and commodities. Communist leaders launched the trade campaign with a major structural problem: a formal commercial sector that was entirely inadequate for handling the volume of retailing necessary for the vast population and changing demographics of the Soviet Union.

The Stalinist regime's decision to move away from its prior emphasis on asceticism and to promote increased consumption levels among the Soviet population was similarly fraught with practical difficulties. Although the regime endorsed a significant increase in the production of consumer goods during the Second FYP (1933–1937), initial target goals were clearly insufficient for meeting mass demand, and were then adjusted downward because of the Stalinist regime's decision to continue to sacrifice domestic consumption for the cause of rapid industrialization.[12] Even these plans proved difficult to meet because of the Soviet Union's insufficient infrastructure for producing mass consumer goods: artisanal manufacturing had collapsed due to recent Soviet economic policies, and industrial manufacturing was oriented overwhelmingly to capital goods production. By assuming responsibility for the expanded mass production of mass consumer goods without the necessary resources, the Soviet regime created a thorny situation. The logistical and planning nightmare of figuring out which regions needed what goods and coordinating the transport and delivery of items did not make the regime's relative commitment to increased consumption any easier.

The ideological task of rehabilitating the legitimacy of retail trade and consumption in the 1930s, and reconfiguring both as "socialist," was also formidable. Political attitudes toward retail trade and mass consumption, which ranged from ambivalence to hostility during the prerevolutionary period as well as the 1920s, made the task even more difficult. In Tsarist Russia many people were critical of the retail sector. Common antipathy existed toward shopkeepers, salesclerks, and petty traders, who were associated with deceptive retail practices and the manipulation of customers.[13] Some people disliked the prominence of Jews and non-Russians in parts of the commercial world. Many members of the aristocracy loathed the growing wealth of merchant elites, which challenged their privileged position in society.[14] Even the very gradual modernization of retailing sparked concerns as it came to be associated with the growing number of foreign stores and retail practices, which some believed threatened Russia's national identity. Critics of modernization counterposed "western" retail practices, such as fixed prices and salesclerks' "icy indifference," to the appealing "conviviality," "disorderliness and freedom" of Russian practices.[15]

Judgmental attitudes about consumption were also carryovers from Tsarist Russia. As a mass consumer culture began to develop in the late nineteenth century, and workers and peasants began to engage in dandyism and a "culture of acquisition," some educated Russians worried about their move away from lives of supposed "simplicity and virtue," and "the corruption of the 'Russian people' by capitalist culture." Many elites were not happy about changing consumption patterns, particularly in the realm of clothing, because they lessened visible distinctions among the classes. Upper-class anxiety about the increasing democratization of dress joined nationalist anxiety that Western clothing styles were displacing Russian styles and contributing to the loss of Russia's distinctiveness.[16] Some critics associated mass consumption with vice and changing gender roles. They feared that shopping for nonessential items unleashed in women an insatiable and almost sexual passion to consume further, leading them to abandon "appropriate 'female' behavior," such as restraint, for "deviant" female behavior, such as greed, which culminated in women's financial ruin and moral downfall.[17] Members of the Russian intelligentsia disavowed the vulgarity and banality (*poshlost'*) of materialism, which hindered a more "spiritually meaningful existence." Russian revolutionaries embraced asceticism as a moral virtue, and renounced the habit of defining oneself and one's social class through one's possessions.[18] Meanwhile, although the lower classes were increasingly involved in a "culture of acquisition," many did not wholly embrace consumerism or the market. The wealth and luxury of the upper classes fueled resentment and social envy, in some cases provoking consumer-oriented protests that led to the ransacking of not only stores but also upper-class homes. In 1897, for example, disgruntled textile workers broke into their director's home, drank his expensive bottles of imported whiskey, smoked his imported cigars, and then lit his house on fire. When provisioning problems became acute, such as during the First World War, popular hostility toward the market and those perceived as profiteers sometimes ended in violence, including the killing of shopkeepers.[19]

Trade policies after the Bolshevik Revolution reflected the new Soviet regime's discomfort with retailing. During the Civil War Bolshevik leaders promoted antitrade policies, and rationed basic foodstuffs and consumer goods. They nationalized and municipalized private shops and made periodic efforts to eliminate petty street trading.[20] In 1921, however, in reaction to economic and political turmoil, Communist leaders adopted the New Economic Policy (NEP), a set of economic policies that reversed many of those instituted during the Civil War, and allowed in the 1920s for the establishment of a mixed economy of state-controlled and privately owned industries, enterprises, and retail trade. Although private trade was technically legal, it was never fully accepted by the Bolsheviks. Throughout the 1920s, private traders and store proprietors faced restrictions, heavy taxation, and prosecution. Communist leaders often identified retail trade with capitalism, corruption, and an ugly materialism, discrediting it as counterrevolutionary and antithetical to socialism. The Soviet press regularly depicted private traders and shopkeepers as greedy and exploitative "Nepmen" (those associated with private businesses), who charged inordinately high prices.[21] When Communist leaders moved the Soviet economy in yet another new direction in the late 1920s by abandoning the NEP-era mixed economy and replacing it with a more permanent economic model – the administrative-command economy – private retailing came under increased attack. As the Stalinist regime assumed more complete state control of the economy, adopted central planning (via the First FYP, 1928–1932, and subsequent plans), launched a drive for rapid industrialization and the forced collectivization of agriculture, and abolished privately owned stores and businesses, Communists increasingly characterized private retailers as an "ideological and economic menace" that had to be overcome.[22]

The Soviet regime was even divided about the socialist sector of cooperative and state trade that supplemented private retailing in the 1920s. As Communists promoted the growth of this sector with the idea that it would increasingly supplant private trade, they sought to reinforce the socialist nature of cooperative retailing. Suspicions lingered, however, because the cooperative movement had originated in the prerevolutionary period as an alternative mode of capitalist retailing, albeit one that was more collectivist. To reconfigure cooperative retailing as socialist, Soviet officials deflated cooperatives' power as independent public organizations by making them into "subsidiaries of the state," subjecting cooperatives to party-state supervision, conducting purges of politically unreliable elements from cooperative bodies, tying cooperatives more directly to the state distribution system, and securing Communist control of the All-Union Central Union of Consumer Cooperative Societies (Tsentrosoiuz), the main coordinating body and then executive organ for cooperatives.[23] To reemphasize the socialist nature of the state retail sector, officials aimed to distinguish it from the private retail sector by showcasing select "model" state stores, such as the State Department Store (GUM) in Moscow, as "modern" retailers that aided in the revolutionary transformation of the economy and society by allowing ordinary people to purchase both high-quality and inexpensive consumer goods.[24] But despite party-state efforts in the 1920s to improve the socialist sector of retailing, shopping in the majority of cooperative and state trade stores remained a dismal and paltry alternative to shopping in the private sector. Communist leaders argued that the cooperative and state trade system failed to meet consumers' needs because it was overrun with greedy "Nepmen" and speculators, conflating it with the private system. Whether privately owned or state-controlled, the official image of retail trade was overwhelmingly a negative one.[25]

Soviet leaders largely condemned consumption as bourgeois and hedonistic in the 1920s, which complicated their efforts in the 1930s to reconcile consumption with socialism. During the NEP era, the Soviet press, communists, and intellectuals regularly decried petty bourgeois and bourgeois material acquisitiveness. Nepmen and Nepwomen came under particular scrutiny for their conspicuous consumerism, but all self-indulgent consumers were excoriated. Communist leaders promoted an antimaterialist aesthetic, rejecting decadence and urging a focus on production, not consumption. The Soviet press, books, and films reinforced this message, contrasting noncommunists as consumers of frivolous and luxury items and communists as uninterested in material items.[26] The newspaper, *Komsomol'skaia pravda*, carried out a campaign against "domestic trash" in the late 1920s to discourage the masses' banal taste for petit-bourgeois objects, urging readers to rid their homes of useless "bric-a-brac."[27]

Official discourse about consumption, however, was contradictory during the NEP era. Communist leaders encouraged Soviet people to consume in a *socialist* way by shopping in cooperative and state stores, instead of private shops, and by purchasing state-manufactured goods, instead of privately made and foreign commodities. Soviet authorities used "agitational" product marketing and advertisements to promote the sale of state-produced merchandise as well as a variety of political messages. State candy wrappers, for example, featured revolutionary terms, images, and slogans, such as "Proletarians Unite." Soviet advertisements politicized consumption by exhorting consumers to purchase goods from cooperative and state stores, depicting Nepmen negatively, and emphasizing the importance of consumption for securing an alliance (*smychka*) between cities and the countryside, between workers and peasants.[28] Constructivist artists sought to replace the capitalist commodity with the socialist object, to replace the fetishized possession with the "comradely object of socialist modernity." Liubov' Popova, for instance, promoted rational clothing designs that celebrated industrial production, replacing "petty bourgeois little flowers" on fabrics with "new and unexpectedly strong and clear patterns."[29] In their efforts to promulgate a new Soviet *byt'* (everyday life) Communists generally castigated materialism, but they also began to link the acquisition of certain items, such as modest clothing, spoons, and soap, to the development of the New Soviet Person.[30] This association of material objects with a new *byt'* became much more pronounced in official discourse in the 1930s, and was critical to legitimizing and redefining consumption as socialist. But despite some ambiguity in its messages about consumption, official discourse in the 1920s overwhelmingly tied consumption to capitalism, and characterized consumerism as contrary to socialism. Moreover, when Communist leaders launched the first FYP in the late 1920s, they prioritized production over consumption and sacrificed citizens' material conditions for the cause of rapid industrialization. As material conditions for the ordinary person declined and scarcity plagued the economy, Soviet officials increased rhetoric about the virtues of self-sacrifice and ascetic living.

Contradictory attitudes about retailing and consumption in prerevolutionary Russia and the 1920s made the 1930s drive to incorporate them into the socialist project particularly challenging. Lingering hostility and suspicion of both created an imperative that they be redefined as socialist, recast as trustworthy, and legitimized within existing ideological frameworks. Communist leaders, trade reformers, and the Soviet press exerted considerable energy and resources to remake retailing, to replace its negative image as a site of backwardness, corruption, and counterrevolutionary personnel with a far more positive image. They sought to redefine consumption by linking it to broader Soviet objectives: industrialization, "democratization," the effort to catch up to and overtake the West, and particularly the party-state campaign to promote *kul'turnost'*, the campaign to civilize people and daily life.[31] Soviet authorities also aimed to legitimize consumption by promoting new consumer practices. These practices were intended not only to further retail reform, but also to remake Soviet consumers into valuable participants in the collective project of building socialism.

Soviet trade and the Stalinist revolution

How should we understand the Soviet dream world of the 1930s? In combination with other changes in Soviet policies and official culture during the mid-1930s (such as the criminalization of abortion and the repudiation of avant-garde cultural production), the Stalinist regime's new approach to retailing and consumption can be viewed as confirmation of the regime's "great retreat" from, if not betrayal of, original revolutionary values and goals, and the "embourgeoisement" of Stalinist policies and attitudes. As Nicholas Timasheff asserts, "The restoration of the freedom of consumption was a conspicuous item in the Great Retreat."[32] The new approach can also be seen as the origins of the "Big Deal" that Vera Dunham argues was firmly established between the Soviet regime and the middle class in the years following the Second World War, in which the regime provided improved material conditions and enhanced consumption opportunities to an expanding middle class in exchange for political and social support.[33] Certainly the Stalinist regime's decision in the 1930s to endorse socialist retailing and Soviet consumerism contributed to the infrastructure and ideological foundation necessary for the regime's postwar promotion of what Dunham views as a more conspicuous and elitist consumerism. Moreover, the new politics of retailing and consumption in the 1930s can be read as a concession to an emerging Soviet elite and their "middle class values," since they benefited the most from the new fancy stores, greater supply of mass consumer goods (including "luxury" goods), and legitimization of consumerism.

Nevertheless, characterizing the new Soviet approach to retailing and consumption in the 1930s as a "retreat" from revolutionary values or socialism is problematic for several reasons. Works by Timasheff, Dunham, and other scholars who reproduce this narrative about the Soviet 1930s have provided important insights about Stalinism. Yet embedded in this interpretation is the idea that the Bolsheviks had a coherent economic trajectory from the outset of the Revolution that they subsequently abandoned. I argue that in fact the trade campaign and consumer policies of the 1930s were the first full-fledged attempt by Communist authorities to address the issues of distribution and consumption under socialism. "War Communism" (the set of economic policies pursued during the Civil War) and the "New Economic Policy" (those of the 1920s) were at best a hodgepodge of contradictory approaches to the question of how to run an economy in an incipient socialist state. While the policies of War Communism and the NEP helped the regime to focus on specific national economic priorities, they did not address the more general and difficult question of how to organize a domestic socialist economy, including retail trade. The regime's new approach to retailing was *not* a retreat from some original revolutionary plan. Moreover, although the Stalinist regime's new approach to retailing and consumption ultimately contributed to Soviet elitism, this approach was initially adopted to manage an economic crisis, not to placate elites. In addition, this new approach reinforced a larger revolutionary goal that remained consistent throughout the early Soviet decades and fluctuations in various policies: to create a new socialist order by building an economy, state, and society that was defined *in opposition* to capitalism.[34]

The narrative of retreat and embourgeoisement is also problematic because it obscures the many ways in which the Stalinist regime's new approach to trade and consumption served to extend the Soviet revolutionary project. As this book shows, authorities promoted the trade campaign to modernize and rationalize the retail sector – a broader socialist objective for the entire Soviet economy – and linked the development of "Soviet trade" to a form of industrialization and state building that was meant to be morally as well as technically superior to capitalist ways. Soviet trade was part of the process by which a rational and efficient industrial socialist order would be achieved. Soviet authorities similarly linked increased consumption and "cultured" consumerism to the building of socialism. They also regarded the trade campaign as a mechanism for Sovietizing people: for incorporating them into the sociopolitical order and inculcating cultured behavior and socialist values. In the 1920s Communist leaders often viewed retail workers, customers, and women as "un-Soviet," as politically ignorant and potentially counterrevolutionary persons. But in the 1930s Communist leaders reconfigured them as Soviet. This book explores this significant shift. How could the rude, unkempt, and politically ignorant salesclerk of the past become a New Soviet Person? How could the irrational and selfish consumer of earlier times be transformed into a socialist consumer? How could the "unproductive" woman of the 1920s become a productive member of society in the 1930s? By deploying negative methods, such as increased *kontrol'* (regulation and surveillance), scapegoating, and repression, and by using more positive methods, such as education, incentives, and a labor hero movement, the campaign exerted pressure on retail employees and trade functionaries to alter their practices and reform the retail sector, and helped to reconstitute them as legitimate Soviet subjects. At the same time, by recognizing the Soviet people as consumers, and not just workers, and by repositioning consumers' role in the broader polity, the Soviet party-state produced a new positive consumer identity. By bringing women into the retail sector as idealized workers, "controllers" (inspectors), and consumer activists, the trade campaign also bolstered women's official status.

Moving beyond traditional studies of industrial workers and peasants to consider a different part of the social landscape of the 1930s, this book shows how the mobilization of hundreds of thousands of retail employees and ordinary Soviet people on behalf of the trade campaign brought many individuals and groups previously left out of the Soviet experiment into the crusade to build socialism. This is not to deny the ways in which the new approach to retailing and consumption contributed to embourgeoisement by enabling some individuals to purchase goods more easily than others, or by helping some people to "fetishize" commodities and use them to distinguish their supposed superiority over others. Indeed, many ordinary people in the 1930s expressed consternation about the conspicuous consumerism of Soviet elites. But for many other individuals the regime's new approach encouraged legitimate consumer pleasure, and allowed them to acquire galoshes, phonographs, eau de cologne, and mass-produced ice cream, all symbols of and vehicles for their transformation into more modern and cultivated Soviet citizens. For retail employees public controllers, and customers, the trade campaign resulted in new prescribed roles and legitimacy. In the Soviet dream world of retailing and consumption, salesclerks could become celebrated labor heroes, public controllers could become important crusaders for "socialist" retail reform, and customers, particularly non-wage earning housewives, could become valuable socialist activists. By adopting a new approach to retail trade and consumption in the 1930s, Soviet authorities helped to enlarge the parameters of socialism.

This book responds to a growing scholarly interest in distribution, retailing, and consumption during the Stalinist 1930s. Until recently these topics were largely overlooked because of a scholarly emphasis on economic planning, industrialization, collectivization, and the politics of repression and the Purges during this decade.[35] Although this book is informed by this recent scholarship, it has a different emphasis. It focuses on the central institutional, cultural, and social changes wrought by the trade campaign, and their implications for the consumer economy, politics, gender, and the history of the Soviet Union. It examines the processes and dynamics of the trade campaign (and the Stalinist system more generally) both "from above" (from the perspective of Communist leaders, Soviet officials, and trade reformers) and "from below" (from the perspective of retail employees, public controllers, consumer activists, and customers). It explores how the Stalinist regime's new approach to retailing and consumption contributed to the emergence of new discourses and social identities, institutions, trade policies, retail strategies, and consumer practices, all of which had numerous, far-reaching, and often contradictory effects. This historical study of the Stalinist response to a problem that continued to plague the Soviet Union to its end – poor retail conditions and goods shortages – straddles economics and politics, and helps to explain ordinary people's growing frustration with the Soviet regime both in the 1930s and in subsequent decades, as they lived under "really existing socialism."

Throughout the book's discussion, two themes in particular will become apparent: how the efforts of trade reformers were shaped and frequently thwarted by socialist ideology and Communist leaders' broader political and economic objectives; and how in producing new social identities and roles for retail employees, public controllers, and consumers, the trade campaign expanded both ordinary people's responsibilities as Soviet citizens to the party-state *and* their possibilities for agency and legitimacy within the Stalinist system. The trade campaign allowed different groups and individuals to shape the new institutions, discourses, practices, and social identities associated with the regime's new politics of retailing and consumption. Of course a caveat is necessary when talking about agency and Stalinism. The agency that the trade campaign made possible coexisted with most people's glaring *lack* of agency in the economy – as Soviet policies consigned them to an often shoddy retail sector and shopping regimen of long lines, shortages, and poor-quality goods. Still, the trade campaign merits closer scrutiny because of what it did *and* did not make possible.

Unlike other studies, *The Soviet Dream World* explores the centrality of gender and women in official narratives and policies about retailing and consumption. As a result, it adds to broader scholarship that uses gender as a category of historical analysis. By exploring how perceptions of sexual difference informed women's mass entry into the retail workforce in the 1930s, this study shows how the feminization of the retail sector contributed not only to a greater number of female workers but also to the gendering of the definition and practices of Soviet trade.

Highly valued attributes of the new Soviet dream world of retailing became coded by authorities and others as "feminine." This study also examines how Soviet officials, trade employees, and the press characterized women public controllers (voluntary regulators) and women consumers as having a particularly valuable role to play in furthering retail reform. But even though women were often idealized as public controllers or activist consumers, the "new Soviet consumer" that was constructed during the trade campaign was never identified primarily or only as female. As a new "socialist" consumer culture emerged in the 1930s, both men and women were expected to shop in a rational, modern, and "cultured" way, and to become *productive* consumers actively involved in economic transformation and state-building. Nonetheless, the positive meanings ascribed to women's paid retail work, voluntary monitoring of the retail sector, and consumer activism afforded women new authority and opportunities. They also reinforced a larger transformation in official Stalinist discourse about women's roles and womanly characteristics in the building of Soviet socialism.

Examining the Soviet dream world of retail trade and consumption is important for understanding not only Soviet history but also the general history of retailing, consumption, and politics in the twentieth century. In the last two and a half decades, the study of consumer societies has flourished. This scholarship has offered a significant window onto the social and cultural aspects of consumption, particularly their importance for group and individual identities, class, and gender. Largely investigating the United States and Western Europe, much of this scholarship has focused on the purchase of goods, the meanings attached to certain commodities, and the new "palaces" and strategies of retailing associated with the emergence of modern consumer societies. A tendency in this literature has been to conflate the rise of mass consumer culture with the triumph of more-or-less liberal democratic political systems, the capitalist marketplace, and American-style retailing and consumerism (despite some acknowledgment of resistance to the latter, and hence the persistence of minor although not unimportant national variations).

More recent scholarship has turned to retailing and consumption in non-Western and nonliberal democratic societies, upsetting the presumed linkage between the development of modern and mass consumer economies with the development of certain political and economic structures and traditions. It has also focused more on the politicization of consumption by political leaders, professional groups, business interests, consumer associations, civic organizations, social movements, and even transnational groups, bringing politics back into discussions of consumption, and highlighting the intersections among governments, ideology, and consumer cultures. *The Soviet Dream World* adds to this growing literature on retailing and consumption in non-Western and nonliberal democratic societies, showing how a socialist system and Eurasian society also promoted a version of modern retailing and mass consumer culture. The Soviet response to the retail crisis of the 1930s provides an illuminating case study of a communist regime's efforts to create a noncapitalist system of distribution that would perform many of the economic functions hitherto provided by capitalism as well as a new kind of consumer: a productive, rational, "cultured," and nonselfish "socialist" consumer.

The Soviet Dream World situates Soviet retailing and consumer culture in a broader international context. Its exploration of the similarities as well as the differences between retailing and consumer cultures in the Soviet Union and advanced industrial countries (especially the United States, Britain, and Nazi Germany) provides insight into both Soviet socialism and the political and socioeconomic systems of other countries. By focusing in particular on government involvement in consumer economies, this book's comparative analysis underscores how other modern governments in the interwar era, like the Soviet government, sought to utilize mass distribution and consumption as tools for mobilizing citizens and promoting political integration, economic stability, and certain cultural values.[36] But it also demonstrates how Soviet interventionism in the consumer economy had important differences from its Western counterparts.

* * *

Soviet trade, which the Stalinist regime officially sanctioned in the 1930s, was an enduring component of Soviet policy and Communist ideology, and helped to frame the institutions and premises of Soviet society for decades to come. Although it reinforced many Communist objectives, it also had unintended effects that worked against the regime's interests and the larger goals of a socialist society. The program of Soviet trade was launched in conjunction with other, equally ambitious economic transformations, specifically the forced collectivization of agriculture and rapid industrialization. Even under ideal conditions, building a state-controlled retail system for a population of approximately 150 to 160 million people would have been a technical and political challenge. When undertaken by a regime that was unwilling to dramatically alter its economic emphasis on industrialization or its political reliance on coercion, the project was Herculean indeed.

The great irony of the 1930s campaign to establish Soviet trade is that it successfully politicized retailing and consumption while failing to provide the Soviet people with a significantly improved retail system or an abundance of consumer goods. Shopping remained an arduous and frustrating experience for most ordinary citizens. Shortages continued to plague the Soviet economy. Given the considerable gap between the rhetoric and reality of retailing and consumption, it is easy to conclude that the new Stalinist approach to both ended up being little more than an ineffective strategy aimed at shoring up socialism in the 1930s. Yet its historical implications are much more significant. During the Cold War, improving the consumer landscape and material conditions of ordinary citizens became central to the competition between the Soviet Union and the West.[37] Meanwhile the Soviet dream world of retail and consumer modernity promoted by the Stalinist regime during the 1930s was never realized in the post-Stalinist Soviet Union. The failure to achieve this dream contributed to the delegitimization of Soviet socialism – and ultimately to its collapse.

1
A New Approach to Retailing and Consumption
The Campaign for Soviet Trade

> I must say that we have really magnificent stores now, both in design and contents. The meat, fish, vegetable, and delicatessen departments are stocked with a wide assortment of high-quality goods. They can be a bit off, but even then only occasionally. But there's plenty of poultry, mutton and fish, with a lot of variety. Lots and lots of canned goods of all kinds, the likes of which we had never heard of before. ... Of course I wouldn't want to say that the stores in Moscow look luxurious, of course not, except the so-called model stores, but in any case over the past 20 years the stores have completely changed and are now unrecognizable. All of them without exception, especially food stores, are clean and orderly, and all the clerks wear white smocks. ... In general people do buy a lot.... When you recall the first years after the revolution and the way things were back then, it's just exhilarating to think that all this has been achieved in just 20 years.[1]
>
> Excerpt from the diary of Galina Vladimirovna Shtange, member of the Soviet intelligentsia, December 1937

Galina Shtange's comments offer a window onto the retail situation in Moscow only six years after the new program of Soviet trade became official policy. Even if Shtange's shopping experience would have seemed fantastic to many Soviet citizens, whose own dingy shops usually had a limited selection of poor-quality merchandise, and even if those familiar with the "magnificent" stores Shtange describes might have disagreed that "in general people do buy a lot," her observations provide a useful snapshot of the government's attempt to deal with the consumer crisis of the late 1920s and early

1930s. Shtange depicts an imperfect but nonetheless transformed retail landscape made possible by the regime's campaign to establish "Soviet trade."

The Stalinist regime's endorsement of Soviet trade in the 1930s was not preordained. As Communist leaders moved away from the NEP-era mixed economy in the late 1920s and essentially destroyed the formal private retail network, the future of Soviet retailing was unclear. There was no grand design for organizing a domestic economy in a socialist system. Economists focused on the failings of capitalist systems "instead of on an economic theory of socialism."[2] As one noted, "little" work had been done regarding "the theoretical realization of the peculiarities of the Soviet economy."[3] Although most Bolsheviks presumed that "product exchange" and "distribution in kind" would be central to a fully developed socialist system, there was little agreement about when or how those those features would be implemented.[4]

Nonetheless, as the formal private retail system collapsed in the late 1920s, many Soviet leaders hoped that money and retailing would soon be replaced with a new "socialist" direction for the domestic distribution of goods: a moneyless system of planned commodity transactions. A government decree in February 1930 appeared to confirm this direction, referring to an upcoming transition "to planned socialist product-exchange."[5] Economists emphasized the need to replace retailing with distributive operations and a nonmonetary system.[6] In November, authorities reorganized the People's Commissariat of Foreign and Internal Trade into the People's Commissariat of Supply (Narkomsnab) and the People's Commissariat of Foreign Trade. The decision to call the new domestic-oriented agency a commissariat of supply rather than of internal trade underscored the regime's profound ambivalence about retail trade, suggesting its future abolition.[7] Yet in 1931 Soviet leaders rejected what had seemed to be the favored direction – the imminent transition to a moneyless system of commodity transactions – for a new direction: the development of a "socialist" retail system that they called "Soviet trade."

The official endorsement of Soviet consumerism in the 1930s, which accompanied the campaign to develop socialist retailing, was also far from inevitable. During the 1920s the Communist leadership had largely dismissed consumerism as self-indulgent and anti-Soviet, and in the drive for rapid industrialization during the First Five-Year Plan (FYP), it emphasized sacrificing consumption on the altar of industrial progress. But in the early 1930s, the regime began to move away from an emphasis on asceticism and to shift the balance between consumer products and heavy industry. Although political leaders still prioritized heavy industry, they sanctioned people's right to better living standards and directed industries to increase the production of foodstuffs and consumer goods. The unfolding campaign to establish Soviet trade legitimized consumer needs, mobilized consumers on behalf of retail reform, and promoted "appropriate" Soviet consumerism.

The Stalinist regime recast both retailing and consumption as integral parts of the Soviet project in the 1930s. An examination of official discourses and policies shows that Communist authorities first promoted Soviet trade and increased consumption primarily for pragmatic reasons, envisioning them as solutions to the major distribution and goods crisis, and as necessary steps for rapid industrialization and continued economic growth. Over time, however, authorities linked them to additional goals, such as fulfilling the material promises of socialism and promoting "democratization." They also assigned cultural importance to Soviet trade and consumption, seeing them as symbols of and vehicles for the modern and civilized transformation of everyday life. In the Soviet dream world of retailing and consumption, Soviet trade and Soviet consumerism became intertwined with the building of socialism, in terms of not only economic imperatives but also social, cultural, and political objectives.

Initial response to the consumer crisis

By the fall of 1929 and the winter of 1930 a major distribution and goods crisis plagued the Soviet Union. Abysmal retail conditions, high prices, and empty store shelves were widespread. Consumers stood hours in lines, even overnight, to purchase ordinary goods. In Grishin, for example, women slept on the streets as they waited their turn to buy apples.[8] Many consumers left stores empty handed. When a cooperative store received a shipment of linen, consumers waited in a long line for three hours, only to be told by the manager that the store would not be selling linen that day. To make matters worse, the scenario was repeated the following day. In response to this treatment, a customer concluded: "This is straight-on mockery."[9] Although this customer did not hold the Communist leadership directly responsible for retail problems and shortages (at least not publicly), many Soviet citizens did. When workers at the Puchezh Mill heard rumors about local difficulties with supplies, they blamed the Soviet regime and threatened "to lay siege" to the cooperative if they did not receive their bread rations. They concluded that the "only difference" between 1905 and 1930 was that when they asked for bread "the tsar treated us to bullets" whereas "the Communists treat us to words."[10]

The Communist leadership's eventual decision to embrace "Soviet trade" was not apparent in its first attempts to deal with this consumer crisis of the late 1920s. Central authorities initially responded by expanding the rationing that local officials had first established in major urban areas in the winter of 1928/1929. As the crisis worsened, policymakers' efforts culminated in a January 1931 decree to establish an all-union system of rationing for the most essential foodstuffs and manufactured goods. But this "all-union" system was by no means comprehensive. The majority of the population, the peasantry, did not receive ration cards, nor did politically stigmatized groups (priests, former Russian aristocrats, and other "social aliens").[11] This system was also notoriously unequal, establishing what scholar Elena Osokina has dubbed a "hierarchy of consumption." In the name of carrying out proper "class" provisioning and rationalized distribution, the government instituted differentiated allocation categories. "Industrial pragmatism" and political interests guided party-state efforts: workers who directly advanced industrial production received a wider assortment of rationed goods and higher ration norms than those who did not; employees in industrial centers received better rations than those in nonindustrial regions; and members of the military and secret police received superior rations. The party-state also privileged its own; top party, government, military, and intellectual elites received better goods and higher ration norms than the most valued industrial workers. But even for those lucky enough to receive ration cards or higher ration norms, rationing failed to meet people's subsistence-level needs.[12]

Authorities additionally responded to the crisis by identifying and repressing scapegoats. In February 1930, party-state organs initiated a purge of personnel from several economic institutions, including Narkomtorg and the All-Union Central Union of Consumer Cooperative Societies (Tsentrosoiuz).[13] In subsequent months many officials and personnel in the cooperative and state trade system were charged with economic crimes like embezzlement, speculation, sabotaging food supplies. In some cases charges ended with execution.[14] As Soviet officials searched for "wreckers" and "embezzlers," they launched a strong critique of consumer cooperatives, which constituted the bulk of the official retail sector at the time.[15] The government directed party, trade union, and state organizations to improve the work of consumer cooperatives, seeing this as critical to managing broader economic and political concerns.[16] At the Sixteenth Party Congress, Stalin criticized consumer cooperatives (and implicitly their personnel) for their "bureaucratism" (excessive bureaucracy) and "Nepman spirit" (profiteering). He claimed this spirit was apparent in cooperatives' preference for "supply[ing] workers with more 'profitable' goods," such as haberdashery, over less profitable but more essential merchandise. Stalin sarcastically queried, "Who needs this kind of consumer cooperative…?"[17] To root out "Menshevik-SR," "bureaucratic," and other "alien" elements in state supply organizations and consumer cooperatives, and to replace "tens of thousands" of "alien" employees "with new, fresh, proletarian forces," Soviet authorities endorsed both punitive measures – greater oversight over and punishment of personnel – and nonpunitive measures – new recruitment and educational efforts.[18] An important part of the subsequent trade campaign, these measures were intended to produce Bolshevik cadres, to turn "a huge army of supply workers" "into a genuinely Bolshevik army."[19]

Retail trade becomes a socialist ideal

By 1931 the Communist leadership's response to the consumer crisis had turned into an explicit campaign to develop "Soviet trade." In February authorities and the press began to use the term "Soviet trade" when discussing the need to transform the existing system of distribution and trade into one of socialist retailing. A *Pravda* editorial asserted that cooperative workers needed to pass through "the school of Soviet trade" and learn to carry out trade "in a Soviet way."[20] The Fifteenth All-Russian Congress of Soviets called on consumer cooperatives to "develop Soviet trade"[21] In May the government asserted, "The abolition of private trade presupposes an all-out expansion of Soviet trade and the development of the network of cooperative and state trade organizations all over the USSR."[22] In July Stalin rebuked cooperative workers for losing their "taste for trade" because they had "won the battle" against private traders. By echoing his own February 1931 proclamation to industrialists about how "technology decides everything" and arguing that workers needed to pursue Soviet trade because "now retail trade decides everything," Stalin ascribed a newfound importance to retailing. The leadership's new mandate to develop Soviet trade was widely covered in the press.[23]

What was this "Soviet trade"? Initial references were vague. Communist leader P. S. Zemliachka argued that most consumer cooperatives had not pursued Soviet trade because "to distribute [was] far easier than to trade." Instead cooperatives manifested "Oblomovism" (laziness), resorting to "mechanical distribution."[24] An October 1931 party resolution similarly counterposed the "mechanical distribution of goods" to Soviet trade. It also declared that Soviet trade had been hindered because "neither the Nepman soul" nor "bureaucratic elements" in the trade system had been vanquished, resulting in the "violation of price policies," the "pursuit of high profits," and "a lack of genuine concern about the consumer."[25] As these comments suggest, authorities envisioned Soviet trade as retailing without corruption, dishonesty, or a "Nepman spirit." They saw it as "cultured" trade, which unlike bureaucratic and mechanical distribution, would be attentive to customers' needs.[26]

Soviet leaders argued that a new system of "cultured Soviet trade" necessitated the elimination of "Asiatic methods" and the adoption of more modern European methods of retailing. These ideas reiterated Lenin's earlier ideas, when he had asserted that to be a competent and cultured trader the Soviet citizen had to adopt a European (as opposed to Asiatic) manner of retailing. Soviet comments also echoed those of prerevolutionary retail modernizers, who contrasted "Asiatic" or "Russian" methods of retailing like trading rows and haggling with more "civilized" European methods like formal stores and fixed prices. Prerevolutionary retail modernizers, Lenin, and retail reformers of the 1930s rejected the disorderly, irrational, and squalid methods they associated with "Asiatic" methods of retailing.[27]

Communist authorities claimed that Soviet trade was unique. It was "socialist and planned trade, in contrast to private free trade." It differed from capitalist retailing like the "sky from the earth" because it furthered socialist construction, strengthened the dictatorship of the proletariat, and improved the position of the working masses.[28] As Stalin explained in January 1933, "Soviet trade is trade without capitalists, big or small; trade without profiteers, big or small. It is a special form of trade which history has not known before and which only we, the Bolsheviks, practice under conditions of Soviet development."[29] At the Seventeenth Party Congress in January 1934, Stalin reasserted the legitimacy and uniqueness of Soviet trade, reminding his audience that "Soviet trade is our own Bolshevik affair," and chastising those who misunderstood this and held a "haughty and scornful attitude" toward it.[30]

Political leaders, economists, and the press often justified the ideological correctness of the turn to Soviet trade by citing Lenin's instructions to Bolsheviks to "Learn to trade" (*uchites' torgovat'*).[31] In the early 1920s Lenin repeatedly asserted that cooperative and state trade workers needed to learn to trade to compete with and eventually replace private traders.[32] By the early 1930s the Stalinist regime had destroyed the official private retail network, but economists asserted that Lenin's slogan still remained relevant. Lenin, they explained, had articulated this slogan not only to strengthen the "struggle against private traders" but also to improve customer service, an objective not yet realized.[33]

Soviet authorities used political and economic arguments to substantiate the trade campaign. As the previous comments suggest, they tied the development of Soviet trade to the removal of politically dangerous and alien elements from the system, and to the eradication of speculative, bureaucratic, and other bad practices. They linked its development to effective labor production and economic growth. The Seventeenth Party Conference in January–February 1932 underscored this last point:

> The development of commodity circulation is of paramount importance for guaranteeing the Bolshevik tempo of growth for the entire economy and for better satisfying the demands of the general public of the cities and countryside in relation to mass consumer goods. The development of commodity circulation, above all retailing ... is an important stimulus for bringing to light the huge and still far from utilized internal resources in our economy ... and itself strengthens the material base of all socialist construction.[34]

The expansion of Soviet trade would stimulate socialist forms of labor and decrease high rates of labor turnover, leading to even greater economic progress. The growth of Soviet trade would also play "an important role in guaranteeing the correct interrelations between town and country," serving as a valuable *smychka* (link) "completely necessary for the socialist reconstruction of agriculture and the success of socialism."[35]

The campaign to develop Soviet trade marked the leadership's rejection of an imminent move to a moneyless system of direct product exchange, reaffirming the continuing role of a monetary economy and retail trade in the socialist order. Trade, so long as it was "Soviet trade," was reconciled with the building of Soviet socialism. Economist Lev Gatovskii, a proponent of direct product exchange in 1930, articulated the regime's new position in 1931, and argued that the final socialist goal of moving to a moneyless system would not be possible until several conditions had been met. This transition required massive accumulation

of manufactured consumer goods, possible only after full-scale industrialization ushered in a post-scarcity economy, and a reconstructed
distribution apparatus – efficient, rational, and customer-oriented –
which would develop via the "school of Soviet trade." The current
system would also have to develop a modernized technical-industrial
base and new methods of inventory management and accounting.[36]
Advocating the implementation of direct product exchange and the
abolition of money in the immediate future now became considered
"anti-Bolshevik." Stalin and others excoriated individuals with these
views. Like "Don Quixote," Stalin asserted, those who held these unre-
alistic "leftist petty-bourgeois" views did not understand that a distribution system based on direct product exchange could emerge only
after Soviet trade had been established.[37]

In July 1934 the Stalinist regime publicly heralded its new commitment to Soviet trade by renaming and reorganizing Narkomsnab into
the People's Commissariat of Domestic Trade (Narkomvnutorg) and the
People's Commissariat of Food Industries (Narkompishcheprom).
Already reclaimed as a legitimate Bolshevik affair, trade was reinstated
in the name of one of the major government agencies in charge of
distributing consumer goods.

Rationing is not a socialist ideal

The rejection of direct distribution in a moneyless economy implied
a repudiation of rationing. Indeed, from the beginning of the trade
campaign authorities characterized rationing as a temporary reaction
to economic crisis, indicating that it would have no place in a fully
developed socialist economy. In May 1931 the government withdrew
most manufactured goods from the rationing system. In October,
A. I. Mikoian, Commissar of Narkomsnab, argued that "rationing
[was] not a socialist ideal" and called for its elimination "as quickly as
possible."[38] The Seventeenth Party Conference in early 1932 designated the abolition of rationing a key goal of the Second FYP, and
soon after, rationing was curtailed even further.[39] Thus, shortly after
the government established a central rationing system, it decided
that this system could not remain an essential feature of the Soviet
economic landscape. Although the centralized supply of rationed
goods was not completely eliminated until the mid-1930s, economic
policy moved in that direction from 1931.

The regime's inability to honor its responsibility to provide
rationed supplies was undoubtedly one reason it decided to repudiate

rationing.[40] But Communist leaders also rejected rationing because they saw it as engendering corruption. In 1931 Stalin lamented:

> How in a worker's government can the supply organs allot rations for workers, but along the road between the workers and the supply organs...the [rations] are stolen? One month, another, a third, fourth, and fifth, there are no rations. The workers are robbed. How can this be?

The rationing system emboldened too many people to steal, gave "shelter to thieves," enabled speculation.[41]

Authorities also considered the rationing system impractical. In 1931 Stalin spoke about its irrationality: "For some reason people have decided that it is not necessary to trade any more," and that "every resident and worker should have their own personal warehouse" so that rations can be allocated "for a month [at a time]." This was "lunacy," because when recipients received their monthly rations all at once, they would receive an impossibly large amount of goods.[42] Moreover, typically rations were not available for purchase throughout the month but for only a few days at a time, contributing to terrible lines and crowds during distribution time. As Mikoian noted, for "ten days a store [was] overloaded" and "the rest of the time the store [was] empty." This was a "bureaucratic system of distribution" that did not safeguard "workers' interests."[43]

Critics lamented the bureaucratic work habits that rationing fostered. In particular they decried the tendency of workers to distribute goods in an "automatic way," without seeing before them a "live buyer," "a customer with individual tastes and needs." "The code of ethics that developed among many trade workers" under rationing was "take what is given." Rationing failed to provide good customer service.[44] In Stalin's view, the elimination of rationing would force trade organizations "to respect the consumer and recognize him as a human being."[45]

Rationing was also unacceptable because it symbolized to the international community the nascent Soviet system's economic difficulties. Stalin told workers:

> A worker's delegation comes from abroad, looks around, and is then directed towards a closed distributor somewhere. It [the delegation] scurries about the city and sees it is impossible to get anything.... Do you think that this order can continue for long? It cannot. The time will come when we will declare all closed stores open, when we will

abolish this rationing system. It is not because of prosperity that we have this rationing system, keep in mind that is it not from prosperity!...We will end this rationing system after one to two years, perhaps.[46]

The repeal of rationing would demonstrate the "growth of the Soviet Union's strength."[47]

Rationing was problematic for two additional reasons. It was expensive to organize. It "require[d] a huge apparatus for distribution," which cost the government approximately 300 million rubles a year. It also impeded labor productivity. Workers received ration coupons regardless of how well they worked, so there was little incentive to work hard. And as Osokina notes, because rationing was inefficient and forced people to waste valuable time in pursuit of their rations, "[p]roduction lost millions of working hands."[48] As the trade campaign progressed, Communist leaders increasingly criticized rationing for thwarting the genuine development of Soviet trade. In 1935 and January 1936, policymakers officially abolished the rationing of bread and any other remaining foodstuffs or manufactured goods still distributed by ration coupons.

The retail infrastructure and consolidation of Soviet trade

As the ideal of a moneyless economy faded from official discourse, it was replaced by a range of institutional solutions that coexisted under the umbrella of "Soviet trade."[49] Initially Soviet trade included closed stores, which first formed in 1930 to ensure proper "class distribution" and to improve the supply of deficit goods to industrial workers.[50] The Communist leadership extended the principle of closed distribution to elites as well, and established special closed stores for party, government, and trade-union officials, industrial managers and engineers, and employees of state agencies.[51] But even though closed stores were a significant retail force in the early to mid-1930s, authorities argued that they would not last as Soviet trade developed.[52] Economist Nosov claimed that closed workers' cooperatives and closed distributors were the best form of distribution given the existence of a "sharp class struggle" and goods deficits. But they were not an "ideal organizational form of socialist distribution," and once a certain level of productivity had been achieved, all capitalist elements had been vanquished, and goods deficits were no longer a problem, they would be eliminated.[53] They were not considered ideal because they fostered mechanical distribution instead of cultured Soviet trade. As a government official explained, many workers in the closed network mistakenly concluded that "it was only in the open trade network that it was necessary to offer cultured service, attentive customer consideration, good quality and a large variety of goods, and cleanliness."[54] Moreover, closed trade purportedly fostered a "propitious environment for bureaucratism and abuse of power."[55] Although closed forms of trade remained a part of the economic landscape until the mid-1930s, authorities rejected them as enduring components of Soviet trade.[56]

Soviet trade included a state network of "open" commercial stores, which sold goods to anyone at higher prices than most stores. They were first established in 1929 to provide provisions to groups ineligible for rationed goods, "the non-working population," and to serve as an "essential source of revenue" for the government. But chronic shortages and problems with other forms of distribution and trade quickly led the general public to patronize these stores.[57] As the trade campaign advanced, these open stores proliferated, despite their higher prices. Not surprisingly, policymakers emphasized positive reasons for their expansion, arguing they were an important resource for ordinary people and linking their growth to the actualization of genuine Soviet trade, especially cultured retailing. Open stores were invaluable "for introducing cultured methods of trade, for cultivating trade cadres who had the ability to trade in a new way."[58] They exerted a positive influence on the rest of the retail sector by serving as the model of the new cultured Soviet trade. Authorities also claimed that these stores helped drive down costs at *kolkhoz* ("collective-farm") markets.[59]

Consumer cooperatives were a significant part of the Soviet trade system as it evolved. In principle, consumer cooperatives were controlled by voluntary cooperative members who elected boards of directors and participated in decision making at periodic cooperative meetings. In practice cooperatives were subordinate to the executive organ Tsentrosoiuz, which effectively served as another state-controlled commissariat. In the early 1930s, cooperative stores were far more numerous than state stores, and served as the focus of the trade campaign's efforts. But as state trade expanded and became increasingly identified with cultured retailing, the centrality of consumer cooperatives to Soviet trade declined. In September 1935, the regime reorganized consumer cooperatives, consigning them to the countryside and transferring those in urban areas to Narkomvnutorg (which ended up being a real boon to the state trade infrastructure). Reorganization was supposed to strengthen trade in rural areas, where cooperatives rather than state stores were the major suppliers of goods, by allowing Tsentrosoiuz and its subordinate bodies to concentrate their efforts on rural cooperatives.[60] But reorganization weakened the position of consumer cooperatives overall, and by 1937, they accounted for about 20 percent of total retail turnover, down from 59.2 percent in 1932.[61] Moreover, reorganization exacerbated the differences between cooperative and state trade, and the differences between rural and urban retailing. Throughout the trade campaign of the 1930s, the state trade sector in urban areas received a disproportionate share of consumer goods and resources, making it easier to realize positive retail changes.[62]

Reforms associated with the new Soviet trade extended to *kolkhoz* trade ("collective-farm" trade) as well. When the Stalinist regime could not eradicate peasant bazaars in the late 1920s, it recast them as *kolkhoz* trade, and allowed collective farms, collective farmers, and independent peasants to engage in the petty sale of their agricultural products at government-regulated outdoor markets (at first according to governmental pricing policies and then according to "prices formed on the market").[63] Because *kolkhoz* markets permitted petty trade by independent peasants, which looked a lot like "private" trade, in 1932 the government expressly forbade the opening of stores and small shops by private traders, reaffirming there would be no formal private retail network as there had been during the NEP years.[64] The leadership justified *kolkhoz* trade by arguing that it provided an invaluable *tovarnaia smychka* (goods link) between urban and rural areas. As Stalin noted, *kolkhoz* trade provided urban areas with much needed goods and it provided the collective farmer with "an additional source of income and strengthened his economic position," operating as an important stimulus for agricultural productivity and the development of collective farms. Yet Stalin and others acknowledged that *kolkhoz* trade was subject to misuse by private traders and speculators. Because *kolkhoz* trade could provoke "private-ownership appetites," party leader Molotov explained, it sometimes turned "individual groups of collective farmers and even entire collective farms into speculators at the market." These dangers necessitated strict regulation of prices at markets, severe punishment of abuses, and increased socialist-educational work among collective farmers.[65] But despite massive government surveillance, frequent crackdowns on violations, and the application of a range of punitive measures (including the deportation of unlicensed petty traders to labor camps or worse), *kolkhoz* trade operated as an "oasis of market trade."[66] Sellers often engaged in profiteering and speculative practices – against Soviet laws – and the outdoor markets were dominated not by collective farms or collectivized farmers but by independent peasants and private hawkers.[67]

Soviet trade and increased consumption

The trade campaign had an immediate and far reaching effect on the official attitude toward consumer goods. As political leaders and policymakers called for the development of Soviet trade, they endorsed the legitimacy of better material conditions for the populace, including improved access to consumer goods. As with retail trade, this new approach to consumption was initially advocated for economic and political reasons.

In 1931 Stalin legitimized consumption by placing the material needs of workers at the center of the drive for industrial expansion and validating the provisioning of these needs as a critical incentive for workers. In a speech about the "new tasks for economic construction," he lectured that bettering material conditions would strengthen workers' ties to enterprises and mitigate high rates of labor turnover.[68] This emphasis on the economic rationale for improving consumption levels was reiterated in subsequent years. As Stalin explained in 1934, goods were made "not for production, but for consumption," and if they "did not reach consumers," industry and agriculture would lose "stimulus" for increased production.[69] Stalin also provided a political rationale in 1931 for why Soviet workers deserved better material and cultural lives: they no longer lived under the "yoke of capitalism." Because the Soviet government had a different political contract with workers than did capitalist regimes, it was the government's responsibility to improve consumption levels.[70]

Throughout 1932 the government took steps to promote greater production of foodstuffs and consumer goods. At the Seventeenth Party Conference, authorities approved increased production, advocating that the supply of basic consumer goods at the end of the Second FYP exceed by two to three times the supply at the end of the First FYP.[71] Heavy industries, light industries, and producers' cooperatives were directed to increase the manufacture of mass-produced consumer goods. The party-state also passed a series of incentives to stimulate greater goods production among artisan cooperatives.[72] These steps were in part a response to official anxiety about popular unrest and diminished labor productivity, which the Stalinist regime continued to confront, particularly in April 1932 when anger among textile workers flared and turned into a wave of strikes.[73] In September–October 1932, the Party chastised industries and producers' cooperatives for not doing enough to increase goods production.[74] Party leaders criticized those who did not understand that "for every Bolshevik the improvement of supply for workers is a responsible and honorable task." They argued that industrial leaders and workers needed to realize that mass consumer goods, even frying pans, were necessary for future socialist construction.[75]

The Stalinist regime's new commitment to improving consumption levels for the general populace had its limits, however, as reflected in the mass famine of 1932–1933 in Ukraine, many Volga regions, and the North Caucasus. Millions of Soviet citizens starved to death as party and government officials forcibly collectivized peasant farms and demanded excessive and compulsory grain deliveries. As the famine unfolded, the government took some steps to ameliorate conditions, such as reducing grain collection quotas and providing a limited quantity of food and seed to rural areas, but these efforts were far too little and too late. During this time a significant number of Kazakhs also died from hunger when Soviet authorities tried to force nomadic farmers into collective farms. In the context of collectivization, Stalinist agricultural policies clearly took priority over rhetoric and plans for improving material conditions – even at the expense of people's lives.

Although Stalinist leaders did not address the stark contradictions in their economic policies or publicly acknowledge the tragic famine of 1932–1933, official rhetoric and plans for improving material conditions were not merely propagandistic. While the party-state did not meet its target goals for consumer goods production during the Second FYP, there was nonetheless significant growth during the mid-1930s.[76] According to Soviet historian G. Dikhtiar, by 1937 the overall production of consumer goods was approximately twice that of 1932, and for some consumer items the increase was even higher: sugar cubes increased by 2.9 times; silk cloth by 2.7 times; bicycles by 4.5 times; and cameras by 11.8 times. For a population of approximately 150–160 million, the production of 500,000 bicycles in 1937 was still inadequate. Yet the limited increase in consumer goods production in the mid-1930s signaled progress compared to the miserly output during the First FYP. Moreover, reportedly the mass production of many consumer goods in the Soviet 1930s compared favorably to production levels under the Tsarist regime.[77] The availability of public consumer goods, such as daycare facilities, rest homes, movie theatres, and public transportation (e.g., the Moscow metro), similarly grew in the 1930s. Shortages persisted, the output of foodstuffs and manufactured consumer goods never satisfied consumer demand, and most Soviet people continued to experience lives of privation. Nonetheless, the Stalinist regime took steps toward becoming a mass consumer society.[78]

Socialist objectives and ideological linkages

Communist authorities linked the new approach to retailing and consumption to broader socialist objectives. As will be explored further in subsequent chapters, they saw the mobilization of retail employees, public controllers and consumers on behalf of retail reform as a mechanism for socialist transformation, for better incorporating these groups into the Soviet polity. They viewed improved retailing and increased consumption as a means of advancing not only economic goals, particularly industrial productivity and socialist construction, but also social, cultural, and political goals.

Soviet consumerism became a political imperative in the context of the Communist leadership's broader competition with the West, its desire "to catch up with and overtake" capitalist powers. In 1932 the president of the State Planning Commission, V. Kuibyshev, noted, "With reference to consumption the Soviet Union will be the most advanced country of the world [by the end of the second FYP]."[79] In 1935 Stalin rhetorically asked why socialism could and would conquer capitalism. He answered, "Because it will provide society with more products and will be able to make society wealthier than the capitalist economic system."[80] In March 1939 Stalin praised the recent industrial gains in catching up to and over-taking capitalist countries, but noted that progress remained incomplete. It was only when the country was "fully sated with consumer goods" and people had an "abundance of products" that the "transition from the first phase of communism to the second phase" would be possible. Even in the 1930s, Communist leaders linked increased levels of mass consumption to the Soviet drive to surpass the West.[81]

Official discourse validated Soviet consumerism by presenting it as more democratic than consumerism in capitalist societies. Economists claimed that Soviet workers and peasants, instead of just the wealthy, enjoyed access to high-quality consumer goods. In earlier times "galoshes had been a luxury for the majority of peasants, owned chiefly by the kulak-prosperous part of the village," whereas under Soviet rule "galoshes had come into general use" by the peasantry.[82] I. Plotnikov explained, "goods that yesterday were consumer items of the bourgeoisie and their servants have today become available to a wide mass of workers."[83] In an effort to match rhetoric with reality, policymakers pursued policies to make "luxury" goods more widely available to the general public. Thus the mass production of inexpensive versions of champagne, cognac, and higher-quality chocolate and candy became priorities in the mid-1930s.[84] For instance, in 1937 the state reportedly produced 48,600,000 bottles of eau de cologne, compared to 9,100,000 bottles in 1932. By 1937, the production of portable gramophones reached 675,000 units, 11.6 times the output in 1932.[85] Although the mass production of "luxury" consumer goods often fell short of target plans, many ordinary people began to acquire such goods in the 1930s because they were cheaper and more plentiful.

Communist authorities and the press also justified the new emphasis on consumption by linking it to modernization. This claim was not difficult to make, for industrial and scientific achievements provided consumers with an array of modern goods: rayon cloth, margarine, home radios, and electric irons. Purchasing the newly available and often industrial items was characterized as a sign of modern rather than bourgeois taste.[86] New industrial food plants and manufactured-goods factories facilitated this argument, because they allowed for mass production, thereby providing goods to a wider cross-section of consumers. In the mid-1930s, for instance, the People's Commissariat of Food Industry borrowed technology from American firms and built several industrial ice cream plants in the Soviet Union. The goal was for ice cream – "a delightful and very nutritious food" which previously had been "eaten on high days, in bourgeois families, at weddings and birthday parties" – to become a daily, year-round, and inexpensive food product "of the masses."[87]

According to official discourse, the acquisition of modern consumer goods was not merely a result of modernization, but also a vehicle for it. Canned goods helped to modernize people's lives: they diversified diets and lessened waste from food spoilage. Food concentrates (such as potato puree) allowed for quick but healthy meals, fitting for a modern tempo of life (Figure 1.1). Ready-made clothing, semi-prepared food products, and other commodities helped the Soviet people pursue new tasks, modern adventures, and pleasurable activities formerly restricted to the wealthy. In 1937, for example, the Soviet press argued that bouillon cubes had aided the "heroic" crew in their recent flight from Moscow to North America. Journalists also claimed that semi-prepared foodstuffs made it easier for working people to relax and go to the countryside, *dachas* (summer cottages), and health resorts.[88]

Soviet authorities particularly emphasized the ability of consumer goods to transform women's lives. Deputy trade commissar Z. S. Bolotin claimed that semi-prepared food products would "free the Soviet

Figure 1.1 A full meal in 20 minutes! Buy food concentrates
Source: Unknown artist, 1939 (Russian State Library).

woman from the kitchen, creating greater leisure time for her, and
giving her the opportunity to participate in socialist construction."[89]
Economists argued that modern consumer goods assisted women's
efforts to become engaged in the productive sector because they helped
working women juggle wage labor and household tasks.[90] Numerous
advertisements reinforced these messages, pointing to the women and
mothers who benefited from new food products that clearly made their
lives easier. An ad from 1937, for example, showed a modern-looking
smiling woman, stylishly dressed, with prepackaged meat in her hand.
The ad proclaimed, "Pre-packaged meat. It saves time. It guarantees
quality and cleanliness."[91] Women's advocates, such as A. V. Artiukhina,
a former head of the Women's Department (*Zhenotdel*) of the Communist

Party, reinforced official rhetoric about the link between consumer goods and women's lives by arguing that the increased production and improved quality of children's goods, electrical home appliances, cookbooks, and suitable women's clothing would aid women in their multiple roles and tasks as mothers, housewives, and workers.[92] By depicting it as a means for increasing people's opportunities in general, and women's emancipation in particular, consumerism could be reclaimed as socialist.

When viewed as a vehicle for inculcating socialist values, the legitimacy of Soviet consumerism was incontestable. Consumers who purchased books, posters, and newspapers in official state venues, for example, could learn about socialist ideas and party-state slogans and initiatives, including Stalin's pronouncements "Life has become better, life has become more joyous" and "Cadres decide all." (Figures 1.2 and 1.3) Consumer

Figure 1.2   Book kiosk, Fergana 1939

Figure 1.3 Department store, Tashkent 1936

goods were deemed particularly valuable for molding children as proper socialist citizens. State officials, salespeople, and customers envisaged toys as a "powerful means for communist education," a mechanism for acquainting children with "important branches of the national economy," and a critical means for influencing the "formation of children's thoughts."[93] They argued that technical toys were especially advantageous, as they helped foster "technical habits" and "technical education," and thereby played an important role in the "first stage in the life of a future builder of communism."[94] Toy tanks, parachutists, and similar items were useful for preparing the younger generation for national duties, "which at any moment" might have to "take up a position on behalf of the defense of its homeland." Not all toys, however, were viewed positively. Because some older toys were not "suitable" for the new socialist epoch, the government's "Toys Committee" advocated their removal from retail circulation.[95] Soviet dolls with "fat legs, short arms, and disgraceful trunks" and crudely made mechanical toys were considered problematic, because they thwarted an important objective: to impart good taste and a love for "beautiful things" in children.[96] Although many Soviet children in the 1930s had no store-bought toys of any kind, Communist authorities endorsed the greater consumption of educational, technical, attractive, and high-quality toys that would help to create a New Soviet Person and society.[97]

Communist leaders also rationalized their new approach to consumption by arguing that increased prosperity, tied to the revolutionary goal of providing the people with a decent standard of living, was critical to the very definition of socialism. In early 1934 Stalin explained:

> Socialism means not destitution and deprivation, but the elimination of destitution and deprivation.... It would be stupid to think that socialism could be built on the basis of destitution and deprivation, on the basis of the curtailment of personal needs and the lowering of the conditions of people's lives to the level of poverty. ... This would not be socialism, but a caricature of socialism. Socialism can be built only on the basis of a rapid growth in the productive forces of society, on the basis of an abundance of products and goods, on the basis of a prosperous life for workers, on the basis of a fast rise in *kul'turnost'* (culturedness).[98]

Stalin's formulation of socialism stood in stark contrast to the association of socialism with asceticism and self-sacrifice, widely promoted by Communist leaders during the early years of the first FYP. But the defeat of various oppositionist groups, significant progress toward meeting the goals of collectivization and rapid industrialization, and the victory of the socialist system – trumpeted by Stalin and others at the Congress of Victors (Seventeenth Party Congress) – allowed socialism to be associated with material prosperity.[99] After declaring in 1935 that "Life has become better, comrades, life has become more joyous," Stalin claimed:

> Our revolution is the only one that has not only broken the chains of capitalism and given people freedom, but has also succeeded in providing people with the material conditions for a prosperous life. In this [lies] the strength and invincibility of our revolution. Of course it is good to drive out the capitalists, the landowners, and the Tsarist *oprichniki*, as well as to take power and receive freedom. ... But, unfortunately... [i]f there isn't enough bread, butter and fats, or manufactured goods, and living quarters are bad, then freedom alone won't get you very far... [T]o be able to live well and happily, it is necessary for the blessings of political freedom to be supplemented by material blessings.[100]

Making material prosperity a barometer of the revolution's success allowed the Stalinist regime to sanction Soviet consumerism as ideologically compatible with socialism.

The Soviet press and many individuals reinforced the relationship between the Bolshevik Revolution and consumerism by comparing the materially impoverished lives of ordinary people under the Tsarist regime with their purportedly much better lives under the Soviet regime. As a news article explained, under Bolshevik rule the "well-being" of people had risen, as had their cultural level, so that people had new consumer tastes and demands. "Before the revolution male and female workers and peasants could not decorate their living quarters or acquire good dishes, furniture, and clothing, because they didn't have the means." What did that mean in practice? It meant that many Russians had only "one clay or wooden bowl" or "one spoon" for the entire family.[101] Under the Tsarist regime, A. E. Bazhanova recounted, she did not have a bed. But after the revolution, she had acquired not only a bed, but also curtains, tables and chairs, and a radio.[102] The supposed advancement of ordinary people's material conditions under Soviet rule made consumerism acceptable, even if such improvement was limited.

The Communist leadership's new discourse about the importance of realizing the material promises of socialism coincided with a broader effort to promote a more "joyous life." In the mid-1930s, the party-state endorsed "officially sanctioned entertainment and gaiety" and greater leisure opportunities, such as vacations at rest homes, participation in a physical culture movement, and Soviet musical films.[103] Authorities sponsored a more celebratory culture, intended not only to win the emotional loyalty of citizens and to educate the populace about socialist achievements (such as aviation feats) but also to foster an image of happiness and prosperity. In 1935, they reinstated New Year's Day celebrations (banned in 1928) and reintroduced the fir tree and Grandfather Frost (Russian version of Santa Claus). They also established new celebrations – such as the hundredth anniversary of Pushkin's death in 1937. To promote these holidays and celebrations as festive events, the Communist leadership explicitly tied them to increased consumption opportunities and stocked stores with extra goods in the days immediately preceding them. With its tree ornaments and children's gifts, New Year's Day was particularly linked to consumer goods. Stores selling merchandise for this holiday, for example, featured "Father Frost" dolls (Figure 1.4)

To be sure, most Soviet people in the 1930s continued to struggle to make ends meet, and many responded angrily to rhetoric about the "good life," viewing it as empty propaganda or something that primarily benefited the elites. As one worker noted, "Much is written about the achievements of Soviet power, while the reality is that before a worker drank tea with white bread while now he gulps down water,

Figure 1.4   New Year's Eve in *Gastronom* No. 1, Tashkent 1937

and as for the *kolkhozniki* – there's nothing to say."[104] But despite cynicism about the regime's "accomplishments," the new approach to consumption apparently offered many individuals a modicum of pleasure. The comments of Valentina Bogda, an engineer in Rostov who was critical of many Soviet policies, illustrate this effect.

> Signs of the approaching New Year's Eve were everywhere. Christmas tree ornaments had appeared in the stores, and even though the most beautiful and interesting ones were quite expensive, people were in a hurry to buy them. Almost every evening, after work, I would take Natasha out shopping for new and interesting toys and decorations. That year we bought a large silvery glass star to go on top of the tree, and a whole family of brightly colored birds. They were no longer selling angels, but one could buy fairies and sparkling dresses with wings. Once, when we walked into our local grocery store, we spotted that traditional Christmas treat and decoration: oranges. Oranges had become a rarity; they had to be imported from abroad, and because precious hard currency could not be spent on such things, we had been doing without them for many years. "Where do these beauties come from?" "From Spain. We are helping our Spanish friends, so it's a sweet deal all around," laughed the clerk. "At least we're getting something in return," I said to myself as I bought a whole crate of oranges – fifty of them altogether![105]

A vehicle for *kul'turnost'*

As the Soviet trade campaign continued, authorities increasingly assigned cultural importance to retail trade and consumption and linked both to the party-state campaign for *kul'turnost'* (culturedness). The campaign for *kul'turnost'* burgeoned after 1934, and consisted of a "complex of practices" that constituted part of the "Stalinist civilizing process." In Vadim Volkov's view, the campaign was a strategy for countering one of the major effects of forced industrialization, the "ruralization of the cities" and its negative effects. In other words, it was a method for edifying and managing the mass influx of purportedly undisciplined and uncouth peasant-workers in urban and industrial areas.[106] *Kul'turnost'* bespoke a new, presumably socialist, way of life. As the Stalinist regime sought to transform people by making them more "cultured," that is, more modern and civilized, people's clothing, personal hygiene, language, personal possessions, cultural interests, and daily habits served as markers of socialization.

The *kul'turnost'* ideal envisioned a modern, rational, and hygienic retail environment where employees provided consumers with attentive and friendly customer service, new retail amenities and services, creative displays, and a wide variety of goods. Cultured stores with cultured goods and new "mother and children's corners" would allow women to buy all that they needed (Figure 1.5). The association of

Figure 1.5 Mother and children's corner, store for cultured goods, Tashkent, 1933

retailing with *kul'turnost'* intensified as the abolition of rationing loomed closer in 1934. In late December 1934, Kaganovich explained that the end of rationing meant that "The consumer, buying goods in whatever shop he wishes, for his own money, will set higher requirements," which ultimately would result in more cultured trade.[107] In 1935 Bolotin explained, "We have liquidated the private trader in retail trade. We have liquidated rationing. ... Now Soviet trade can and should become cultured."[108] Authorities and the press argued that if consumer cooperatives, closed stores, and open stores wanted to be competitive, their salespeople would have to become "capable of trading in a genuinely cultured Soviet way."[109] Cultured Soviet trade was supposed to entail a newfound "respect for the consumer, for his interests."[110]

According to authorities, cultured Soviet trade was not only a reflection of but also a vehicle for increased *kul'turnost'*, because in this idealized retail environment salesclerks would act as advisors to consumers and help to promote "cultured" consumption, a "new Soviet taste." As the economist Stushkov explained, a key objective of cultured Soviet trade was to combat the "gustatory and aesthetic conservatism of consumers" and introduce them to new goods (including the "modern" ones mentioned previously).[111] In the mid-1930s party and government leaders increasingly emphasized that cultured Soviet trade would offer instruction to buyers and enlighten the populace.[112] The press covered retail workers' new roles as advisors, and trade leaders trumpeted retail workers' responsibility not only to meet consumers' needs, but also to teach "new habits" and foster "new consumer demands."[113] Speaking on this topic, a professor at the Plekhanov Institute of the National Economy commended what he saw as "one of the most successful and correct examples of trade information": an advertisement for canned corn in *Pravda* that detailed different dishes that could be prepared using canned corn, what foods the corn could replace, and where it could be bought.[114] Retail instruction about new products, both in stores and via advertising, was supposed to foster cultivated and modern consumers. It would help the Soviet people overcome "the old custom of living on cabbage soup and mush."[115]

The narrative of the transformative power of Soviet trade was predicated on a specific conceptualization of consumer goods and their cultural significance. Certain consumer goods were considered hallmarks of *kul'turnost'* and socialist modernity. For example, possession of "urban" clothes, home furnishings, and cultural items, such as books, radios, watches, and phonographs, distinguished a cultured and modern person from an uncultured and premodern one. The purchase

of toothpaste and other toiletries supposedly signaled a person's growing awareness of the importance of hygiene. (Figure 1.6) According to
Soviet authorities, the increased demand for particular items denoted
"backward" workers, peasants, and nationalities into modern Soviet men
and women. Economist I. Plotnikov noted that the cultural growth of
workers had resulted "in a sharp reduction of the consumption of vodka"
and a "sharp increase in demand for cultured goods." Communist leader

Figure 1.6 Demand our tooth powder, tooth paste, perfume, face cream,
powder

Source: Unknown artist, 1930s (Russian State Library) (in Azerbaijani and Russian languages).

Molotov similarly claimed that the great demand among *kolkhozniki* for "iron beds, hanging clocks, silk dresses, and so on" showed that they were "no longer" peasants.[116] According to A. Pavlovich, another economist, the rural demand for *bast* (straw) shoes and sandals had fallen whereas rural demand for sets of matching knives and forks, iron enamelware, and watches had risen. "Backwardness," he maintained, was being overcome due to the "influence of cultural habits acquired in the Red Army, at socialist construction sites, and in the city."[117] Commissar of Domestic Trade, I. Veitser, also linked *kul'turnost'* and modernization with consumption, arguing that increased interest in household articles, such as saucepans and coffeepots, demonstrated the "elimination" of cultural "backwardness" among the peasantry.[118] These ideas resonated with the general public; many Soviet citizens, such as the worker M. Diukanov, publicly promoted the ideal of the cultured person by listing those material goods that would help workers live a cultured life: "bicycles, pianos, phonographs, records, radio sets."[119]

Positing consumer goods as expressions of *kul'turnost'* helped authorities and ordinary people legitimize Soviet consumerism and underscore its civilizing force in building socialism. Government officials particularly applauded peasants who adopted urbane consumer interests as well as national minorities who demanded European or Russian consumer goods.[120] A 1936 book on Soviet trade in Central Asia celebrated Uzbeks' increased demand for goods like gramophones, radios, and bicycles as a sign of their "cultural growth."[121] An article in *Pravda Vostoka* similarly characterized changing consumer demand in Central Asia as a measure of economic and cultural progress.[122] Although the language of cultural development suggested official interest in imposing a particular model of taste and consumer demand on diverse Soviet peoples, political leaders and trade officials did not support the abolition of *all* regional and national variations in consumer demands. Yet while acknowledging that differences would remain, they nonetheless viewed increased consumer demand for urban, Russian, and "European" goods as a sign that peasants and national minorities were becoming more civilized. Mikoian argued in 1936:

> Life is becoming more cultured. Comrades, take for example Uzbekistan. There today many still dress in an Uzbek way. But already in Uzbekistan in the near future they will wear the same clothes as Muscovites. The same may be said about the populace of other regions, for example, about Riazan peasants. There do women

combine and tractor drivers now really dress in the clothing of a Riazan girl? No. Already we have women in the countryside wearing good city clothing. They buy good perfume and fragrant soap because life has become more cultured.[123]

The supposed dissolution of stark consumer differences between the urban and the rural consumer as well as between the Russian and non-Russian consumer represented the success of party-state efforts to modernize and civilize the masses.

*   *   *

In the 1930s, Soviet trade became firmly linked with the socialist project of transforming the economy and society, and extending revolutionary progress into the material culture of everyday life. If at first Soviet officials emphasized primarily economic and political reasons for the campaign for Soviet trade – and for the regime's new emphasis on retailing and consumption – during the course of the trade campaign they began to point to additional social, cultural, and political reasons. They reconfigured the retail sector and consumer goods as expressions of and vehicles for the realization of a variety of socialist goals, including the advancement of *kul'turnost'*. They promoted Soviet trade and Soviet consumerism as positive forces for the building of socialism.

2

The *"Perestroika"* of Retail Trade
Visionary Planning for
Revolutionary Retailing

Organized explicitly like a "Five and Dime" in the United States, the unit price store that opened in April 1937 on Moscow's Kirov Street was a model of innovation, efficiency, and convenience compared to most Soviet stores.[1] It featured a panoply of manufactured goods, including haberdashery, household items, and toys. It sold merchandise that was premeasured and sorted, allowing for speedier sales transactions. Because the store displayed merchandise on open shelves with premarked prices, customers could see goods and their costs without the assistance of a salesclerk. The store's distinguishing feature was its policy of selling all merchandise according to eleven fixed prices of "2, 3, 5, 8, 10, 13, 15, 18, 20, 23, and 25 rubles." This scheme simplified things for store employees and customers alike by obviating the need to deal with small change.[2] The unit price also introduced "bundling," a "new way of selling goods" that involved selling different items together in a set. One toy set "Voroshilov gunner," for example, featured a toy helmet, mini-cannon, rifle, and other accessories which could not be purchased separately. Standardization of prices allowed for further rationalization of the customer experience. Instead of the department store norm of standing in different lines and interacting with different employees to assemble purchases, customers paid the salesclerk directly, a practice which was believed to reduce the average transaction time to less than two and a half minutes. The unit price store's emphasis on efficiency was even built into the building design: unlike most Soviet retail establishments, the store had a basement storage area as well as three cargo lifts to facilitate the transfer of goods for commercial distribution. Employing the modern retail practices of standard low prices, high turnover, and customer-centered convenience, the store broadcast the regime's goals to sell an assortment of "small and relatively inexpensive consumer goods with mass demand" and to introduce commodities that an increasingly "cultured Soviet consumer could not do without."[3] The store's focus on supplying inexpensive merchandise reflected the regime's normative vision of modernity and consumption that sought plenty while downplaying the many symbolic distinctions that marked differences in purchasing power among shoppers.

The number of customers who frequented the unit price store suggests its success. During a typical week in 1938, the store had approximately 40 to 45,000 weekday and 75,000 to 80,000 weekend visitors. But despite the store's relative success and appeal, the store was by no means perfect. Shortages were common. Officially the store promised consumers access to an assortment of 3,184 different goods, but in reality it provided regular access to fewer than 2,000 goods. Nor was the store's "rational" and "convenient" approach to sales always appreciated by its consumers. As one exasperated customer explained, she had to purchase multiple sets of needlepoint canvases with needles and thimbles because canvases were not sold separately.[4] The unit price store also suffered from overcrowding. Notwithstanding its challenges, the store's general features and retail practices underscore some of the main attributes that trade authorities associated with their project to transform and modernize Soviet retailing: technology, scientific rationalism, and *kul'turnost'* (culturedness).

The unit price store was a product of the campaign to develop socialist retail trade. This campaign, conducted without a clear roadmap, was supposed to distinguish the Soviet Union. Party leaders envisioned a new system of "cultured" retailing that would be "trade without capitalists." They provided some instruction about how to establish the new Soviet trade – e.g., to enlarge the retail network and strengthen its "technical base."[5] But party leaders did not provide details on how this enterprise was to be carried out. They instead assigned to trade authorities the task of imagining its particulars and implementing necessary reforms.[6]

Pursuing myriad strategies to achieve a common goal that some called the *perestroika* (reconstruction) of retailing, trade authorities imagined the details of a new retail infrastructure that they saw necessary for the Soviet economy.[7] How should the retail network be organized? How should goods be sold? How exactly should retailing's technical base be strengthened? Trade officials and store managers held countless meetings to grapple with these and other questions, which also became important topics for professional economists, and graduate students at institutions of higher learning.

Trade authorities did not turn to Lenin or Marx and Engels in order to rethink their retail operations; rather, they looked abroad. I. Zelenskii, the president of the All-Union Central Union of Consumer Cooperative Societies (Tsentrosoiuz) explained: "If we take machinery from America, if we utilize the experience of capitalist governments for industry and transportation, then why should we refrain from using the experience of capitalist countries in the matter of handling goods?"[8] Another high-level trade leader put it this way: if Soviet industry could draw on the experience and techniques of industrial enterprises in capitalist countries, why couldn't the trade sector?[9] Despite the many negative attributes trade authorities associated with foreign capitalist retailing, this retailing represented modernity: technological innovation, rationalization, efficiency. And just as Party leaders aimed "to catch up with and overtake" the modern industry of advanced capitalist powers in the drive for industrialization, trade authorities aimed to "catch up with and overtake" the modern tools and techniques of capitalist retailing.[10]

Using capitalist retailing to build (the great future of) socialist retailing

As trade authorities looked for ways to modernize retailing, they sent hundreds of delegates to capitalist countries "to study" foreign trade.[11] Engineers, architects, store directors, managers of retail departments studied contemporary retail design and commercial practices at a variety of stores known for progressive retailing, including Piggly Wiggly, Woolworth's, and Macy's in the United States, Printemps in France, and Selfridge in England. Soviet delegates also visited factories engaged in the manufacturing of mass consumer goods and retail tools. By visiting retail establishments and factories, and collecting samples of merchandise and technologies for possible reproduction, Soviet delegates came back with a sense of what to make, how to make it, and how to distribute it. They purchased ice cream machines from the United States, for example, to introduce industrially produced ice cream to the Soviet world.[12] They also imported German machinery for the manufacture of paper plates and cups to facilitate the mass distribution of foodstuffs.[13] The technology transfer that resulted from these trips abroad was substantial. The acquisition of foreign retail devices, machinery and fixtures all served the mandate "to acquire examples of [trade] equipment" for imitation and use that would improve Soviet retailing.[14] Authorities emphasized the pragmatism of their focus on the West, arguing that it made sense to "borrow the best from the experience of American and European capitalist firms."[15]

Although the Soviet trade establishment explored the retail sector in a variety of capitalist countries, some countries garnered more attention than others. Trade reformers admired retail tools and practices found in Britain, particularly those associated with London's modern department store Selfridge, which consciously strove to break away from class-based marketing and dispense with class segregation.[16] But because the dominant image of England was as a "realm of small shopkeepers," it was never viewed as a serious retail model.[17] France of course had produced the first modern department store, the *Bon Marché*, but it was the country's high-end consumer goods, such as champagne and *haute couture*, rather than its retailing that attracted attention. France may well have been too upscale for the Soviets: the French writer Emile Zola had popularized the grand bourgeois view of modern French commerce when he had described the French department store as a "ladies' paradise" brimming with new opportunities for upper-class women.[18] Soviet attention to France's consumer goods was also related to interest in democratizing luxury by reproducing inexpensive versions of luxury goods for ordinary people.[19] Trade reformers took German retailing, particularly its technologies and window displays, more seriously than French retailing. This tendency may have been a product of earlier Russian associations of Germany with efficiency and competency.[20]

Undoubtedly, United States retailers left the deepest imprint on the Soviet trade campaign. In envisioning a new Soviet retail system, trade authorities most frequently referred to the value of American examples.[21] Delegates returning from abroad repeatedly emphasized the merits of American retail techniques and machinery, and the press even published cribbed versions of articles from the American business press, such as those printed in the journal "Chain Store."[22] From the more striking and unusual practices of capitalist retailing – store agents who went to people's homes to help them with interior decorating, store employees who tried to engage consumers in taste testing, loudspeakers that notified consumers about new products – to the more mundane and common aspects – standardized retail fixtures and labeling devices – American retail methods captured the imaginations of reformers.[23] They served as a model of retail modernity from which the Soviets could borrow.

In certain ways America had long symbolized economic modernity. This had been true in Tsarist Russia and continued through the revolutions.[24] In 1924 even Stalin himself called for the joining of "American efficiency with Bolshevik ideology," with the implied goal of making American methods compatible with socialism.[25] Despite their disdain for its perceived capitalist excesses, Communist leaders held up America's rapid economic development as a model of dynamism, productivity, and inventiveness.[26]

Soviet officials were not alone in associating modernity with American retailing. For many European entrepreneurs, the United States held a double symbolic quality, representing both the promises and dangers of retail modernity. Some American innovations, such as the mechanized cash register, promised more accurate and efficient financial practices. But European retailers were far more ambivalent about other innovations, such as the variety chain store. On the one hand chain stores represented rational enterprise. Unlike department stores, they moved beyond traditional urban retail centers to outlying districts and small towns. They also garnered large profits because they had fewer overhead costs and "revolutionize[d] pricing" by offering goods at "low fixed prices."[27] On the other hand, variety chain stores made shopping more convenient and accessible to all people, and thereby lessened differences in purchasing habits among different classes. Moreover, chain stores, like other forms of large-scale retailing, sapped business from small retailers. Europeans who were interested in protecting their own businesses, or in maintaining a bourgeois regime of consumption as opposed to a "Fordist" or mass model of consumption, greeted modern American retail practices that promoted mass consumption with anxiety and hostility if not outright opposition.

If a fascination with economic modernity informed trade reformers' plans, so too did Communist anxiety about the purity of the body politic. From the first days of Soviet rule Communists worried about the presence of counterrevolutionaries, class enemies, and anti-Soviet elements. In the 1930s these concerns culminated in redoubled efforts to purge such forces from the general population. The trade campaign coexisted with a terror campaign against counterrevolution: trade authorities scrutinized themselves as well as retail employees and customers for politically disloyal and anti-Soviet practices. Innumerable reports about the treacherous activities of trade officials, store personnel, and consumers exacerbated the difficulty of realizing a good Soviet retail policy, and fueled attempts to improve retailing by ridding it of "speculators," thieves, and others hostile to socialism.[28] This political atmosphere of distrust shaped trade authorities' plans for retail reconstruction, even thwarting the adoption of potentially useful strategies for achieving improvements.

Modernizing retail tools and technologies

The idea of building a modern retail network throughout the Soviet Union made sense not only as socialist policy, but as a goal of modernity itself. Though the ideology and the macroeconomics of Soviet retailing suffered from the instability of transition, trade officials had two powerful safe harbors for productive work toward their collective goal: they could immerse themselves in the details and technologies of retail reform, and they could pursue the broad, intermediate goals of "modernization" that at times seemed identical with socialism. But even if the focus on "modernizing" and "rationalizing" retail spaces, production and distribution technologies, and store practices had an almost universal appeal, trade authorities' methods of implementing reform had a distinctly Soviet character to them that produced notable successes in some areas and great failures in others.

Soviet visions of modernization often revolved around the idea of the machine. This was no less true in the retail realm, where new tools and technologies served as a kind of first principle for the vision of a reconstructed retail system. Reformers emphasized three main reasons for their necessity. First, new tools and technologies were iconic. Their presence would instantly distinguish the Soviet trade experience from its antiquated precursors in prerevolutionary Russia and during the NEP era of the 1920s. Soviet stores lacked cash registers and modern scales, modern heating and lighting, sophistication of design and packaging.[29] The "archaic" equipment and low level of technology underscored the "very primitive" technical-material base of trade relative to the technological advancements of industry.[30] Trade leader Zelenskii complained that Soviet retailing used "the same counter, the same scoop, and the same scales" employed "100 years ago." Second, the adoption of new tools and technologies would make Soviet trade more competitive with capitalist retailing. As trade leaders noted, retail networks in Western Europe and America were increasingly outfitted with modern technical equipment whereas the Soviet system used the "most backwards trade equipment and instruments," leading to a discrepancy "between contemporary industrial technology and the technology of the circulation of goods."[31] Finally, the "complete reconstruction of [the trade system's] technical-material base" was instrumental in a broader sense: updated equipment would facilitate the development of cultured Soviet trade. In particular, trade authorities noted, mechanization and technical reconstruction would enhance "the quality of customer service."[32]

The trade establishment favored the adoption of technical devices that would increase labor productivity, accuracy, and worker accountability – goals that were not only common in other industries at this time but were also a product of reformers' interest in advancing Soviet retail modernity and in reducing the unscrupulous retail practices associated with the NEP era and rationing. Trade commissar Veitser, for example, argued that meat-slicing machines and electric knives promoted greater efficiency and precision.[33] Reformers hoped to increase and improve the manufacturing of weights and scales because all too often "salesclerks had to wait [to use] necessary weights or scales," and because the unreliability of existing devices contributed to frequent errors and allowed deceptive practices.[34] The People's Commissariat of Domestic Trade (Narkomvnutorg) was particularly interested in manufacturing the dial-balance scales already common in the United States, Germany, and Sweden, as such scales were more time-efficient. Moreover, since they allowed consumers to read the dials themselves and catch "mistakes," they prevented fraud.[35] Mechanical cash registers promised similar benefits to a Soviet retailing sector still largely dependent on the abacus.[36] As of late 1935 there were only 10,000 to 12,000 cash registers, primarily older foreign models, in use.[37] More were needed to speed up the sales process and solve an endemic problem with Soviet retailing: long queues. The more sophisticated machines provided accountability, recording on paper the item purchased, its cost, sales department, and assisting salesclerk. They were seen "not [as a mere] money box, but as an apparatus for the quick accounting of current store operations." Slippage, tagging mistakes, and theft could be tracked to individual salesclerks or departments.[38]

If the mechanized scale and cash register were central to reformers' vision of modernization, so too was the refrigerator. The visible presence of insects and rodents in stores seemed to underscore the missing prerequisite to modern and cultured trade, proper sanitation.[39] The flies that plagued so many stores and warehouses seemed especially to cry out for technological improvements.[40] Cultural comparison pointed to the dearth of Soviet refrigerators and cold counters. N. Shinkarevskii explained, "the one inalienable particularity of the American food store, its soul, is the cold…." Refrigeration solved a "very important problem – the struggle with flies," that apparently caused no difficulty in American shops.[41] Refrigeration improved not only retail sanitation but also extended food life, even on "hot days," allowing for continuous turnover of perishable goods.[42] Foreign stores also regulated relative humidity and ensured proper ventilation, which helped preserve perishables, especially vegetables and fruits.[43] Commissar Veitser recognized that it would be a massive undertaking to achieve greater refrigeration and improved ventilation in Soviet retailing. In the mid-1930s, most Soviet shops had little or no refrigeration: in 1935 only 24 percent of meat and fish stores and 17 percent of dairy shops in the consumer cooperative system had iceboxes or cold storehouses, and only 7 percent of food stores in Moscow had any refrigeration. Nonetheless, Veitser argued that in Soviet stores the salesclerks were freezing and goods were warm, and if this could be reversed, everybody would reap the benefits.[44] With the goal of universal refrigeration in mind, trade officials pursued greater domestic production while simultaneously importing more foreign equipment.[45]

As reformers looked at modern retail tools and technologies used in the capitalist West, they became particularly enamored with the prepackaging of merchandise, especially foodstuffs.[46] Trade officials argued it would allow for "greater hygiene" and greater efficiency by lessening the need for the weighing, measuring, and wrapping of products, thereby economizing retail workers' and customers' time and energy. M. P. Smirnov asserted that the prepackaging of goods in American stores increased capacity by "7–10 times."[47] Prepackaging served "order and cleanliness" in the handling of dry goods by reducing messes and the need for big storage bags and barrels, and by decreasing transport losses and on-site contamination.[48] Officials had reason to be concerned about the hygiene of bulk food sales given the general scarcity of packaging materials. One customer reported a store had wrapped his sugar in "filthy paper from an old book," a dictionary of Church-Slavonic.[49] Worse, there were reports of wastepaper from hospitals and medical offices being reused for on-site food packaging.[50] Interest in prepackaging led authorities to direct heavy industry to increase the production of both wrapping materials and related machinery. Cellophane, used in capitalist countries, was particularly prized for its efficacy, practicality, and association with modernity.[51]

These new tools and technologies were viewed as necessary instruments for a revolutionary, technological transformation of the entire retail infrastructure. This change was conceived of in very basic terms. While trade officials were undoubtedly enchanted by Western showcase items such as the elevators and escalators of the *grands magasins*, they also seized on more utilitarian technologies, such as refrigeration and sanitary packaging. The absence of the technological in Soviet retailing underlined its failure to provide basic amenities – proper lighting, plumbing, heat, and ventilation – which in turn discouraged customers from home and abroad. Apparently these daily failures constituted nothing less than a poor bill of health. Store director Nechaev explained how bad ventilation in his Leningrad store occasionally made it necessary "to call the ambulance" for salesclerks and customers. He considered conditions unbearable, even criminal, for "heart attacks" could result from the lack of appropriate ventilation. Such conditions not only threatened the health of employees and customers, but also contributed to labor turnover, which Nechaev claimed reached 70 percent during the summer.[52] Trade union leader G. Moroz argued that the paucity of "elementary things" in stores, such as lavatories or rest areas where employees could sit down and have a smoke, diminished labor productivity.[53] Another trade union leader pointed out that poor store conditions constituted a "political" matter:

> When representatives of foreign governments come to Moscow and visit the Central Department Store, they will first direct attention to the work conditions of the Soviet salesclerk... What can the [store] boast of?... Air – from which salesclerks faint and customers try to escape quickly to the street.[54]

Because of poor store conditions, trade reformers argued, it was important to draw upon the "rich foreign experience in the construction of huge department stores" so that questions of lighting, heating, ventilation, and fire prevention could be better addressed.[55]

Scientific rationalism and better organization

Plans to reconstruct the retail infrastructure included extensive discussion about rethinking retail space, retail time, and retail motion. The pursuit of scientific rationalism in other sectors of the economy encouraged trade reformers to pursue "rationalizing" strategies in retailing through increased standardization, planning, and centralization. In searching for new strategies, trade reformers turned their gaze to the West as they had done in their search for new retail tools and technologies. Reporting his findings from a research trip, trade leader Gumnitskii openly admired the advances within the American retail industry. Acknowledging the error in his preconceptions of a mechanized retail sphere dominated by "conveyor belts," he saw "the orderly system of [trade] organization" as the real American retail innovation. If Soviet retail space could be better organized and presented, Gumnitskii reasoned, the Soviets could "catch up to and surpass America."[56]

Rationalizing the external and
internal design of stores

The aesthetic impulse in modernizing the old retailing infrastructure was largely destructive: reformers wanted to eliminate the system's backwardness, idiosyncrasy, and antiquated disorder. Moscow trade leader M. Epshtein explained the reasoning behind this impetus. He noted that out of approximately 3,000 shops in Moscow, 2,560 had been constructed before 1917. Each bore the unfortunate imprint of prerevolutionary trade: "Tasteless" and "motley" store exteriors suggested that private merchants had merely "fantasized" as they decorated and designed their shops. These formerly private urban stores were ugly and garish.[57] Trade union leader G. Moroz similarly lamented the random internal décor of many stores, which he claimed underscored their "complete Asiaticness [sic]." This equation of clutter with backward "Asianness" was an old prejudice, but it took on new meaning in the 1930s precisely by combining with new visions of modernity.[58] Tobacco stores decorated through Ukrainian craftsmanship seemed part of "the olden days," and therefore inappropriate. A Moscow confectionary store seemed wrongly feminine, lacking only the requisite "flowers and small couches," before "one could sit and smoke [as if] in [a woman's] boudoir." For Moroz and others, such cluttered feminine ornamentation communicated backwardness, tastelessness, and impracticality.[59] As a deputy trade commissar pointed out, it made no sense to decorate a store with carved wood that absorbed dust easily and was difficult to clean.[60]

Such aesthetic and practical concerns came together in the mass condemnation of existing retail establishments. Epshtein disparaged the many older "dwarfed shops" that resembled "narrow kielbasa," because they did a poor job of accommodating even a small number of customers. According to Epshtein, the retail sector had "clung" to these old shops without taking the initiative to make them more useful or logical. In order to meet "the most elementary needs of Soviet trade," he proposed tearing down the walls between small shops to create larger, more rationally planned retail establishments. Other trade authorities similarly advocated the transformation of "old, squalid, and unsightly" rural shops into standardized, larger, and "cultured" district rural stores.[61] Typically, the motivation for this proposal went beyond aesthetic considerations. Rural shops frequently had narrow windows, and hence poor light, which made it easier for personnel to cheat customers.[62]

Foreign stores again served as a model for the scientific retail future. Gumnitskii enthused about the new Sears and Roebuck department store in Chicago. He explained how the building was uniquely designed: its only windows were the first floor displays. Windowless floors apparently had 35 percent more space for the sale of goods, which allowed for "every little piece of the store [to be] used rationally."[63] Gumnitskii noted that such rationalism was often incorporated into foreign stores' equipment and furnishings. Soviet stores, by contrast, were poorly planned and filled with wasted space. Unnecessary columns blocked access to valuable sales counters, and sales areas too narrow to accommodate display cases were widespread.[64] A more extensively planned architecture would allow for better interior organization, liberating salesclerks from haphazardly arranged retail furniture, marathon distances from counters, or excessively cramped quarters that impeded efficiency.[65]

The next step after rationalizing space was to standardize equipment. Embracing the standardized and mass-produced shop equipment already used abroad, reformers aimed to purge the "Asiatic" furnishings produced by decentralized craft manufacturing.[66] In their view, the benefits of standardized and mass-produced store furniture were numerous. It could replace unsightly, expensive, and "difficult and cumbersome" store furnishings.[67] Trade leader M. Smirnov attacked artisanal furnishings, saying it was "time to stop the pointless waste of resources on individual, often tasteless, and always expensive furniture that no one needed." The savings could, for example, be redirected to the purchase of machinery that was universally useful, such as those for the in-store preparation and sale of hot sausages and cutlets.[68] Standardized, mass-produced equipment also promised greater efficiency and convenience. Stores could order and receive it quickly instead of having to wait for artisan cooperatives to finish custom orders. If constructed as it was abroad, store furniture could be flexible and modular: counters and shelves would then be simpler to move and reassemble. Uniform display counters could also allow customers to scan shops more easily, since counters would be of uniform height.[69]

This spatial logic could further be applied to improve the movement of people in stores. Deputy trade commissar Bolotin endorsed greater uniformity in the interior layout of stores, seeing the American trading firm, the Atlantic and Pacific Tea Company (A&P), as a positive model. As he noted, each of its 15,000 stores had the same design. Consequently, "if matches were placed on the right [side of the store], then matches would be situated on the right [side] in all the stores." Bolotin argued that such uniformity of layout would be beneficial for both customers and salesclerks. Customers would be "easily oriented" in stores, knowing in advance where goods were situated. This rationally organized space would promote greater labor productivity, since salesclerks would not "get confused" or "make mistakes." Hence they would "work calmly," and overall their work would "go better." A clearly structured layout would also distinguish the new Soviet store from its predecessor, in which merchandise and retail departments were arranged in an "unsystematic and disorderly" manner.[70]

Rationalizing the display of merchandise

As trade reformers sought to improve the external and internal organization of stores, they also aimed to improve the display of Soviet merchandise. Moscow trade leader Epshtein summed up what many reformers saw as a problem when he complained, "When I was in America I saw the following: There a bad product is displayed in such a way that it looks good. We have the opposite – a good product is displayed in such a way that it looks bad."[71] To enhance the display of goods, reformers extended the principle of scientific rationalism to the organization of merchandise and looked to the West for ideas. Gumnitskii, for instance, applauded capitalist stores that arranged clothing according to size, which made the selection of goods "much easier and simpler."[72] Reformers particularly liked the capitalist strategy of "ensembling" goods, that is, displaying kindred merchandise together. By the 1920s, ensembling took on new forms in the capitalist West because "accessorizing" became a common practice in department stores.[73] As merchants accessorized primary consumer goods, such as dresses, with secondary items, such as handbags, retail departments featured primary commodities along with a lesser collection of supplementary items. As a Soviet article on foreign department stores noted, ensembling encouraged customers to buy a "suit in one department" along with the coordinating shirts, handkerchiefs, "and other small items without wasting time searching for these articles in [other] departments, often located on a different floor."[74] If used in the Soviet Union, this practice would serve the customers' interests, increase sales, and be more logical. Moreover, ensembling would contribute to the trade campaign's goal to "educate" the consumer. As one store director explained, it made sense for soap and tooth powder to be located next to perfume. Ensembling did a wonderful job of "orienting the customer" by helping consumers find what they were looking for and reminding them of additional related items.[75]

Capitalist merchandise displays emphasized dynamism and novelty, and this impressed trade reformers. By exhibiting "different novelties in action" or offering food samples, common especially in America, customers would be introduced to new items.[76] At Woolworth's, for example, as a saleswoman stood on display and pulled out hairpins to demonstrate her new curls, she was "showing the hairpins in action," which helped to increase hairpins sales. "This system of demonstrating goods," Gumnitskii concluded, was "undoubtedly right" for the Soviet system.[77] The proactive showcasing of the broadening array of Soviet foodstuffs and mass consumer goods would educate consumers and contribute to healthy economic turnover.

The fascination with the West reached a point of excited contradiction in the Soviet trade reformers' comportment over window displays. Seen as important vehicles for communicating with customers, indeed as "the cheapest form of advertising," window displays were considered highly effective advertising that was nonetheless socialist.[78] What constituted a "good" display, however, was however far from self-evident. Officials were painfully aware that Soviet merchandise was not always presented in an attractive and pleasing manner, and they encouraged the study of foreign techniques for organizing such displays, promoting albums with positive examples from Soviet and foreign stores.[79] But trade reformers also worried about borrowing wholesale from the West, for storefronts and window displays, like capitalist advertising, seemed more ideologically charged than questions of rational store organization or cultured ensembling. It was best if such concerns did not need to be stated negatively, but turned into a virtue. Thus an article in *Sovestskaia torgovlia* warned that it was necessary "to carefully take into consideration foreign experience and then create our own Soviet style."[80] But when the appeal to a unique style failed, there was no hesitation to point out the dangers of direct emulation: like capitalist advertising, Western window displays aimed to deceive consumers, and this needed to change. As M. Shereshevskii explained, some displays were composed of "special installations" that bore "the imprint of treachery," bearing no clear relation to the actual product. Socialist window displays, he reasoned, should be honest and informative, eschewing all deception: they should be educational and intriguing without manipulating desires.[81]

So emerged a complex aesthetic mandate. Displays in Leningrad were judged negatively for being so lively and gaudy that the customer remembered the attraction "but forgot the product." Other displays were so complicated and crowded that customers became confused about what was being exhibited, or their excessive adornment blocked light and made it difficult for customers to discern the quality of merchandise. Dynamic displays were worthwhile only if they "informed the customer and publicized goods" in a coherent and tasteful manner.[82] When all else failed, officials could point to a comforting feature of many capitalist window displays: the fact that many were centrally planned through marketing "campaigns." Such central planning could help rid the Soviet system of haphazard and ill-thought out displays. Reformers additionally favored the adoption of narrative techniques that embedded goods in a history that seemed educational, such as "the history of women's bags." Such techniques not only attracted the passerby, but could also deliver a political message. Popular in this regard were themes that conjoined mass production and collective endeavor: the Moscow Central Department Store's display on "the party and government's concern about children of our socialist motherland" presented a visual statement about Soviet progress. Finally, reformers admired the standardized and mass-produced equipment used in capitalist storefronts and window displays.[83]

Rationalizing the sales process

The next logical step was to scrutinize the sales process, hoping to organize it in a more efficient and rational manner. As with other features of Soviet trade, there was no clear "socialist" answer about how to streamline the movement of customers and goods through stores. Some proposals garnered more support than others, but all involved negotiating the perceived tensions between potential greater efficiency and the enduring suspicions concerning the trustworthiness of retail workers and customers. Discussions about self-service shopping, a retail innovation that was spreading in the capitalist West, galvanized these concerns. The "open" counters and shelves that allowed customers to look at merchandise freely and without assistance were applauded as the essence of modern aesthetics and both time and labor efficiency.[84] Researchers at Tsentrosoiuz's Central Scientific-Research Institute of Soviet Trade, for example, marveled at the orderly and compact design of American self-service "Piggly Wiggly" grocery stores. Although small and narrow, these stores nevertheless allowed crowds of consumers to select goods themselves, and thereby lowered overall fixed costs.[85] It is telling that despite clear agreement on the efficiency of this system, retail reformers did little to adopt it. [86] Implementation concerns and the accepted imperatives of social control mingled with ideological suspicions to make self-selection seem unfeasible in a society with severe shortages. As one journalist pointed out, although a self-service fruit and vegetable store on Moscow's *Arbat* operated effectively, this was impossible for stores with enormous crowds. Too many customers in stores with open shelves led to inventory slippage.[87] Given the acute scarcity that continued to mark the 1930s, trade authorities doubted that consumers would act responsibly if they had easy access to merchandise, and they opined that speculators might easily take advantage of such systems.

Concerns about the balance between efficiency of operations and distrust of customers and workers shaped efforts to reform the sales process in another significant way. Trade leaders decided to retain the Soviet *kassa* (cash box) system that required customers to wait in three distinct lines to make a purchase. First they had to request an item and procure a slip of paper listing its price. They then had to pay at the designated cashier. Finally it was necessary to take the receipt to the original sales counter or a designated counter where purchases were distributed in order to claim the item. If the store was divided into departments, this could be particularly tortuous because customers were not allowed to pay for items from different departments at a single cash box. Customers objected to the *kassa* system, viewing it as unnecessarily time-consuming, and researchers acknowledged that in small stores the *kassa* system slowed the shopping process, but the system was retained with the justification that in large stores it supposedly lessened the amount of time customers spent making purchases. Using the language of the trade campaign, researchers also argued it was rational to have "trained" cashiers accept money when there was a great mass of consumers. But more fundamentally, researchers believed that the *kassa* system reduced theft and graft, since fewer employees were entrusted to handle money, and none handled both goods and money.[88] This was presented as offering increased protection for the customers.[89] While it retained the *kassa* system, the trade establishment did introduce a concession to consumers in some larger stores, the "mixed" cash box (*sbornaia kassa*), which allowed customers to pay for all purchases at once even as they continued to stand in separate lines to order and receive merchandise.[90]

As trade reformers explored ideas for reconstructing the sales process, they pointed to the practical convenience of selling goods by the piece and not by weight. Citing Western experience, trade officials and store managers argued that this practice increased efficiency and promoted cleanliness. Customers who purchased "piece goods" (*shtuchnye tovary*) were allowed to pay a salesclerk directly, bypassing the time-consuming *kassa* system altogether. Salesclerks were relieved from the weighing and sorting of goods. And because piece goods (like macaroni) were often prepackaged, this retail practice fostered greater hygiene.[91] According to trade leader Shinkarevskii, selling goods by the piece also reduced opportunities for errors in or manipulations of the actual weight of a product.[92] Trade official I. Isaev agreed, noting that in America, the sale of *shtuchnye tovary* had precisely this effect.[93] Along with interest in this new sales technique came interest in advance-ordering and home delivery, both of which in principle could economize retail employees' and customers' time.[94] The latter practice particularly captured the imagination of trade authorities because they considered it a standard and modern convenience offered in capitalist countries. In addition, Soviet customers liked home delivery, and it broadened the geographical boundaries of stores, allowing them to serve larger populations.[95]

To further rationalize the sales process, trade authorities acknowledged the importance of expanding the parameters of retailing. In the mid-1930s most urban stores and stalls were still centrally but not necessarily conveniently located. To compensate for this and the overall shortage of retail venues, reformers advocated mobile delivery systems, often embracing older and distinctly nonmodern methods, such as handcarts and hawker's trays, which could be supplemented with more modern forms, such as mobile booths and "auto-stores." They supported the development of auto-stores – vehicles with merchandise – because they could sell goods along routes lacking permanent shops. In developing these plans, here too reformers turned to the experience and models of foreign firms that utilized mobile retail trade.[96]

Rationalizing the organization of distribution

One of the recurring issues in trade reform was the question of how to organize national distribution in a more rational and effective way. Meeting with press representatives in 1933, trade leader Zelenskii explained a recent decision to focus the bulk of retail expansion in urban and regional centers: he feared that spreading distribution evenly throughout the country would dilute its psychological impact. For example, if the total number of goods produced was increased by 15 to 20 percent but distributed throughout the rural network of consumer cooperatives with its 130,000 shops, increases would not be particularly noticeable. He claimed that peasant-collective farm workers (*kolkhozniki*) would be disenchanted, failing to see clear improvements in rural retailing. They might even begin to think that authorities were lying about purported changes. If distribution was concentrated instead on urban and regional centers, and collective-farm workers knew that they could travel to a regional center and find necessary goods, they would see the logic and the success of the retail system. According to Zelenskii, the recent government and party decree to open 2,000 new stores in regional centers would ultimately open up opportunities to *kolkhozniki*.[97] While *kolkhozniki* probably disagreed with Zelenskii's conclusions, there was an underlying (though perhaps faulty) logic to his thinking.

Another answer to the question of how best to organize national distribution was to expand the network of specialized stores that focused on specific categories of consumer goods, such as haberdashery or readymade clothing, and to give them preferential allocations of merchandise.[98] Specialized shops engaged in "open" or commercial trade and sold goods at higher prices than most stores. They also concentrated their efforts on the sale of nonrationed goods. Trade reformers ascribed rationality to their support for specialized distribution. Economist V. Stushkov argued that not every store should sell every kind of merchandise. It was more logical for some goods to be centralized and sold in specialized stores located in urban and regional centers and made available for delivery to outlying districts via postal trade. It was better for the consumer "to have a rich assortment" of goods in a specialized store focused on "furniture, winter coats, cameras, expensive wine, and so on," rather than a poor selection from a general store next door.[99] Trade leader Epshtein also favored greater retail specialization because he deemed the general store (*univermag*) impractical. Reportedly 90 percent of these stores failed to stock an adequate assortment of goods. As a result, he noted, it was unclear what a *univermag* sold, and too many customers wasted time in the *univermag* hoping they might find a given product. This frustrated customers and often caused commotion in stores.[100] He might well have added that the largely empty general stores also underscored the persistence of shortages. It was probably this realization that prompted Epstein and others to promote specialized stores as a way to increase concentrations of available merchandise and make shopping more predictable. But even if specialization could define rationality, it was only with difficulty that it could be reconciled with egalitarianism. Not all consumers had equal access to the small but growing network of specialized stores and their specialty goods. Trade authorities acknowledged this shortcoming, but reasoned that highly constrained goods were already hard to find in general stores, so a trek to a specialty store would constitute no more of a hardship. For consumers who could make their way to the specialized shops, goods shortages would be less onerous (at least in principle). Moreover, because employees with more specific merchandise training and knowledge were supposed to work in specialized stores (to deal with the store's specialty), consumers would also receive better customer service than in most general stores.[101]

The drive toward the rationalization of distribution advanced the development of "model" stores in both the specialized and universal retail sectors. In 1933 the trade establishment opened the *Gastronom* groceries, which sold delicacies, tobacco, and liquor (among other items), the *Bakaleia* food shops, which featured dry goods like cereals and pasta, and "model" department stores.[102] As scholars have noted, resources poured into these model stores at the expense of ordinary stores. "Instead of effectively organizing the conditions of regular trade all over the country in a less grandiose manner," Jukka Gronow points out, "a few luxurious model shops opened in Moscow and other big cities, serving as hallmarks of the supposed new abundance."[103] It was extravagant for the Soviet regime to outfit the premier food store in Moscow, *Gastronom* #1, with multiple modern retail technologies and to stock it (reportedly) with 117 different kinds of fish, 52 different sausages, and 223 varieties of wine and vodka, when so many ordinary stores suffered from inadequate infrastructure and largely empty shelves.[104] The policy of favoring high-price model stores had similar effects to the focus on certain regions: it imposed a "hierarchy of consumption" among sectors of the populace.[105] Differences in consumer wealth and regional access fostered an uneven system of national distribution. But the hope was that the logic of rationalization would allow the model shops, like the specialized stores, to transcend the zero-sum problem by providing consumers with more consistent access to goods: either specific foodstuffs or a diversity of department store products. To promote this objective, the party-state prioritized model stores' supply of consumer goods and hoped they would operate as a vanguard force for cultured retailing. Leading by example, they would encourage nonmodel shops to improve their service, abandon their mechanical distribution of products, and embrace new retail methods.[106] Model stores' distinctive status was supposed to be temporary: they would become less noteworthy as more were established and as other stores improved their customer service and retail practices. Trade officials claimed that for this reason model stores would need to be opened in ever-more distant and dispersed locales.[107] Wholly of a piece with trade reformers' conception of cultured retailing, the model stores mixed high-brow and populist logics in with modernist and rational-bureaucratic tropes in a distinctly Soviet style.

From planning to implementation

In the 1930s the retail infrastructure expanded even as good shortages persisted. In 1932 alone, the People's Commissariat of Supply (Narkomsnab) established 7,100 new stores and 5,900 new trading stalls. Tsentrosoiuz opened 13,100 new shops and 22,500 trading booths.[108] Throughout the 1930s, the Soviets excelled at creating distribution networks. This expansion was uneven, benefiting some regions and republics more than others, especially the Russian and Ukrainian Republics. Nonetheless, if in 1928 there were 155,241 stores and stalls in the cooperative and state trade system, by 1940 there were 407,204.[109] Mobile methods of trade likewise expanded.[110] Progress was also made in renovating stores, depots, and other retail venues. In 1937, for example, the cooperative network in the countryside reported repairs to approximately 30,000 stores and small shops. Although specialized stores continued to constitute a small percentage of the overall trade network, their numbers expanded, and by early 1936, there were almost 43,000 specialized stores in urban areas.[111] Some chains experienced significant growth. By the end of 1936, the model specialized *Gastronom* and *Bakaleia* stores dotted approximately 250 major industrial and urban landscapes across the Soviet Union.[112] Other specialized stores multiplied primarily in the Soviet Union's capital cities, especially in Moscow. The first specialized crystal store made its debut in Moscow in January 1936, selling over one hundred different types of glasses. A "dietetic" store, in which nurses and doctors sold special "health products" alongside health advice, opened on Moscow's Arbat in January 1937.[113] Although plans to open new unit price stores in the late 1930s were never realized, unit price departments and kiosks within stores experienced rapid growth.[114]

The practical implementation of reformers' ambitious plans to modernize retail trade via mechanization and retooling was greatly thwarted by endemic problems in obtaining raw materials and moving them through the production system. Narkomvnutorg, for example, anticipated increased production of scales and cash registers in the mid-1930s.[115] But party-state directives to advance the manufacturing of retail technologies were not well realized: in 1935, for example, the goal of producing 3,000 dial-balance scales yielded a disappointing 900 units. Factories not only failed to meet production plans, but they tended to manufacture the more "technically backward" scales and cash registers (compared to those found in the capitalist West), presumably because they were easier and cheaper to produce.[116] Meanwhile, faulty and expensive equipment abounded. New scales, for example, often failed by their "third day" in operation.[117] Desperate for intermediate devices, trade organizations continued to import foreign technologies.[118]

The Communist leadership's continued emphasis in the 1930s on heavy industry and capital goods production undermined retail reform efforts. New retail technologies were difficult to develop without the necessary capital investment. To a lesser extent this was also true for strategies for rationalization. Some improvements required only a detailed plan and the political will to implement, while others required significant resources. Moreover, consumer goods shortages, due largely but not exclusively to the emphasis on industrial goods, challenged the efficacy of organizational innovations. Officials clearly wanted window displays that were "honest" and "informative." But when such displays showcased unobtainable goods, they undercut both the practical and the ideological function of these displays. They served neither to communicate the availability of the goods in question, nor to bolster the image of a rational and honest retail sector.[119] The shortcomings of the trade campaign were obvious and public, reported widely by the media. Authorities made no pretense of success. They repeatedly drew up new plans and decrees designed to address the limitations of reform efforts. They modified plans and resorted to practical compromises. They adopted measures to increase public accountability for reform goals. But despite these efforts, the regime's ability to expand the retail infrastructure outstripped the ability to make it function smoothly, to have goods to deliver, and to stimulate the rationalization that it sought to emulate from the West.

The human element and limits of rational planning

The campaign to transform retailing seemed to authorize officials to blame workers whenever things did not go well. During the paranoid political climate of the 1930s, the many troubles in the retail network seemed proof of sabotage. Such charges corresponded with Soviet discourse on the need to purify society of "enemies."[120] Perversely, these charges always reappeared to bolster the cause of failed reforms: if the goal was to construct a retail network free of the kind of "enemies" symbolically represented in the stereotype of the unscrupulous and exploitative Nepman, all failures could be ascribed to the ongoing power of this shadowy enemy. Authorities accused workers of malfeasance, of being "backwards," and of lacking modern sensibilities necessary for rationalizing retail trade. Trade reformers could reaffirm their commitment to the cause of Soviet trade through trumped-up recrimination of retail employees, even if the resulting punitive responses (e.g., dismissals) undoubtedly undercut reform and contributed to chaos and labor turnover.

The scapegoating of class aliens and "wreckers" was an integral part of the Stalinist 1930s. In this respect, the retail sector differed little from other spheres. But trade authorities decried what they saw as serious human barriers to reform efforts. Corruption was one problem. Another problem was resistance to change. Reformers noted that the adoption of new tools, technologies, and organizational strategies sometimes failed because retail employees and trade administrators lacked the proper attitude about these matters.[121] Trade Commissar Veitser argued that many "qualified salesclerks" possessed "strong anti-mechanical tendencies" and viewed new retail technologies as competition.[122] Even some trade leaders "underestimate[d] the role of technology in trade," disdained it, and "sometimes even sabotage[d] mechanization." For almost two years various trade organizations in Kiev neglected to deploy a whole array of labor-saving devices. One local trade leader responded to this discovery with hostility, saying, "Brigades arriving from Moscow only confuse and bother us. Take your automatic scales, band-saws, and ham-slicers, and then we will say that you have helped us. We don't want them and we will not set them up."[123]

The fact that trade policy was far from ideologically exciting and did not necessarily provoke enthusiasm was another cause of concern. Trade authorities were continuously outraged by employees' indifference to retail reform. M. Epshtein chastised retail personnel for not caring about the plagues of flies infesting their stores. In pointing to the absurdity of this failure, he referred to the battle against White generals during the Civil War: "We defeated Denikin, we defeated Kolchak, but we can't deal with flies, we retreat from flies." Refrigeration was lacking, to be sure, but apathy seemed to be in great supply, and reformers puzzled as to why proper storage and retail sanitation moved so few people.[124]

Unable to solve deficits of scarce resources, authorities repeatedly blamed individuals for not doing more to improve the system. In response to those who claimed that lines resulted from the paucity of cashiers, wrapping paper, and tape, Epshtein proclaimed that lines were due to "the lack of concern for the customer and the habits of trading in an uncultured manner." Instead of combating lines, store managers and salespeople accepted them. Epshtein recounted his experience of going into a store with an adequate supply of wrapping paper and multiple cashiers. Confronted with a line of 30 people, he asked the store director why it existed. Apparently the store manager replied that a line of this size was "nothing." Epshtein concluded that managerial negligence was the main problem.[125] The editorial staff for *Sovetskaia torgovlia* agreed: those who argued that lines were inevitable needed to employ techniques by which salesclerks could "liquidate lines." But to do this, they had to care.[126]

Reformers recognized that the reconstruction of retailing required the transformation of the human element of trade. Scientific rationalism could contribute to more logical retailing and technologies could boost efficiency, but neither could transform trade employees who had unhygienic habits or indifferent attitudes toward embracing new tools, practices, and the official vision of cultured Soviet trade. As a consequence, trade officials expanded their efforts to educate employees and to integrate them into the trade campaign. They also turned to strategies for incorporating customers into reform efforts. They aimed for cadres of dedicated workers and consumer activists to compensate for the limitations of rational planning and structural insufficiencies.

* * *

In envisioning a reconstructed infrastructure, reformers embraced the Soviet objectives of technological modernization and scientific rationalism, and turned to the West for models of modern retail design and practice. Despite visions for a major *perestroika* of retailing, including its "nuts and bolts," plans for reconstruction resulted in a characteristically uneven mixture of relative success and absolute failure typical of the Soviet system. Some stores received new devices for slicing meat or measuring swaths of cloth; most stores relied on laborious and time-consuming human processes. Some retail establishments featured fancy new cash registers and a wide assortment of merchandise; most shops relied on the abacus and a limited selection of goods. Some shops boasted innovative and attractive window displays and a rational arrangement of goods; most stores featured grim displays and the disorderly and sometimes dangerous arrangement of products (such as kerosene on sale next to food items). The more successfully reconstructed stores usually charged higher prices and were located in the downtown areas of urban and regional centers, which restricted access to them. That reformers' plans were in many ways well-intentioned but ultimately failed the people of average or lesser means whom they hoped to serve was unfortunately a familiar refrain.

Had Communist leaders provided the trade establishment with more resources to implement reforms, such as increased funding, better access to constrained materials, and a greater supply of new tools of modern retailing, and had macroeconomic policy been geared less toward the production of armaments or capital equipment and more toward the production of mass consumer goods to put in stores, reformers' efforts to realize a modern revolution in retailing would have been more effective. But plans for retail reconstruction faltered, and as they did, trade authorities directed their focus toward one area over which they seemed to have greater control: the "human resources" of the retail world. They emphasized tactics for transforming the retail sector that relied more heavily on the labors of retail employees and consumers.

3
Legitimizing Soviet Trade
Gender and the Feminization of the Retail Workforce

> The first thing the shop owner or manager says when you ask for a job is: "Are you ticklish?" If you bat your eyes or nod your head suggestively, the job is yours. But if you don't agree, you might as well forget it.
>
> Shop clerk, 1908

> Year-round, we have to work a fifteen- or sixteen-hour day. We don't get any time off for lunch... [Our] long hours and low wages force us to turn to the shameful trade. Our wages do not give us enough money to survive, but the bosses still demand that we dress fashionably. We can't fight this because Petersburg is full of girls who are willing to work fifteen hours a day just to get a crust of bread. The bosses want only good-looking girls.
>
> Salesclerk from a pastry shop, 1908[1]

Women retail workers in Tsarist Russia were treated poorly. They worked long hours for terrible wages, and were subjected to sexual harassment. Moreover, because of their miserly pay, and the concomitant expectation that they dress attractively, women often resorted to prostitution to make ends meet. Researcher A. M. Gudvan confirmed this general picture. He found that "in most cases, women had to pay their prospective employers 'in kind' to get a job in the first place. Their only recourse was to turn to prostitution, and what began as occasional prostitution would become a permanent source of income."[2]

The Soviet press in the 1930s publicized the exploitation of women salesclerks in prerevolutionary Russia and argued that they had been denied rights and "condemned" to lives of "degradation and prostitution."[3] It also painted a grim picture of the abusive working conditions that women retail workers in capitalist countries endured.[4] These depictions underscored the great fortune of Soviet women retail workers. In the 1930s, Soviet women became a significant part of the retail labor force, and during the campaign to establish "socialist" retailing, women employees came to symbolize the remaking of the retail system. Described as a "great force," women retail workers received widespread acclamation for their achievements.[5] The state rewarded them with financial bonuses, vacations, the Badge of Honor, and even the Order of Lenin, the highest Soviet award.[6] It recognized tens of thousands of women in retailing as labor heroes: exemplary workers (*otlichnitsy*), shock workers (*udarniky*), and Stakhanovites.[7] "From the veil to shock worker status," trumpeted the title of an article on women retail workers in Baku.[8] Women's stores, shops staffed primarily or exclusively by female personnel, were idealized as paragons of the new Soviet trade and praised for their successful commodity turnover, "ideal cleanliness," "accurate" display of goods, and excellent customer service.[9]

In some respects the feminization of the Soviet retail sector paralleled the feminization of the retail workforce in the capitalist West. As societies industrialized in the nineteenth century and a new commercial landscape developed, the retail workforce expanded dramatically and became increasingly feminized. Although women had long worked in small family shops (with little or no pay), few were initially employed in the new, larger-scale, and more modern retail venues in major Western European countries and the United States. But over time their numbers grew, and by the 1920s, women constituted the majority of salesclerks in the United States, Britain, France, and Germany. Retailers turned to women as men began to leave the retail sector for new opportunities and better-paying jobs in the expanding professional and industrial spheres. Retailers also hired women because they were a less expensive and less political labor force than men.[10] As women entered the paid retail workforce in greater numbers, many contemporaries worried about their susceptibility to materialistic temptations and vice in the face of advances by male customers, coworkers, and storeowners. Concerns began to fade, however, as retail trade and consumption were refigured as vehicles for the propagation of bourgeois and national values and taste. Saleswomen were reimagined as respectable and even talented employees who mobilized their "feminine knowledge" and maternal nature to promote sales. The woman salesclerk, along with the woman shopper, came to epitomize mass consumption and modernity.

Women's increased employment in the Soviet retail sector was also the product of extensive economic changes. And like their Western counterparts, Soviet women were touted as having particular womanly attributes that could improve retailing. Unlike them, however, their employment did not signify the success of capitalist consumerism. Rather it denoted the dawning of a new socialist era of rapid industrialization and the development of a noncapitalist system of retailing. Women's employment became linked to a broader Soviet objective: the transformation and legitimization of the Soviet retail sector. The growing presence of women workers in the retail sector came to represent the "Bolshevization" of retail cadres.

Indeed, the feminization of the Soviet retail workforce resulted in more than an influx of women workers; it turned out to be critical to the regime's campaign to remake retailing, and it contributed to the gendering of Soviet trade. As the trade campaign got under way and the female retail workforce grew, authorities and women workers themselves rationalized women's employment by proposing that women were better equipped for work in the retail sector than men. They constructed an image of a new woman retail worker whose "feminine" qualities could be used to promote excellence in retailing and the "new" practices promulgated in the trade campaign. In the process, highly valued attributes of the idealized new Soviet trade that reportedly distinguished it from both capitalist trade and the already existing state-controlled system became coded as "feminine." Communist authorities and the press praised women workers' purported "feminine" practices, such as solicitous customer care, and associated these practices with the ideal new retail worker, male or female. The new retail system that emerged in the 1930s was officially legitimized, at least in part, because of its feminine face. Significantly, the feminization of the retail sector had important implications not only for the incipient "socialist" trade system but also for the Soviet project as a whole. Because this feminization was accompanied by a new discourse of women's retail work that involved the reimagining of the feminine and the domestic, it reinforced a broader official move to reconceptualize women's roles and womanly characteristics in the 1930s. It contributed to the Communist government's efforts to attribute new importance to women as well as to the feminine and domestic in the crusade to build Soviet socialism.

Background: Women in the 1920s

How did women and a concept of femininity come to play a role in the campaign to transform and legitimize trade? After all, public applause for women retail workers in the 1930s stood in stark contrast to the

Communist regime's ambivalence about women in the 1920s. Although in principle the leadership supported women's emancipation and passed laws and policies to establish women's civic and legal equality after coming to power, in actuality many Soviet leaders continued a long-standing tradition of associating women with backwardness. Because in the 1920s the majority of women remained outside the regulated productive sector and official politics, it was easy for leaders to perceive of women as "backward." Communists viewed wage labor and political engagement as necessary for women's emancipation and full inclusion in the Soviet polity.[11] While an official discourse of equality promoted the "sameness" of women and men and informed early legislation, a parallel discourse focused on gender differences between men and women, and presented women's particularities as a problem. Women's continued dominance in the private sphere of the household, for example, heightened suspicion about their activities outside the home, because of concerns that the private contaminated the public.[12] Soviet authorities mobilized contradictory discourses, fluctuating between characterizing "woman" as a comrade or a *baba* ("backward" woman).[13] Woman was the new wage earner who had joined the revolutionary struggle as well as the worker who was not Soviet enough. She was the politically enlightened proletarian and the passive religious peasant. She was the self-sacrificing mother as well as the self-indulgent woman susceptible to petty-bourgeois habits. Communists ultimately remained uncertain about how to incorporate women into the socialist order as modern Soviet subjects, fearing that women's economic, political, and social "backwardness" would thwart revolutionary change. Even though the new government claimed that it supported gender equality, official discourse often represented women as backward and identified them with a narrow domestic purview.

The association of women salesclerks with the positive transformation of retailing is also surprising because retail work was not typically a woman's job when the Bolsheviks first came to power in 1917, nor was it in the 1920s. Although they probably constituted a larger percentage of the private retail workforce, women constituted only about 11 to 13 percent of the cooperative and state trade workforce in the mid-1920s. Moreover, most women employees worked as secretarial or cleaning help. The relatively few who worked in stores did so primarily as cashiers and not as salesclerks. By 1929 women's employment in cooperative and state trade had increased to 16 percent, still relatively low in comparison to women's percentage of the workforce in other service industries, such as public catering. Their participation as laborers in the socialist sector of retailing fell far short of the total percentage of women employed in the general labor force, which was 27.2 percent in 1929.[14]

The reasons for women's limited employment were twofold. First, while the party-state made some efforts to hire female employees in the 1920s, its main emphasis in the retail sector was on recruiting women to join consumer cooperatives and shop in cooperative and state stores (as opposed to private ones).[15] Soviet authorities assigned particular importance to women's membership in cooperatives, arguing that it weakened the influence of the private retail sector. They also saw it as an instrument for altering the everyday practices and consciousness of women. As cooperative members, women had access to cooperative facilities, like public canteens and laundries, which would move them "closer to full equality."[16] Active participation in cooperatives would introduce women to "public work," helping to "widen [their] horizons" and integrate them into the project to build socialism. As a women's group in Tashkent explained, membership was important because as Lenin had said, "Cooperation is the path towards socialism."[17]

The party-state's emphasis on getting women to become members of and shop in consumer cooperatives had implications for women's retail employment in Soviet Central Asia in the second half of the 1920s. Because Muslim women were not supposed to appear in public alongside men, consumer cooperatives began to organize "women's stores."[18] At many of the stores which opened in Uzbekistan (43 by October 1927), shoppers had access to tea-drinking opportunities, "red corners," "mother and children's corners," political discussions with *Zhenotdel* activists and store personnel, and lectures about "motherhood and infancy."[19] These stores also organized special women's shop commissions so that women could become cooperative activists. Because the stores offered Muslim women political instruction, health education, and opportunities to become active participants in the "socialist construction of the USSR," many cooperative officials and *Zhenotdel* activists concluded that these stores were useful vehicles for the destruction of old ways.[20] Although women's stores were established to draw Muslim women into consumer cooperatives, a secondary effect was the greater recruitment of women workers, albeit in small numbers. Moreover, women's stores proliferated throughout the Soviet Union in subsequent years, and during the trade campaign they served a new purpose: to highlight the successes of women retail workers.

The employment of women in the retail sector in the 1920s was also limited because retail work was perceived by many as men's work. After all, it entailed labor in unheated and dirty stores and warehouses, including strenuous duties, like lifting boxes and carrying heavy bags. Soviet authorities and male trade workers naturalized women's qualities to explain why women were not appropriate for retail work, using language that associated women's "drawbacks" with biological deficiencies, and criticizing women's lack of necessary physical strength, "natural timidity," and tendency to get ill. They pointed to women's ostensible backwardness, adding sociocultural reasons for not employing them: women had less know-how and lower rates of literacy than their male counterparts and were allegedly more religious and prejudiced.[21] As these comments suggest, many Soviet authorities and male employees saw women as less capable than men, and were dismissive of and actively hostile to women workers. As one male cooperative leader claimed in 1928, "Women know only how to wag their tongues, and they are not capable of doing anything."[22] A male manager in 1930 explained a woman worker's mistakes as a result of her "woman's head, woman's brains."[23] Given the low percentage of women workers in the "socialist" retail sector in the 1920s, and the many disapproving attitudes about them, the subsequent influx and celebration of women retail workers in the 1930s indicate major shifts in official policy and discourse.

Mobilizing women and rehabilitating retail trade

During the 1930s the Stalinist regime adopted a new approach to women. In 1928 there were approximately three million women in the paid workforce. By 1940 there were over thirteen million.[24] The dramatic increase in women's employment was due primarily to demographic and economic changes prompted by rapid industrialization and forced collectivization. Unemployment of the 1920s gave way to a significant and unanticipated labor shortage in 1930, which jeopardized not only the fulfillment of the First Five-Year Plan (FYP) but also the stability of the economy as a whole. To meet economic goals, in 1930–1931 the government revised its plans for the mobilization of women's labor, and composed a list of jobs and occupations for the predominant or exclusive employment of women, including many in cooperative and state trade.[25] The goal was to replace men with women so the men could be redirected to skilled and physically intensive industrial work. The new policy for women's involvement in the labor force was based on the concept of "integration through segregation," that is, the (re)gendering of entire sectors of the economy as female.[26]

The regime also made a more sustained effort than in the previous decade to mobilize non-wage earning women into various social and cultural initiatives. This move was expedient: women's unpaid labor as activists underwrote industrialization and served as a training ground for their possible move into wage labor. It also helped to socialize non-wage earning women by getting them out of the home and incorporating them into Soviet initiatives. Political leaders especially promoted women's participation in the wife-activists' movement and the party-state campaign for *kul'turnost'* (culturedness), encouraging women to get involved in myriad activities, including literacy work, workplace inspections, auxiliary labor, political agitation, and cultural uplift.

Rhetorical shifts accompanied women's new roles in wage labor and the public sphere. As women moved en masse into the workforce, official Soviet discourse about women's work changed. Whereas in the 1920s economists, labor analysts, and party officials often emphasized women workers' alleged physical weakness, inexperience, and lesser productivity, in the early 1930s they began to highlight women workers' achievements, even honoring female labor heroes.[27] They argued that many physical and skills barriers to women's employment had been removed due to mechanization and educational initiatives. And they ascribed positive attributes to women that provided additional reasons for employing them throughout the economy, such as women's greater efficiency and work discipline compared to their male counterparts.[28] Official discourse about non-wage earning women also changed. If in the 1920s it had generally characterized these women as unproductive and backward, in the 1930s it reconfigured them as valuable assets. In 1934 Soviet authorities promoted a wife-activists' movement, and urged wives' groups to assist their husbands in the construction of socialism, particularly the remaking of everyday life. As tens of thousands of wives became activists, authorities praised them for their participation in state-building efforts. They extolled wife-activists for their "social mothering" and "social cleaning," expressing widespread appreciation for the possibilities of women's supposed maternal disposition and household expertise in the public sphere, especially in regards to the drive to civilize and modernize the general populace.[29] Associating women activists with refined manners and cultivated behavior, political leaders depicted them as important symbols and agents of the transformation of ordinary individuals into cultured Soviet citizens.

The Stalinist regime's new approach to women in the 1930s had important ramifications for retail trade. In response to the 1931 directive to feminize many jobs in the retail sector, cooperative and state trade organs and the Trade Union of Cooperative and State Trade Workers (PRKGT) increased efforts to recruit women workers. Regional and local branches of these bodies pledged to meet the newly decreed responsibility "to hire women exclusively, replacing men's labor with women's," and to disallow "the reduction of women in the trade apparatus," except for when they violated rules.[30] The imperative to hire women was given a boost by the Soviet leadership's decision to launch a trade campaign: the development of Soviet trade required an expanded workforce. As a result of the regime's directive to promote women's mass employment in certain sectors, the trade campaign's labor needs, *and* women's own search for increased employment, the retail sector became increasingly feminized in the 1930s. By 1939, women comprised approximately 60 percent of salesclerks and 70 percent of cashier workers in urban areas as well as 38 percent of the overall retail workforce.[31]

Initially authorities targeted non-wage earning wives and daughters of workers as well as women already in the workforce (but in other spheres) for employment in the retail sector.[32] This recruitment strategy allowed for the economizing of resources in urban and industrial areas; the employment of these women did not necessitate as much expenditure on new services as did other groups, such as peasants. According to Communists, these women were also more reliable than other potential recruits because they were already of the working class.[33]

In seeking to explain women's mobilization, Soviet officials emphasized pragmatic reasons. First, men's labor was needed for industry. Second, retail work had become more appropriate for women because of the benefits of technology and rationalization. Though the mechanization of retail trade was still in its infancy, trade authorities proposed that it would facilitate the "widespread introduction of women's labor" by making some aspects of trade work easier. The mechanization of the transport and storage of goods, for example, meant that men's "strength" in retailing could be redirected to industry. The introduction of machines also allowed for the deskilling of certain tasks, such as the slicing of meat, which enabled unskilled workers, including women, to take on jobs in a relatively quick manner that had previously required lengthy training. A more rational division of labor likewise permitted women's greater employment in the retail sector. If men carried out tasks that required more physical strength, then women could take on the remaining duties.[34]

The Stalinist regime's valorization of women's attributes to justify their greater employment in the 1930s was reproduced by cooperative and state trade officials as well as trade-union authorities. Instead of explaining women's mobilization in the retail sector by referring merely to practical and economic exigencies, they chose instead to reframe women's work by arguing that women workers were actually better suited than men to meet the requirements of the new retail system. Imagining Soviet trade as honest, modern and rational, responsive and edifying, efficient and cultured, officials constructed a new woman retail worker whose merits would promote this vision of socialist retailing. Her virtues were grounded in gender stereotypes operating at two levels: those based on allegedly innate or essential characteristics of women and those based on presumptions about their domestic experience. In contrast to the 1920s, when women's ascribed qualities had supposedly hindered their ability to work effectively in retail trade, they apparently contributed to their successes in the 1930s.[35] The greater employment of women offered the promise that they would exert a positive influence on retailing by extending their womanly disposition and domestic skills to the trade sector. Casting women retail workers in the role of helpmates, authorities suggested that they would advance the trade campaign's goals to transform the existing system and alter the negative social meaning and practices of trade. Although some critics continued to raise the same objections to women's employment in the retail sector that were voiced in the 1920s, the emphasis in official discourse shifted from a negative to positive evaluation of women retail workers, contributing to efforts to give a more legitimate, modern, and Soviet image to both retail trade and women. Not surprisingly, women in the retail sector bolstered this discourse by emphasizing women's newly valid feminine and domestic characteristics in worker reports and at trade-union meetings. They deployed gender stereotypes to underscore their value as workers. Women leaders in the trade apparatus in particular underscored women's supposed feminine and domestic attributes to explain why more women should be hired and placed in managerial and leadership positions. Female salesclerks were "more polite and cultured" than male ones, a consumer cooperative chairwoman explained, and therefore should replace the already existing male employees. Another woman trade leader reminded her audience that even good men workers, on account of their drinking binges, were "weaker" than women workers and not always appropriate for leadership roles. Reportedly "most women," by virtue of their "character," were more capable than men of performing well in the retail sector.[36] Although women's comments about women retail workers' positive qualities and work practices in the 1930s were not exactly new (since some women in the retail sector had tried to make similar claims in the late 1920s), such remarks acquired new resonance during the trade campaign. In the 1930s, women's interest in promoting a more affirmative image of women retail workers converged with party and government interests.

Politically naïve

In the context of trade reform efforts, one stereotype about women's "backwardness," their supposed lack of political consciousness, was explicitly reframed as a positive feature. It was considered a boon in an economic sector that had supposedly been populated by "alien and enemy elements," "counterrevolutionaries," and "SR-Menshevik elements."[37] The Secretary of the All-Union Central Council of Trade Unions argued that "the involvement of workers" wives and family members' as workers in cooperatives would help "secure their liberation from alien elements and wreckers."[38] Similarly, a high-ranking trade official called for the greater recruitment of women "to render the cooperative apparatus [politically] healthy."[39] Because "there [were] more foreign elements among men than among women," a trade leader argued, it was necessary "to train women and promote them to higher positions" so that they could replace the foreign elements.[40] Embedded in these statements was the assumption that women could "enliven" the system because they were not members of any real or imagined opposition, unlike many of their male counterparts. Another assumption was that women's "lesser" political awareness made them less susceptible to anti-Soviet political affiliations than men. In the early 1930s this characterization of women's political innocence rhetorically facilitated efforts to recruit them; in the context of the Purges in the mid-1930s, this perceived political innocence gained even greater public value. Symbolically, women's increased presence in trade highlighted the decreasing number of politically suspect men, and underscored the integration of the retail sphere into the political mainstream.

Essentially good

Official discourse championed women as "good girls" who would bolster the regime's campaign to remake retail trade.[41] Assertions about women's moral probity served as a core rationale for their employment. Trade administrators, journalists, and women workers claimed that "theft was less common" in stores and consumer cooperatives staffed by female salesclerks, store directors, and consumer cooperative leaders. They argued that men were the ones overwhelmingly responsible for "abuses of power," including the cheating of customers.[42] In speaking about her work experience, one woman cooperative leader explained why she had established a women's activist group: because she and other women had had enough of the "men-embezzlers who reign in our village store."[43] Another trade leader maintained that "experience [showed] that when it came to honesty," retail work was "a womanly affair."[44] The president of the All-Union Central Union of Consumer Cooperative Societies (Tsentrosoiuz) essentially dictated the new party line on women workers to representatives of the press in 1933:

> It is necessary to say that where there is a woman store manager, where there is a woman chairperson of a rural cooperative store, things are better and we do not have such theft and embezzlement. Here [with women] we have a very big reserve and the central question now is how to activate the recruitment and participation of women.[45]

Newspapers, trade-union meetings, and worker reports underscored the achievements of new women employees by noting the absence of customer complaints and charges of embezzlement or theft levied against them.[46] Because a key component of the trade campaign was the repeated insistence on the need to replace dishonest workers with upright and dependable ones, all of the talk about (and seeming proof of) women's integrity was significant. It suggested that women would serve as a valuable moral force in a sphere plagued by traces of the greedy "Nepman spirit." In addition, it justified women's recruitment, for countless male trade officials and workers had been fired, punished, arrested, and tried for allegedly stealing, embezzling, and "wrecking." Regardless of women's actual level of integrity, the image of ethical women workers allowed for symbolic contrasts with both the crimes of immoral Soviet male trade employees and the alleged dishonesty of capitalist retailing. The mass entry of women in retailing signaled that "virtuous" women were replacing "corrupt" men, and that a new non-capitalist retail system was in the process of being realized.

Women were also characterized as "good girls" because of their supposed self-discipline. Proponents of women workers pointed in particular to their reliability and sobriety.[47] They suggested that women workers shirked work less often than their male counterparts, which made them more dependable. They also depicted drunkenness on the job as a male problem, with the implication that if more women were hired, fewer drunkards would spoil the retail sector. Since authorities considered insobriety to be one of the "main reasons for theft" in the trade apparatus, and viewed drunkenness as a sign of a person's lack of *kul'turnost'*, the employment of *sober* women workers provided clear advantages.[48] By not skipping out of work as much as their male coworkers and by remaining sober, women offered the likelihood of greater productivity, less corruption, and more cultured behavior in the retail sector.

Cultured behavior

Representations of women worker's virtues were directly tied to the government campaign for *kul'turnost'*. As mentioned in previous chapters, as the Communist leadership pursued its plans for rapid economic transformation in the 1930s, and sought to build socialism, it aimed to transform people by inculcating in them a set of behaviors, attitudes, and values that fit with leaders' image of the ideal New Soviet Person. Cultural activists promoted the importance of sobriety, personal hygiene, proper speech, basic literacy, and political awareness. Women came to have a salient role in the government campaign to civilize and modernize the masses. Communist leaders paradoxically identified women with economic and political backwardness (particularly in the 1920s) at the same time they associated them with *kul'turnost'*. In their opinion, women tended to have a more cultivated sensibility than men. In the 1930s, they mobilized women's alleged civilizing influence to advance the campaign for *kul'turnost'*. So did trade authorities. Depicting women's *kul'turnost'* as an innately feminine virtue in the context of trade reform, they underscored women's propensity to be tidy and organized, courteous and attentive, and tasteful. According to them, these attributes helped improve the retail sector. Women's *kul'turnost'* had obvious value for official efforts to overcome negative images of the retail system as dirty, unresponsive, and crude.

As trade functionaries and retail employees discussed women in retailing, they characterized "cleanliness and tidiness" as naturally more common in women than in men. Reportedly women rooted out dirt and kept workplaces more sanitary and better organized than their male coworkers.[49] A store director in Uzbekistan summed up a common perspective when he opined, "Where a woman works the workplace is always cleaner, tidier, and better."[50] The press likewise asserted that "almost everywhere" female trade employees "introduced elements of culture," including cleanliness, in their workplaces.[51] Women's apparent attention to detail and sanitation, key elements of *kul'turnost'*, became important to descriptions of progress in stores. Ridding the retail sector of flies, grime, and the irrational and inefficient display of goods served as markers of the construction of Soviet trade. As trade reformers envisioned the ideal new retail system as hygienic and orderly, they commended women workers for helping to realize this vision.

Women's supposed tendency toward solicitude was another reason the trade establishment and press credited them with the ability to improve retailing. Concern for others was presented as a critical component of quality customer service: a hallmark of Soviet trade. The economist and editor of the journal *Sovetskaia torgovlia* argued that affairs ran more smoothly and "the approach to the needs of customers was more attentive" in stores and consumer cooperatives with female directors and leaders.[52] Journalists proposed that "female labor [was] often more effective than male labor, especially with respect to the quality of service for the customer" and that women had an aptitude for "servicing the consumer in a cultured way."[53] They applauded shops staffed exclusively by women, where one could feel "caring concern about the enterprise and the consumer."[54] Trade authorities claimed that women handled consumer goods "more thoroughly and carefully" than men.[55] Casting women as "natural" caretakers (which was linked to broader representations of and assumptions about women's motherliness), they repeatedly emphasized women's capacity to provide polite and solicitous service.[56] Notably, women's attentiveness contributed to their "authority" and helped them to earn "the trust" and "respect" of customers. This served not only to legitimize the retail system but also to secure greater consumer activism, which further helped to improve retailing.[57] Women's proclivity for providing good customer care was additionally characterized as advancing the trade campaign's goal of eradicating "distributionism," a legacy of the older cooperative and state trade system, in which apathetic trade workers were indifferent to customers' needs, product quality, and the general shopping experience.[58] By this logic, women's employment in retailing promoted "cultured Soviet trade."

Women's refined taste was yet another element of their *kul'turnost'* that trade authorities decided could be used to remake retailing. Ostensibly women retail workers had better taste than male employees, which was significant because of the cultural imperatives of the new Soviet trade.[59] In contrast to capitalist retailing, which purportedly worked against consumers' welfare, Soviet retailing was supposed to work on behalf of consumers by assisting in their cultural uplift. Retail employees were expected to introduce customers to new items, to instill "Soviet taste" for contemporary, cultured, and rational commodities (which would ideally replace an irrational and petit-bourgeois taste for useless, extravagant, or overly ornate goods).[60] Because of their propensity for good "taste," women were deemed particularly qualified to promote cultured consumption.

Domestic skills

Proponents of women in the retail sector recast not only "essentially" feminine and even matronly attributes as positive, but also women's formerly suspect role as keepers of the household.[61] In essence, they proposed that women's presumed know-how in domestic affairs provided them with invaluable knowledge and skills, making them "natural" retail experts. According to one woman cooperative leader, women's household experience prompted women workers to be more economical than men, "looking after every kopeck."[62] A labor analyst argued that more workers' wives needed to be recruited into the retail workforce so that a new sector of the working class could be brought "into socialist construction," which would simultaneously help to introduce more of "a housewifely eye" in the trade apparatus. An assistant store manager of a women's store claimed, "We [women] are all involved in the household economy," and consequently, "we know well that a poor-quality commodity hurts the consumer."[63] As the imperative to employ women workers intensified, the logic behind recruiting women workers became the same as the logic that had long been used for recruiting women cooperative members and volunteer retail activists: women's "housewifely eyes" and consumer experience as "the principal buyers of all that [was] necessary for the family" made them well suited for addressing retail problems.[64] Trade authorities continued to applaud many male retail workers for their talents. According to official discourse, however, both women's "nature" and their everyday domestic chores meant that they had a special aptitude for retail work. Women's domestic expertise could be mobilized to promote retail improvement.

Representations of women workers highlighted their skills in offering product information and domestic advice. These skills were deemed important because trade leaders directed store personnel not only to introduce customers to new consumer goods and "Soviet" taste but also to provide them with basic instructions, such as how to prepare canned food or clean certain fabrics.[65] Employees in the new trade system were expected to teach consumers how to utilize new foodstuffs and consumer goods. Although the Soviet press and trade-related reports noted that men as well as women advised consumers, they underscored women workers' successful efforts at consumer education. Often this success was explicitly or implicitly linked to women's domestic knowledge, such as food preparation.[66] The implication was that women's duties in the "private" sphere of the household made them extra capable of meeting retail responsibilities in the public sphere.

Women workers beget women activists

Another reason for employing a greater number of women in the retail sector was their apparent success in recruiting women activists. During the trade campaign, both men and women retail workers were expected to draw consumers into retail reform, to get customers to become active volunteers. Trade officials and trade-union functionaries put particular stock in women's ability to foster consumer activism. In many of their descriptions of women workers, they underscored women's ability to establish strong women's activist groups (*zhenskii aktiv*) in stores, or to recruit women into shop commissions. Women workers frequently noted their efforts to recruit women activists, confirming the association between women workers and women activists.[67] Women workers' apparent skill in generating volunteer activists was no small matter. Women activists served not only as a valuable source of unpaid labor, but also as a "chief source and reserve" for recruiting women workers. As the Tsentrosoiuz leader, Zelenskii, explained, "the selection of cadres of salesclerks, heads of small shops and so on, and in particular the selection of women cadres," should be drawn from women's activist groups.[68] To promote actual employment, the trade establishment and trade-union organizations enrolled women activists in short-term training courses so that they could become semi-skilled paid trade employees. But even without formal training, Soviet authorities deemed women activists eligible for promotion into non-entry level jobs because of their practical experience in the retail sector.[69] Throughout the 1930s, trade officials hired nonemployed women activists, with and without training, to become paid trade personnel.[70] Thus another benefit of women retail workers was that they fostered the ranks of women activists who often then became retail employees themselves.

Recruitment efforts and their limits

Despite the mandate to hire women and the new official discourse about the benefits of women workers, women's entry into the retail workforce was not a seamless process and the number of women workers in the cooperative and state trade network varied considerably throughout the Soviet Union in the 1930s. Fewer women in rural areas worked in the system than in cities. Women in non-Slavic regions did not make as many inroads as their counterparts in Slavic areas.[71] These employment variations were likely due to complex regional differences: religious practices, cultural norms, general job opportunities, child care possibilities, existing economic infrastructure, history of retailing, and level of administrative integration with and bureaucratic proximity to Moscow.[72]

Women also did not move evenly into all sectors of the retail workforce. This was partly because government organs and trade leaders fostered a gender-based division of work. For example, when the government advocated women's employment in cooperative and state trade and generated a list of suitable jobs, this list explicitly excluded women from meat-slicing work.[73] Associated with strength and skill (since slicing machinery was still relatively rare), meat-slicing was often considered men's work in 1930 and in later years.[74] Similarly, in 1931 the governing board of *Kievtorg* was unwilling to send textile goods and readymade clothing to a women's store, because the board members considered the sale of these goods to be a "man's business."[75]

As more women moved into the retail sector, the gender-based division of work both changed and remained the same. By the mid-1930s the sale of textile goods and readymade clothing was no longer viewed as a man's job.[76] But despite some modification of women's work roles, a gender-based division of labor persisted. Men continued to dominate meat-slicing jobs. They also constituted the majority of warehouse workers. When in the mid-1930s Chulkova became the first woman to work in storage in her depot, she was laughed at because such work was "not a woman's affair."[77] The division of labor remained substantially gendered in another way. Although the overall number of women workers increased significantly in the 1930s, the percentage of women in management and leadership positions remained disproportionately low.[78] Thus in 1934 women comprised 28.3 percent of employees in consumer cooperatives, but only 6.9 percent of their leadership.[79] In 1935 they constituted 45.3 percent of salesclerks but only 15.8 percent of store directors, assistant store directors, and heads of sections and departments.[80] In 1939, women constituted approximately 18 percent of all store directors, whereas they comprised 60 percent of salesclerks and 70 percent of cashier workers in cities.[81]

The trade establishment issued repeated decrees to advance women workers. In 1933 and 1935, for example, Tsentrosoiuz called for the "more bold and decisive promotion of women into leadership positions." In 1936 it called for additional measures to help fulfill this mandate.[82] Trade leaders emphasized the "positive results" achieved by women who had been promoted.[83] They also tried to protect women in leadership positions (cooperative chairpersons, store directors) by instructing regional and local officials not to fire them without the explicit permission of higher bodies. The People's Commissariat of Domestic Trade (Narkomvnutorg) and Tsentrosoiuz established educational initiatives so that a greater number of women could be trained and then promoted into leadership positions.[84] Nevertheless, while some women in the 1930s gained responsible and high-status posts, plans and directives to promote women were not well implemented. The trade establishment itself failed to promote women evenly in its administrative apparatus. Out of all the cooperative and state trade organizations in the USSR in the mid-1930s, women comprised 4.6 percent of management personnel versus 68.1 percent of clerical staff.[85] Men continued to dominate the more powerful and authoritative positions in Soviet trade.

Despite women's mass entry into the retail sector in the 1930s, and the new rhetoric that praised women's labor, central and local targets for the recruitment, training, and promotion of women retail workers were underrealized. The vision of and rhetoric about women workers' contributions to Soviet trade often declined to indifference. Trade-union reports and women workers reported that "not enough attention" by cooperative and state trade organizations, party organs, and trade unions was paid to meeting plans and to recruiting, training, and advancing women. All too often women worked by themselves, without any official guidance.[86] Targets were also hampered by lower-level opposition to women's employment. Many personnel officers and store managers resisted hiring women.[87] Some local trade officials ignored the new mandate to recruit women. When, for example, a local official was asked how many women's stores had opened in his regional consumer cooperative system, he dismissively replied that "this business" had already ended. In other words, in his opinion the opening of women's stores and similar initiatives to recruit women had been temporary tactics that no longer warranted any energy.[88] Sometimes even after women completed training courses and started new jobs they were dismissed for no apparent reason. In some cases, women were also the first workers fired when there were cutbacks.[89]

Discrimination and animosity posed limits on the advancement of women to high-level posts and on the acceptance of their authority once promoted. Women encountered particular contempt when they challenged traditional gender roles by moving into leadership positions.[90] When a rural party organization recommended N. Federova become the new chair of a rural cooperative society, cooperative members, "particularly the male ones," expressed skepticism about her abilities. The male chair of the rural soviet did not support her candidacy, saying: "How can this illiterate *baba* be expected to manage such affairs."[91] V. F. Polozhenskaia recounted a similar story of ill will from her male colleagues who resented her appointment as store manager and "did not want to help" her.[92] Women workers promoted as Stakhanovite instructors likewise experienced suspicion and hostility.[93] Even some trade leaders remained resistant to the idea of promoting women, stating that "Any hastiness in terms of advancing women to responsible posts could turn out to be very harmful"; after all, "a woman is [just] a woman."[94]

In addition to discrimination and hostility, insufficient child care negatively affected women's employment. Although Communists had pledged to free women for wage labor by developing state-run communal institutions that would assume many of women's domestic functions, in the 1930s women suffered from the lack of necessary resources with which to juggle their dual roles as mothers and workers.[95] Like women workers in other parts of the economy, women retail employees had little access to child care. Despite party-state efforts to establish additional child-care options for retail workers' children, and despite the actual growth of facilities in the 1930s, the network of child care remained wholly inadequate.[96] In 1936, 2074 women worked at the Moscow Central Department Store, yet the store did not have its own crèche and its nursery school served only 50 children.[97] Similarly, in 1937 *Glavtorg* RSFSR had 15 kindergartens with a total of 2,000 spaces for its approximately 126,000 employees. Moreover, the child care that was available was often of low quality. In a nursery school in Michurinsk, for example, children suffered from deficient nutrition as well as a lack of blankets for naps.[98]

Inadequate funding hindered efforts to expand child care. Even when the Central Committee of the Trade Union of State Trade Workers

(PRGT) doubled its expenses for child care in 1936 compared to 1935, the outlay remained unsatisfactory.[99] Indecision and confusion about funding and problems securing necessary materials also affected construction.[100] In October 1936, for example, the PRGT faulted trading organizations for failing to pursue the building of child-care facilities that had been recently decreed. Part of the blame lay with Narkomvnutorg for issuing no instructions about how to finance construction or procure scarce materials, such as cement.[101] Nor did institutional struggles for limited resources help matters. In 1937 city soviets (elected governmental councils) in Gorky, Iaroslavl, and Cheliabinsk handed over some of Narkomvnutorg's child-care facilities to municipal health departments to use as children's hospitals. When Commissar of Domestic Trade Veitser protested this decision by explaining that Narkomvnutorg SSSR had "satisfied an extremely negligible percent of its [child care] needs," the transfers were revoked.[102] Trade workers in Iaroslavl were not so fortunate. A kindergarten for their children was seized and used as a hospital.[103]

Lack of child care impeded women's training and education. As one woman worker explained, women had to rush home after work to feed their children, even though some had a "great desire to study."[104] It hindered women workers' ability to attend and complete classes, limiting their chances for being hired.[105] And it affected women's chances for upward mobility, since additional training was often linked to promotions. According to some trade authorities and workers, the paucity of child care also impaired women's work performances. One worker who made this case asked his audience to imagine a cashier who had to go to work and leave her child at home without supervision. In this situation, he argued, the quality of her work would be diminished. Instead of thinking about how to provide better service to the consumer, the cashier would worry about "what was going on with the child."[106] A store manager confirmed this scenario when he discussed why one saleswoman's work performance was so poor. Because she had to leave her young child at home alone, she "thought more about her child than about work." Once the store manager found a place for her child in a nursery school, her work performance improved dramatically.[107] Problems with child care affected not only women workers and their children but the entire trade apparatus. In select cases, women brought their children to work when their child-care plans fell through, as did the salesclerk Gavzheeva, for 16 days, when her mother could not care for her six-year old. The situation of child care was so "catastrophic" that many women workers ended up leaving their jobs, exacerbating the retail sector's existing problem of high labor turnover.[108]

*   *   *

Notwithstanding the limits of recruitment, women moved en masse into cooperative and state trade in the 1930s. The feminization of the retail sector buttressed the trade campaign by contributing to the gendering of Soviet trade. As women entered the retail workforce, authorities identified ideal characteristics of the new retail system as womanly. This move shaped the new trade and further legitimized it, distancing it from previous retailing. It also provided women with opportunities for new professional identities, labor hero status, and recognized public roles for feminine and domestic work.

The new meanings ascribed to women's retail work reinforced a broader change in official discourse about women. The Soviet regime's increased emphasis on women's "womanly" roles in the 1930s, including in retail trade, in conjunction with the abolition of the Women's Section of the Communist Party in 1930, the outlawing of abortion in 1936, and new pronatalist policies, have generally been interpreted by scholars as proof of a retreat from women's liberation under Stalinism. Paradoxically, however, these changes were accompanied by the regime's greater recognition of women as workers and unpaid activists. Women were integrated as productive citizens into Soviet society. Although negative images of women continued to circulate in the 1930s, representations of women as a paid or voluntary force actively assisting in the construction of socialism gained ascendancy.[109] Women received great kudos for their contributions to industry, agriculture, retail trade, collective voluntary activities, and the metamorphosis of everyday life.[110] The predominant public image of woman was transformed from *baba* to comrade, albeit an often overtly "feminine" comrade.

Significantly, women's involvement in the remaking of retail trade, like their mass participation in wage labor and volunteer initiatives, broke the monopoly of the masculinized proletarian as the ideal. For example, women became retail labor heroes by attending carefully to the needs of customers and offering useful domestic advice. In the process, they gained social legitimacy that in the 1920s had been restricted primarily to men and industrial workers. In the 1930s, authorities celebrated both the industrial and skilled male labor hero and the solicitous and cultured female retail hero. The celebration of the latter underscored a newfound validity of retail work, women, and the feminine. Indeed, the official acknowledgment of women's contributions and the promotion of Soviet retail heroes epitomized women's transformation from "symbol of backwardness" to "symbol of modernity."[111]

Although both retail trade and womanly traits were publicly valorized in the 1930s, it is important not to overdraw the point: neither the retail sector nor feminized customer service were as venerated as heavy industry and masculinized industrial productivity. While retail work was proletarianized and promoted by Stalin as "revolutionary Bolshevik work," it was never considered as revolutionary as skilled industrial labor.[112] Still, retail trade, womanly attributes, and women retail workers were incorporated actively into state building and mobilized on behalf of Soviet socialism.

The regime's promotion of the feminine and the domestic was contradictory: it allowed for a certain disruption of traditional gender discourses even as it reaffirmed them. Femininity could be exalted, while the naturalizing of women's qualities and experiences, and even the rewarding of them, could also work to reinforce gender differences between men and women, and thereby facilitate gender segregation and gender hierarchy in the workforce, including in retail trade. The Soviet regime succeeded in drawing women workers into retailing, but not in providing them proportional entry into managerial and leadership positions. Unexamined stereotypes and discrimination played a role in this, but no doubt so did the emphasis on women's feminine qualities and domestic experience. Underscoring women's differences may have reinforced the popular stereotype of women workers as first and foremost mothers and wives who would not be reliable and long-term workers.[113] In other words, emphasis on the womanly may have served to justify women's entry into the trade sector *and* to limit its scope. Trade authorities and others often invoked women's womanly attributes to justify their employment in stores, but not usually to justify their employment in other trade-related positions, such as administration, management, or economic planning. In the retail industry, women became associated with service whereas men became identified with leadership and management.

New understandings of the feminine and the domestic, nonetheless, including in the retail sector, contributed to a regendering of Soviet subjectivity. They facilitated the incorporation of women into the socialist order as well as the feminine and the domestic into the public sphere. In the 1920s the regime often effaced the feminine and domestic in its pursuit of gender equality, assuming male characteristics as universal (and supposedly gender-neutral) and encouraging women to become more like men. Or the political leadership construed the feminine and the domestic as negative in its criticism of women's essential limits and "backwardness." In the 1930s, by contrast, the regime applauded "womanly" attributes and suggested they could bolster Soviet goals. In some instances it even encouraged men to adopt these characteristics. The discursive shift in official understandings of the feminine and the domestic also altered ideals for men. In the retail sector both men and women received acclaim and reward for feminine behavior, and the ideal Soviet retail worker was expected to combine positive feminine traits of attentive service, honesty, and *kul'turnost'*, with more traditionally masculine traits of efficiency and productivity. Thus the regime's broader reevaluation of the feminine and the domestic fostered both the feminization of the retail workforce as well as the gendering and recharacterization of trade, and ultimately helped to promote the increased feminization and domestication of Soviet socialism.

4

"Revolutionary Bolshevik Work"
Stakhanovite Retail Labor Heroes

In November 1935, Serafima Borisova was awarded a thousand-ruble bonus and a portable gramophone in recognition of her accomplishments as a Stakhanovite labor hero. Unlike Aleksei Stakhanov, for whom the honor was named, Borisova did not mine coal; she sold women's clothing. As an exemplary saleswoman, Borisova carefully organized clothing displays, beautified her sales section, procured new designs and fabrics to meet consumer needs, and informed industries and cooperative *artels* what consumers wanted. In addition to meeting norms for sales, she provided excellent customer service.[1]

The Stakhanovite labor movement developed after the coalminer Stakhanov hewed 102 tons of coal instead of the daily norm of 6.5 tons in August 1935. In response to this Herculean achievement, the Stalinist regime promoted the emulation of Stakhanov's efforts. The ideal of a "Stakhanovite" model of work emerged in heavy industry. Soviet authorities applauded the super-productive, technically skilled, and individually heroic industrial Stakhanovite, who exceeded labor expectations and contributed to the national drive for industrialization. The Stakhanovite movement also spread to light industry and agriculture.[2] Surprisingly, it became a significant presence in retail trade as well.[3] Salesclerks like Borisova were some of the least likely workers to become proletarian labor heroes. After all, they worked in the service industry, and compared to the labor of the archetypal productivist and skilled industrial worker, their work was "nonproductive" and "unskilled." Moreover, as noted in other chapters, retail workers suffered from a legacy of stigma from the NEP and prerevolutionary years. Despite party-state efforts in the early 1930s to recast the official image of trade workers by expanding their training, promoting their social integration, and hiring a great number of "solicitous" and "honest" women, many people still viewed those who worked in retailing as corrupt and politically suspect. Party members complained that even fellow Communists did not appreciate the importance of Soviet trade and continued to treat retail workers in a dismissive and contemptuous manner.[4] At the Seventeenth Party Congress in 1934, the head of the All-Union Central Union of Consumer Cooperative Societies (Tsentrosoiuz) referred to trade employees as "an army of one and a half million workers" who should be looked at as a "necessary link" in the "struggle for the strengthening of socialism." Yet, he lamented, trade workers were devalued.[5] At the same congress, Stalin addressed the still prevalent negative perceptions of retail workers by asserting that Soviet trade was a "genuine Bolshevik cause" and that honest salespeople were the "bearers" of this "revolutionary Bolshevik work."[6] Stalin's much-publicized remarks made it clear that trade had become a legitimate socialist pursuit and that retail workers were no longer pariahs. In a subsequent published letter to Stalin, retail workers fondly referred to Stalin's remarks as a source of legitimization and inspiration. They noted:

> We remember well those unforgettable days, when from the high tribune of the Seventeenth Party Congress of our Communist Party you sternly ridiculed people who arrogantly relate to Soviet trade. You called these [arrogant] views not Bolshevik views but those of the impoverished nobility.... Your simple and wise words that "trade workers, including counter workers, provided that they work honestly, are bearers of our revolutionary Bolshevik work" – were imprinted in the minds of every one of us. These words cheered us, raised our energy, and made us work better.[7]

The development of Stakhanovism in trade reinforced the party-state campaign to transform "trade employees" (*torgovye sluzhashchie*) into trade workers (*rabotniki torgovli*).[8] Indeed, the image of the heroic, cultured, and hyper-competent Stakhanovite retail worker underscored the sea change in official discourse about trade employees.[9] Stakhanovism also reinforced broader Soviet efforts to transform retailing and consumption. By establishing and widely publicizing new professional norms, and by offering workers new social and material incentives, Stakhanovism redefined retailing as a matter of labor achievement, and fueled new and improved retail practices. By strengthening the association between retailing and the Soviet campaign to produce *kul'turnost'* (culturedness) in everyday life, Stakhanovism helped to *recast* Soviet retailing and consumerism as modernizing, cultured, and socialist.[10]

The new labor hero in retail trade

The Stakhanovite exemplified the ideal new retail worker. According to I. Ia. Veitser, the commissar of the All-Union People's Commissariat of Domestic Trade (Narkomvnutorg), a Stakhanovite trade worker was more than a shock worker (*udarnik*) or an outstanding worker (*otlichnik*). S/he was a "new figure, a new hero," namely "a hero of the epoch of mastering trade," capable of combining all the work elements necessary for "unfolding Soviet cultured trade."[11] More explicitly, a Stakhanovite trade worker was:

> the *udarnik*, the *otlichnik*, who reconstructs his system of work via new creative work methods, and who achieves an expansion in work load, an increase in labor productivity, and a rise in the quality of consumer service via: the refashioning of all [of one's] work, the rationalization of one's work place, the application of even elementary machinery, the correct arrangement of goods, the appropriate use of the assortment of goods, and so forth.[12]

L. M. Khinchuk, the Russian Republic's commissar of domestic trade, differentiated Stakhanovites from shock and outstanding workers, arguing that Stakhanovites did more than fulfill and overfulfill plans: they searched for "novel methods to improve their work."[13]

In October 1935, Commissar Veitser convened a meeting with trade officials and store managers to discuss the distinguishing features of Stakhanovism in trade. He began the meeting by pointing out the two defining characteristics of Stakhanovism in industry: (1) exceeding output norms and (2) increasing labor productivity via the mastery of work techniques and technology. Veitser argued that if the main imperative of Stakhanovism in industry was to produce greater output, this could not be the case with Stakhanovism in the retail sector, "because in trade work the salesclerk or counterworker interacts with the consumer, and how he serves the consumer plays a big role in determining the quality of [his] work." If Stakhanovism in trade was based primarily on surpassing norms (gross sales) and improving productivity, "this might elicit negative results from the point of view of servicing the customer."[14] Too much emphasis on productivist objectives might adversely affect customer care. In Veitser's opinion, the pursuit of quality customer service as well as these other goals needed to serve as the basis of Stakhanovism in trade.

When Narkomvnutorg convened the first reception for Stakhanovite and outstanding retail workers in mid-November 1935, Commissar

Veitser delineated the central components of Stakhanovite work that had emerged in recent meetings: an increase in labor productivity and work load via the introduction of new work methods and the rationalization of existing methods; the introduction and mastery of trade technologies; and the better servicing of customers.[15] The first two components were similar to Stakhanovite work methods in other spheres. Not surprisingly, during the initial onset of Stakhanovism in the retail sector, and in subsequent months and years, trade officials and store managers posited that the deployment of more rational processes would yield positive results. They claimed that better productivity could be achieved via the optimal division of labor among salesclerks, the scientific organization of goods, the preweighing and prepackaging of products.[16] The trade establishment exhorted retail employees to devise and implement rationalizing measures to maximize efficiency. It also urged workers to learn to utilize technical devices, such as meat-slicing machines, associated with improved productivity and customer service.[17] Deputy Commissar of Domestic Trade Z. S. Bolotin stated, "Without the complete use of technical devices, Stakhanovite methods are impossible. And what is more, Stakhanovites should be initiators in the introduction and mastery of new trade technologies."[18]

The third component of Stakhanovite retail work – the provisioning of quality customer service – denoted the special niche occupied by salesclerks in Soviet society and the national economy. "Customer service" distinguished Stakhanovism in trade from Stakhanovism in industry and agriculture. The predominant criterion in determining a Stakhanovite in industry and agriculture was norm overfulfillment, notwithstanding the problems associated with that approach. Although other criteria sometimes factored into whether or not an industrial or agricultural worker was recognized as a Stakhnovite, "cultured service" was not one of them.[19] By contrast, Stakhanovite retail workers were expected to care about their customers and serve them well. Referencing Stalin's remarks about honest salesclerks being "bearers of revolutionary Bolshevik work," a *Pravda* editorial explained, "Honest work and Stakhanovite labor in trade is composed of genuine concern about consumers, the quick gratification of his demands."[20] The provisioning of quality customer service was the *sine qua non* of Stakhanovism in retailing.[21]

Stakhanovism in the retail industry *was* similar to Stakhanovism in other spheres in that it was not merely defined from above.[22] Exemplary retail workers as well as top trade authorities helped determine the standards of Stakhanovism in the retail sector. As workers pursued their own techniques for improving retailing, many of their practices defined Stakhanovite methods and were formally recognized as such. Authorities particularly praised and promoted workers' innovative "Stakhanovite" techniques. Stakhanovite Sirot, for example, received positive press attention for constructing a device for unrolling cloth that significantly shortened the time spent on such a task. In the first half of 1936, the Soviet press reported that authorities had accepted many Stakhanovites' ideas for improving department stores, specifically 32 of 46 "rationalizing proposals."[23] Cognizant that employees were a source of potential ideas and practices for bettering retail processes, including customer service, trade authorities encouraged Stakhanovites to exchange their thoughts and strategies with others by arranging meetings for this explicit purpose. At such a meeting among Stakhanovites in the All-Union Trade Organization for Fur in December 1937, Stakhanovite Stepanova proposed how to improve matters in her store:

> Hats, received from [the hat workshop in a factory] are of standard style, crumpled, and soiled. My wishes for future work: it is imperative for the head of the workshop to maintain contact with us, to frequent the store more often, to consult with us about fashions. It is necessary to make sure that the transfer of hats from production to the depot and from the depot to the store happens in boxes.[24]

Ultimately both trade leaders and retail workers emphasized the critical importance of translating the ideals of increased labor productivity (via rationalization and the adoption of new technologies) and quality customer service into the practices of the new socialist trade. They agreed that Stakhanovites were supposed to surpass output norms for gross sales or merchandise turnover while simultaneously providing consumers with a cultured retail environment as well as valuable information, instruction, and advice.

Trade leaders directed Stakhanovites to furnish quality customer service in many different ways. One idea they encouraged was for Stakhanovites to act as liaisons between producers and consumers. Since the Soviet trade apparatus did not have a "market" mechanism for regulating supply and demand, consumers could not exercise their influence in market fashion. Stakhanovites were supposed to study consumer demand by soliciting customers' opinions daily, organizing special goods exhibits, and convening in-store customer conferences, and then serve as consumer advocates by conveying relevant information to store managers, factories, and other enterprises.[25] A Stakhanovite explained, "If a customer doesn't like some style of clothing, then we present this problem to our manager and either cease distributing this style or alter it."[26] By engaging in these activities, Stakhanovites allegedly helped consumers affect the production of goods, at least indirectly.[27]

Part of providing good customer service included educating and advising consumers. These roles were necessary, Veitser explained, because customers were not "merchandise experts." When customers purchased readymade clothing, they needed information about "how to wash [the clothing]" and "how to clean stains, and so forth."[28] Consumers also required instructions about how to use everyday electrical devices, such as radios, or how to cook semi-prepared food, such as canned corn or frozen dumplings. Some customers even needed advice on how to prepare simple vegetables such as squash and celery. Ostensible consumer ignorance along with the proliferation of new products associated with an improved economy and modern industrial society dictated new responsibilities for salesclerks. Trade leaders expected Stakhanovite salesclerks to know how to treat a product (cook, wash, turn on, repair) and "to know a commodity well – the quality of a good, where and how it was produced – and to know the factory and brand of a product" in order to impart necessary knowledge and tips to consumers.[29]

As educators and advisors, Stakhanovite salespeople were supposed to introduce customers to new items, "to cultivate the taste of the consumer."[30] More specifically, they were to nurture a "new Soviet taste."[31] In essence, Stakhanovites were obliged to promote Soviet consumerism. Deputy Commissar Bolotin explained, "Our consumer is not familiar with many goods. It is necessary to instruct him toward new tastes, to stimulate new needs."[32] A Kharkov trade official similarly argued that because there were numerous products unfamiliar to the customer, such as new fabrics, the Stakhanovite salesclerk needed not only to sell consumer goods, but also "to organize the taste of the customer."[33] As "organizers," a trade leader in Uzbekistan elucidated, salesclerks had a responsibility "to raise the cultural life" of customers.[34] The Stakhanovite Beznogov served as a model, convincing a customer to buy eau de cologne, perfume, and children's toys in addition to the wine he had originally planned to purchase.[35] By cultivating "Soviet taste" and the wider consumption of specific types of merchandise, Stakhanovite salesclerks helped to confer a more modern and cultured lifestyle in previously "backward" workers and peasants while promoting commodity turnover. This Stakhanovite approach to selling served to advance *both kul'turnost'* and economic growth.

Stakhanovite retail workers were also assigned responsibility for introducing consumers to "new" and "better" items "so that they could live better, so that they could live more happily."[36] Stakhanovites could help people realize Stalin's platitude: "Life has become better, comrades; life has become more joyous."[37] The trade-union leader Moroz used this logic to explain why Stakhanovites should teach consumers about a new type of industrial and mass-produced ice cream in the mid-1930s: "Eskimo" ice cream. "Eskimo" was a part of this better life; it was tasty as well as healthy. But because most people were unfamiliar with Eskimo ice cream bars, they did not eat them. It was therefore incumbent on retail workers to become "advisors to consumers."[38] By informing consumers of the new ice cream and other novelty products, such as cornflakes, folded pocket umbrellas, and electric samovars, and by promoting the sale of mass-produced and inexpensive luxury goods, such as champagne, authorities envisioned salesclerks, especially Stakhanovite salesclerks, advancing a Soviet consumerism that was about pleasure as well as cultural transformation.[39]

Providing good customer service necessitated concern for consumers' welfare. Trade-union leader Moroz suggested that this concern distinguished Stakhanovites from non-Stakhanovites. Before, he noted, "a salesclerk silently took a receipt [showing payment] from a consumer, and silently weighed and distributed products. He was indifferent to what a consumer took." In contrast, "Stakhanovites of trade help customers pick out what [is] the best."[40] Stakhanovites were solicitous, taking care of customers in an "attentive" manner and selecting goods for them "with great love."[41] When a Stakhanovite salesclerk selected fruits for her customers, she made a special effort to pick out fruits that would not spoil quickly. The Stakhanovite store manager Danilin conscientiously looked after small children and ensured that they purchased the "best fresh bread."[42]

Soviet authorities also claimed that Stakhanovites rendered good customer service by promoting "cultured trade."[43] One element of cultured trade was the provisioning of consumer conveniences, such as prepackaged goods, or even something quite simple as a place for customers to sit down. Stakhanovites in a rural cooperative store, for instance, decided to make their store more comfortable by providing visitors with a table, chairs, and a copy of the newspaper *Sovetskaia torgovlia*.[44] Another sign of culturedness was the beautification of retail spaces. Borisova furnished her department with a "cultured look" by setting up an attractive and well-lit showcase so that customers "could see the dresses in all their beauty."[45] V. Ia. Iakovleva displayed food in an artistic manner, winning an award for her effort.[46] Increased attention to the aesthetics of retailing purportedly distinguished the emergent new system of cultured Soviet trade from prior systems.

Stakhanovites additionally promoted cultured trade by modeling *kul'turnost'* themselves: by being hygienic, punctual, orderly, well-mannered, well-dressed, and hardworking. Industrial and agricultural Stakhanovites were also expected to model *kul'turnost'* in their workplaces and everyday lives. But because those in the retail sector worked in more "public" spaces and were supposed to promote *kul'turnost'* among the broader Soviet populace, greater importance was attached to their personal deportment. As trade-union leader Moroz explained during a speech on Stakhanovism, high quality cultured trade could only be achieved by increasing the cultural level of salesclerks. "Here you yourselves yell cleanliness! Hygiene! For milk, the personal hygiene of a salesclerk decides all. For meat, personal hygiene plays a decisive role. Not only hygiene in stores but also the hygiene of a salesclerk is a vital thing." In Moroz's view, "cultured salesclerks" were critical for the development of the Stakhanovite movement.[47]

Stakhanovites elaborated on what constituted cultured customer service, helping to clarify what constituted "Stakhanovite" practices. They repeatedly emphasized the importance of not using the word "no" to a customer's query about whether or not an item was available. It was better to help consumers choose something else when the product they originally wanted was not in stock. By proposing another item, the customer would "remain very satisfied." According to the head of a department store's sales section, cultured customer service entailed "winning over the customer." This required salespeople leaving their "bad moods" at home.[48] Stakhanovites were not merely polite or helpful retail workers; they actively fought for customers' satisfaction.

Trade authorities credited Stakhanovite retail workers with two other attributes: resourcefulness and creativity, both of which bolstered commodity turnover (hence retail productivity) and customer service. Deputy Commissar Bolotin underscored the importance of enterprising vitality when he argued that Stakhanovites were obliged to "fight in a Bolshevik way not only for the quality and the range [of goods], but for new goods." Instead of relying on an existing supply of merchandise, Stakhanovites needed to demonstrate "initiative" and "inventiveness" by negotiating with local industries and *artels* to receive new or additional goods. Or they could procure scarce goods elsewhere, such as the

Stakhanovite Kumskov, who bicycled from the city to rural cooperative stores in search of bay leaves, successfully located an excess supply, and retrieved the bay leaves for sale in his establishment.[49] This emphasis on Stakhanovites' "initiative" had two contradictory effects. By applauding Stakhanovites' ability to obtain new or supplementary goods, Soviet authorities acknowledged the persistence of goods shortages and the failure of industries to provide necessary products. At the same time, by emphasizing Stakhanovites' successes in overcoming the limitations of the planned economy, party-state authorities reinforced official rhetoric that the development of cultured Soviet trade (including the provisioning of goods) was impeded not so much by broader economic shortcomings but by the lack of energetic activism on the part of individuals.

Unlike the trade employee of the past or a less inspired fellow employee, the Stakhanovite retail worker also demonstrated ingenuity in sales. Salesclerk Kreitz gained recognition as a Stakhanovite because of his innovative and skillful assembling of haberdashery commodities in "sets." His least expensive set for women consisted of different sewing accessories. Retail creativity allowed Stakhanovites not only to overfulfill norms for commodity turnover but also to sell more than other salesclerks handling the same array of products.[50] Ingenious sales strategies benefited customers as well as the Soviet economy. When a store was loaded down with summer galoshes that would no longer sell because the fall season had commenced, Stakhanovite salespeople advised customers to combine the summer galoshes with felt boots (*valenki*) and sold the remainders.[51] When customers in Voronezh were unwilling to buy beds because of their dark and "gloomy" colors, Stakhanovite salesclerks repainted them and successfully sold fifty in just a few days. Stakhanovite "counter engineers" likewise added oil and chalk to "trifles," namely, the remainders of hard and oil paints, creating a useful putty that sold "like hotcakes," particularly since putty was a scarce commodity.[52] The Stakhanovite ability to come up with imaginative solutions to problems expanded the possibilities of a limited and often frustrating retail landscape.

The actualization of Stakhanovism in trade

As the industrial Stakhanovite movement expanded in the fall of 1935, Stakhanovism spread to the retail sector. Stakhanovite retail workers made their debut when two saleswomen in Moscow exceeded their norms for daily gross sales by 2 to 3 times.[53] The all-union and Russian

Republic commissars of domestic trade sponsored the first official meetings among trade workers in mid-November 1935 to discuss Stakhanovite work methods.[54] As Narkomvnutorg, Tsentrosoiuz, the People's Commissariat of Food Industries, and trade-unions promulgated Stakhanovism in the retail sector, many officials and employees in the cooperative and state trade system began to take up the charge in earnest.[55] Retail workers pledged to adopt Stakhanovite techniques, some even making their pledges directly to Stalin. In a public letter to Stalin, a group of exemplary workers explained, "We are obliged to work in a Stakhanovite way and we are pleased to report to you that the Stakhanovite movement has found a warm response among us trade workers."[56] Although 1936 was the banner year for publicizing Stakhanovism in the retail sector and in other industries, the trade campaign continued to promote Stakhanovism throughout the remainder of the 1930s. In December 1937, for example, the commissar of Domestic Trade argued that the task for 1938 was to move from "individual Stakhanovites" in the retail sector to the establishment of "Stakhanovite stores": stores composed primarily of Stakhanovites.[57]

Soviet authorities tried to convince trade officials and retail workers of the importance of Stakhanovism. They argued that it was tied to the redefinition of retail workers. Khinchuk, the Russian Republic's commissar of domestic trade, told retail workers that Stakhanovism would demonstrate that they were "capable of working in their own sector no worse than Soviet miners and factory workers in their spheres."[58] The secretary of the All-Union Central Council of Trade Unions declared that Stakhanovite salesclerks could be "labor heroes just like Stakhanovites of heavy and light industry."[59] At a meeting among Stakhanovites, trade-union leader Moroz connected the development of Stakhanovism to a new and improved self-perception among salesclerks. He claimed:

> Now we have different people than before. Earlier (I have worked five years), [they] were poor specimens, who were ashamed of and embarrassed by their professions. It is not a secret for anyone that salesclerks were kept down. Take three or four years ago, when a metal worker of the Stalin workers' factory [was] asked "where do you work," he would answer with pride: I work at the Stalin factory. But when they asked our salesclerk, he would answer in a half-voice, quietly, so that no one would hear him: I work in a district consumer cooperative. Now in our industry we have sent these workers to the devil. Now the situation has changed. Even Comrade Stalin said that

so long as counter workers work honestly, they are doing our Bolshevik work.[60]

Stakhanovite salesclerks represented a new breed of workers, a new "Bolshevik" specimen.

The Soviet press used the burgeoning Stakhanovite movement to highlight the positive redefinition of those involved in retailing. Newspapers and journals featured urban and rural Stakhanovite retail employees and their attendant work practices, representing them as hardworking and honest laborers who were no longer excluded from the general Stalinist *Zeitgeist*.[61] An editorial in *Sovetskaia torgovlia* made this point explicit by declaring that trade workers had not remained uninvolved in the Stakhanovite movement – the "great movement of the masses." The already renowned Stakhanovite salesclerks, "Nikolaeva, Molokutskii, Naryzhnyi, Borisova, Shlepneva, Karakhan and others" served as proof.[62] "Not only trade workers," a different editorial pointed out, "but many thousands of customers" were familiar with Stakhanovite notables in retailing.[63] Stakhanovite cadres had "destroyed the opportunistic theory that Stakhanovite methods in trade, as a mass movement, could not develop."[64]

Official discourse linked Stakhanovism in retailing not only to the redefinition of retail workers, but also to the redefinition of retail trade. Commissar Veitser contended that the Stakhanovite movement was the means by which trade could move from its "backward position" to an "advanced" one in the national economy. It was the "lever" that could be used to rid the trade apparatus of bad tendencies and "distribu-tionist" remnants.[65] Another official stated that Stakhanovite techniques "would make Soviet trade worthy of the great Soviet government."[66] Journalists alleged the development of Stakhanovism in retailing would make it "one of the finest sites of socialist construction."[67] Stakhanovism was essential for realizing the objectives of the trade campaign.

Scores of retail workers participated in the first all-union "Stakhanovite day" of work on January 11 1936, and in similar all-union and local initiatives repeated throughout 1936, 1937, and 1938.[68] Young Stakhanovite retail workers joined in the Communist Youth League's all-union raid of "light cavalry" to promote the Stakhanovite move-ment in stores and warehouses.[69] Commissar Veitser directed trade officials and workers to arrange a "Stakhanovite salutation of May first," just as the Commissar of Heavy Industry had instructed those in the industrial sector to do.[70] By paralleling industrial Stakhanovite campaigns, retail Stakhanovite campaigns underscored that trade workers were a part of broader worker initiatives.

A main goal of Stakhanovite campaigns was to motivate trade workers to improve retail trade, and in many cases this objective appears to have been realized, at least during the actual campaigns. During the Stakhanovite month in March 1936, a group of salesclerks organized *subbotniki* (voluntary unpaid workdays) to make retail arenas more hygienic, while others tried to "rationalize" stores by reorganizing layout and equipment. Store directors held meetings to evaluate Stakhanovite progress. Salesclerks offered new forms of customer service, such as the direct selling of prepackaged goods at fixed prices. Some stores even sent brigades of Stakhanovite salesclerks to food manufacturers and suppliers, such as the *Bol'shevik* cookie factory, to improve merchandise assortment and quality by exerting influence on production. Although workers in goods' warehouses and retail transport did not mobilize for the Stakhanovite month as much as salesclerks did, some were sufficiently inspired to pursue improvements.[71]

Participation in the first Stakhanovite month and similar campaigns was uneven, but these initiatives did result in an increasing number of officially recognized Stakhanovite retail workers and "Stakhanovite stores."[72] Data for Moscow showed a threefold plus increase in Stakhanovite retail workers during the first quarter of 1936.[73] Salesclerks and store managers testified that media accounts about Stakhanovites, including ones in the retail sector, prompted them to rethink their jobs and to adopt Stakhanovite methods.[74] While only 7 percent of the "1.5 million" trade workers had become Stakhanovites by October 1936, the percentage among those who actually handled customers directly was much higher, over one-third in some cities and regions.[75] According to a survey of 23 provinces (*oblasti*), as of January 1 1937, 36.5 percent of salespeople, store directors, store department managers, stall managers, cashiers, and chairs of village cooperative stores in Odessa, 41 percent in Moscow, and 35.2 percent in the Kharkov *oblast'* had been designated as Stakhanovites. Not all regions could claim such success. In the Kirov *oblast'* a mere 4.3 percent of such workers achieved Stakhanovite status. Ultimately, 21.3 percent of those surveyed had become Stakhanovites by the beginning of 1937. This percentage was slightly lower than the average of 25 percent reported for industrial workers *circa* January 1937.[76]

Although retail workers in stores were more likely than other employees in the state and cooperative trade system to become Stakhanovites, the likelihood of workers achieving this status was partly a function of

the location and type of store in which they worked.[77] Reportedly
27.9 percent of employees in model department stores were
Stakhanovites as of January 15 1937.[78] In Leningrad, 60 percent of retail
workers in the model *Bakaleia* food shops were Stakhanovites in late
1936.[79] Because model stores received more and better-quality consumer
goods than regular stores, their employees had an easier time becoming
"model" workers. Plus, the greater attention paid to model stores resulted
in the greater recognition of "Stakhanovites." Still, workers in regular
stores could compete as Stakhanovites, even if the stores received less
attention and fewer resources. Workers could arrange products creatively,
adopt rational practices, and provide quality customer service. In regular stores run by a Saratov municipal trade organization, for example,
21.7 percent of trade workers had gained the appellation Stakhanovite
by the beginning of 1939.[80]

To help spread Stakhanovism in trade, in 1936 Narkomvnutorg organized
the best Stakhanovites to serve as "instructors for introducing"
Stakhanovite work practices.[81] After attending a few months of prepara-
tory courses, instructors worked in the field, visiting stores and helping
others "to master Stakhanovite methods of work." By the summer of 1936,
there were approximately 100 such instructors in Moscow alone.[82] In
introducing workers to new "Stakhanovite" practices, instructors helped
clarify the developing standards of socialist retailing, and provided useful
advice and information that would enable workers to do better.
Stakhanovite instructors were an important supplement to educational
initiatives not only because of the limited scope of the latter, but also
because instructors promoted retail knowledge not necessarily taught in
short courses, educational circles, or lengthier study programs. Instructor
Bakei, for example, showed salesclerks "how to cut kielbasa" and discern
the difference between a "Cracow" and a "Polish" kielbasa.[83]

In 1938, Stakhanovite "schools" were established to spread
Stakhanovite retail methods. At one such school in Novosibirsk,
Stakhanovites attended lectures on subjects such as "The Stakhanovite
store and its work methods" and "Pushkin and his art."[84] Most
Stakhanovite schools, however, appear to have been far less formal than
this one, and were modeled on similar schools in heavy industry, which
usually provided only on-the-job instruction. Serving as teachers, leading Stakhanovites met with "students" in stores and warehouses usually
before or after work, and discussed a variety of topics, including how to
better organize one's work space and provide cultured customer service.
Often Stakhanovite teachers demonstrated their own successful techniques, focusing on practices such as slicing butter efficiently. Reportedly

by October 1939 over 1,500 informal Stakhanovite schools with tens of thousands of students had been organized across the Soviet Union.[85]

Hostility and Stakhanovism

Stakhanovism in retailing differed from Stakhanovism in industry and agriculture not only because of its greater emphasis on *kul'turnost'* and service, but also because it engendered less overt and violent hostility. Many scholars have noted the hostility directed against Stakhanovites as the movement spread in industry and agriculture. The extent of this hostility is not clear, though examples of such hostility were widely covered in the press. Hostility took many different forms. One worker "cursed the Stakhanovite Vlasova for overfulfilling her norm and then threw a spanner that injured her."[86] Other workers poured sulfuric acid on Stakhanovites' clothes on a collective farm in Belorussia. Resistance to Stakhanovism, Mary Buckley notes, "can usefully be categorized along a continuum of undermining behavior as follows: condemnations and rumours behind Stakhanovites' backs; direct belittling, humiliation and baiting; victimization at work by those in authority; acts of sabotage against Stakhanovites' machines, animals, land and homes; threats of physical violence; and actual violence."[87] According to scholars, the motivations behind the antipathy and opposition to Stakhanovism were "varied and complex."[88] Stakhanovism provoked hostility because it "intensified antagonisms within an already fractionalized work force," fostered the growth of a labor aristocracy, and impeded the formation of a cohesive working class. Stakhanovism also appears to have incited resentment because it increased output norms and led to the demotion of some workers to subordinate positions.[89] "Communal and individual resistance to those who were different, deep cultural patterns of envy towards those doing well, patriarchal rejection of changing gender roles," and other factors, such as jealousy, contributed to resistance as well.[90]

Overt and violent acts against Stakhanovites in trade appear to have been relatively rare. Indeed, many reports issued by trade officials and store managers specifically note the lack of "active resistance" to Stakhanovism.[91] Of course there were instances of hostility. Stakhanovite Lebedev, for example "fought against" a coworker's efforts to sabotage the Stakhanovite movement. But instead of rewarding him, a trade official labeled Lebedev a "troublemaker." Ultimately the Trade Union of Trade Workers vindicated Lebedev, punishing both his coworker and the official.[92] Accounts like Lebedev's, however, were not widely reported. Moreover, in the retail sector there does not appear to be evidence of physical acts of aggression against Stakhanovites.

Less overt expressions of opposition were far more common. Commissar Veitser claimed there was resistance from conservatives who did not favor change, "Oblomovites" who suffered from laziness, and skeptics who contended that Stakhanovite methods were not applicable in the retail sector.[93] Trade authorities, retail workers, and the press pointed to acts or nonacts by trade organization leaders, store managers, and trade-union representatives that they interpreted as hostility and opposition to Stakhanovism: indifference to the movement or unwillingness to organize it; insufficient leadership for existing Stakhanovites; mockery of and disrespect toward Stakhanovites; refusal to listen to Stakhanovites' criticism or to implement their proposals; failure to assist Stakhanovite instructors; "undervaluing the meaning of Stakhanovite schools"; inadequate provisioning of incentives to encourage existing Stakhanovites to continue to improve their work; and insufficient mobilization of women as Stakhanovites.[94] When Stakhanovite Efman tried to refuse poor-quality kielbasa from a factory, management began to "yell, insult, and accuse him of sabotage and a lack of desire to work."[95] One trade organization sent Stakhanovites off to Stakhanovite courses "to get rid of" them.[96] But while problems regarding the development of Stakhanovism in the retail sector as well as problems experienced by particular Stakhanovites may have been a result of oppositional attitudes, they may also have been a result of other factors, such as limited resources or personal conflicts. Given the lack of clarity regarding the motives behind the acts and nonacts construed as resistance to Stakhanovism, the level of genuine resistance is difficult to evaluate.

Acrimony between Stakhanovites and non-Stakhanovites was most obvious in two instances: first, when Stakhanovites accused superiors (such as store managers) or coworkers of wrongdoing (e.g., corruption); and second, when non-Stakhanovite store personnel encountered "Stakhanovite instructors."[97] In the first instance, it is likely that the accusations themselves were more significant in provoking hostility than the accusers' Stakhanovite status. After one Stakhanovite complained publicly that the new head of her department section had hired his friends and provided them with more merchandise than Stakhanovites, so that the latter could not meet their sales norms, one of the "friends" threatened the outspoken Stakhanovite, saying she would "pay for this."[98] In the second instance, Stakhanovite instructors appear to have provoked hostility because they played the role of outsiders (usually) who made suggestions about how to do things differently. Stakhanovite instructors reported that some store managers, department heads, and other retail employees perceived them as intrusive and useless busybodies, or worse, as invasive watchdogs. I. Semenychev explained, "several [store managers] treat me as an extraneous person who has arrived 'to give orders' (*komandovat'*)." Semenychev's solution was to show through deeds and "not words" that he was not an outsider.[99] Apparently some retail workers initially thought Stakhanovite instructors had arrived "to draw up charges against or fine" them for bad practices. To stem potentially negative receptions by retail employees, trade leaders warned Stakhanovite instructors not to "put on airs" or approach all workers in the same way.[100] Stakhanovite instructors also complained that store managers and others often treated them in a dismissive and "bureaucratic" manner, not wanting to listen to their advice and not providing them with necessary assistance.[101] The head of a shoe department "rudely silenced a Stakhanovite instructor" who had advocated a useful proposal by telling him "Look after your own shoes." At a department store in Baku, an employee responded to a Stakhanovite instructor by declaring, "Do you really think that you know more than us?"[102] Store managers and department heads may have been particularly irked by the implicit or explicit challenges that Stakhanovite instructors posed to their authority. As one trade official noted, many store managers regarded Stakhanovite instructors as people who had come "to control" them.[103] Whether because of hostility or other reasons, Stakhanovite instructors were not always utilized as instructors, per se, but were instead assigned to different tasks. They were also ignored, which contributed to the demoralization of some instructors. V. Liamin was so exasperated by the isolation and lack of direction in his role as Stakhanovite instructor that he asked authorities to relieve him of his post.[104]

Young female Stakhanovite instructors appear to have encountered particular hostility. At a party meeting among trade workers, Moscow trade official Epshtein asserted that some store directors saw Stakhanovite instructors as "young Komsomol girls" who had nothing to teach them, as they were older and "bearded men with ten years experience." Speaking shortly after Epshtein, a Stakhanovite instructor confirmed this narrative of sexism and ageism and complained that store managers often looked at her disparagingly, as if she was a "little girl." She added that when she informed a store manager about moldy bread that should not be sold, he answered that "he had been working for eight years, and that I was not going to order him around."[105] When a female instructor tried to rid a bread store of specific problems, the salesclerks responded to her advice with "Please, don't teach, we are not going to listen to you!"[106] Female instructors may have elicited particular hostility because they held positions of relative authority, unlike most women retail workers. Their prominence as Stakhanovites also served as highly visible symbols of the encroachment of women in trade as well as the general advancement of Soviet women in the 1930s. Moreover, the influx of women in trade corresponded with an increase in praise for "feminine" trade practices. Trade officials lauded retail workers specifically for what was viewed as traditionally feminine behavior, namely, nurturing and attentive service-oriented work. Salesclerks were rewarded for their "womanly" characteristics, not their brawny strength. As a result, hostility toward female Stakhanovite instructors may have been a response to the "feminization" of the workforce and the gendering of trade practices as much as a reaction to "intrusive" outsiders.

The relative lack of aggressive hostility among ordinary retail workers toward ordinary Stakhanovites (e.g., noninstructors) indicates that Stakhanovism in trade was not as much of a zero-sum competition, with clear winners and losers, as it was in industry. Stakhanovism does not appear to have been as divisive in the retail sector as it was in other spheres. This is likely a product of the longstanding negative status of retailing, which the trade campaign sought to overcome. Though non-Stakhanovite salesclerks may have looked lazy or rude compared to their fellow non-Stakhanovites, the association of Stakhanovism with trade provided retail work with a very clear and publicized official stamp of legitimacy. Stakhanovism in the retail sector may have divided workers by contributing to the formation of a labor aristocracy who received higher wages and greater praise than ordinary workers. But it simultaneously unified retail workers by allowing them all to gain status as proletarians in a Soviet labor movement. Even non-Stakhanovite retail workers profited from the general celebration of nonproductive, service-oriented, and previously suspect work.

Stakhanovism and its uses

If Stakhanovism promoted retail workers' social integration into a larger community of Soviet laborers, it also promoted their greater incorporation into the regime's discourse of blame, which centered on the deficiencies of individuals. Stakhanovism made this discourse appear

more logical, for it underscored the possibility of individual achievements even in a difficult retail landscape. Stakhanovism additionally
provided trade authorities with a new weapon for holding retail workers responsible for problems by establishing a broad set of normative
ideals in a much more public and specific way than ever before, ideals
broadcast in ordinary and trade-specific newspapers. Trade authorities
increasingly faulted retail employees for not pursuing Stakhanovite
methods. They blamed salesclerks for the mechanical and noncreative
distribution of products, the inability to see a "live buyer" instead of a
mere "ration coupon," the display of "uncultured" behavior, and a lack
of initiative. The expansive new Stakhanovite behavioral norms worked
against the less impressive salesclerks and facilitated official efforts to
shift responsibility for shortages onto individual workers and away
from shortfalls in the production of consumer goods. Amid horren-
dous problems of supply, this particular agenda served the regime well.
Party, government, and trade-union leaders repeated the same basic
refrain: "We have a series of goods that our trade apparatus does not
organize so [they] can reach consumers."[107] Such language implied that
if retail workers wanted, they could improve supply.

The Soviet trade establishment used Stakhanovism to exert pressure
on regional and local officials of the trade commissariat, consumer
cooperatives, trade organizations, and trade unions. It reproached them
for not promoting the Stakhanovite movement and intimated that their
disinterest in Stakhanovism was related to their general culpability for
trade-related problems.[108] As the Purges took off and the Terror expanded
in 1937, trade leaders made more spurious claims, arguing that "enemies
of the people" deliberately sought to thwart the Stakhanovite movement. Trade leader M. P. Smirnov argued, "Enemies of the people –
Trotskyist-Bukharin agents of fascism [have] caused significant injury
to our trade, arresting the growth of Soviet trade and the development
of socialist competition and the Stakhanovite movement, and trying to
disorganize supply" in various ways.[109] The Soviet press reiterated this
narrative, and also asserted that there was a connection between the
failure to promote Stakhanovism and other problems, such as the failure to meet commodity turnover norms, the growth of embezzlement
and theft, and an increase in the cheating of customers. Ignoring
Stakhanovism, in other words, had broad consequences for the campaign to develop a new and improved system of Soviet trade.[110] As in
industry, Stakhanovism in trade provided Soviet authorities with new
reasons to criticize managerial-level personnel.

Soviet authorities were not the only ones to use the development of Stakhanovism in trade to advance their own interests. Retail workers, like their industrial counterparts, utilized Stakhanovism to castigate superiors.[111] Presumably trade officials did not find this undesirable since it allowed for the release of frustration at the same time as it reinforced the idea that individuals, as opposed to myriad structural problems, were responsible for retail difficulties. Stakhanovites chastised store managers and heads of retail departments for a variety of offenses. Some salesclerks faulted trade organizations, the managers of factories and trusts, store directors, and shipping clerks for failing to provide stores with available items, which they argued, was a major problem that prevented them from working "even better," in a "Stakhanovite way," or from "becoming genuine Stakhanovites." Others emphasized the need to reorganize the division of labor so that they could be freed from subsidiary work. Ostensibly this would allow them to overfulfill their norms and provide better customer service.[112] According to Stakhanovites, some trade organizations "misconstrued the nature of the Stakhanovite movement" by making employees work excessively long hours and without days off (which also violated labor laws).[113] While the impact of complaints was likely limited, the establishment of norms and expectations via the Stakhanovite movement provided trade workers with a platform and increased authority to challenge authorities.

Stakhanovism in the retail sector provided workers with diverse benefits. By mirroring the benefits extended to Stakhanovite industrial and agricultural workers, these benefits not only created new incentives for workers and fostered expectations of improved worker performance, but they also underscored the official acceptance of retail employees into the ranks of Soviet workers. Thus whereas Stakhanovism in industry and agriculture advertised the super-proletarian productivity of workers, in trade it advertised both exceptional workers and the relatively new legitimacy of retail work.

The most common benefits bestowed on Stakhanovites were material. Trade officials and store managers rewarded Stakhanovites with better remuneration and promotions. Salesclerk Koznakov, like other Stakhanovites, earned a higher salary when he became a Stakhanovite. He claimed that as a result, his material position had become easier, and that he had begun to acquire new things, such as clothing, as well as to pay for his wife's bookkeeping studies. Stakhanovite Braginskaia planned to use her higher wages to greet the upcoming New Year with luxury, with a wide assortment of "expensive dishes." As an expectant mother, she also noted that her increased means allowed her to prepare for her "joyous event long before the child's birth."[114] After becoming a Stakhanovite in the groceries department of her food store, and affecting her coworkers there so positively that all became Stakhanovites, Marusia Soldatova was promoted to the position of assistant store manager.[115] Along with higher wages and promotions, Stakhanovites also profited from money bonuses, gifts, and other perquisites. Narkomvnutorg awarded E. V. Shlepneva a winter coat and a room of her own. A. V. Peredkov gained a child's bed and a paid furlough to a sanitarium (an institution for the improvement of health).[116] Some Stakhanovites earned honorific orders and medals, such as a Soviet medal of honor.[117]

One benefit bestowed on at least some Stakhanovites was increased access to education. The trade establishment and the Trade Union of State Trade Workers allocated funds and organized educational opportunities specifically for Stakhanovites to improve their general education as well as trade-related skills and expertise.[118] After O. A. Il'ina became a Stakhanovite, she was assigned a tutor who helped her to overcome her illiteracy.[119] Stakhanovite Ania Kuznetsova's reward was training at a technical school (*tekhnikum*). In an enthusiastic letter to the newspaper, she explained that she no longer stood behind a sales counter but sat behind a desk, and she vowed to "return to her department store and give it all the knowledge that she had received at the technical training school."[120] Narkomvnutorg's Administration for Educational Institutions promoted courses for Stakhanovites, explaining that after making it through the classes, sales-counter workers "should be able to raise the quality of their work even more and become promoted to leadership work in a store," as a manager of a department, an assistant store director, or even a store director.[121] A variety of courses available to Stakhanovite trade workers allowed them to pursue other fields: accounting, financial planning, and merchandise consulting. In addition, the Trade Union of State Trade Workers sometimes arranged for Stakhanovites to receive special instruction to help them prepare for higher education.[122] Increased education, however, was not only a reward; it was also deemed a necessity. As V. Sheinman asked rhetorically in a news article, could an illiterate or semi-literate Stakhanovite really demonstrate "mastery of the techniques of Soviet cultured trade?"[123]

The higher-profile Stakhanovite salesclerks enjoyed a kind of "celebrity identity."[124] The media featured Borisova and other Stakhanovite retail workers as role models and notables of the new Soviet trade apparatus.[125] Publications such as "Stakhanovite-exemplar trade workers of Minsk," and "The experience of Stakhanovite state-trade workers of the north" extolled prominent Stakhanovites.[126] Some Stakhanovites even became authors, writing pamphlets about their work practices.[127] As trade luminaries, higher-profile Stakhanovites additionally enjoyed travel privileges and fanfare, such as trips to Moscow and other cities as delegates from the provinces and villages to attend special receptions. Stakhanovites expressed satisfaction about their newfound prestige and perks. The store manager Tsalkina from Kharkov enthusiastically summed up her delight, explaining that she never "dreamed" she would see the Soviet capital.[128]

As a result of Stakhanovism in trade, some retail workers expressed new attitudes toward work, new understandings of self, and appear to have experienced their jobs in a new and more dignified way. The Stakhanovite Levin noted that some of his comrades called his retail work "thankless" and insignificant. But Levin disagreed, arguing that it made him happy to satisfy a customer's request. Moreover, he had become a Stakhanovite, and in the process, he felt like a "useful person." Stakhanovite Bukhman had worked for 29 years in the retail sector. Before the revolution, he claimed, he had been a "voiceless person, blindly fulfilling the will of his merchant-master." Under the Soviet regime, however, Bukhman had become a "rationalizer," an inventor of a new system for cutting butter, a Stakhanovite. What did all this mean? In Bukhman's view, "A salesclerk of a Soviet store has a proud ring (*zvuchit gordo*). I love my work and consider it as honorable as all forms of work in our country."[129] For Marusia Soldatova, becoming a Stakhanovite was the "most wonderful event in [her] life."[130] Some Stakhanovites gained a sense of improved social standing, feeling not only useful, but also valued and important. In the words of one salesclerk, they had become "esteemed people."[131] E. S. Shlepnova pointed out how customers "valued her" and bought bread only from her. This loyalty, she claimed, raised her spirits and encouraged her "to attempt to work as best as possible."[132] Another Stakhanovite salesperson boasted, "Customers trust me and don't search for bread on the shelves themselves because they know that I will give them what they need."[133] Work evaluations confirmed the respect afforded many Stakhanovites, recording how they appeared to hold "great authority" among customers.[134]

Rather than reveling in feats of production, Stakhanovite retail workers reveled in their new cultural and pedagogical roles. Sofia Guk offered consumers advice and information about food. After explaining how to prepare a tasty meat dish with peas, Guk claimed that "the number of those who purchased green peas increased with every day."[135] Borisova, the celebrated Stakhanovite mentioned at the beginning of this chapter, taught customers how to remove stains by using a chemical compound, and helped them pick items according to "their budgets." She paid special attention to out-of-town male customers who wanted to buy presents for their wives. She spent additional time with them, "telling them everything and even writing [down]" what she was saying. Offering such instruction to customers, she explained, made them "feel" they were not only being sold something, but that they were being "helped."[136] In contrast to capitalist salesclerks, who ostensibly induced self-indulgent materialism, Stakhanovite salesclerks offered consumers useful knowledge.

*   *   *

The development of Stakhanovism in trade contributed to party and state attempts to recreate the meanings and alter the actual practices of selling and buying in the 1930s. By valorizing retail work and providing it with a level of legitimacy unthinkable only years before, and by reformulating retail work as a matter of labor achievement, Stakhanovism in trade bolstered the trade campaign and publicized the proletarian integration of retail workers as labor heroes in a national movement. This had implications not only for retail workers, but also for Soviet workers in general, for Stakhanovism in retailing helped to transmute the official image of the ideal Soviet worker. While the quintessential icon of the proletariat, the productive and skilled male industrial worker, remained the most dominant image of the Soviet worker, the service-oriented and often female Stakhanovite retail worker began to appear as a paragon alongside him. In conjunction with the feminization of the paid labor force and the widespread public promotion of Soviet heroines in the 1930s, Stakhanovism in retailing therefore contributed to what Choi Chatterjee describes as "the transformation of the Russian woman from a symbol of backwardness to a symbol of modernity in Soviet propaganda."[137] In addition, by establishing new and more public work standards among retail workers that were tied to rewards, Stakhanovism in retailing, as in other sectors, helped to promote a "politics of productivity," as Lewis Siegelbaum aptly puts it. As retailing became a matter of labor achievement, many workers were actively inspired to improve Soviet trade. Unlike Stakhanovism in other sectors, Stakhanovism in retailing also helped to promote a *politics of consumption* because it reinforced the trade campaign's conceptualization of retailing and consumerism as vehicles for civilizing and modernizing the citizenry. Soviet authorities, the press, and retail workers expected Stakhanovite retail workers to act as agents of social and cultural transformation, to act as "transmission belts" for *kul'turnost'* among the broader public both by influencing customer choice and by providing quality customer service in a cultivated environment. As Stakhanovites pursued these duties, and helped make shopping a more edifying and civilizing experience, both the acts of selling and buying were further reconfigured as socialist. Stakhanovism thus played an important role in the discursive reinvention of retail labor *and* consumption in the Stalinist 1930s. Finally, Stakhanovism contributed to the consolidation of the Soviet social order as it incorporated into the revolutionary project those previously on the margins, namely salesclerks and "backward" customers. This is illustrated by the experience of the saleswoman Borisova. After becoming a Stakhanovite, she enrolled in a course on decorative arts and developed dress patterns in factory workshops. Borisova was also chosen to be on the Presidium of the General Moscow Meeting of Exemplary Workers.[138] She served as a customer consultant, clothing specialist, fashion designer, and political representative. Stakhanovism in retail trade allowed for Borisova's transformation. Instead of working as a devalued distributor of clothes, she became a socialist labor hero who brought culture to the consuming masses.

5

The *Kontrol'* of Soviet Trade from Above and from Below

> Constant participation in the work of [soviets'] sections, the use of tens of thousands of the best industrial and white-collar workers for the organization of genuine *kontrol'* of trade work, and the creation with their help of public *kontrol'* around every store – all of this can yield huge results in the improvement of the work of the Soviet trade apparatus and cleanse it of alien elements and enemies of the people – Japanese-German Trotskyite and Bukharinite wreckers.[1]
>
> M. Epshtein, Moscow trade official, 1937

The mass participation of Soviet people in the monitoring and regulation (*kontrol'*) of the retail sector was central to the Communist pursuit of a Soviet dream world of retailing and consumption. Although authorities established official institutions to oversee compliance to rules and directives, they also relied on popular involvement in *kontrol'*. As Epshtein's quote suggests, they believed this mass participation would lead to improvements in retailing, and strengthen efforts to uncover "culprits" who impeded retail reform and economic progress.

Responsibility for the oversight of state agencies, policies, and functionaries is a part of every government, including not only the Soviet government but its Tsarist predecessor. The Tsarist agency *GosKontrol*, for example, monitored the financial affairs of government ministries and departments. The surreptitious surveillance of individuals and groups, sometimes a counterpart to official monitoring and regulation, was also not distinctly Soviet. The infamous Tsarist political police (*Okhrana*) spied on revolutionary groups and repressed alleged subversives.[2] However, the purview of official *kontrol'* and clandestine surveillance was far more extensive under Soviet rule than under the Tsarist

112

regime. Soviet efforts to create a new political order and noncapitalist economy generated a vast bureaucracy responsible for coordinating and auditing new policies and directives. This bureaucracy was influenced by the regime's class-based understanding of politics and society, and its anxiety about the social hygiene of the body politic. Political leaders posited the existence of a continuous struggle against the regime by class enemies or more "elusive enemies" and conducted "purification campaigns" to sanitize society of its "vermin," "saboteurs," "fascist insects," and other foes. Thus while regulatory bodies, such as inspectorates, scrutinized government agencies and economic organizations for compliance to party-state initiatives, these bodies and the political police (and its network of informants) also scrutinized individuals and groups in them (particularly "the usual suspects") for political opposition.[3] As Peter Holquist has pointed out, because the Soviet leadership wanted to know people's ideas and attitudes not only to prevent subversion but also to refashion individuals and build a new socialist world, it extended surveillance efforts to the populace as a whole.[4]

To support an expansive network of Soviet surveillance and regulation, the Communist leadership promoted the secret police as well as three types of official *kontrol'*: party *kontrol'*; state or government *kontrol'*; and social or public *kontrol'*. Authorities advanced party *kontrol'* to reinforce internal party discipline and to assert the Communist Party's dominance over state and public bodies. They promoted state *kontrol'* (via state agencies such as the militia, soviets, and procuracy) to investigate political, economic, and social matters. And they fostered social or public *kontrol'* (also referred to as mass *kontrol'* and *kontrol'* from below) to involve the masses in the monitoring of compliance to state and party directives, regulations, and norms of conduct.[5] Of the hundreds of thousands of citizens (and likely more) who became involved in public *kontrol'* in the mid- and late-1930s, many concentrated their efforts on the retail system as part of the campaign for socialist trade.[6]

This chapter explores the importance of public *kontrol'* in the retail sector, particularly mass participation in regulatory activities sponsored by state institutions, and public organizations and groups.[7] Public *kontrol'* was a product of not merely economic imperatives but also the Soviet leadership's interest in creating a new society. As with efforts to feminize the retail workforce and promote a retail labor hero movement, public *kontrol'* was explicitly understood as a means for transforming retail trade *and* the population-at-large. The goal was to foster a new system of retailing as well as a new "Soviet subjectivity." Soviet authorities aimed to improve the regulation of the consumer economy *and* to produce a new civic persona, the public controller, who unlike the manager or auditor in liberal capitalist societies, was concerned with more than maximizing profits and efficiency or checking compliance to retail-related and other rules. The Soviet public controller was concerned with furthering the collective good and socialist development – politically, economically, and socially. By mobilizing the general populace in *kontrol'* initiatives, authorities also sought to encourage self-discipline among trade officials and retail employees, the objects of this mass observation. Public *kontrol'*, in other words, was supposed to further retail reform and facilitate the construction of both a policing and self-policing New Soviet Person.

The parameters and logic of retail *kontrol'*

The extent of retail *kontrol'* activities grew from the drive to create a noncapitalist economy. In the 1930s, as part of its campaign to *replace* the private capitalist retail network of the 1920s with an entirely state-controlled network, the government advanced an immense array of retail regulations and directives, requiring attendant oversight mechanisms to ensure compliance.[8] Decrees were passed on the trade of specific foodstuffs and manufactured goods (such as bread and knitted goods). Authorities also adopted price controls and issued resolutions regulating retail practices, including advertising, customer complaint and suggestion books, weights and measures. Some directives sought to mitigate problems, such as goods shortages, caused by the nature of the Soviet planned economy and the campaign for rapid industrialization. For example, in the face of persistent goods shortages, the People's Commissariat of Domestic Trade (Narkomvnutorg) decreed that shop windows could not display products unavailable in stores.[9] Other regulations and directives sought to manage issues typically determined by private individuals and businesses in the capitalist marketplace, such as hours for retailing and employees' wages.

Policymakers' plans to create a modern and cultured socialist retail system contributed to the proliferation of regulations: rules focused on not only practical matters but also scientific and aesthetic concerns. This is illustrated by the 50 rules for dairy products that Narkomvnutorg established in 1935. To ensure freshness of goods, retail establishments were not supposed to sell dairy products beyond the following timeframes: 1 day for fresh milk and cream; 3 days for butter during the summer and 5 days for butter during the winter; 5 days for soft cheeses and 10 days for hard cheeses. It was not permissible for employees to use the same knife for cutting butter and cheese. All salesclerks were to undergo monthly medical examinations. Personnel were to carry out "a constant struggle against insects and rodents." In stores that sold dairy products, smoking was not allowed. Shop walls and ceilings were supposed to be "plastered and whitened or painted with a light-colored oil paint." Narkomvnutorg also directed stores selling dairy products to conduct their work on the basis of "cultured customer service."[10]

Soviet understandings of crime further stimulated surveillance and regulatory efforts in retailing. A 1932 law "On Guarding the Property of State Enterprises, Collective Farms, and Cooperatives and on the Strengthening of Societal (Socialist) Property" was intended to hinder theft in cooperative and state trade as well as in other sectors of the economy. Through this law, theft from stores or warehouses was defined as theft of societal property, and became an act against the party-state and the Soviet people. The law outlined severe penalties for theft: execution or no less than a 10-year prison sentence. A companion law, "On the Struggle against Speculation," employed firm measures to enforce officially established prices. It delineated tough sentences of 5 to 10 years imprisonment for those deemed guilty of speculation (buying and reselling goods to make a profit).[11] A later law against fraud was adopted in July 1934, which addressed the "deception of the government and consumers" through the misuse of weights and measures, and violations of price policies, mandating sentences of up to 10 years incarceration for infractions. Punishable offenses even included actions that resulted from negligence rather than deliberate deception, such as forgetting to display price listings or unintentionally using faulty scales.[12]

Such laws against economic crimes, in conjunction with the innumerable retail regulations and directives, provided a broad framework for the surveillance and monitoring of Soviet trade. An expansive network of controllers was necessary to investigate the retail sector for compliance to these laws, regulations, and directives. Communist leaders could have relied merely on party and state organs for this work, enlarging already existing official bureaucracies. But they opted instead to recruit the general populace to investigate the vast realm of potential infractions in the trade system.

Support for mass *kontrol'* in the retail sector was a product of official support for mass *kontrol'* more broadly. Ordinary people's involvement in the *kontrol'* of the state and economy was an important feature of the Soviet system from its inception. Public oversight "grew out of the workers' control movement of 1917–1918 and the flowering of the soviets (elected governmental councils), factory committees and trade unions as agencies of mass democracy in that period."[13] From 1918–1920, regional and local workers' inspectorates monitored the activities of state and economic establishments.[14] The Soviet regime underscored the importance of *"kontrol'* from below" by founding the Workers' and Peasants' Inspectorate (Rabkrin) in 1920 as a national agency to direct and expand public *kontrol'*, and to consolidate state and public investigations by reorganizing the state *kontrol'* commissariat into Rabkrin.[15] The Central Control Commission (TsKK) merged with Rabkrin in 1923 to become TsKK-Rabkrin, combining party, state, and mass *kontrol'* into one body. Throughout the 1920s and early 1930s, TsKK-Rabkrin functioned as an important "institutional symbol" and vehicle for public *kontrol'*, purportedly marshalling hundreds of thousands of ordinary people as activists.[16]

The Party disbanded TsKK-Rabkrin at the Seventeenth Party Congress in 1934, but it did not abandon its support for public *kontrol'*.[17] Indeed, the congress's final resolutions called for the devolution and broadening of responsibility, and instructed soviets, trade unions, and the Communist Youth League (Komsomol) to expand popular involvement in the inspection of state and economic institutions.[18] Nor did the abolition of TsKK-Rabkrin mark the end of ordinary citizens' mass participation in Soviet *kontrol'*.[19] State institutions, like the militia and soviets, and public organizations and groups, like trade unions and wife-activist groups, deployed citizens in monitoring activities.[20] The Soviet populace also voiced public criticism and denunciations at production meetings and party activities, in letters to authorities, newspapers, and journals, and in other forums.[21] While decentralized, this *"kontrol'* from below" became a hallmark of everyday life. Moreover, combined with citizen involvement in clandestine surveillance (as some people worked as covert informants for the secret police), this public *kontrol'* contributed to the repression and the Purges of the 1930s.[22]

From the early Soviet years, Communist leaders championed *"kontrol'* from below" because of its practical and ideological importance. In their view, mass participation in *kontrol'* was necessary for achieving a new socialist order, serving as a valuable tool for promoting the more efficient and scientific administration of the state and economy. Public *kontrol'* would reveal how government plans and directives were *not* being fulfilled. By uncovering shortcomings, abuses, and violations, it would help hold the genuinely subversive as well as scapegoats accountable for misconduct and difficulties. Ideally it would also elicit useful suggestions from below that could help resolve problems.[23] By identifying resistance to state and economic development, public *kontrol'* would additionally contribute to the broader Soviet purification drive. Finally, mass surveillance and regulation would create an army of *unpaid* volunteer controllers.

Public *kontrol'* was also considered a valuable tool for transforming the populace. Authorities argued that the involvement of "millions and millions of workers and peasants" in checking compliance to rules and regulations would promote self-discipline, honesty, and a greater sense of responsibility among those subjected to such *kontrol'*.[24] Party leader Lazar Kaganovich, a major proponent of public *kontrol'*, explained:

> We are trying to cultivate people by correctly organizing the examination of the fulfillment of orders. While it is important for us to punish [people] for infractions, it is more important not to punish infractions, but to prevent them. It is ten times more valuable to prevent a person from making a mistake than to punish him later when the mistake has already been made.[25]

Presumably the knowledge that they were being monitored by the masses, and official party and state agents, would "cultivate" individuals, encourage self-policing, and promote new attitudes. It would discourage citizens from engaging in criminal or anti-Soviet activities. In short, public *kontrol'* would alter everyday habits.

Communist leaders imagined that participating in *kontrol'* would similarly transform controllers. In a 1920 speech to the Moscow Soviet, Lenin instructed his audience:

> You must recruit into the workers' inspection the most diffident and undeveloped, the most timid of the workers and promote them upward, let them gradually proceed from the simplest duties they are able to carry out, at first only as onlookers, to more important roles in governmental affairs.[26]

Giving individuals the opportunity to participate directly in *kontrol'* would involve them in the administration of the government and help them acquire economic and organizational skills. Kaganovich made a similar argument in 1934:

> In the administration of production and the management of a proletarian state, trade unions take part, first of all, in performing their

controlling functions. Through the school of *kontrol'* – the trade unions as well as the Komsomol train cadres of state leaders. A good controller is a good future manager.[27]

Like other Soviet practices of subjectivization, such as autobiographical writing and speaking, Komsomol membership, or educational initiatives, authorities envisioned public *kontrol'* as a mechanism for self-transformation: for training ordinary people, fostering new talents, and inculcating a socialist outlook.[28]

Fostering mass participation in the monitoring and regulation of the state and economy was considered a crucial step toward creating ideal citizens and a participatory socialist democracy. Even before the Revolution Lenin had claimed that under socialism the general populace would take part "not only in voting and elections, but also in the everyday administration of the state."[29] Once Soviet rule was established, Communist leaders sought to mobilize citizens in state affairs through a variety of institutions and processes. *Kontrol'* was one mechanism for incorporating those less likely to be active in public service and governance via trade unions, local soviets, or other organizations into the Soviet polity. Because ordinary people were generally not afforded opportunities to monitor the state under capitalism, mass participation in Soviet *kontrol'* also fostered the illusion that the Soviet Union promoted a more genuine democracy.

As trade authorities, local government officials, and others endeavored to transform retailing in the 1930s, they too emphasized the practical and ideological value of public *kontrol'*. Zelenskii, president of the All-Union Central Union of Consumer Cooperative Societies (Tsentrosoiuz), claimed that it was essential for ridding the retail sector of "aliens, embezzlers and thieves."[30] Commissar of Domestic Trade Veitser argued that it would be impossible to establish effective *kontrol'* without popular involvement: the emergent state-controlled retail system was simply too large for party-state bodies to monitor on their own. "In addition to *kontrol'* by the trade unions," it was necessary for the retail sector to establish more *kontrol'* by consumers, by those from various "factories, enterprises, institutions."[31] Moreover, Veitser argued, to have "every store in its field of vision," the State Trade Inspectorate needed to organize activist groups of public controllers from the ranks of customers, trade workers' wives, and so on.[32] To promote more successful *kontrol'*, and to advance the Stalinist regime's trade campaign, state and public controllers needed to work together.

Trade authorities did not intend for public *kontrol'* to operate merely as a repressive practice. While public *kontrol'* was designed to uncover transgressors, and serve as a cautionary warning to wrongdoers, it was also intended to yield positive changes and genuine improvements in the trade system. Authorities directed public controllers not only "to reveal facts about this or that ugliness or insufficiency," but also to eliminate problems and take actions that would "prevent the possibility that new theft and embezzlement [would] arise," and "strive for the implementation" of measures that would in some way improve Soviet trade.[33] Those engaged in public *kontrol'* were expected to be problem solvers, not only whistleblowers.

Trade officials and trade-union leaders reiterated official discourse about how *kontrol'* would alter individuals subjected to surveillance. The Central Committee of the Trade Union of Cooperative and State Trade Workers (PRKGT) explained that "in every store and stall honest Soviet trade would prevail" if only there were more, and better, public controllers.[34] According to Soviet officials and retail reformers, the daily and omnipresent threat of public *kontrol'* would act as a preventative measure *and* foster accountability, enhancing employees' work.

Authorities in the retail sector also echoed the party line that ordinary people would be transformed by working as volunteer inspectors. According to the PRKGT, the Seventeenth Party Congress decision to have trade unions more involved in *kontrol'* was "a new and mighty lever" for the "communist education of millions of masses."[35] Public *kontrol'* of the retail sector, in other words, would contribute to the construction of a new system of retailing and the forging of "Soviet" subjects – activist citizens engaged in a larger revolutionary project.

The *kontrol'* infrastructure: State institutions and public organizations and groups

The Soviet populace engaged in the public *kontrol'* of retailing by participating in monitoring initiatives organized by state institutions and "public" organizations (such as trade unions and the Komsomol). Because public organizations and groups in the Soviet Union were not truly independent entities separate from the party-state, their monitoring activities were not necessarily spontaneous or organic. Indeed, they were often a direct response to party-state directives. This affected the rhythm of *kontrol'*. Although there was a general drive to increase state and public *kontrol'* during the trade campaign, new government directives provoked a flurry of new activity and energy. Thus, for example, after the law against the deception of the government and consumers was passed in 1934, public organizations dramatically increased their investigations of prices and the use of weights and scales. In just three months over 200,000 counter workers from the ranks of the "best and most honest people of Soviet trade," in addition to other workers, were mobilized for inspections.[36]

Official state bodies involved in the oversight of retailing included but were not limited to the following: the Soviet *Kontrol'* Commission (its Trade Group); the political police (OGPU) and its successor, the People's Commissariat of Internal Affairs (NKVD); the regular police; the procuracy; the judiciary; the soviets; trade organizations' inspectorates; TsKK-Rabkrin, and various all-union inspectorates.[37] These state organs did not rely solely on the surveillance of paid staff but organized and welcomed public *kontrol'*. Ordinary people assisted state organs in monitoring the trade apparatus by forming "assistance groups," joining inspection brigades, and becoming *kontrol'* activists.[38]

Even more so than other state organs, TsKK-Rabkrin, the State Inspectorate of Prices, the State Trade Inspectorate (GTI), and soviets enlisted the general public in their surveillance activities, interweaving party-state *kontrol'* with public *kontrol'*. In 1933, for example, 25,000 Komsomol activists carried out "light cavalry" raids in conjunction with TsKK-Rabkrin officials, inspecting 1,037 stores and 1,173 canteens.[39] A network of volunteers helped the State Inspectorate of Prices supervise the state's system of fixed prices, participating in the inspectorate's mass raids and joining various "*kontrol'*-signal" posts and assistance groups. In April 1933, for example, the State Inspectorate of Prices reported checking prices in 4,611 trading points with the help of 1,472 activists.[40] The GTI relied on a paid staff of hundreds of permanent inspectors as well as tens of thousands of "public inspectors," "*kontrol'*-signal posts" (usually organized at large-scale enterprises and factories) and activists from trade unions, the Komsomol light cavalry, and other groups.[41] In the first quarter of 1935, over 21,000 such volunteers contributed to the work of the GTI, and in the first quarter of 1936, the ranks of volunteers grew to almost 60,000.[42] Activists usually assisted the GTI by participating in mass raids and spot-checks of the retail system, whereas public inspectors and *kontrol'*-signal posts engaged in more consistent work. Provincial, city, and rural soviets deployed the general public in surveillance initiatives via "trade sections," "trade-procurement sections," "cooperative sections," "workers' supply sections," and "trade and financial budget sections." Activists in these "sections" carried out inspections of stores, canteens, and warehouses, and investigated customers' complaints, sales and storage practices, and the implementation of trade-related requests from voters.[43]

The regulation of Soviet trade consisted of party, state, and public efforts, often overlapping and collaborative.

Among public organizations, trade unions were central in fostering public *kontrol'* of the retail sector. This is not surprising since they had long been involved in the policing of other spheres. From the beginning of Soviet rule, trade unions coordinated "workers' *kontrol'*," which granted workers a supervisory role in enterprises by allowing them to monitor production processes, financial affairs, and other matters.[44] During the 1920s, unions participated in many oversight initiatives, including some in the retail sector.[45] From 1930 on, party and state organs called for unions' increased involvement in the *kontrol'* of trade in response to the massive distribution and goods crisis, and the launching of the campaign to establish Soviet trade.[46] In July 1931, for example, the All-Union Central Council of Trade Unions (VTsSPS) ordered trade unions to establish inspection brigades to look into "how the party's and government's decrees about developing Soviet trade were being carried out."[47] In 1933 the Soviet government transferred oversight responsibilities previously assigned to the People's Commissariat of Labor (including the oversight of canteens and stores) to trade unions.[48] When the Seventeenth Party Congress approved the dissolution of Rabkrin in 1934, it instructed trade unions to assume Rabkrin's role "as an organizer of mass *kontrol'*" and to take on many of Rabkrin's former "*kontrol'* functions," including those in the retail sector.[49] In subsequent years, the VTsSPS frequently reminded trade unions of their duty to organize the public *kontrol'* of cooperative and state trade, especially among workers and housewives.[50]

As trade unions gained greater responsibility for retail *kontrol'*, the Trade Union for Cooperative and State Trade Workers (PRKGT) became one of the primary contributors to this effort.[51] PRKGT leaders sought to direct members' energies on the sector in which they worked, and actively organized them in workers' brigades and "signal posts" to investigate a wide array of issues at cooperative and state trade enterprises, stores, stalls, warehouses, and depots. While some workers' brigades carried out regular inspections, many mobilized for specific campaigns and one-time spot checks-ups, such as when they inspected stores for how well they were fulfilling the party-state decree in September 1935 about lowering prices for bread, flour, and other food products.[52] "Signal posts," ideally composed of the trade union's best shock workers and activists, appear to have monitored the retail sector in a more consistent manner, some even on a daily basis. In principle, signal posts were supposed to uncover both the negative and the positive, to reveal "the insufficiencies and mistakes in work as well as the positive experience of work."[53] In practice, signal posts served first and foremost as whistleblowers.[54]

Consumer cooperative societies had long encouraged active member involvement in the administration and regulation of cooperative affairs, but during the trade campaign they directed new attention to public *kontrol'*.[55] Cooperative leaders urged members to get involved by joining revision commissions, shop commissions, cooperative bureaus, or by becoming more general "cooperative activists" who joined activist groups (*koopaktivy*).[56] Revision commissions (aka *kontrol'*-revision commissions) were responsible primarily for monitoring the financial affairs of consumer cooperatives.[57] Shop commissions (aka *kontrol'*-shop commissions) played a direct role in the regulation of stores' general conditions, investigating them on a frequent basis for prices, sanitary standards, salesclerks' behavior, and so on.[58] Tsentrosoiuz also instructed them to "listen carefully to consumer's complaints" and "get to the root" of whatever ugliness had arisen.[59] Cooperative members who joined cooperative bureaus or *koopaktivy* undertook a variety of tasks, including the inspection of stores.[60]

Women and *kontrol'*

In 1938 the working women's journal *Rabotnitsa* illustrated the particular attention that Soviet authorities and the press paid to recruiting women into the regulation of Soviet trade in the 1930s with the call: "Women-workers, wives of industrial and white-collar workers – help trade organizations make trade precise and cultured via *kontrol'*."[61] Efforts to enlist women as controllers in the retail sector were not entirely new. During the Civil War and the 1920s, Soviet authorities appealed to women to get involved in monitoring sectors of the economy that they were presumed to be familiar with, including canteens and shops. In 1919 and 1920, for example, Lenin made repeated remarks about the need to draw women into *kontrol'* work.[62] Emphasis on women's participation as controllers – both in the early Soviet years and during the 1930s – was predicated on the view that women, especially non-wage earning women, would benefit in particular from the training that *kontrol'* work would ostensibly provide. Despite official rhetoric about women's equality, many Communist leaders and others viewed women, especially non-wage earning women, as less educated and politically conscious than men. In part this was because women were less likely than men to be actively involved in public service and the political arena in the 1920s, and this remained true in the 1930s, even as women entered the wage labor force en masse (which was supposed to foster a new political consciousness). The idea was that through participation in *kontrol'*, women would acquire valuable skills that would enable them to take on new civic responsibilities in running the state, and in the process, become full-fledged Soviet citizens. Women's involvement as controllers, Lenin claimed, would therefore lead "to the strengthening of socialist society."[63]

In the 1930s, authorities placed new emphasis on enlisting women in *kontrol'* – repeatedly directing trade unions and other organs to recruit workers' wives, women delegates, and housewife activists into *kontrol'* posts and brigades, shop commissions, and similar groups.[64] Official discourse stressed that women's participation in *kontrol'* was beneficial for both retail trade and the women themselves. A newspaper editorial claimed that the *kontrol'* of stores served as a "school of public work" for female collective-farm workers, and that "thousands of women had passed through the school of cooperative work in shop and *kontrol'*-revision commissions, as well as rural cooperative boards," which had prepared them for "independent work."[65] Noting that many women employees in the consumer cooperative apparatus had initially gained qualifications and education by participating in the work of *"kontrol'*-shop commissions" and cooperative bureaus, a consumer cooperative report concluded that this experience served as a "big public-political school for housewives."[66]

Soviet authorities and women's advocates also supported women's role as controllers because of women's alleged talent for monitoring the retail sector. They reiterated arguments that were mobilized to justify women's recruitment as paid retail employees, professing that as the primary consumers in families and managers of household economies, women had domestic skills that made them particularly capable of working in the retail sector, whether paid or unpaid. As a journal editor explained, it was easy for women to work in soviets' cooperative sections as controllers, because "as customers they c[a]me into daily contact" with cooperatives' "insufficiencies, disorder, and inability" to provide cultured customer service.[67] A news article asserted: "Knowing all the 'ailments (*boliachki*)' of shops, stalls," and so on, "workers" wives provide wonderful results in the *kontrol'* of these parts."[68] A consumer cooperative report discussed women's significant contributions as controllers, noting that housewives were particularly good at inspecting "those areas that they encounter daily as consumers and whose insufficiencies and ailments they know perfectly well."[69] The "penetrating eye of the housewife [controller]," some alleged, could transform retail work.[70] Women's roles in the domestic sphere were presumed to provide them with consumer insight that could be deployed usefully to monitor and fix retail problems.

Wife-activists' groups played a particularly prominent role in the monitoring of Soviet trade. Like other public controllers, they investigated cooperative and state trade for general problems, retail violations, and criminal conduct. They uncovered instances of sales personnel who stole goods and sold them on the side, cheated customers, allowed the sale of defective goods, and treated customers rudely.[71] Often they made such discoveries by carrying out "*kontrol'* purchases," that is, by acting as Soviet versions of contemporary day "mystery shoppers" and hiding their role as controllers.[72] Wife-activists formed brigades to see if the "principles of cultured trade" were being carried out, taking particular responsibility for investigating sanitation and hygiene problems in stores, warehouses, and among workers.[73] Apparently seasoned by their domestic housecleaning duties, they "fought for cleanliness in stores." Even when stores looked free of dirt, the closer inspections of women activists often discovered the presence of dirty smocks and rat droppings on bread shelves.[74] Wife-activists were known to actively seek solutions to the problems they uncovered. One wife-activists' group explained how women formed brigades and "systematically visit[ed] stores, depots, and canteens, not as controllers with a mandate, but as helpers." Upon discovering problems in stores, they "right there, on the spot, sought to eliminate them." Among other things, they "put on aprons and showed how best to arrange goods in store windows," "bought aprons and berets for salesclerks," and cleaned off "trash and dust from shelves."[75] The ideal public controller – as exemplified by the wife-activist controller – was not supposed to be a punitive force, a hierarchical figure of authority such as an official inspector from an inspectorate; she was supposed to be a comrade-in-arms, waging the collective battle to create a new socialist order, including a new socialist retail system.

Limited data suggest that tens of thousands of women became unpaid public controllers in the 1930s.[76] In 1934 over half the activists in the shop commissions of the October district consumer society in Moscow were women.[77] According to a 1935 survey, *kontrol'*-revision commissions in rural consumer cooperatives were made up of about 20 percent women.[78] Women comprised 25 percent of the trade activists in the Kuibyshev City Soviet in 1936.[79] In some regions the number of women *kontrol'* activists increased in the mid-1930s. In the Moscow *oblast'*, 5 percent of cooperative activists on revision committees in 1933 were women, whereas in 1934, women constituted about 25 percent of the activists.[80] Women controllers, including wife-activists were not spread evenly throughout the Soviet Union, but they worked in many different cities, towns, and rural areas in both the Russian Republic as well as other Soviet republics.[81]

Kontrol' and Soviet subjectivity

When it comes to the question of "Soviet subjectivity," the case of women's participation in *kontrol'* is instructive. It suggests that for some people, including many women, involvement in retail *kontrol'* was educational, empowering, and integrative. Controller Tolokonnikova stated, "Checking stores, we ourselves learn. For example, if necessary I could tomorrow stand behind a counter and free [up] a male salesclerk so that he could stand for the defense of our wonderful country."[82] A wife-activist leader asserted, "For thousands of women, who yesterday knew nothing except children and their family's well-being, new horizons have opened, inviting them [to participate] in the active struggle for and success of the socialist front. Diverse and inexhaustible possibilities for the improvement of Soviet trade [including *kontrol'* work] are opening up before the wives of trade workers."[83] A housewife activist and public controller for the retail sector of her city soviet happily concluded that Soviet power "has turned me into an active builder of a new life."[84] Women controllers gained new public roles and legitimacy, and often received attention, praise, and even awards for their hard work.[85] In most cases women's participation in *kontrol'* did not lead, as Lenin had envisioned, to more important management positions in governmental affairs. Nonetheless, by allowing women to become productive citizens in the campaign to remake retailing, this participation served to better integrate women into the Soviet polity. Moreover, it appears to have helped foster a new sense of self, a "Soviet subjectivity" more closely identified with the socialist project, or at the very least, a new publicly expressed presentation of self that was more closely identified with Soviet socialism.

Public *kontrol'* transformed not only some controllers but also many of those who were subjected to its gaze. Combined with party-state *kontrol'*, it worked as a deterrent, at least some of the time. As one trade union leader explained, *kontrol'* was "not only repressive but also prophylactic" for salesclerks had adopted a new attitude toward work, announcing, "We did not pay attention to prices and weights because no one asked us about this earlier; now we are going to pay special attention to this [issue]."[86] Many reports and controllers affirmed this point, claiming that retail establishments showed fewer violations and inadequacies when inspected more frequently and consistently.[87] At the same time, although authorities hoped that the mass observation of public controllers would improve the practices of trade officials and retail employees, and encourage self-policing and the internalization of socialist values, the seemingly endless "crimes" and misconduct that controllers uncovered suggest that these objectives were at best only partially realized. Inspections routinely revealed corruption at all levels of the Soviet trade system as well as unsanitary retail conditions, incorrect pricing, and poor customer service. It appears that in the minds of many, the potential punitive consequences from mass regulation did not outweigh the perceived benefits of underperforming on the job or engaging in retail misconduct.

Nor was participation in public *kontrol'* always transformative for controllers. Although authorities successfully organized mass participation in *kontrol'* via workers' brigades, shop commissions, and other public organs, some of these organs were inactive or rarely active, existing more on paper than in reality.[88] Public *kontrol'* suffered from uneven effort and commitment. As one critic observed, revision commissions "sle[pt] more than they work[ed]."[89]

Such poor performance was not merely a result of apathy or indifference. Public controllers often lacked the necessary leadership, assistance, and training from higher authorities that would have enabled them to pursue their work more effectively.[90] As one person explained, "the bad results" of workers' *kontrol'* were due not only to "enemies of the people" who sought to disrupt *kontrol'*, but also to "the exceptional negligence" on the part of authorities.[91] Indeed, a worker controller noted, some controllers did little or no work because they lacked guidance and did not know their "rights and responsibilities." He added, "In stores we often see cheating and the spoilage of goods, but we aren't able to say anything, because we don't know if we have the right to do so. But if we had instructions, then we would act without fail." Controllers' lack of retail knowledge also undermined their ability to perform certain tasks. Many found it difficult, for example, to evaluate goods given their unfamiliarity with the nuances of merchandise. "It is said that meat has three grades with each grade having a different price," a public controller noted. "How are we able to check it, when we aren't able to understand it, when we don't know which [meat] is the first, the second, or the third grade?"[92] Armed with uncertain authority and limited guidance, some controllers backed away from their responsibilities, while others were probably more disruptive than productive, acting as a meddlesome presence instead of as a discerning eye or helpful assistant.

The efficacy of public *kontrol'* and its transformative potential on those involved in mass regulation were also undermined by the failure of higher authorities to pursue adequate action in the face of information supplied by controllers. Judicial and procuratorial organs did not always carry out their duties in a timely manner, resulting in prosecutorial delays that allowed the accused to continue with their suspect practices.[93] In 1935, for example, Moscow court investigation agencies took 136 days to look into cases of theft or embezzlement.[94] Law enforcement officials often took it easy on offenders: judges granted "lenient verdicts" for many offenses and the police (militia) sometimes released suspects without taking any action.[95] Observing this lack of follow through to misconduct and "crimes" uncovered via *kontrol'*, one controller testified that her desire to work was diminished.[96]

Another issue that detracted from the potentially transformative effects of *kontrol'* work on public controllers was the hostility that many of them confronted. Not surprisingly, trade workers did not always welcome the "help" that controllers were trying to provide. It was not uncommon for salesclerks and store managers to try to block controllers' access to stores and complaint books, question their authority, and treat them rudely.[97] In one store a saleswoman yelled at controllers and tried to stop their investigation, announcing "there is nothing here, there is nothing for you to look at." In another store, when a public controller asked why there was no small change, a problem which was causing a line, a Leningrad cashier "rudely" replied, "there isn't a bank next door and there's no courier to go change [money]."[98] Some salesclerks tried to mobilize customers against controllers by arguing that controllers caused problems, such as lines.[99] Women controllers appear to have experienced particular obstruction of their efforts. They were accused of meddling, "talking rubbish," even thrown out of stores.[100] Women controllers may have encountered more vocal and aggressive resistance than men controllers because of a perception that they were easier to intimidate, or in response to the disruption of traditional gender dynamics caused by their growing involvement in *kontrol'*.[101] Women's increased surveillance of the trade apparatus provided them with newfound power over men as they uncovered malfeasance and incompetence among mostly male trade leaders, store directors, managers of store departments, and warehouse workers, as well as the large contingent of male salesclerks and other store employees.

Whether public controllers encountered a lack of guidance, leadership, training, or responsiveness on the part of higher authorities, or hostility to their efforts, these experiences probably did not foster a sense of pride in the crusade to build socialism or identification with a broader "socialist" community of brothers and sisters. Instead, it appears that these experiences hindered the contribution of *kontrol'* work to the forging of a new "Soviet" self, fomenting feelings of disempowerment and demoralization among controllers, and perhaps even disillusionment with the system.

In some cases, public *kontrol'* was transformative in the wrong ways, and fostered anti-Soviet selves: individuals who engaged in behavior that worked against Soviet objectives. Some public controllers used their positions to elevate themselves, abuse their power, pursue easy profits, and create more corruption, the very problems that regulation was expected to stem. Many took advantage of their roles to avoid long lines or to demand goods in limited supply, while others accepted bribes to remain silent about retail problems or criminal activities.[102] A public controller from a textile factory in Turkmenistan, for example, demanded that store employees give him sugar without a ration card and let him try the alcoholic beverages. Another controller for a Karelia trade organization engaged in "reckless self-supplying" during his first audit of a store.[103] Although public *kontrol'* could and did contribute to the improvement of retailing, it also provided new opportunities for misconduct, which undermined official efforts to transform retailing and forge the New Soviet Person.

The limits of retail reform and *kontrol'*

Mass regulation underscored the limited success of the campaign to remake the retail sector. Throughout their many investigations, controllers frequently found unsanitary conditions, incorrect prices, poor merchandise assortment and defective goods, a lack of complaint books and price listings, obsolete technologies, and poor customer service.[104] They also confirmed that corruption pervaded all levels of the Soviet trade system. Although authorities pursued many measures to Bolshevize trade employees, inspections routinely revealed that the trade system was "clutter[ed]" with "former people" such as private traders and kulaks (well-to-do peasants), and thieves and embezzlers, many of whom had records for previous offenses.[105] Even though controllers identified many offenders, the supply appeared endless. Hiring and firing practices did not help matters. Employers were supposed to hire workers who had clean records and official clearance from attestation committees, but because these committees functioned poorly (if at all), employers often hired workers who had not been reviewed, including those who had already been fired for abuses.[106] Moreover, authorities did not usually fire individuals caught engaging in minor offenses, so small-scale criminals often remained in the system until repeat offenses were discovered.[107]

Another major problem was the dearth of quality retail tools. For example, as controllers mobilized en masse in 1934 to check the accuracy of weights and scales, they found thousands of inaccurate weights and scales, many of which malfunctioned because of deliberate tinkering to facilitate cheating. When they ordered the removal of these weights and scales for repair or replacement, stores often went without them (sometimes for months) because of slow repairs and an inadequate supply of new tools.[108] Even after some weights and scales had been "repaired," many still worked improperly.[109]

Controllers also found that retail employees were unfamiliar with some of the new regulations and instructions emerging from the trade campaign.[110] Such lack of awareness was a serious problem. It would be impossible to realize the ideal new cultured Soviet trade envisioned by policymakers if retail workers did not have a good sense of that vision and what was expected of them. Although there was massive propaganda about the trade campaign as well as the adoption of decree after decree to improve retailing, inspections of the retail sector demonstrated that some of the campaign's key objectives and initiatives were not always well known or understood by the very people who were supposed to implement them.

Although state and public controllers were often successful in identifying retail problems, regulatory and surveillance efforts were undermined by a host of problems. Trade officials and trade-union leaders were well aware of these problems – many of which were systemic to the efforts – even as they publicly pushed for the expansion of monitoring activities. Indeed, the internal records of the trade apparatus and trade-union organs are replete with reports and discussions documenting patterns of negligence, corruption, and incompetence on the part of not only public controllers but also state controllers and local officials. Police members in charge of monitoring the retail sector abused their positions, letting their relatives cut into long lines or extracting payments to tolerate speculation.[111] Even the State Trade Inspectorate (GTI), the state agency whose *raison d'être* was to promote effective *kontrol'*, struggled to establish a productive focus and was criticized for inspecting too many matters, straying from primary tasks. Worse yet, some members of the inspectorate hid "actual conditions" and ignored or covered up inspectors' findings.[112]

Despite problems, particularly the ones with public *kontrol'*, Soviet authorities remained committed to expanding retail regulation, and took steps in response. They organized competitions to combat inaction and apathy among controllers, using material awards (including cash) and vacations as incentives. In Samara in 1934, for example, authorities sponsored a three-month competition to promote better public *kontrol'*, setting aside 35,000 rubles for 76 prizes, of which 40 would be awarded to rural consumer cooperatives with exemplary *kontrol'*-shop commissions.[113] They chastised local officials for their negligence and lack of leadership, and called on trade unions to take more responsibility for supervising and training controllers. In a pamphlet on mass *kontrol'*, the Trade Union of Cooperative and State Trade Workers quoted Kaganovich: "It is necessary to learn how to *kontrol'*." It then urged local trade-union organizers "to bind themselves" to controllers on a *daily* basis, "to know, educate, and encourage the best of them, to look after and worry about *kontrol'* activists, and to raise controllers' qualifications."[114] The PRKGT and other organs, like Narkomvnutorg, organized short-term courses and seminars, and convened instructional meetings for controllers to exchange experiences and learn about "the tasks of lower-level *kontrol'*." They also disseminated educational materials for controllers through the Soviet press and in pamphlets and books.[115]

Ultimately, public *kontrol'* turned out to be a blunt instrument for the regulatory oversight of the nascent Soviet trade system, and it was mired in contradictions. By uncovering "transgressors" in the retail network, public *kontrol'* helped to rid the system of alleged criminals. But the vast number of offenses it uncovered (in addition to those uncovered by state *kontrol'*) was overwhelming. As authorities faced a flood of reports about criminal activity, they faced a difficult situation. As a Tsentrosoiuz report acknowledged, "Not sending the cases [of very small-scale embezzlement and theft] to the courts weakens the fight against embezzlers, and sending these same cases and having them looked into in an established juridical manner makes more difficult [the work of] the court investigation agencies and deprives them of the possibility of quickly looking into and solving more important cases." To make matters more complicated, some of the smaller-scale cases consisted of individuals who made mistakes from inadequate qualifications and experience rather than bad intentions.[116] In other cases, those charged and punished for theft and embezzlement were simply more qualified workers in charge of sections or departments, whose positions of oversight made them responsible for losses, such as theft, even when they were not personally guilty of wrongdoing. Punishing these people did little to address the actual crimes, and likely made recruitment of employees to these supervisory positions more difficult.[117]

By identifying overly bureaucratic procedures and personalities, public *kontrol'* helped to undermine bureaucracy. Yet by producing report after report after report, *kontrol'* exacerbated the very bureaucracy it was supposed to diminish. In recognizing this problem, a GTI functionary became hostile to the idea of energetic assistance from public controllers. He argued, "If in my *oblast'* there are 300–400 public inspectors who work, and every one of them looks into five stores, I will receive 2,000 documents [from them]. And what should I do with them, with these documents?"[118] In many respects, *kontrol'* simultaneously fostered and hindered reform efforts.

* * *

Despite its inefficiency and unevenness, *kontrol'* did have an impact on the retail sector. As state and public controllers identified problems, central and local authorities sought to address them. Thus, for example, they removed faulty equipment from retail establishments to be repaired or replaced, fixed the incorrect pricing and labeling of goods, and promoted greater retail hygiene.[119] They also held tens of thousands of personnel accountable for trade violations and criminal offenses. Disciplinary actions included verbal reprimand, small fines, job loss, criminal proceedings, imprisonment, even execution.

Soviet authorities' emphasis on mass enlistment in *kontrol'* also furthered the trade campaign's efforts to redefine the retail system as socialist, and served as a mechanism for social integration. Under capitalist regimes in the interwar era, ordinary people were not expected to play a significant role in the official monitoring of retailing. Soviet retailing, by contrast, encouraged ordinary people to bolster the system by participating in a vast array of regulatory activities, forging them as public controllers engaged in the remaking of retailing and the construction of socialism. For some individuals, particularly women from the so-called "unorganized" part of the Soviet population (non-wage earning wives), this participation appears to have been especially transformative, fostering a new sense of self and a new identification with the socialist project. But while the public *kontrol'* of Soviet trade may have contributed to the production of "Soviet" selves, including the development of ideal socialist public controllers, it also contributed to the production of subjects who engaged in explicitly subversive and "anti-Soviet" behavior. Moreover, even if some people understood their participation in *kontrol'* in ways that the Communist leadership hoped, as democratization of the state or as an important civic contribution to the building of socialism and the regulation of the state and economy, others undoubtedly saw this participation as a thankless chore.

Regardless of whether or not public *kontrol'* helped to produce a new sense of self, particularly an ideal Soviet self, it shaped the language of public controllers, helping to constitute Soviet subjects who "spoke Bolshevik" (at least some of the time).[120] Whether upstanding and proud, corrupt, demoralized, or indifferent – public controllers alike reproduced official discourse about retail trade and the economy. Controllers' reports often followed a standard format, limiting controllers' focus to an established set of concerns and categories of interest, which stifled investigations and frank discussions of other issues.[121] Soviet authorities directed public controllers to monitor adherence to existing laws and directives, to uncover violations. They did *not* encourage public controllers to identify structural shortcomings or economic policies in need of revision. They did *not* encourage public controllers to make connections between local difficulties and broader Soviet priorities. When controllers sought to explain problems in reports, at meetings, on the radio, or in newspapers, they perpetuated the party line by assigning blame to individuals: to the lackluster performance or negligence of trade officials and employees (both at the store level and in cooperative and state trade organizations) who did not do enough to advance cultured Soviet trade; or to the "wreckers" and "enemies of the people" who actively hindered progress by engaging in theft, embezzlement, and speculation. By replicating official discourse, controllers reaffirmed the legitimacy of Stalinist narratives and helped the Soviet regime locate scapegoats for retail problems.

By bringing the retail sector into the broader culture of surveillance that was developing during the 1930s, the public *kontrol'* of Soviet trade had another important effect: it contributed to an awareness of self (often new) among those who were objects of scrutiny. The mass monitoring of trade organizations and retail venues helped teach trade officials and employees that their actions and "selves" mattered. They were being watched – not only by official party and state organizations and agents, or by more surreptitious secret police members and covert informants, but by their peers – by a broader collective.[122] The widespread publicity about this *kontrol'* that was promoted via the press, radio, and "show processes" (trials) about speculation or theft reinforced this message.[123] Such publicity allowed the regime to propagandize about real changes being made in the retail system, but it also reminded potential offenders (and the Soviet people more broadly) of two things: first, that there was an elaborate and multilayered if somewhat dysfunctional system of *kontrol'*; and second, that violations could result in serious consequences.

Public *kontrol'* of the retail sector enlisted the general Soviet populace in the disciplining of others. This made citizens themselves complicit in the making of a particular kind of Soviet subject who was aware of the regime's explicit mobilization of not only hierarchical observation but also a more egalitarian observation (mass scrutiny by fellow citizens) to examine individual attitudes and practices. When combined with similar efforts to involve the general public in the monitoring and regulation of coworkers and neighbors, particularly during the Terror of the mid-to-late 1930s, the *kontrol'* of the retail sector advanced a broader Stalinist goal: the construction of a society of mutual surveillance, a Soviet version of the panopticon.[124] In addition to promoting improvements in the retail system, mass participation in the monitoring of cooperative and state trade therefore contributed to both the subjectivization *and* the subjugation of individuals.

6

The Making of the
New Soviet Consumer

In October 1936 the Stakhanovite Kondrasheva spoke at a conference on the latest exhibition of children's consumer goods in Moscow. She complained:

> Displayed here are children's strollers. I'm interested in the question – who had so little conscience as to put them on display? Look at the crude work. How can I put a well-dressed child in such a stroller? It is completely incomprehensible. ... If a child is not a freak, a hunchback, then he will have a hump after he is ambled about in this stroller. The question is how does such a product come to be sold in a store?[1]

Kondrasheva's criticism was articulated at one of an expanding number of officially sanctioned forums for consumers' voices in the 1930s. Her comments joined a litany of public consumer complaints. Instead of repressing consumer grievances about retail trade and consumption, authorities explicitly supported such negative feedback.

The public expression of citizens' opinions in the 1930s, some laudatory but most critical, was not unique to the retail sector. The Communist leadership invited individuals to express their opinions about production problems, abusive practices by superiors, and other matters in a variety of venues, including soviets (state organs of elected representatives), production meetings, and letters to the Soviet press.[2] Soliciting criticism was a valuable tool for exercising social control. It provided displeased citizens with a cathartic outlet for dissatisfaction, serving to dissipate popular frustration.[3] Official advocacy of citizens' complaints appeared to show concern for people's grievances, offering a pretense of state responsiveness.[4] On a more cynical level, public criticism also operated as a vehicle for denunciation, which allowed the Stalinist regime to enlist individuals' "malice, self-interest" and "quest for justice" in its official obsession with rooting out "wreckers" and neutralizing "enemies of the people."[5]

Soviet authorities encouraged consumers like Kondrasheva to express their grievances to mitigate popular discontent, demonstrate official interest in citizens' views and welfare, *and* involve ordinary people in the party-state drive to unmask economic and political "culprits." But the party-state's mobilization of consumer criticism had greater significance, with broader functions. Government leaders promoted it to further economic progress: to improve manufacturing and retailing. They endorsed it to regulate criticism and reinforce official narratives about problems in the retail sector. Authorities also viewed consumer participation in officially sanctioned forums for criticism as a useful vehicle for producing a "new" Soviet consumer. The drive to create a new Soviet consumer was part of a broader effort to create a New Soviet Person: to transform "backward" peasants into collective farmers, *baby* ("backward" women) into modern and politically astute women, religious believers into Marxist secularists, native "savages" into socialist citizens, and the uncultured and illiterate masses into civilized comrades.[6] But creating a new Soviet consumer who could be reconciled with socialism would do more than transform individuals. It would also further the Communist pursuit of a Soviet dream world of retailing and consumption. Unlike the consumer of the past, whom Soviet authorities characterized as an unproductive and selfish individual who contributed nothing to the public good, the new Soviet consumer would be a legitimate and productive member of society, a positive force in the building of socialism.

The Stalinist regime pursued several strategies for refashioning consumers and repositioning them within the Soviet polity. As it launched the trade campaign, it recognized people as consumers, not merely workers, and asserted a new relationship between the party-state and consumers, publicizing the party-state's duty to respond to consumers' interests. Joseph Stalin publicly declared it the regime's responsibility to do a better job meeting people's material needs and providing them with an abundance of consumer goods. Echoing Stalin, the press and trade authorities affirmed citizens' expectations for a comfortable and modern lifestyle, endorsing the consumption of semi-prepared foodstuffs, canned goods, ready-to-wear clothing, electrical devices, and pocket watches. Soviet leaders also moved away from their earlier emphasis on the virtues of asceticism, and during the Second Five-Year Plan (1933–1937), they approved the expanded production of basic foodstuffs and manufactured goods. Subsequent increases in manufacturing did not come close to meeting overall demand, and shortages continued to plague the Soviet economy. Nonetheless, the rhetorical and policy changes regarding the provisioning of commodities legitimized consumers' interests.

Official Soviet discourse proclaimed that citizens were entitled to a greater number and selection of consumer goods *and* to a better retail experience. This included a more efficient and expanded retail network, and good customer service, themes underscored as the government promoted its trade campaign. A *Pravda* editorial, "Respect for the Soviet Consumer," validated people's desire to obtain material goods "without any particular waste of time and energy." *Pravda* argued that the "consumer had a right to demand conditions" that would allow him or her "to calmly choose and purchase" whatever needed. Paraphrasing Stalin, *Pravda* noted that the task before the Soviet trade apparatus was "to genuinely turn its face toward the consumer, to learn to respect the consumer."[7] Indeed, "respect for the consumer, for his interests" was the "basis" of the new cultured Soviet trade.[8] An editorial in *Sovetskaia torgovlia* approvingly pointed out that customers now "demanded that trade workers treat them with the same respect as that which befits a Soviet citizen."[9] Under the new retail system, salesclerks and other employees would ideally demonstrate not only respect but also "deep concern" and even "love" for the "Soviet citizen-customer."[10] Amidst the trade campaign's hyperbole, and perhaps good intentions, two principles were established: (1) citizens deserved an improved system of retailing, including a better supply of consumer goods; and (2) state functionaries and retail employees had an obligation to promote consumers' needs.

In their effort to produce a new Soviet consumer, Communist authorities urged consumers to adopt new practices. Soviet citizens were instructed to consume in a "socialist" way that reinforced the logic of the regime's political objectives. They were not supposed to be conspicuous consumers like the petty-bourgeois and bourgeois consumers of the past. Nor were they supposed to cling to "primitive" and "backward" material desires that ostensibly characterized prerevolutionary and peasant culture. For example, buying *bast* (straw) sandals, a commodity that symbolized rural backwardness, was frowned upon. Official discourse bombarded the populace with messages that citizens should be civilized and rational consumers who displayed "Soviet taste," a modern, urban, and practical aesthetic, when making their purchases. This kind of consumption of mass-produced products would demonstrate the transformation of the citizenry and the advancement of Soviet socialism.

Soviet authorities also encouraged consumers to contribute to the remaking of retail trade. They urged consumers to be better mannered when shopping, to model civilized behavior and thereby improve the retail environment.[11] Store signs instructed customers "Demand politeness of salesclerks and be polite to them."[12] Authorities exhorted consumers to get involved in retail reform on an institutional level, by joining store committees or activist groups, or by engaging in the *kontrol'* (monitoring and regulation) of retailing via state and public organs. Consumers were additionally pressed to offer individual "criticism from below." Specifically, the government promoted consumer feedback in officially sanctioned venues, including, "consultations" with consumers about manufactured goods, the Soviet press, in-store complaint and suggestion books, and "customer conferences" that brought together trade officials, store managers and employees, and customers. Soviet authorities stressed that customers had a "duty and right to help improve work in the trade apparatus."[13] Citizen participation in these forums allowed the Stalinist regime to herald the emergence of a "new" socialist consumer who actively contributed to economic modernization and state-building. It advanced a Soviet version of consumer citizenship, which served the regime's interests but also afforded ordinary people new authority and agency, albeit limited.

"Consultations" with consumers about manufactured goods

In the 1930s, Soviet authorities organized "consultations" with consumers to gather feedback about manufactured goods: conferences with producers and/or sellers, and goods exhibits. As trade leader Veitser explained at one of these forums, the role of consumers was to "evaluate the quality of manufactured goods," indicate which commodities were not made or sold in sufficient quantities, and comment on what items "needed to be made in the future."[14] Consumers' opinions, including their more critical remarks, would then shape production and sales to better reflect demand. By promoting the idea that consumer demand was worthy of study, and by inviting consumers to articulate this demand proactively, these conferences and exhibits underscored the new official rhetoric that the party-state championed consumers' inter-ests. They also contributed to the redefinition of consumers, emphasiz-ing their role as stakeholders and socially responsible citizens, who unlike selfish shoppers of the past, helped to improve manufacturing and retailing.

In the early 1930s, branches of the Trade Union of Cooperative and State Trade Workers (PRKGT) organized "three-sided" conferences about goods among producers, sellers, and consumers.[15] To elicit consumer participation, organizers publicized the conferences in newspapers and at workplaces. In 1931, for example, 3,000 notices were sent out to enterprises in Azerbaijan to advertise a "three-sided" conference on leather goods. Conferences emphasized the importance of consumer feedback regarding the assortment and quality of products, and focused primarily on the problem of poor-quality and defective goods, including measures that could be taken to improve matters.[16] After approximately 450 individuals, including over 100 consumers, attended two conferences in January 1932 in Vitebsk, a brigade of shoe workers and store personnel checked 400 pairs of shoes at a warehouse and discovered that 335 pairs were defective. Four showcases of defective products were also organized around the city.[17]

As the trade campaign progressed, similar conferences discussed not only defective goods but also consumer desire. What models and styles did consumers want? In 1935, for example, the Moscow atelier "House of Fashions" convened meetings with clothing workers, trade representatives, and consumers, to gain a better understanding of the latter's wishes. As a result, a news article proclaimed, "the best girls of our country who have been awarded the order of Lenin – parachutists, weavers, collective farm workers – resolved the question of what the dress of a Soviet girl ought to be."[18] In 1936, model department stores in Moscow sponsored conferences with customers and industrial representatives to discuss merchandise possibilities for the following year. Newspaper ads inviting the public to participate underscored that "all the wishes of customers will be taken into account during the drawing up of orders."[19] The task of consumers, these conferences suggested, was to help local officials determine supply.

Soviet authorities also convened goods exhibits in the 1930s. Geographically diverse and organized throughout major cities, these exhibits showcased a wide variety of consumer goods, such as shoes, furniture, and children's goods. Many exhibits drew large audiences, attracting tens of thousands visitors, and sometimes more. For example, roughly 130,000 people, including many children, attended an exhibit on children's toys at the Children's Movie Theater No. 1 in Moscow in the winter of 1936/1937.[20] Along with the construction in the 1930s of the grandiose metallurgical complex, Magnitogorsk, and the Moscow

Metro, these exhibits promoted a "dream world" of industrial modernity. They served "didactic" purposes by lauding "Soviet industrial achievement" and "the improved standard of living that its products would bring about."[21] They reinforced the regime's legitimization of consumption by displaying consumer goods, like tractors and other industrial products, as yardsticks of socialist progress. The exhibits likewise promoted a "dream world" of consumption by inculcating desire among attendees for many of the displayed products.[22] Even though the products were often difficult to procure in real shops, the exhibits constructed an appealing image of the promises of socialism. Spectators could engage in the fantasy of acquisition and imagine a life with leather shoes, hand watches, fashionable hats, or talking dolls – a world of greater comfort and pleasure.

The goods exhibits emphasized the transformation of consumption from a private affair into a public matter, in which consumers played a key role. Visitors were not merely passive participants at these commodity spectacles. Exhibit workers actively solicited visitors' opinions, even those of children.[23] Visitors were also encouraged to express feedback in visitors' albums and at related exhibit conferences and meetings.[24] In the summer of 1935, the People's Commissariat of Light Industry held an exhibit of leather shoes, wool shawls, and textile, silk, and knitted goods in Tashkent, which 47,256 individuals attended. Exhibit workers gathered opinions from 2,086 attendees. An additional 1,578 opinions were recorded in visitors' albums.[25] Typical comments focused on the selection, style, and attributes of items on display: "The flannel from No. 500 irritates the eyes terribly; it is tasteless"; "The eastern fabrics aren't typical, they don't reflect the East, and some fabrics, like No. 404, resemble wallpaper"; "The shoe section far from represents the union shoe industry, which is a drawback of the exhibit and shows how poorly it was prepared. There are no national shoes."[26] A report summing up visitors' comments pointed to many "national" and regionally specific needs and desires. Visitors wanted "to decorate clothing sent to Central Asia with more resilient and chemical colors, since they quickly lose color under the scorching sun's rays"; "to increase the output of velvet for *tiubeteiki* (a skull-cap worn in Central Asia)"; "to increase the output of weekend eastern slippers," "to increase the output of eastern silks." Such commentary can be read as expressions of resistance to Communist efforts to modernize Uzbek clothing and impose a more urban, Russian, and European aesthetic on national minorities. Whether consciously oppositional or not, this feedback suggests that at the very least some visitors thought of themselves as Central Asian or Uzbek citizens with different consumer needs and tastes than Russian or Soviet citizens. In discussing the exhibit's results, industrial and trade authorities concluded that the "consumer had issued completely concrete demands in terms of patterns, colors, and styles," and considered it their duty to incorporate these demands into future plans.[27]

It is not clear to what extent consumer input affected production. Communist authorities and the press acknowledged that consumer feedback was often ignored.[28] But they also provided many examples of consumer influence, of how positive remarks about certain models, for example, affected manufacturing. One Soviet functionary asserted that opinions expressed at goods exhibits in Tashkent, Ashkhabad, and Frunze in 1934 continued to influence the production of commodities even in September 1935.[29] One must be skeptical of Soviet pronouncements about consumer influence. Consumers' opinions did not change macroeconomic plans. Nonetheless, they did offer trade organizations, industries, and planners valuable information about consumer demand, which could be incorporated into economic decision making at the margins, at a more local level.

Consumers' letters in the Soviet press

During the trade campaign the Soviet press played an important role in promoting the regime's new focus on retailing and consumption, frequently publishing articles and editorials about efforts to enact retail reforms, and providing extensive coverage of consumer concerns articulated at goods exhibits, in complaint books, and at customer conferences. Although the press publicized the trade campaign's many ostensible successes, publicity was not always positive. A review of newspapers from 1931 to 1939 illustrates a wide diversity of reportage about consumer goods and retailing, including much criticism.

Newspapers became central venues for consumer feedback when they expanded the publication of consumers' letters in the mid-1930s. Although letters from consumers were by no means new, beginning in 1935 major newspapers (such as *Pravda, Pravda Vostoka, Vechernaia Moskva*) showcased consumers' voices by initiating new columns: "customer letters," "the consumer writes," "customer notes," "the consumer presents a claim," "the customer demands." Because the Soviet press was a powerful institution with a mass audience, these columns underscored the new official legitimacy of consumers. They also elevated consumers' letters from an informal to a formal means of consumer feedback, and sent a clear message that the party-state considered consumers' concerns to be of importance to the general Soviet public. Moreover, they promoted the idea that consumers had a particularly valuable voice that needed to be heard. After all, the press did not establish similar columns for workers or artists or party members to express their opinions. During the 1930s, consumers' letters also began to be published more regularly in some of the already established spaces for citizen letters, such as "letters to the editor" and "signals from below."

The expanded publication of consumers' letters provided writers with a vehicle for expressing their discontent about retailing and consumer goods, aiding Soviet efforts to maintain social control. Yet letter writing was not merely cathartic. It offered consumers the possibility that their concerns would be addressed. Although official responses to letters were not guaranteed, consumers' letters and other pieces of writing were often forwarded to suitable agencies for examination, such as the Trade Union of Cooperative and State Trade Workers (PRKGT) or trade organizations.[30] These examinations sometimes garnered additional response. For example, after a series of children's letters about consumer goods were published in *Komsomol'skaia pravda*, the Presidium of the Central Committee of the PRKGT ordered a series of city-wide meetings among salespeople and children to address the latter's concerns. It also instructed trade-union committees to examine children's goods in different stores.[31]

The Soviet press made a point of publicizing some of the official reactions to consumers' letters (both published and unpublished). The Moscow evening newspaper, for example, reported how a consumer's letter about the alleged wrongdoing of the head of a store's bakery section had led to an inquiry, a confirmation of the charges, and the subsequent removal of the offending individual.[32] After receiving a letter from a consumer who complained about the lack of small baby blankets and asked why trade organizations did not care about newborns, a journal published the government's response: the People's Commissariat of Trade (Narkomvnutorg) was working with the sewing industry in the letter writer's region to increase the production of children's sheets and blankets.[33] Reportage of official reactions demonstrated party-state responsiveness, and was likely intended to appease consumers who did not receive replies to their published or unpublished grievances. But it also emphasized that consumer criticism was critical for achieving improvements in the consumer economy.

Consumers' published letters helped to reinforce the Soviet regime's discourse about problems with consumer goods and the retail sector.

Although consumers' letters were usually quite negative and thus gave the appearance of being uncensored, they were in fact censored. While published letters could be quite accusatory, they offered a more restrained expression of popular criticism than unpublished ones. Take for example A. Matveev's letter, published in *Ferganskaia Pravda* in 1939:

> In the trade network nepotism and self-supply flourish.... The assortment of goods, particularly groceries, confectionaries, and perfume, is sparse, even though at the depot there is an adequate supply. In the stores it is filthy. Window displays are not changed on a monthly basis, and individual salesclerks are slovenly and rude to customers. All of this is well known by the leaders of the municipal trade organization, as well as party and trade-union organizations, but no one has taken any measures...[34]

Why was this letter accepted for publication? By focusing blame on individuals, local officials, and local groups rather than on broader economic or political reasons such as the planned economy, the letter reinforced the prevailing official narrative, which placed responsibility for retail problems on incompetent, corrupt, and hostile individuals and groups. The letter functioned to validate the Soviet system. Moreover, it did not express the degree of dismay with or vitriol against Communist leaders or Soviet power that could be found in unpublished letters. In an unpublished newspaper letter, for example, an unemployed mother asked, "Is it really possible that Soviet power will allow for my husband, me, and my children to die from hunger?"[35] As for why the Uzbek people had to wait in long lines for hours in order to purchase bread, another unpublished letter concluded, "It's because 'Ferganskaia Pravda' is sleeping, along with the Bolsheviks in Fergan'."[36] By censoring many consumers' letters, but publishing ones that were quite disapproving and negative, the press fostered the illusion of an unregulated public sphere, and produced a palatable discourse of complaint.

In-store complaint and suggestion books

In-store complaint and suggestion books, like consumers' letters, predated the trade campaign.[37] Nonetheless, reports from the early 1930s suggest that their use was far from widespread, and that official reaction to complaints was often negligible.[38] As the trade campaign developed, Soviet authorities began to place more importance on complaint and suggestion books as a primary vehicle for consumer feedback. But problems with them persisted, as 2 illustrations accompanying a 1933 article cleverly pointed out. The first illustration depicts a male customer with pen in hand, who cannot access a store's complaint book because it is under lock and key. The caption reads, "It is difficult to get to the complaint book." The second illustration shows a store manager smoking a cigarette made out of rolled paper torn from a complaint book. It reads: "And if you do reach it, then your complaint will be used for a smoke."[39] These comments and others like it suggested that problems with Soviet trade stemmed from indifference and hostility to consumers' concerns. In one case, a newspaper pointed out, a store's administration even tried to intimidate consumers by sending a complaining customer to the local police for her "legitimate" complaint.[40]

To compel stores to take consumers' concerns more seriously, and to establish a more reliable forum for customers' grievances, in April 1935 Narkomvnutorg passed a decree making complaint and suggestion books obligatory in all retail trade establishments and public catering facilities under its direction.[41] In addition, government agencies and public organizations, such as trade unions, conducted repeated investigations to hold cooperative and state trade stores responsible for carrying these books. Subsequent decrees reinforced the mandate to establish a functioning complaint-book system. Even though many retail establishments failed to carry books or to make them easily available to consumers, the increased emphasis on them in the mid-1930s underscored the trade campaign's valorization of consumers' voices.[42]

The trade establishment viewed complaint books as an invaluable mechanism for helping to promote retail reform via "control from below," that is, via the surveillance and regulation by customers who shopped on a daily basis.[43] An editorial in *Sovetskaia torgovlia* explained: "The complaint book is a mirror in which daily the work of an entire store is reflected: the productive and public face of its collective, the interrelation between counter worker and customer."[44] Officials encouraged consumers to use complaint books, arguing that it was not "slander" for them to lodge complaints but "healthy Bolshevik criticism."[45] Complaint books played an important role in identifying retail problems in stores, like poor customer service or incorrect pricing. Moreover, they apparently contributed to "solutions" – such as the hiring of additional salesclerks to improve service, and the disciplining of trade workers.[46] Indeed, when complaint books included more serious allegations against store managers and employees, ensuing investigations often led to fines, firings, and more draconian punishments.[47] Although many trade workers were no doubt aware that consumers' complaints were often ignored, complaint books increased the possibility that bad behavior would be officially recorded (and perhaps punished), which may have contributed to better work practices.

Although complaint and suggestion books were often used to discipline store employees, they were also used to paint a positive picture of workers, a particular store's performance, or retail reform more generally. Trade officials and employees began to cite a lack of complaints as proof of a worker's or store's merit. In addition, they referred to positive customer reviews recorded in complaint and suggestion books as evidence of the good work of an individual worker or an entire store.[48] One of the first Stakhanovite labor heroes in retail trade, for example, bragged at a reception for exemplary trade workers that she and her coworkers had received written praise from customers, accumulating 16 commendations in a one-month period.[49] Trade officials also pointed to decreases in the number of complaints to underscore the success of retail reform.[50]

More often than not, however, trade officials cited problems with the implementation of the complaint books to underscore the difficulties in reforming the retail sector. They did so both internally and publicly. In the fall of 1935, the State Trade Inspectorate issued a dismal report on complaint books to the trade establishment. Inspectors had examined books in the Leningrad, Moscow, Ivanovo, and Western provinces (*oblasti*), the Azov-Black Sea, Saratov, and Siberian administrative territories (*kraia*), and in Belorussia and Turkmenistan, only to discover that most retail venues had either ignored the April decree altogether or failed to enforce the complaint-book system effectively.[51] At meetings with party members and trade workers, trade officials lamented what they saw as bureaucratic incompetence, negligence, and abuse. They recounted stories of store managers who maintained two different books, one for customers and one for inspectors, or who allegedly told customers, "you want to write a complaint, go ahead and write it. ... There are 200; there will be 201."[52] Newspapers relayed similar stories to the general public about store managers and local trade authorities who ignored consumers' complaints, failed to answer in a polite and timely manner, or responded in an overly bureaucratic way.[53] The press noted how "callous," "hooliganistic," and "anti-Soviet" treatment of complaints meant that not only consumers, but even state investigators, were denied access to complaint books.[54] Media coverage of problems with complaint books was in some ways counterproductive for the regime, insofar as it showcased the failures of retail reform. Yet press coverage was simultaneously productive, for it reinforced the idea that authorities took trade difficulties seriously. Moreover, the media continued to focus blame on the "scandalous ugliness in the work of the trade network" – on local conditions in general, and the failings of individual officials, managers, and employees in particular – rather than on larger systemic causes.[55]

Customer conferences

In January 1936 Commissar Veitser ordered all *oblast'*, *krai*, and municipal branches of Narkomvnutorg to organize conferences for customers who shopped in a particular store. Customer conferences provided consumers with *public* venues for airing grievances that they might otherwise have recorded in complaint and suggestion books. The goal of customer conferences was to attract a "wide circle of customers to the work of a store" to provide consumers with the possibility of directly influencing retail affairs.[56] In this respect the conferences were similar to consumer cooperatives' meetings at which members articulated concerns about retail conditions and other matters. But attendance at the new customer conferences was not restricted to cooperative members. Moreover, customer conferences were administered by a state organizational hierarchy rather than local cooperatives, in principle promoting greater accountability. Narkomvnutorg instructed its branches as well as store managers to take quick and effective measures to address customers' concerns. As a "new" consumer forum that was an explicit product of the trade campaign, customer conferences also received much greater press attention than consumer cooperative membership meetings.

Customer conferences highlighted the active role that trade officials expected consumers to assume in the trade campaign. The Soviet press and trade establishment emphasized the importance of these conferences in terms similar to those used to describe the function of the complaint and suggestion book – as a form of "*kontrol'* from below." They characterized customer conferences as a particularly important form of "people's *kontrol'*" given the inherent challenges of managing the trade apparatus from above.[57] Consumers had a better sense of retail problems and potential solutions than "Soviet officials and inspectors," who visited stores for only "a few minutes and could not notice" everything that was going on. Store management did not always see "the defects" that daily customers recognized. Trade officials and store managers encouraged customers to offer "serious Bolshevik criticism," to identify a store's shortcomings, including "instances of impolite, uncultured behavior" on the part of the staff. Consumers were also asked to provide "practical proposals" about how to improve a store's work. "You customers are our friends," one trade official argued, "and it is your criticism alone that will help us to better our work."[58] An editorial about customer conferences asserted that the "weighty word of the customer" was a "mighty lever for liquidating the insufficiencies of trade."[59]

Trade officials, store managers, and retail workers identified women as especially valuable participants in customer conferences because of their daily shopping duties. At a meeting among exemplary trade workers in Ashkhabad one speaker explained, "It is necessary to convene these conferences in tens of stores with the participation of housewives, because housewives, comrades, are a 'huge force,' and it is necessary for them to speak out, to say what they need." An official from the Trade Union of Trade Workers argued that "it was necessary to invite housewives, who frequent the stores and buy products, so that they can talk about the conditions of a store," about its bad attributes or what was "necessary to eliminate."[60] During opening remarks at conferences, authorities appealed specifically to women shoppers to speak up.[61] In the emerging new retail order of the 1930s, trade authorities conferred new authority on women, and recast their domestic roles and experiences from negative to positive, from being a source of "backwardness" to a source of knowledge and insight.[62]

Customer conferences were explicitly conceived of as mechanisms for promoting retail reform *and* for incorporating consumers into public life and the Soviet polity. Conferences constituted a "new form in the organization of Soviet public work (*obshchestvennost'*) around trade," which would "guarantee the participation of a large number of people in *kontrol'*, a high[er] level of criticism, and a great reckoning of the diverse demands and needs of a store." Customer conferences fostered not only public activism, but also political integration. They constituted a "new form in the evolution of Soviet democratism," a vehicle for achieving what the "proletarian government aims at: that every citizen actively participates in the resolution of all questions pertaining to economic, cultural and everyday construction."[63] The Soviet press and trade officials promoted this connection between customer participation and democratic inclusion. As one newspaper noted, consumers did not participate in the various forums as "foreigners" or as "guests," but as "Soviet citizens" who were invested in making "every Soviet enterprise" work well. Even customers, the editorial implied, had been integrated into Soviet society by taking on new civic responsibilities.[64] The Soviet consumer had begun to think of himself "as a participant in the great socialist project" and wanted to exert influence on retailing via the customer conferences.[65] Some customer conferences reinforced the conflation of customer involvement with national pride and political participation by opening or closing the conferences with the *Internationale*, the Soviet anthem in the interwar period.[66]

Trade authorities, store managers, and the press also depicted customer conferences as an important vehicle for consumer influence. They did not overdraw the point, acknowledging that consumers' remarks at conferences often went unaddressed. But they also argued that consumer remarks resulted in concrete changes. At a customer conference in November 1936, a store's deputy director reminded participants of their influence. He claimed, "Comrades, at the last conference many [people] presented, and their presentations helped us a lot. We have implemented the proposals that were made and this has very much furthered our good work." Trade official Shinkarevskii asserted that there were numerous examples of how the customer, via the customer conference, "exerts influence upon a store, improvements in its work, elimination of its shortcomings, and introduction of culture in trade."[67] Consumer feedback reportedly affected various aspects of the retail experience, such as the physical layout of stores, the supply and design of goods, store hours, and the distribution of scarce technological equipment.[68] Although it is impossible to know how much influence consumers exercised via customer conferences, consumers' suggestions and complaints elicited responses from appropriate authorities at least some of the time. Some customer conferences afforded consumers additional influence when trade officials and store managers invited participants, often housewives, to form commissions to work on solutions to customer concerns.[69]

Customer conferences provided consumers an opportunity to challenge trade authorities and retail personnel in front of a larger public. The back and forth exchanges that were made possible at customer conferences held trade officials and retail personnel more directly accountable than other forums for consumer feedback. For example, customer Martynchenko challenged a store director's explanation for why his store had no fruit by saying that it was "completely untrue." He then challenged a trade official's rationale for the same problem by arguing that it was "an extremely naïve explanation." Martynchenko also dismissed the trade official's argument that the store had no herring for sale because it was unavailable, asking, "Then why do neighboring stores have herring?"[70] Martynchenko clearly did not accept official excuses. Similarly, after a salesclerk complained at a conference about how some consumers wasted salesclerks' time by asking to look at items they did not need or intend to buy, customer Dudaleva replied, "It is necessary, comrades, not to frighten customers or declare that we bother you. We bother and will [continue to] bother you, and you [will] treat us tactfully and in a friendly and comradely manner."[71] The open nature of the customer conference allowed Dudaleva to reprimand the salesclerk and remind him of his duties, and suggested that the forum was an unregulated public sphere, in which citizens could express opinions freely. But the customer conference, like the consumer letter, was not unregulated. Minutes from customer conferences indicate that participants engaged in self-censorship, self-regulation. Although at times customers directly challenged other participants' statements or explanations, customers did not speak without restraint. In their comments they reproduced official Soviet discourses and followed established norms for acceptable criticism.

Consumer participation and voices

Consumer participation in the venues for feedback served key practical and ideological functions for the Stalinist regime. It helped authorities to better understand and meet consumer demand, and to advance retail reform. It helped the regime to measure the progress and failure of the trade campaign, internally (among trade organizations) and publicly. Consumer participation publicized the party-state's new commitment to retailing and consumption, and overwhelmingly reaffirmed official narratives about problems in the consumer economy. By participating in the venues, Soviet citizens also bolstered the idea that they had new rights and duties as consumers.

Consumer participation in the venues was extensive. Conservatively, hundreds of thousands of people throughout the Soviet Union attended conferences about manufactured goods as well as goods exhibits. At least tens of thousands of these individuals expressed their opinions publicly or in visitors' albums. Countless consumers wrote letters to newspapers and journals, and even to higher authorities. Though incalculable, the number of people who recorded complaints, suggestions, or praise in the complaint and suggestion books was large, as was the number of people who attempted to record comments in these books but were denied access to them. Tens of thousands of people attended the hundreds of customer conferences organized in the mid-to-late 1930s.[72] Unlike mandatory workers' political meetings[73] or collective-farm meetings, "where attendance was expected and absence was construed as a political statement,"[74] the new and expanded forums for consumer feedback did not coerce participation, either directly or indirectly.

What does widespread participation in the venues signify? It does not signify consumers' conviction that Soviet authorities were "really" going to address their interests. Indeed, some customers expressed skepticism about the venues' ultimate value. At one goods exhibit, a visitor commented, "The exhibit is interesting, but I would like these elegant things to be on sale sometime this year. Only then would this exhibit make any sense."[75] Still, widespread participation points to a combination of public curiosity, people's increased identification with a consumer identity, and their desire to influence changes in the commercial landscape. It shows how consumers utilized the forums, along with hoarding, queuing, and other practices, as a tactic for managing difficult retail environments. In some cases consumers even used multiple forums to insist that their grievances be heard. Housewife Stepanova, for example, first turned to the in-store complaint and suggestion book to voice her concern about incorrect pricing that cheated customers. After no response, she appealed to a workers' brigade inspecting the store. Although the brigade confirmed the veracity of Stepanova's allegations, no action was taken. Stepanova noted, "Then I realized that the head of the local trade-union committee, Blinov, doesn't take any measures in response to customers' complaints." Finally, Stepanova wrote a letter to the newspaper *Trud*, which was published.[76]

Whatever consumers thought about the socialist system or the authenticity of retail reform, they used the new identity of the Soviet consumer, and the official venues for consumer feedback, to present themselves as valuable participants in efforts to transform the consumer landscape. This may have been more meaningful for some people than others, especially housewives who remained outside of trade unions, the Communist party, and other Soviet institutions, for it provided them with public authority. In January 1937, for example, 15 housewives attended an exhibit and taste-test sponsored by confectionary and bread industries in Moscow. The housewives provided feedback about the samples they tasted. They also submitted their own samples of strudel, cookies, and cakes so that the industries could benefit from their expertise and recipes. Many of the housewives' samples were so delicious that the confectionary and bread industries apparently decided to send them (along with the housewives' recipes) to factory laboratories for further study, and in many cases, for eventual mass production and sale in stores. By participating in the food exhibit and taste-testing, these housewives influenced industrial food production and received official applause, even press attention, for their efforts.[77]

Analysis of consumers' voices in the various forums shows that consumers often fashioned themselves as active citizens integrated into the fabric of the Soviet social order and public life. They expressed familiarity with official discourses and campaigns, with socialist ideology and objectives. They positioned themselves as deserving citizens, rather than mere supplicants or simple purchasers, whose consumer needs and desires, if better met, would reinforce and further Soviet interests.

Language of the trade campaign

Consumer feedback often reproduced the language of the trade campaign, in both positive and negative commentary. When consumers expressed optimism about the new consumer goods or Soviet retailing and used the same categories and conceptualizations of the trade campaign, their commentary reinforced the legitimacy of the campaign and suggested that the Stalinist regime was "selling" its new approach to retailing and consumption.[78] Take, for example, the comments of P. A. Olenev:

> Now you go into a store with joy. There are beautiful showcases, cleanliness, and the main thing is that with every passing day there are more goods. In the store you feel like a master – that this is our Soviet store.[79]

These comments illustrate the success of the trade campaign, in terms of actual retail improvements and the dissemination of new understandings of the retail sector. As authorities promoted retail reform, they repeatedly urged consumers to become masters of their stores, that is, to claim ownership over their stores and envision the retail sector as their own, as Soviet – as working on their behalf and the behalf of socialist goals – unlike the private retail sector.[80]

Reproducing the more positive language of the trade campaign did not make consumers dupes of the regime. By using this language, consumers articulated new expectations, and put additional pressure on manufacturers, trade administrators, and store employees to do better. Using this language also served to underscore consumers' new authority in evaluating the retail sector. Customer Slobozhanikov wrote the following in a store's complaint book:

> On account of the selection of goods, and more importantly, given the exceptional attentive treatment by salespeople and the excellent, capable servicing of customers, the store produces a wonderful impression. The saleswoman Comrade Khan'kovskaia knows her work so well and knows how to serve a customer in such a talented manner that via her wonderful attitude to customers she is a model worker of Soviet trade.[81]

Slobozhanikov's comment transcended mere praise. It bolstered his role as the one who recognized when a salesclerk provided such excellent customer service that she was a "model worker." It positioned him, and by extension other consumers, as the legitimate arbiters of Soviet retailing.

Consumers also used the language of the trade campaign to articulate their grievances and frame their complaints. They moved their focus from goods shortages to the campaign's promises to provide a wider array of high quality merchandise. In a newspaper letter, consumer Petrushko asked, "Why does our store give out sugar that is so dirty that it is impossible to use? It is damp, yellow, and filthy."[82] Petrushko was unimpressed with the simple provisioning of sugar; he expected quality sugar. Another customer complained about the lack of different grades of food products in her local store: "in our store the assortment of goods should be no less than that in the best *Gastronom* store."[83] Model food stores, like the *Gastronom* chain, were this customer's yardstick for proper provisioning.

Lamenting poor retail conditions and employee practices, consumers invoked the trade campaign's pledge to produce "cultured" Soviet trade, a much publicized goal. Retail establishments were supposed to be much more than mere places to purchase goods. They were supposed to provide consumers with a modern and cultivated environment as well as excellent customer service. But, consumers noted, retail trade was far from cultured. One customer explained, "Great energy is needed to carry out shopping in this department store. There are huge lines for galoshes and manufactured goods. I leave the department store perspiring, like from a bathhouse, and of course, I try to visit the store as little as possible."[84] Another consumer griped, "The salesclerks undervalue and ignore the question of decorating the store. Not enough attention is paid to price listings and labels on goods."[85] While some customers underscored problems with retail conditions, others emphasized the vexing issue of poor customer service. Customer Strel'nikov objected that even though a store had suffered from huge lines, only two salesclerks handled customers while a third "chewed a tomato in a melancholy way."[86] For another consumer, it was a "big problem" that salesclerks knew so little about the many new food products that had recently appeared. He wanted salesclerks to provide critical information. What did products taste like? How should products be stored and preserved? Some customers focused less on the need for qualified and educated personnel and more on the simple need for personnel with hygienic habits. In Cheliabinsk, a consumer sarcastically noted how a salesclerk provided "cultured trade" by picking his nose and then cutting bread with the same hand.[87] Soviet consumer complaints raised the bar on retail performance, and held the regime responsible for the trade campaign's goals.

The need to respect the consumer, a major slogan of the trade campaign, was also embedded in people's criticism. Nineteen consumers wrote to a Tashkent newspaper to complain about how they had been mistreated in a store, ending their letter by exclaiming, "It's impossible not to call this trade anything other than a mockery of customers!"[88] Repeatedly told that they were deserving citizens with valid consumer interests, consumers demanded better treatment.

Politicizing consumption

Customer commentary demonstrates how people mobilized not only the rhetoric of the trade campaign, but also other Soviet rhetorics, to strengthen the validity of their consumer demands and complaints. Women in particular pursued this strategy. Citizens implicitly and explicitly linked their personal consumer interests to broader political and ideological priorities of the Soviet regime, and attached their interests to hegemonic party-state discourses. In so doing, they politicized their needs and promoted the idea that consumption transcended individual materialism. They reaffirmed the official identification of retail trade and consumption with the socialist project.

Some Soviet consumers politicized their interests by associating them with longstanding public state initiatives and goals. Working women connected their interests to the regime's emphasis on engaging women in wage labor, which was supposed to advance women's emancipation. For instance, A. Nalatova criticized existing footwear and clothing in the working women's journal *Rabotnitsa*, arguing that thoughtless products impeded women's ability as workers. Unable to find shoes without heels, she asked, "Is this really suitable footwear for female factory workers or for female peasants?" She was "breaking her legs with these heels." Nalatova also pointed out how existing clothing styles were similarly inappropriate. Dresses and skirts were "either too short or too long," and skirts with flounces "only interfered with walking, particularly around machines." According to Nalatova, it was high time for a functional and comfortable Soviet style to develop that would meet the needs of working women.[89] Other working women demanded the increased mass production of everyday electrical devices, such as electric irons, saucepans, and kettles, and a greater supply of collectively used machines, such as vacuum cleaners and floor polishing devices, arguing that they "would ease the work of women immeasurably."[90]

P. V. Artemova, a Stakhanovite weaver, framed her consumer needs in terms of her desire to study and become a "politically educated person," a much publicized goal of the Soviet regime for all of its citizens, but particularly for women, whom Communist leaders saw as less educated than men. Artemova's work, plus the daily tasks of foraging for her children in stores and cooking for them, took up too much time, some of which could be used instead for "interesting work, for studying." If home delivery of foodstuffs was made more affordable, and if a greater quantity of children's clothes were made available without waiting in long lines, her overall responsibilities would be more manageable. If Soviet trade could be properly organized, it would mitigate some of the demands of Artemova's daily life as a working mother.[91]

Some consumers attached their interests to the socialist imperative to create a classless, egalitarian society. They pointed to the unequal retail conditions and service that workers encountered. Three housewives from an industrial district in Moscow noted that when they walked by the area's 20 factories, they rejoiced "in the success of our socialist industry." Such success, however, was not mirrored by their local retail stores, which failed to meet their needs and did not match the standards of stores in downtown Moscow. They demanded that the "all regions of the capital be supplied in an exemplary manner."[92] Customer Konoplitskaia lamented that more "prominent customers," those who had larger purchases, received special treatment at the expense of customers, like her, who had lesser purchases.[93] A Stakhanovite praised the "attentive and polite treatment" he had received in a shoe store despite his worker's uniform, implicitly pointing to the discriminatory retail practices that industrial workers encountered. He concluded, "My wish is that this kind of service would be carried out throughout our trade system."[94]

Other citizens associated their concerns with a variety of newer campaigns and political objectives. In particular, consumers appropriated rhetorics associated with three party-state campaigns in the 1930s: the campaign for *kul'turnost'*, that is, the drive to civilize everyday life and increase the cultural level of ordinary people; the campaign to promote motherhood and women's maternal obligations, which the Stalinist regime advanced via pronatalist language and various measures, like the criminalization of abortion and the introduction of a new family law in 1936; and the campaign to legitimize housewives by ascribing importance to the domestic sphere and mobilizing them to extend their domestic talents into the public sphere via a wife-activists' movement.[95]

Official Soviet discourse promoted the importance of living a cultured life, which authorities admitted was facilitated by the purchase of nonessential "cultured" commodities. Consumers reaffirmed this linkage, and complained that their aspirations to lead a more cultured life were thwarted by the poor state of the consumer economy. As one customer explained,

> We live well, in a cultured way, but we want to live still better. Yet the store is resting on its laurels. Therefore, it is often necessary for us to go to the city center for foodstuffs.[96]

Another consumer pointed out, perhaps with a bit of sarcasm, We live prosperously, we eat well. We would also like to dress better. But in the store, you often can't find what is necessary.[97] Engineer Gavrilov tied his consumer interests to the drive to promote *kul'turnost'* by arguing that "the cultural importance" of keeping a few bookstores open later in the evening "is undoubtedly very great."[98]

Mothers often referred to women's "motherly" responsibilities, emphasized in official discourse about motherhood. At a closing conference for a goods exhibit, one woman expressed frustration about her difficulty finding clothes to dress her child "in a cultured manner." Although she was pleased to see all the beautiful children's items at the exhibit, she was vexed because "it was impossible to find them in stores."[99] Embedded in her commentary was the idea of mothers' obligation to instill in their children a cultured way of living. Another woman linked her consumer concerns to her motherly duty to educate her children politically. In a newspaper letter, she described how officials had advised parents to celebrate the anniversary of the "Great Proletarian Revolution" by giving a gift to their children. In response, she had searched for an appropriate toy for her nine-year old, without success. An inadequate supply of toys had stymied her efforts to commemorate the regime's political holiday with her child.[100]

The newly publicized social duties of wives were also embedded in consumers' comments. M. P. Klimova complained in a newspaper letter about her household's lack of basic culinary tools and crockery due to a shortage of kitchenware. She was not grumbling about unessential "trifles," such as "dessert spoons," but basic commodities such as frying pans upon which the family depended. She reminded readers that "family mood" was connected to how well the household worked. It was "clear" that when family members were dissatisfied with their home environment, they "could not work well" outside the home. To create a cultured and satisfactory home environment, as well as an effective labor force, Klimova asserted the need for rudimentary household supplies.[101]

From individual to collective, from personal to public

Consumers further politicized consumption, converting it from an individual to a collective affair and from a personal to a public matter, when they asserted that their personal needs reflected the interests of larger groups. Consumers used plural pronouns "we" and "our" in their criticisms to situate themselves more explicitly in a group identity. Worker Ivanov extrapolated from his own personal experience to represent workers' broader interests: "Before going to work many workers buy milk, but now it is impossible to find." In complaining about the poor retail conditions in a worker's region, another worker, Ians, concluded his letter: "The workers demand an end to this outrage."[102] Both Ivanov and Ians constructed their personal desires as collective desires on the part of workers.

Women consumers in particular appear to have spoken on behalf of larger groups. The housewife Shebekova began her comments at a customer conference by stating, "I want to speak on behalf of housewives."[103] In a newspaper M. Makarova argued that the "housewives of Moscow" were pleased with the successful efforts of the Commissariat of Food Industries to provide "delicious and diverse food products." But, she added, misleading product instructions and recipes often resulted in the spoiling of food.[104] When the housewife Prokopenko demanded the mass production of affordable household items, she spoke explicitly for a broader group: "On behalf of all housewives I appeal to our Soviet community, to our scientists, technicians, doctors: help rationalize housework!"[105]

Some consumers spoke explicitly on behalf of regional ethnicities and identities. In a letter to an Uzbek newspaper, a consumer complained how none of the five new bread stores in his district sold *obinon*, traditional Uzbek bread. This lack of bread did a disservice not only to the native population, but also to the "European" population, the Russians and Ukrainians who had recently moved to the area.[106] At a customer conference in Baku, customer Lazarev presented himself as the voice of a larger regional and ethnic community when he proposed that a vegetable department be organized next to the meat department. In his words, "We are an Eastern people, and without fail, we ought to have greens."[107] Comments such as these underscore how Soviet citizens were empowered to speak not only as individual consumers, but as members of a deserving group with particular consumer needs.

Consumers also politicized consumption by tying their interests to the general welfare of the Soviet people. In 1935, 45 female collective farmers (*kolkhoznitsy*) wrote a collective letter to I. A. Zelenskii (the President of the All-Union Central Union of Consumer Cooperative Societies), which was published in a newspaper. The women echoed recent proclamations about the significance of cultured consumption, saying that their children needed "good linen, individual beds, enamel dish ware," so they would not be uncultured.[108] The *kolkhoznitsy* claimed that the local store did not have these items or other ones "necessary for the cultural development of [their] children." Nor did the rural shop sell the most basic things, "like children's powder, cotton wadding, and petroleum jelly." Given the Soviet regime's anxiety about the "backwardness" of the peasantry, and the drive to promote *kul'turnost'*, the women's appeal to Zelenskii was powerful. They asked him to urge industries to produce more mass consumer goods and to organize the distribution of children's goods more fairly. In concluding, they gave their "Bolshevik word to raise a hearty, healthy, and cultured generation of future builders of communist society." By closing their letter this way, the 45 women linked the provisioning of children's consumer goods to the well-being of the nation. If given access to these goods, the letter implied, they would be better equipped to raise modern and cultured socialist citizens. These women consumers asserted themselves as protectors of the public good.

*   *   *

In the 1930s, Soviet citizens continued to be subjected to shortages, inferior products, long lines, and poor customer service, and many consumers lived lives of extreme material deprivation. And yet Communist authorities promoted the identity of the new Soviet consumer, argued that the Soviet people had legitimate consumer needs and desires, and attempted to mobilize consumers of behalf of socialist initiatives. As authorities reconfigured consumers' role in the Soviet polity, built on the idea that consumer practices and roles were central to economic and political policy, and promoted consumers' "rights" and "obligations," a Soviet version of the "citizen-consumer" emerged.[109] The term "citizen-customer" was even used during the trade campaign. Many Moscow food stores, for example, hung announcements appealing to the "citizen-customer" to use a new retail service.[110] Of course citizen-consumers in the Soviet Union had neither political nor economic freedom. Choice was not central to consumer agency (as it was for many in capitalist countries). But during the 1930s trade campaign, consumers gained a new positive status and civic responsibilities as participants in retail reform and the crusade to build socialism.

Soviet consumers bolstered and shaped the emergence of this citizen-consumer identity, taking advantage of the new and expanded venues for criticism to assert the legitimacy of their interests, and the right, indeed the obligation, to articulate these interests. The tactics employed by consumers to justify their needs and desires can be considered "weapons of the weak," because of the limited nature of consumer criticism and influence.[111] Nevertheless, the relationship between consumers and the party-state was dynamic, and offered consumers the opportunity to discipline workers, transform local retail conditions, become involved in public life, and lay claim to a new relationship with the Soviet government.

7
Soviet Retailing and Consumer Culture in Comparative Perspective

It is tempting to view the Stalinist regime's new approach to retailing and consumption in the 1930s as a uniquely Soviet story, a product of totalitarian aspirations to establish party-state control of the economy, the general populace, public organizations, and other aspects of life. At first glance, the Soviet government's intervention in the retail sector and its mobilization of consumers appear to support this narrative. After all, the historical development of modern retailing and consumer cultures is typically associated not with socialism and the state but with capitalism and the bourgeoisie. But if one accepts the arguments presented in recent scholarship about the importance of government involvement in the development of retail sectors and consumer cultures, then the Soviet approach to retailing and consumption can be understood as part of a broader historical story about how advanced industrial societies and states have responded to the challenges of mass distribution and consumption. Indeed, the Soviet approach can be understood as part of what Victoria de Grazia has pointed to as the "diversity of trajectories" to consumer modernity.[1]

The late nineteenth and early twentieth centuries in advanced industrial societies witnessed the simultaneous rise of mass consumption and the interventionist state. As governments confronted a new "age of the mass" – mass production, mass culture, mass politics, mass consumption, and mass warfare[2] – and the new challenges that this age engendered, they became increasingly concerned with transforming, regulating, and mobilizing populations for broader purposes. Governments aimed to produce national citizens who identified with broader state interests, for example, and to quell social unrest arising from the problems of industrialization and urbanization. State officials were aided in their efforts at social engineering by nonstate professionals, who exercised new forms of knowledge (e.g., medical) and new technologies of social intervention (e.g., health campaigns) to help refashion society. One result of efforts to manage populations was the emergence of the modern welfare state, with its policies and programs designed to protect people's welfare and further national economic and political objectives. States passed unemployment and accident insurance schemes, for example, to safeguard workers, maximize labor productivity, and counter the growing influence of socialism. Governments also endorsed pronatalist measures to foster women's reproduction, address demographic concerns about decreasing populations and national security, and stem the appeal of burgeoning women's movements.

The rise of the interventionist state had important implications for retail trade and consumption. As mass production and consumption became a new reality, retailers and governments began to transform retailing and distribution. Many entrepreneurs and large corporations adopted more modern retail systems and marketing techniques to promote efficiency and increase profits. A commercial revolution unfolded, although as de Grazia notes, this was not a seamless, uniform, or uncontested process. In the face of changing consumer landscapes, governments began to intervene more actively in economies, including in the sphere of the marketplace, and to respond to concerns raised by the production and sale of mass consumer goods. They also began to confront the questions – To what extent should the government respond to the consumer needs and desires of citizens? And how did satisfying, ignoring, actively shaping, or subordinating consumer needs and desires serve particular economic and political interests? During the First World War, these questions became particularly salient, and governments dramatically increased their interventions in the marketplace as they sought to manage economic and social upheavals, and to advance national objectives.

Anxieties about the dangers of mass culture and consumption surged amidst the economic tumult of the interwar era and became intertwined with concerns about national identity, economic and political stability, and women's changing roles in society. In the 1930s market economies collapsed in the face of worldwide economic depression. In the Soviet Union the market economy also collapsed, although this was deliberate government policy – a product of Stalin's Revolution from Above. As governments sought to manage the fallout from the consequences of relatively unrestrained capitalism, or in the Soviet case to construct an alternative economic model, they became even more involved in the regulation of the retail sector and consumption, and as this chapter shows, in the mobilization of consumers. Political leaders and policymakers began to recognize consumers as central to economic and political systems.

This chapter places the Soviet government's intervention in retailing and mobilization of consumers in a comparative context, focusing overwhelmingly but not exclusively on similar phenomena in the United States, Great Britain, and Nazi Germany. In the interwar era, the United States served as the paragon of capitalist economic modernity, including retail modernity; Great Britain was an advanced industrial capitalist society that pursued retail modernization, but not to the same extent as the United States; Nazi Germany was a dictatorship that exerted a strong hand on the economy, including the retail sector; the Soviet Union was a self-proclaimed socialist system, defined in part by its anticapitalism. How did these different countries' governments react to the challenges of mass distribution and consumption? How did they help to transform consumption from a private to a public matter? How did they attach notions of rights and duties to consumption? Through comparative analysis, this chapter sheds light on how specific economic, social, and political environments, as well as differing ideologies, informed interventionist approaches to retailing and consumption in both the Soviet Union and elsewhere.[3] While different in each case, this interventionism had particular implications for women. It also contributed to the increased politicization of consumption and the making of consumer cultures.

State regulation of retailing

Although the tenets of liberal capitalist theory espoused the value of keeping government hands off the economy and promoting a free market, in the late nineteenth and early twentieth centuries advanced industrial states with capitalist systems became more interventionist in the sphere of the marketplace. As societies became more industrialized and urbanized, and as urban populations were increasingly subjected to urban food processing, mass manufacturing, and modern retailing practices (e.g., advertising), local and national governments adopted regulations that affected the production and sale of consumer goods, and established corresponding government agencies to monitor compliance.[4] The purpose of much of this state intervention was to protect consumers from the dangerous or fraudulent production and sale of foodstuffs and consumer goods. In Great Britain, for example, the Sale of Food and Drugs Act of 1875 prohibited the sale of adulterated food and drug products and a 1912 Act prevented the use of preservatives in milk. The British Parliament also passed a Milk and Dairies Bill in 1914 to improve milk safety, but the war postponed its implementation.[5] In the United States the Meat Inspection and Pure Food and Drug Acts of 1906 established minimum standards for the safety and quality of products; and the Clayton Act and the Federal Trade Commission Act of 1914 promoted antitrust measures to thwart monopolies and their unfair retail practices.[6]

The economic and political chaos caused by the First World War prompted further state intervention in consumer economies. Governments in most of the war-affected countries adopted food control measures in an effort to maintain social order and ensure continued production for war ends. The British government, for example, instituted the rationing of basic foodstuffs in 1918 to dissipate growing popular frustration with long lines, shortages, and high prices. In the face of a "milk famine" and the sale of unsafe milk, the Local Government Board (a national body) began to "regulate conditions of sale and distribution of milk to assure sanitary standards and prevent the addition of water and colouring."[7] Food-related unrest contributed to the German government's decision to establish a virtual "food dictatorship" in 1916, run by the War Food Office. This office attempted, though not very successfully, to organize centralized control over food distribution.[8]

Economic collapse in the interwar era, particularly during the Great Depression, fueled state regulation of capitalist commercial sectors. As governments endeavored to rebuild economies, they felt increased pressure to address the consumer needs and demands of citizens, such as the problem of high prices. The United States Congress passed the Food, Drug, and Cosmetic Act of 1938, which provided additional regulatory legislation of consumer goods to safeguard citizens from hazardous products. In the 1930s, the British government established marketing boards and tariffs to regulate retail trade via prices and other controls; the fascist Italian government established a central committee for price control to determine "maximum price lists for staple foods and other products"; and the National Socialist regime in Germany set up the Office for the Supervision of Prices to institute "a more effective system of price control" under the Four-Year Plan. The Nazi government also prohibited "sensational, manipulative or deceptive advertisements."[9]

State regulation was usually framed as an issue of public safety, as a measure to protect consumers from the dangers of unfair or unhealthy business practices. Nonetheless, broader ideological and economic concerns shaped state regulation, including understandings of the potential political and social hazards of modern retailing and mass consumption. In the mid-1920s, for example, the fascist government in Italy "prohibited the opening of any new form of bar, café, public house, pastry shop and night club," in an effort to curb a perceived problem: "voluptuous" consumption.[10] Many Western European governments, with "Austria and Germany in the lead," passed laws in the interwar era that "directly or indirectly sought to restrict and limit the development of the multiple-shop, variety chain stores, and other forms of large-scale retailing." These measures, which helped to defend traditional retailing practices against the incursions of more modern and "international" practices, were intended to shore up political support among small shopkeepers *and* safeguard national identity.[11] Many of these same governments also established production quotas and/or fixed prices for certain goods "to restrain competition" and defend small competitors.[12] In some cases the ideological objectives behind state regulation were particularly obvious. To protect the German *Volk* from the alleged contamination of Jews and to further its anti-Semitic agenda, the Nazi government passed a new ordinance after *Kristallnacht* in 1938 that "formalized and accelerated the aryanization of Jewish property that was already taking place," and transferred ownership of department stores and other enterprises by Jews to non-Jews.[13]

Increased state intervention in the consumer economy was, to a considerable extent, a response to public pressure from a variety of groups and interests, including professional experts, business groups, journalists, social reformers, women activists, and consumer groups. Although members of these groups all emphasized the importance of protecting the broader populace from various dangers, some clearly acted on behalf of a combination of public and private interests. Scientists and medical experts who lobbied for greater state control over the unsafe adulteration of foodstuffs, for example, were interested not only in advancing public welfare but also their own economic or professional interests. Many ended up employed by industry or government as regulatory authorities.[14] Business interest groups, such as butter producers in late nineteenth-century Britain, pushed for the regulation of margarine to defend buyers from the fraudulent sale of margarine as butter *and* to protect the butter industry.[15] Muckraking journalists in the United States uncovered problems in food industries, which boosted their own careers and played an important role in upping the ante for state intervention. Upton Sinclair's 1906 expose of the horrors of the meat industry detailed the lack of hygienic working conditions and the use of diseased cows in meat processing, contributed to growing pressure from Progressives for government measures to protect consumers.[16] Acting on behalf of the public welfare, Progressives convinced the federal government to adopt greater food control and antitrust legislation before the First World War, and during the New Deal Era in the 1930s, women's associations and consumer groups successfully pressed the federal government to support consumer-safety by expanding national regulations.[17] In Germany, housewives implored the government for fair prices and other protections during the First World War.[18] In Britain the People's League of Health sought to make the pasteurization of milk compulsory in the 1930s.[19] These groups and others helped to change the relationship between the state and the consumer economy. Instead of depending on the self-regulation of the free market to protect consumers, governments mobilized to establish greater standards and controls for the production and distribution of foodstuffs and consumer goods. Nonetheless, despite expanded state intervention, particularly in times of political and economic crisis, governments in capitalist societies generally maintained an ideological commitment to "free markets" and assumed limited regulatory roles.

In the late 1920s, the Stalinist leadership abandoned the mixed economy of the 1920s, turning instead to a state-controlled command economy. As the formal private retail sector collapsed, and a major distribution and goods crisis emerged, the Soviet regime confronted the imperative to develop a modern system of mass distribution and consumption. It sought to monitor and regulate that system by adopting various laws and regulations, and by developing mechanisms to ensure compliance. Like capitalist laws that sought to abolish the sale of adulterated food and drugs, Soviet laws aimed to stop the sale of spoiled foodstuffs and defective goods. Soviet regulations also endeavored to protect public health by enacting more stringent sanitary standards. Nonetheless, despite some similarities with regulatory efforts in advanced industrial states in the West, socialist ideology and objectives shaped Soviet efforts in important ways. First and foremost, official *kontrol'* (regulation and monitoring) of the retail sector was pursued not only to protect consumers from the potential hazards of mass distribution and consumption but also to promote the development of a state-controlled noncapitalist system of retailing. As a result, Soviet interventionism was more extensive than in capitalist countries, incorporating a wider array of laws and punitive sanctions. In addition, the Communist leadership's promotion of mass participation in *kontrol'* contributed to an expansive system of regulatory oversight.

In trying to establish a new system of "socialist" retailing, the Soviet government was responsible not only for enforcing a regulatory framework but also for transforming and managing the trade apparatus. As the party-state assumed formal control of goods distribution for the entire Soviet Union, it faced enormous challenges in building a comprehensive network, challenges exacerbated by the desire to distinguish the new Soviet trade from what had existed before. To achieve their dream world of a rational, modern, honest, and cultured system of Soviet socialist retailing, Communist leaders realized that it was not enough to destroy the formal private retail network. The new system would need to be modernized, workers would have to be remade, many more women would have to be hired, and "anti-Soviet elements" and corrupt employees would have to be weeded out. Because *kolkhoz* (collective farm) trade operated as a sphere of semi-state directed market trade, it would need to be monitored extra carefully to constrain potential profiteering and "capitalist" appetites. To promote cultured Soviet trade, stores and employees would need to meet sanitary and other requirements. The endeavor to realize a new dream world of Soviet retailing resulted in a proliferation of retail-related laws and regulations as well as oversight mechanisms to check compliance.

A "socialist" understanding of crime contributed to the expansive nature of surveillance and regulatory efforts in the Soviet retail sector. Without private corporations and managers responsible for monitoring incidents of theft or embezzlement, these common problems fell under the purview of the government, requiring party-state surveillance. Soviet authorities also viewed the resale of consumer goods at higher than original purchase prices as "speculation," an objectionable and illegal activity. Such "speculative" activity was intolerable: it exploited consumers, contributed to social inequality, led to excessive profiteering, and undermined socialism. It was a terrible scourge that required state intervention. This was a different understanding than in the West, where economic and political elites usually understood such activity as one of the vagaries of the marketplace (even if they sometimes characterized it as unsavory and unscrupulous). During times of major economic and political crisis, governments in capitalist societies sometimes took steps against excessive speculation. Public agitation against perceived profiteers during the First World War, for example, eventually led the British government to pass a 1919 Profiteering Act, which in principle allowed the Board of Trade to pursue the more active protection of consumers from extreme profiteering.[20] But in general, capitalist governments tolerated "speculative" activity.

Perhaps the most distinctive feature of Soviet intervention in the consumer economy was the degree to which it encouraged popular involvement in surveillance and regulation. While ordinary citizens in capitalist countries certainly protested retail problems and lobbied against perceived excesses, and more commonly exercised a form of monitoring and regulation when they "voted with their feet" and stopped shopping in particular retail establishments, very few participated in formal regulatory initiatives.[21] In the Soviet Union, by contrast, hundreds of thousands of ordinary people participated in the official regulation of retailing in the 1930s. As detailed in Chapter 5, they aided state organs in their surveillance efforts, acted as controllers for state-directed public organizations, and participated in monitoring initiatives sponsored by the Soviet trade system, such as shop commissions. Soviet citizens also engaged in "*kontrol'* from below" by reporting on retail conditions in stores' complaint books, in letters to the press, and at customer conferences. Combined, these efforts added up to a vast volunteer regulatory network. Of course Soviet citizens continued to engage in the unofficial regulation of the consumer economy – for example, via unsanctioned protests. But Soviet leaders actively encouraged mass participation in the official monitoring of retailing as part of a broader effort to get ordinary people involved in the auditing and managing of the state and economy. They also promoted this participation as a practical response to the immensity of the regulatory challenge of the state-controlled retail network and as a means of social control (to help to diffuse consumer frustration). And according to Communist authorities, mass participation was an important vehicle for transforming people, inculcating socialist values, and integrating them into the Soviet body politic. In the end, mass involvement in the regulation of the retail sector served an additional function: it contributed to authorities' efforts to redefine the sector as socialist. Soviet retailing became distinguishable in part from capitalist retailing because of its monitoring by "the masses."

Mobilization of consumers

Increased state intervention in the consumer economy in the interwar era was accompanied by increased state mobilization of consumers. Political leaders and policymakers in many countries, including the Soviet Union, began to recognize consumers as a distinct group that could be deployed for various goals, and to advance a new relationship between consumers and the state. Governments promoted a new politics of consumption – acknowledging their greater responsibility for promoting consumers' alleged interests, and assigning greater accountability to consumers for promoting national interests. As political leaders and policymakers reconceptualized consumers' role in the broader polity, consumers were reconfigured as citizen-consumers, gaining "rights" and "responsibilities" in official government discourses.

The new relationship between states and consumers had its roots in the late nineteenth and early twentieth centuries as well as the First World War. As discussed above, it was during this time that local and national governments began to intervene more actively in domestic economies to protect and promote consumers' interests by adopting controls over the production, sale, and distribution of foodstuffs and consumer goods. The First World War was a particular turning point as political leaders sought to contain the social unrest that accompanied severe provisioning crises. Many governments ended up establishing rationing systems for the distribution of essential commodities as well as maximum food prices. In some cases they even included consumers as representatives in the government offices and councils that were set up to deal with provisioning policies. The British government, for example, instituted an advisory Consumers' Council under the aegis of the Ministry of Food (which was disbanded in 1921).[22] Members of the general populace, including those from trade unions, the Social Democratic Party, and women's organizations, were invited to serve on the executive committee of the German War Food Office.[23] But even though these measures signaled governments' recognition that they had some responsibility for protecting consumers and providing a modicum of consumer representation in policymaking, most political leaders did not view consumers as a distinct constituency with political rights and responsibilities.

Still, consumer activism during the First World War and in the immediate pre- and post-First World War period contributed to the new relationship that emerged between governments and consumers in the 1930s. Of course the popular protests against high prices during these times – expressed via food riots and local boycotts – were nothing new. As E. P. Thompson and others have noted, there was a long tradition in many countries of public unrest and direct action related to perceived violations of the "moral economy," of inordinately high prices, for example, that went against local traditions and understandings of "just" prices.[24] What was new was the emergence of the consumer as an explicitly social identity and political force. In the United States, for example, both in the pre- and post-First World War period, consumer activists promoted "ethical consumption" by underscoring the connection between production and consumption, and directing consumers to purchase goods that were produced in labor environments with "better" work conditions. Proponents of free trade in Edwardian England appealed to consumers as political actors, urging them to support free trade in the face of potential tariff reform so as to protect the collective good. During World War I urban Germans began to conceive of poorer consumers not only as "those of lesser means" but also as "representatives of the nation," as citizens who deserved to have their basic food needs met.[25]

But even though there was a history of activism "at the point of consumption" before the 1930s, and even though the consumer had already begun to emerge as a social identity and political force before this time, it was only during the economic collapse and political instability that followed in the wake of the Great Depression that there was a sea change in thinking about consumption among a significant number of political leaders and policymakers in Europe and the United States.[26] As the failures of free markets and the reality and challenges of mass consumption became more apparent, political elites began to reconfigure consumption, and to actively support it as a vehicle for political integration and civic participation. They began to view consumers differently, associate them more broadly with the public interest, and grant them greater authority and political legitimacy. In the process, a variety of governments in the interwar ear began to link consumption with citizenship – admittedly to lesser and greater extents – and to pay more attention to consumers' "rights." One way they did so was by passing additional protective legislation: food and drug regulations, price controls, antitrust measures (see previous section). Although such legislation was not entirely new, the legislation of the 1930s marked an important expansion of earlier initiatives.

In the United States and Britain, the "right" to greater consumer protection was accompanied by the "right" to greater consumer representation in official government affairs. Federal agencies in the United States were particularly energetic in establishing consumer offices and advisory boards in the 1930s, including in the newly formed National Recovery Administration (NRA) and the Agricultural Adjustment Administration (ARA). The president's wife, Eleanor Roosevelt, even sponsored a Consumers' Conference at the White House in December 1933, underscoring the greater importance assigned to consumer concerns. President Roosevelt explained the new approach to consumers by arguing that they had the right "to have their interests represented in the formulation of government policy." Ultimately, however, the United States federal government did not establish a "Department of the Consumer" in the 1930s, which some consumer advocates wanted.[27]

Consumers in interwar Britain were never afforded the same rights of representation as consumers in the United States. Although the government created a Food Council in 1925, a watchdog agency that included some consumer representation, the council was largely ineffective. Efforts to pass Consumers' Council Bills were defeated in both 1930 and 1938. And when the British government established Agricultural Marketing Boards in 1931 to regulate trade for select products, and attached an advisory Consumers' Committee to the boards, this new body apparently had little influence. The weak nature of consumer representation appears to have been a result of British economic and political culture. Matthew Hilton argues that "powerful [business] interests ensured that the consumer was largely seen as a rational individual unit whose sphere of activity belonged purely within the economic confines of the market in the side of the mass manufacturer." The otherwise progressive labor movement's greater interest in protecting production rather than consumption likewise lessened consumers' political power.[28] Difficulty decoupling "free trade" from its historical association with the growth of civil society and "the freedom of society from the state" may have also limited the political rights gained by British consumers in the 1930s.[29] Before the First World War, consumer activists and many others had essentially defined Free Trade as the best "safeguard of the public interest." As attitudes began to shift during the war, and consumer activists began to promote state retail regulation as a better defense, this constituted a major ideological shift from the prewar aversion to an interventionist state. As a result, British consumers in the interwar era likely had a more difficult time than their American counterparts in convincing officials that they should have their voice incorporated into official governmental bodies assuming more proactive policies vis-à-vis the consumer economy.[30] Nonetheless, however limited consumer representation was, and whether it was largely symbolic or not, the inclusion of consumers in state agencies in the interwar era marked an official acknowledgment by both the American and British governments that consumers had some right to have their voices incorporated into policymaking. In the process, these governments helped to legitimize and institutionalize the political identity of the citizen-consumer.

The Nazi regime also repositioned consumers' role in the body politic in the 1930s, promoting its own version of consumer citizenship. This might seem surprising. Nazi leaders, after all, were hostile to mass distribution and consumption, associating both with American materialism and international "Jewish" capitalism. Nazi economist Gottfried Feder noted, "The large retail stores, all in the hands of Jews...depend on 'charm,' 'display,' 'bluff,' and the awakening of wholly unnecessary 'demands' for 'luxuries.'"[31] But when the Nazi regime came to power in 1933, it confronted the problem of high prices and good shortages, common problems in countries affected by the interwar depression and already overwhelming in Germany during the Weimar period. To quell popular frustration and win public support, Hitler and other Nazi leaders promoted greater consumer protections. They also promised economic revival, including enhanced purchasing power. This pledge of increased consumption, however, did not fit easily with the Third Reich's interest in rearmament and the establishment of an autarkic economy. In an effort to demonstrate governmental support for consumers' interests while at the same time suppressing the population's overall level of consumption, Nazi officials acknowledged that consumers were entitled to the increased consumption of certain items, such as canned goods, frozen foods, and synthetic fabrics. As the newest modern commodities, these products were a testament to German industry, and more importantly, they would help to make the nation more impervious to potential blockades. The state also subsidized the mass purchase of small household radios so that consumers could have access to mass entertainment as well as propaganda about the advances for which the Fatherland was supposedly responsible.[32] To underscore every person's right to own an automobile, which had previously been a privilege of the wealthy, and to overcome Germany's backwardness compared to the United States when it came to mass motorization, the Nazi leadership launched a campaign to produce and market an affordable "people's car," the *Volkswagen*.[33] Although this campaign was largely rhetorical (because mass production of "people's cars" did not begin until after the Second World War), it underscored the legitimacy of consumers' needs and desires. The regime's emphasis on boosting consumption in at least some spheres (though not all) offered a pragmatic response to consumers' frustrations by reinforcing the message that German citizens had a "right" to more material goods, while promoting the broader economic goals of the state.

It is important to note that the Nazi regime did not guarantee *all* consumers' rights, which the American and British governments did, at least in principle. Jews, who were excluded from the Nazi national community (*Volksgemeinschaft*), were denied the same consumer rights as racially "valuable" citizens. For example, the state provided subsidies for furniture and other household goods via "marriage loans" to young "German" couples, so they could easily establish new homes and procreate. Jews were not entitled to these loans and associated merchandise, since they did not qualify as "German." The Nazi leisure organization "Strength through Joy" (KdF), which provided millions of Germans with various forms of "noncommercial consumption," such as sports programs and 2 to 3 day excursions, explicitly barred Jews from these benefits.[34] By affording privileges or "rights" to some but not all consumers, Nazi policymakers aimed to consolidate a racially harmonious and unified nation, a vision based on racist exclusions. They advanced a racialist consumer politics.

Governments in the 1930s era consolidated the identity of the citizen-consumer not only by acknowledging that consumers had some rights but also by expecting consumers to fulfill certain obligations. In the United States these obligations were essentially twofold. In granting consumers the right to government representation, New Deal officials assigned them the responsibility to help formulate state responses to mass consumption, economic problems, and the limits of the free-market economy. Consumer representatives were directed to carry out this duty not only on a federal but also on a local level by serving on county consumer councils whose primary mandate was to investigate and resolve charges of unfair prices (and if necessary, to report back to higher authorities). Although American citizens were not as involved as their Soviet counterparts in the official regulation of the consumer economy, they nonetheless assumed a greater role in regulatory efforts. Exercising one's purchasing power also became an American civic responsibility. When the President established the National Recovery Administration (NRA) in 1933 and urged American businessmen to pursue fair labor practices and fair prices, he appealed to consumers to support the recovery act by *only* purchasing goods from businesses that demonstrated their compliance.[35] As the 1930s progressed, economists and policymakers increasingly adopted Keynesian thinking and viewed underconsumption as one of the main reasons for the lingering depression. As government officials linked mass consumption to economic recovery, and viewed "consumer empowerment [as] integral to the nation's political and economic health," they argued that the government had an obligation to adopt strategies that would facilitate such empowerment *and* that consumers had an obligation to exercise greater purchasing power (when and if they were able to).[36] The American government's new approach to consumers in the 1930s helped to make citizen and consumer "permeable categories" in American political culture.[37]

The British government similarly exhorted consumers to fulfill their civic obligations by purchasing national goods, launching an "official, government-sponsored" "buy British" campaign in 1931. Significantly, the British Cabinet endorsed the President of the Board of Trade's remarks during this time: "It is the plain duty of every British citizen at the present time, to give all the help he can to British industry by buying British goods." Through various propaganda posters and pamphlets, the Empire Marketing Board (EMB), which was in charge of the buy British campaign, explained to consumers that purchasing national goods would help not only to promote industrial growth but also to correct the country's "adverse balance of trade" and to help resolve problems of unemployment.[38] Although the government abandoned the "buy British" campaign when it introduced new tariffs in the mid-1930s, effectively pricing many non-British goods out of the consumer market, the campaign helped to link consumption to citizenship by transforming the private act of buying into civic duty.

The Nazi government, like the American and British governments, also conceived of consumer purchasing as a civic obligation in the 1930s. But it did so somewhat differently. In an effort to establish a self-contained economy, pursue war mobilization, and unite the *Volk*, the Nazi state urged consumers to think of purchasing in a "racial-political light."[39] Political leaders and policymakers encouraged Germans to strengthen the *Volksgemeinschaft* by supporting Aryan-owned businesses, and boycotting Jewish retailers and commodities produced by Jewish manufacturers. They also directed citizens to buy from traditional small-scale retail establishments instead of modern department and chain stores, because the latter were associated with either foreign ownership or foreign retail practices. To facilitate the consolidation of an autarkic economy, the "regeneration of the national community," and the preservation of an "authentically pure" German culture the Nazi regime tried to redirect consumer demand, entreating consumers to buy domestic (often ersatz) products to replace imports, such as cellular wool made out of chemically treated wood. State functionaries characterized these products as "patriotic, more 'natural,' healthier, and abundantly available because they were indigenous to Germany."[40] Doctors and Nazi departments of public health argued that the consumption of certain indigenous foodstuffs would "strengthen the racial community." What was one way to decrease "disease and degeneration?" Eat "wholemeal" bread![41] The scope and fervor of the Nazi "buy German" campaign, as well as the institutional resources devoted to it, distinguished the Nazi campaign from the purchasing campaigns advanced in the United States and Great Britain. So too did the explicitly racialist discourse that underwrote it.

Nazi consumer politics differed from American and British consumer politics in two additional ways. Whereas American and British policymakers protected consumers' individual freedom by acknowledging their right to free-market choice, German policymakers restricted consumers' marketplace choices. Nazi leaders did not completely eliminate the import of foreign goods, such as coffee, because of anxiety about alienating consumers. But they did limit imports, which made some items very difficult to procure. The Nazi regime additionally constrained consumer choice by abolishing the production and sale of particular items. In the mid-1930s, for example, the "addition of synthetic fibres to textiles" became compulsory, ending the commercial manufacture of "pure cotton or woolen textiles." Because of fat, butter, and margarine shortages, the Nazi regime also banned whipped cream and cream cakes from the market. Unlike American and British governments, which encouraged consumers to increase personal consumption to further economic growth, the Nazi regime aimed to suppress overall levels of consumption. Nazi propaganda exhorted citizens to live more simply by buying fewer items and recycling items, because reduced consumer demand would allow the economy's resources to be reoriented to other national priorities, namely, war preparations. Political leaders also launched savings campaigns to decrease personal consumption, arguing that money saved in the short term would allow for easier and increased expenditures later.[42] As these examples suggest, although the Nazi regime actively protected and promoted some consumers' "rights," the new relationship between consumers and the state was dominated by an expansion of consumers' civic obligations.

As governments in the United States, Britain, and Nazi Germany turned their gaze to consumers, and characterized consumer spending or *not* spending as a patriotic duty that would contribute to the collective good, they often imagined consumers as female. In the United States, for example, when the Women's Division of the NRA organized consumer drives to champion the president's plan to support business with fair labor practices and prices, it targeted women, giving them an important role in safeguarding economic objectives. As the head of the Women's Division explained, "the buying power of the country" was in women's hands.[43] In Britain, the "buy British" campaign assigned women particular responsibility to promote the public good, as illustrated by the EMB's pamphlet "Why Every Women Ought to Buy British."[44] As the Nazi regime encouraged citizens to purchase different items (from usual) and adopt new consumption habits, it too focused on women consumers. In 1938, for example, officials organized approximately 85,000 cookery courses to teach women how to prepare meals with replacement food products, such as "Quark," which was a domestic substitute for margarine or butter.[45] Similarly, when it initiated a massive campaign against waste to convince citizens to consume less, the Nazi regime targeted women to contribute to this effort, distributing 18 million postcards with the slogan "Fight waste" "for women to use in their private correspondence."[46] As German propaganda appealed to housewives to adopt patriotic consumer and household practices so that the state could pursue broader economic objectives, Hermann Goering, the top Nazi leader in charge of the economy, acknowledged women's new civic roles as consumers by calling them "trustees of the nation's wealth."[47] Because of women's role as primary household consumers, state functionaries in all three countries rendered women's consumption habits a matter of national importance, a matter of civic responsibility.

As governments in the 1930s began to conceive of consumers differently, and to mobilize them on behalf of political and economic goals, politically marginalized groups used consumer issues to enlarge their public influence and political voice beyond the confines of high politics. Consumer activists – particularly women – bolstered the emerging identity of the citizen-consumer by asserting themselves as political actors. In the United States, for example, women consumer activists moved their boycotts and protests beyond local neighborhoods, coordinating larger-scale actions at citywide and national levels and forcing local and federal governments to take action. They forged new coalitions, crossing ethnic, racial, and class boundaries, and claimed a role "as guardians of the public welfare."[48] Millions of women activists took up consumer issues through already existing national women's groups (e.g., the National League of Women's Voters and the General Federation of Women's Clubs), which had previously focused on other social concerns. As women activists strengthened demands for state intervention in the sphere of consumption, and played an important role in getting the new Federal Food, Drug, and Cosmetic Act of 1938 passed, they helped to "turn consumption into a new realm of politics, and its policing into a new kind of political mission for themselves."[49] As the Great Depression and racial discrimination in the workplace led to high rates of unemployment, activists in black communities also began to mobilize African American consumers. By organizing "Don't Shop Where You Can't Work" campaigns, these activists used black purchasing power to highlight racism and put pressure on white-owned businesses to change their discriminatory practices.[50] In Britain women too played a salient part in promoting the identity of the citizen-consumer.[51] For example, when Labour Party women and the Women's Cooperative Guild gathered "700,000 signatures from housewives in protest against high prices in their 'Cost of Living Campaign' in 1938," they associated high prices with "questions of public health and welfare (nutrition)."[52] As they framed the issue, unfair prices were not merely a cause of concern for the private consumer; they were a cause of concern for the national interest. Even women in Nazi Germany used official efforts to politicize consumption and mobilize consumers to gain greater public authority in the 1930s. For example, many women from housewives' organizations, which in the 1920s had promoted similar ideas as the Nazis about the need to reject big department stores, boycott imported goods, and cut back on private consumption, joined government efforts to modify daily consumption habits, such as those sponsored by the Nazi women's organization, *Deutsches Frauenwerk* (German Women's Work). As women activists assisted state functionaries in targeting housewives to redirect and reduce consumption – e.g., by distributing written materials on how to prepare delicious meals with "German staple foodstuffs" – they carved out new official roles for women *and* reinforced the idea that specific acts of consumption were civic acts. In their new roles, these women activists characterized consumers, especially women consumers, as protectors of the general public, as citizen-consumers.

   In the Soviet Union a new relationship between the government and consumers emerged in a very different economic and political context than in other countries. There was no Great Depression, nor were there new understandings of capitalist systems and their obligations to the masses. Instead there was a consumer crisis fueled by Stalin's Revolution from Above and a grand crusade to build socialism. The former was a cause of significant unrest, and the latter included a campaign to establish "socialist" retailing, a move to reconcile the retail sector and consumption with Soviet socialism. During the trade campaign of the 1930s, the Stalinist regime advanced its own version of the citizen-consumer, reconfiguring consumers' role in the socialist endeavor. Consumers gained an official legitimacy that they had been denied previously. Up until that point, consumers had largely been left out of the socialist project for two reasons: first, because of the identification of consumers with conspicuous consumption and the materialistic Nepmen and Nepwomen of the 1920s (those associated with private entrepreneurship and retailing); and second, because of Communist leaders' valorization of workers and production. But in the 1930s consumers gained standing as "productive" players in the socialist project, and were integrated into the broader Soviet polity as they gained new "rights" and "responsibilities."

Soviet consumers never gained the kinds of freedom of choice in the marketplace that their American and British counterparts did. The politics of the domestic economy, like Nazi Germany's, imposed serious constraints on the goods available to individual consumers. Nonetheless, even if consumers faced serious constraints and continued to wait in long lines and suffer from goods shortages, the trade campaign of the 1930s acknowledged ordinary people as consumers, not merely workers, and promulgated consumers' "right" to a better retail experience. Soviet officials and the press instructed retail personnel to respect consumers, and to treat them in a more polite, efficient, and even loving way. This was not only propaganda. To promote new attitudes and retail practices, Soviet policymakers launched massive initiatives to increase the training and sociocultural education of salesclerks, to feminize the retail workforce (because women were supposedly more honest, hardworking, and hygienic than men), and to promote a labor hero movement in retailing.

During the trade campaign Soviet leaders sought to respond to the political and economic destabilization of scarcity, publicizing the party-state's duty to respond more effectively to people's material needs by improving the provisioning of consumer goods. Socialism, Stalin firmly declared, was not about poverty; it was about prosperity and abundance. The Second Five-Year Plan (FYP) in the mid-1930s devoted far more resources to the manufacture of foodstuffs and consumer goods than the First FYP, even if industrial development remained the plan's priority. Karl Marx and subsequent communists had long trumpeted the slogan, "From each according to his ability to each according to his need," harkening to a future society of abundance in which all persons would live in comfort. But when Soviet leaders assumed power, they had emphasized asceticism as a revolutionary virtue. Thus, official pronouncements in the 1930s about the legitimacy and necessity of improving living standards, along with new economic policies, marked a new Soviet approach to consumption. Mass manufacturing during the Second FYP never came close to meeting the vast population's consumer needs, although the production of some commodities witnessed significant expansion. Still, in terms of rhetoric, if not reality, Soviet consumers gained the "right" to purchase *more* even though they never obtained the right to purchase *as much* as they needed or wanted.

If in the United States, Great Britain, and Germany the emphasis of consumers' civic obligations was on what they did *or* did not buy, in the Soviet Union this was not the case. Instead the Stalinist regime emphasized consumers' responsibility to reach beyond individual acts of purchasing and become actively involved in state building, particularly the reform of retailing. This emphasis is not surprising, given the terrible scarcity that continued to plague the Soviet economy throughout the 1930s. By emphasizing the primacy of consumer participation in the remaking of retail trade, the Stalinist regime helped to redefine the practices of consumption as socialist, as productive and useful for the socioeconomic order as opposed to bourgeois acts of consumption deemed unproductive and selfish. Trade officials articulated a vision of consumer citizenship, arguing that it was customers' "duty and right" to improve Soviet retailing.[53]

The state encouraged customers to contribute to reform efforts in a variety of ways: by participating in the regulation of retailing via state and public organizations; by becoming unpaid consumer activists in stores; and by publicly articulating ideas and complaints about consumer goods and the retail sector in various state-sponsored forums for consumer feedback.[54] As citizens-in training, the Soviet party-state even mobilized children consumers on behalf of the trade campaign, soliciting their opinions at goods exhibits and customer conferences. Through these forums the Soviet populace learned that rather than being considered slanderous and antisocialist, it was a civic responsibility to rail against the corrupt store manager, the intoxicated salesclerk, or the scourge of flies buzzing around foodstuffs. The articulation of public consumer disapproval was reconfigured during this time as "healthy Bolshevik" behavior.[55]

As in other countries, Soviet officials emphasized the value of women's contributions to the trade campaign, targeting them to become paid employees and unpaid controllers and consumer activists, and appealing to women, particularly housewives, to voice their criticism in forums for consumer feedback. In part, this emphasis was because women had long been at the center of popular unrest over retail conditions. But it was also because trade reformers proposed that women's "womanly" characteristics, such as their "natural" concern for others, and their "housewifely eye(s)" and domestic experiences as household managers and primary shoppers, meant that they had an important role to play in identifying retail problems.

As ordinary Soviet people exercised their rights and obligations in the retail economy, they contributed to the construction of the new "socialist" consumer: the activist citizen-consumer. Hundreds of thousands of Soviet citizens, if not more, engaged in retail regulatory initiatives, became consumer activists, and offered consumer feedback via the various state-sponsored forums. The party-state's mobilization of consumers in the 1930s provided Soviet citizens, including women and especially the ranks of housewives, with expanded opportunities for involvement in the public sector. This mobilization granted consumers, both male and female, a new language and authority with which to place demands on the party-state, castigate local authorities, and affect local retail conditions. While there were limits to public consumer criticism, the new relationship that emerged between the Soviet regime and consumers allowed ordinary people to define consumer needs and lobby for a more responsive government. It allowed them to speak as deserving citizens representing the general good. For example, a group of 214 mothers from Belorussia published a newspaper address in 1937 in which they linked their own material interests with national objectives. They explained "to all mothers with multiple children in the Soviet Union" that they were raising their "sons and daughters as Soviet patriots, dedicated to the affairs of Lenin and Stalin." They pledged to help fulfill the regime's new 1936 law "in support" of mothers and children, which criminalized abortions, restricted divorce, extended maternity benefits, and increased incentives to mothers to reproduce. To be able to serve and educate their children in the best way possible, they demanded that stores respond to the needs of mothers and children. In their words, "Our collective farm rural consumer cooperatives should have all that is necessary for mothers and children (children's layettes, beds, small bath tubs, individual goods, and so on)." If they were to advance the socialist goal of producing loyal and politically conscious sons and daughters, they needed certain material goods. What is more, these mothers did not merely speak their mind. Their address provoked an official response – a new push among consumer cooperatives to improve customer service to mothers and children and to better meet their material needs.[56]

*   *   *

In the 1930s government intervention in commercial sectors intensified, and a new relationship emerged between many states and consumers.

Governments recognized and mobilized consumers as citizens as they grappled with the problems produced by the excesses of capitalism, or as they sought to build a noncapitalist economy, and as they confronted a new age of the mass and its potential benefits and perils for advancing national interests. As this chapter has shown, despite some commonalities, the broader economic and political objectives of different governments as well as their differing ideologies informed processes of state intervention and notions of consumer-citizenship. Thus in the United States and Great Britain consumer citizenship was connected primarily to individual purchasing power, and to a lesser extent to government representation; in Nazi Germany it was associated mostly with advancing a self-sufficient economy and uniting the *Volk*, which rested upon an explicitly racialist conceptualization of consumer politics; and in the Soviet Union it was linked largely to the collective construction of socialism and the promotion of a participatory consumer politics (of a limited sort). Consumer-citizenship did not necessarily involve an equitable balance between consumers' rights and responsibilities, and in Nazi Germany and the Soviet Union, its conceptualization relied more heavily on consumers' duties to the government. Moreover, while the new "rights" and protections granted by the liberal capitalist countries were clearly limited by lax oversight and enforcement, the "rights" allowed consumers in Nazi Germany and the Soviet Union were directly compromised by people's broader lack of political and economic rights.

Government recognition of consumers as central actors in economic and political affairs particularly affected women. It provided women, who were mostly excluded from the formal institutions of the state and high politics, with public authority and new civic roles. But political leaders' focus on women's contributions as the primary shoppers was both a blessing and a burden. It valorized women at the same time that it held them more responsible than men for carrying out certain consumer acts which would safeguard the public good. If American and British women didn't exercise their buying power properly, the national economy would suffer. If German women bought too much butter or frequented Jewish-owned stores, their fellow citizens would be jeopardized. If Soviet women didn't offer their womanly insight via public consumer criticism, the campaign to establish socialist retailing would be weakened. The new relationship that emerged between governments and consumers in the 1930s afforded women greater opportunities for public agency as well as greater responsibilities for advancing the public good, but it also led to their greater regulation as consumers. Government recognition of women consumers' central economic and political roles, moreover, served as a vehicle for regulating their femininity. Were they good mothers or good women? That depended in part on whether they engaged in conspicuous or unpatriotic consumption, whether they purchased wholemeal bread, whether they volunteered as store activists or spoke up at a conference about children's goods.

State interventionism in consumer economies in the 1930s politicized consumption in new ways, and shaped the development of mass consumer cultures. Implicit in most conceptualizations of mass consumer culture is the idea of the sovereign consumer who has freedom of choice in a market (capitalist) society of abundance.[57] The assumption is that if the masses can not exercise their purchasing power freely or articulate their individuality through the consumption of particular products, then there is no mass consumer culture. This conceptualization allows one to conclude, regarding the Soviet Union in the 1930s, that "only in relation to books and especially movies can one discern the outlines of a mass consumer culture."[58] But this conceptualization is problematic for many reasons. It errs in equating mass consumer culture with an American-style consumer culture. It does not take into account how mass consumer culture is about more than buying things in the marketplace and using the acquisition of goods to define social identity. In particular, this conceptualization avoids the role of the government, and state–consumer interactions, in influencing domestic political and economic cultures, and affecting the norms and practices of mass consumption. As a result, it fails to recognize the multiplicity of paths to consumer modernity and mass consumer culture. As this chapter has shown, in the United States, Great Britain, Nazi Germany, and the Soviet Union, governments in the 1930s promoted a particular culture of consumption for the masses. These consumer cultures varied in their focus on consumer sovereignty and understandings of legitimate consumer needs and desires. Nonetheless, in each country a culture developed which helped to shape the identities, ways of operating, and rhetorics of consumers, and to inform consumers' relationship to state and society.

Conclusion

In Russia today it is not uncommon to walk into a store and see a pamphlet or flyer about consumers' rights protection laws posted on the wall, often behind a glass or plastic enclosed case. Many retail businesses also have a "complaint book" or a "book of suggestions and complaints," which give customers an opportunity to express their opinions. When the Soviet Union collapsed in 1991, the postcommunist Russian government passed many new laws regarding consumers' rights, starting with a Russian Federation Consumer Protection Act in 1992. More recently, various businesses have organized "mystery shoppers" in major Russian cities, in which consumer advocates pose as regular customers to investigate and report on sales practices, particularly customer service. It would be easy to assume that all this attention to consumers and the consumer experience is new, a product of Russia's move to a capitalist system and market economy in which consumers have legitimacy and "rights." This assumption also appears logical because under the Soviet socialist economy consumers did not have it easy. During bad economic periods, shortages were common and Soviet consumers waited in line for hours to purchase basic foodstuffs and other necessities from often rude salesclerks. Moreover, Soviet policies contributed directly to the starvation of millions during three major famines in 1921–1922, 1932–1933, and 1946–1947. When deemed necessary, the Communist leadership sacrificed consumer needs, and even lives, for economic and political objectives.

But despite the Soviet Union's notoriously impoverished and inadequate consumer economy, the mode of attunement to consumers in contemporary Russia is rooted in the Soviet past. During the 1930s, the Stalinist regime endeavored to establish an explicitly noncapitalist system of socialist retailing, "Soviet trade." This was uncharted territory, an unprecedented experiment. As authorities embarked on their trade campaign, they recognized the Soviet people as consumers, and touted consumers' "rights" and responsibilities. The trade campaign institutionalized the in-store complaint book, and promoted a Soviet version of the "mystery shopper" – the ordinary citizen turned public controller who investigated stores, issued reports, and sometimes acted incognito as a customer to unearth deceptive practices.

The Stalinist regime tried to bolster itself and the campaign to establish Soviet trade via customer collaboration. But from the regime's perspective it was ultimately counterproductive to foster a new relationship between the party-state and consumers by acknowledging consumers' needs, and encouraging the development of active citizen-consumers. As consumers embraced their new civic responsibilities and participated in the forums for consumer feedback and other initiatives aimed at promoting retail reform, they increasingly demanded that the government live up to its promises and implement rhetorical and policy changes regarding consumer goods and retailing. The problem was that the government's new pledge to meet consumers' needs was *always* constrained by broader economic imperatives. Unwilling to alter its industrial goals significantly, the Stalinist leadership increased the production of foodstuffs and consumer goods during the Second Five-Year Plan, but did not commit the necessary resources to allow for massively expanded production and material abundance. Nor did it provide the necessary finances for widespread retail reform, so despite some successes of the trade campaign, retail improvement remained uneven and limited. For Soviet citizens who lived outside of major metropolitan areas, retail reform was particularly minimal and ineffectual. Thus the Stalinist regime widely touted but by no means guaranteed consumers' "right" to the improved provisioning of consumer goods and a better retail experience. The Soviet dream world of retail and consumer modernity coexisted with a dream world of industrial modernity, and as Communist authorities often recognized, these dream worlds were intertwined. But ultimately the drive for industrial modernity took precedence, at the expense of the drive for retail and consumer modernity.

By politicizing retailing and consumption during the trade campaign, and promoting consumers as a legitimate constituency, the Stalinist regime advanced a social contract with its citizens in which the consumer economy became an important component of the regime's legitimacy. By failing to meet consumers' needs, the regime opened itself up to the possibility of severe public reproach. Konovalov, a trade worker, grasped part of the problem when he explained to a group of fellow trade workers why they needed to become Stakhanovite labor heroes. If a worker is badly served in a store, he asserted, "He will be embittered not only at us, but also at Soviet power. ... Often the wives of workers stand for a long time in line, and then they say: What is this Soviet power, which forces us to stand in line?" In short, he reminded his audience, there were political consequences to "bad customer service."[1] G. Moroz, the Chair of the All-Union Trade Union of Soviet Trade Workers, similarly noted how problematic it was that people heard all this talk about life improving and yet they still encountered scarcity. In his opinion, people might conclude, "All the talk [about life getting better] amounts to nothing." According to Moroz, the salesperson therefore had a particular duty to act as an agitator for Soviet power and to work against the spoiling of the "political mood of the masses."[2]

During the 1930s, the Soviet dream world of retailing and consumption often spoiled the mood of the masses because it coexisted with the lived reality of the consumer economy. There were successes, to be sure: the trade campaign was not all illusion. Stores were built and renovated, new modern retail technologies and rationalizing practices were introduced, and the retail workforce was expanded and increasingly feminized. Women's greater presence in the cooperative and state trade system – as trade officials, employees, public controllers, and consumer activists – appears to have improved and even "civilized" retailing (at least to some extent). Stakhanovite labor heroes helped transform retail work into "revolutionary Bolshevik work." Mass participation in the surveillance and regulation of retailing, and in retail reform, integrated many new people into the project to build socialism, and encouraged new senses of self. The party-state's new relationship with consumers served to promote a more collectivist and productivist consumer culture (even if it coexisted with a more individualistic and selfish culture of consumption) and to produce a Soviet version of the citizen-consumer. But the trade campaign also had *many* failures, arousing consumer discontent as it increased expectations and further politicized retailing and consumption. While consumer discontent did not lead to any mass uprisings, it did much to hollow out the authority of the Stalinist regime, particularly in light of the trade campaign's valorization of consumers' interests. It was one thing for the Soviet system to have unhappy consumers. It was quite another thing for it to have unhappy consumers who were repeatedly told that they had a right to expect better provisioning and retailing, and who were repeatedly encouraged to articulate their grievances. In the decades after the Second World War, the issues of consumption and ordinary people's material conditions became central to the Cold War. The continued failure of the Communist leadership to meet consumers' needs, and manage the challenges of mass distribution and consumption more effectively, undermined Soviet socialism and facilitated the demise of the Soviet experiment.

Notes

The following note format is used throughout the book: ARCHIVE *fond/opis'/delo: listy.*

Abbreviations used in notes:

Archives

RGASPI – Rossisskii gosudarstvennyi arkhiv sotsial'no-politicheskoi istorii (Russian State Archive of Socio-Political History)

RGAE – Rossiiski gosudarstvennyi arkhiv po ekonomiki (Russian State Archive on the Economy)

GARF – Gosudarstvennyi arkhiv Rossiiskoi Federatsii (State Archive of the Russian Federation)

TsAGM – Tsentral'nyi arkhiv goroda Moskvy (Central Archive of the City of Moscow)

TsAOPIM – Tsentral'nyi arkhiv obshchestvenno-politicheskoi istorii Moskvy (Central Archive of Socio-Political History of Moscow)

TsGAMO – Tsentral'nyi gosudarstvennyi arkhiv Moskovskoi oblasti (Central State Archive of the Moscow *Oblast'*)

GASO – Gosudarstvennyi arkhiv Saratovskoi oblasti (State Archive of the Saratov *Oblast'*)

TsDNISO – Tsentr dokumentatsii noveishei istorii Saratovskoi oblasti (Center for the Documentation of Recent History of the Saratov *Oblast'*)

TGA – Tashkentskii gorodskoi arkhiv (Tashkent City Archive)

TsGARUz – Tsentral'nyi Gosudarstvennyi Arkhiv Respubliki Uzbekistan (Central State Archive of Uzbekistan Republic)

Periodical Literature

SKT	*Snabzhenie, kooperatsiia, torgovlia*
ST	*Sovetskaia torgovlia*
VST	*Voprosy sovetskoi torgovli*
VM	*Vechernaia Moskva*
PK	*Planovoe khoziaistvo*
PE	*Problemy ekonomiki*
ZKU	*Za kul'turnyi univermag*
ZTKP	*Za tempy, kachestvo, proverku*

Introduction

1. Slavenka Drakulić, *How We Survived Communism and Even Laughed* (New York, 1993).

2. Elena Osokina, *Za fasadom "Stalinskogo izobiliia": Raspredelenie i rynok v snabzhenii naseleniia v gody industrializatsii, 1927–1941* (Moscow, 1998), 83. For similar examples, see 81–5.
3. For more on provisioning-related labor unrest, turnover, and decreased productivity, see Lewis H. Siegelbaum and Andrei Sokolov, *Stalinism as a Way of Life* (New Haven, 2000), 37–41; Wendy Z. Goldman, *Women at the Gates: Gender and Industry in Stalin's Russia* (Cambridge, 2002), 84–5; Jeffrey Rossmann, *Worker Resistance under Stalin: Class and Revolution on the Shop Floor* (Cambridge, MA, 2005), 118–19; Moshe Lewin, *The Making of the Soviet System: Essays in the Social History of Interwar Russia* (New York, 1985), 220–1; Stephen Kotkin, *Magnetic Mountain: Stalinism as Civilization* (Berkeley, 1995), 95–9; R. W. Davies, *The Industrialization of Soviet Russia 3: The Soviet Economy in Turmoil 1929–1930* (Cambridge, MA, 1989), 279–80; Arup Banerji, *Merchants and Markets in Revolutionary Russia, 1917–1930* (New York, 1997), 147–8.
4. Rosalind Williams, *Dream Worlds: Mass Consumption in Late Nineteenth-Century France* (Berkeley, 1982), 91.
5. By 1940 there were approximately 407,000 stores and stalls in the cooperative and state trade system (vs. approximately 155,000 in 1928). The number of trade workers grew from 855,000 in 1932 to 1,382,000 in 1940. Tsentral'noe statisticheskoe upravlenie, *ST – statisticheskii sbornik* (Moscow, 1956), 7, 113, 137, 140–1.
6. G. L. Rubinshtein, *Razvitie vnutrennei torgovli v SSSR* (Leningrad, 1964), 7, 15; Julie Hessler, *A Social History of Soviet Trade: Trade Policy, Retail Practices, and Consumption, 1917–1953* (Princeton, 2004), 21.
7. For the "degradation of trade," see Hessler's excellent discussion in chapter 1.
8. Alan Ball, *Russia's Last Capitalists: The Nepmen, 1921–1929* (Berkeley, 1987), 92–4; Hessler, 105–6.
9. Ball, especially 56–82, 100–8, 127–45; Sheila Fitzpatrick, "After NEP: The Fate of NEP Entrepreneurs in the 1930s," *Russian History/Histoire Russe* 13: 2–3 (Summer–Fall 1986), especially 198–207; Davies, *The Soviet Economy in Turmoil* 76–7, 287–8; I. Ia. Trifonov, *Likvidatsiia ekspluatatorskikh klassov v SSSR* (Moscow, 1975), 225–30.
10. Hessler, *A Social History of Soviet Trade*, 195.
11. Hiroaki Kuromiya, *Stalin's Industrial Revolution* (Cambridge, 1988), 306.
12. Alec Nove, *An Economic History of the U.S.S.R.* (Middlesex, reprint 1986), 228.
13. For popular disgust regarding retail tactics and the commercial sphere, see Marjorie Hilton, "Commercial Cultures: Modernity in Russia and the Soviet Union, 1880–1930," Ph.D. diss., University of Illinois, 2002; Steve Smith, "Popular Culture and Market Development in Late-Imperial Russia," in *Reinterpreting Russia*, eds., Geoffrey Hosking and Robert Service (London, 1999), 145–6.
14. Hilton, 38–9, 44, 56.
15. Quotations from Christine Ruane, "Clothes Shopping in Imperial Russia: The Development of a Consumer Culture," *Journal of Social History* 28: 4 (1995): 767–8; and Robert Gohstand, "The Internal Geography of Trade in Moscow from the Mid-Nineteenth Century to the First World War," Ph.D. diss., University of California, Berkeley, 1973, 703. For more on anxieties about modern forms of retailing, "foreign" merchants, and Russia's identity, see Gohstand, 121, 632; Hilton, 36–8, 89. For more on the contrast between

the older Russian-style of retailing and the newer and often foreign style of retailing, see Joseph Bradley, *Muzhik and Muscovite: Urbanization in Late Imperial Russia* (Berkeley, 1985), 60–5, 82–6.

16. Christine Ruane, "Clothes Make the Comrade: A History of the Russian Fashion Industry," *Russian History/Histoire Russe* 23 (1996): 318, 321; Jeffrey Burds, *Peasant Dreams and Market Politics: Labor Migration and the Russian Village, 1861–1905* (Pittsburgh, 1998), 167–9; Peter Stearns, *Consumerism in World History: The Global Transformation of Desire* (New York, 2001), 78; Steve Smith and Catriona Kelly, "Commercial Culture and Consumerism," in *Constructing Russian Culture in the Age of Revolution, 1880–1940*, eds. Catriona Kelly and David Shepherd (Oxford, 1998), 112–13, 136–7. For more on the development of a mass consumer culture, see Sally West, "The Material Promised Land: Advertising's Modern Agenda in Late Imperial Russia," *The Russian Review* 57:3 (1998): 345–65.

17. Ruane, "Clothes Shopping," 770–5; Hilton, 57–64. Hilton makes the fascinating point that some individuals worried that the commercial world also fostered "wayward" men.

18. Svetlana Boym, *Common Places: Mythologies of Everyday Life in Russia* (Cambridge, MA, 1994), especially 41–63; Christina Kiaer, *Imagine No Possessions: The Socialist Objects of Russian Constructivism* (Cambridge, MA, 2005); David Hoffmann, *Stalinist Values: The Cultural Norms of Soviet Modernity, 1917–1941* (Ithaca, 2003), 120.

19. Burds, 180–4; Smith, 149–51; Barbara Alpern Engel, "Not by Bread Alone: Subsistence Riots in Russia during World War I," *The Journal of Modern History* 69: 4 (1997): 696–721.

20. Rubinshtein, 123–45; Mary McAuley, *Bread and Justice: State and Society in Petrograd, 1917–1922* (Oxford, 1991), 280–304; Lars Lih, *Bread and Authority in Russia, 1914–1921* (Berkeley, 1990); Mauricio Borrero, *Hungry Moscow: Scarcity and Urban Society in the Russian Civil War* (New York, 2003), especially chapters 1–3, 7; Hessler, chapters 1–2.

21. Ball, especially 165–6, 170–2; Banerji, especially 44–5; Trifonov, *Likvidatsiia ekspluatatorskikh klassov v SSSR*, 225–30; L. F. Morozov, *Bor'ba protiv kapitalisticheskikh elementov v promyshlennosti i torgovle: dvadtsatye – nachalo tridtsatykh godov* (Moscow, 1978); Hessler, chapters 3 and 4.

22. Ball, 171.

23. Hessler, especially 53–61, 87–94; S. P. Dneprovskii, *Kooperatory: 1898–1968* (Moscow, 1968), especially 320–50; Rubinshtein, 176–83, 227–30.

24. Marjorie Hilton, "Retailing the Revolution: the State Department Store (GUM) and Soviet Society in the 1920s," *Journal of Social History* 37: 4 (2004): 939–64.

25. Ball, 166–8; Fitzpatrick, "After NEP," 192, 198; Hessler, 101, 109, 153–4; Randi Cox, "NEP without Nepmen! Soviet Advertising and the Transition to Socialism in the 1920s" in *Everyday Life in Early Soviet Russia: Taking the Revolution Inside*, eds. Christina Kiaer and Eric Naiman (Bloomington, 2006), 128–9; Hilton, "Retailing the Revolution," 943, 954–7; idem, "Commercial Cultures," chapter 5.

26. Ball, 165–6; Hilton, "Commercial Cultures," 326–34; Eric Naiman, *Sex in Public: The Incarnation of Early Soviet Ideology* (Princeton, 1997), 138–9, 208–24; Hoffmann, 122–3; Cox, "NEP Without Nepmen!," 121–2; Karen

Kettering, "'Ever More Cosy and Comfortable': Stalinism and the Soviet
Domestic Interior, 1928–1938," *Journal of Design History* 10: 2 (1997): 120–5;
Anne Gorsuch, "Moscow Chic: Silk Stockings and Soviet Youth," in *The
Human Tradition in Modern Russia*, ed., William Husband (Wilmington,
2000), 65–76.
27. Boym, 35–7.
28. Hilton, "Retailing the Revolution," 940, 946; Cox, "NEP Without Nepmen!,"
127–33.
29. Kiaer, especially 137; John E. Bowlt, "Constructivism and Early Soviet
Fashion Design," in *Bolshevik Culture: Experiment and Order in the Russian
Revolution* (Bloomington, 1985), Abbott Gleason, Peter Kenez, and Richard
Stites, eds., 203, 206, 210–17.
30. Hoffmann, especially chapter 1; Kiaer, chapter 2.
31. Vadim Volkov, "The Concept of *Kul'turnost'*: Notes on the Stalinist Civilizing
Process," in *Stalinism: New Directions*, ed., Sheila Fitzpatrick (New York,
2000), 210–30.
32. Nicolas Timasheff, *The Great Retreat* (New York, 1946), especially 133–40;
Leon Trotsky, *The Revolution Betrayed: What is the Soviet Union and Where is
it Going?* (New York, 1937; Reprint 1972); Sheila Fitzpatrick, "Becoming
Cultured: Socialist Realism and the Representation of Privilege and Taste,"
in *The Cultural Front* (Ithaca, 1992), 216–37; idem, *Everyday Stalinism:
Ordinary Life in Extraordinary Times: Soviet Russia in the 1930s* (Oxford, 1999),
107; Julie Hessler, "Cultured Trade: the Stalinist Turn to Consumerism," and
Volkov, "The Concept of *Kul'turnost'*," both in *Stalinism: New Directions*,
182–209 and 210–30, respectively.
33. Vera Dunham, *In Stalin's Time: Middleclass Values in Soviet Fiction* (enlarged
and updated edition, Durham, 1990), especially 49. For a similar point, see
Lewis Siegelbaum, *Stakhanovism and the Politics of Productivity in the USSR,
1935–1941* (Cambridge, 1988), 246.
34. Kotkin, *Magnetic Mountain*, 356–7.
35. In addition to works already cited, see Elena Osokina, *Ierarkhiia potrebleniia: o zhizni liudei v usloviiakh stalinskogo snabzheniia, 1928–1935 gg.*
(Moscow, 1993); *Za fasadom, 'Stalinskogo izobiliia': Raspredelenie i rynok v
snabzhenii naseleniia v gody industrializatsii, 1927–1941* (Moscow, 1998); *Our
Daily Bread: Socialist Distribution and the Art of Survival in Stalin's Russia,
1927–1941* (Armonk, 2001); Catriona Kelly and Vadim Volkov, "Directed
Desires: *Kul'turnost'* and Consumption," in *Constructing Russian Culture in
the Age of Revolution: 1881–1940* (Oxford, 1998); R. W. Davies, *The
Industrialization of Soviet Russia 4: Crisis and Progress in the Soviet Economy,
1931–33* (London, 1996); Oleg Khlevniuk and R. W. Davies, "The End of
Rationing in the Soviet Union, 1934–1935," *Europe-Asia Studies* 51: 4
(1999): 557–609; Randi Cox, "All This Can Be Yours! Soviet Commercial
Advertising and the Social Construction of Space, 1928–1956," in *The
Landscape of Stalinism: The Art and Ideology of Soviet Space*, eds. Evgeny
Dobrenko and Eric Naiman (Seattle, 2003): 125–62; Alena V. Ledeneva,
Russia's Economy of Favours: Blat, Networking, and Informal Exchange
(Cambridge, 1998). This explosion of interest in distribution, retailing,
and consumption has not been limited to the 1930s, as many of my
previous footnotes suggest.

36. *Soviet Dream World* joins a growing body of recent scholarship that uses a comparative perspective to better understand Soviet socialism. See Peter Holquist, "'Information is the Alpha and Omega of Our Work': Bolshevik Surveillance in its Pan-European Context," *Journal of Modern History* 69: 3 (1997): 415–50; David L. Hoffmann, "Mothers in the Motherland: Stalinist Pronatalism in its Pan-European Context," *Journal of Social History* 34: 1 (2000): 35–54; Stephen Kotkin, "Modern Times: The Soviet Union and the Interwar Conjuncture," *Kritika* 2: 1 (2001): 111–64; Forum: Adeeb Khalid, "Backwardness and the Quest for Civilization: Early Soviet Central Asia in Comparative Perspective," Adrienne Edgar, "Bolshevism, Patriarchy, and the Nation: The Soviet 'Emancipation' of Muslim Women in Pan-Islamic Perspective," Peter A. Blitstein, "Cultural Diversity and the Interwar Conjuncture: Soviet Nationality Policy in its Comparative Context," and Mark R. Beissinger, "Soviet Empire as 'Family Resemblance'," *Slavic Review* 65: 2 (2006): 231–303.

37. This literature is extensive. For a start, see Andre Steiner, "Dissolution of the 'Dictatorship over Needs'? Consumer Behavior and Economic Reform in East Germany in the 1960s," and Ina Merkel, "Consumer Culture in the GDR, or How the Struggle for Antimodernity was Lost on the Battleground of Consumer Culture," in *Getting and Spending: European and American Consumer Societies in the Twentieth Century,* eds. Susan Strasser, Charles McGovern, and Matthias Judt (Cambridge, 1998), 167–85 and 281–99, respectively; Susan E. Reid and David Crowley, *Style and Socialism: Modernity and Material Culture in Postwar Eastern Europe* (Oxford and New York, 2000); Susan E. Reid, "Cold War in the Kitchen: Gender and the De-Stalinization of Consumer Taste in the Soviet Union under Khrushchev," *Slavic Review* 61: 2 (2002): 211–52; Greg Castillo, "Domesticating the Cold War: Household Consumption as Propaganda in Marshall Plan Germany," *Journal of Contemporary History* 40: 2 (2005): 261–88; Uta Poiger, *Jazz, Rock, and Rebels: Cold War Politics and American Culture in a Divided Germany* (Berkeley, 2000); Judd Stitziel, *Fashioning Socialism: Clothing, Politics and Consumer Culture in East Germany* (Oxford and New York, 2005).

1 A new Approach to Retailing and Consumption: The Campaign for Soviet Trade

1. Quotation from Eds. Veronique Garros, Natalia Korenevskaya, and Thomas Lahusen, *Intimacy and Terror: Soviet Diaries of the 1930s* (New York, 1995), 209.
2. R. W. Davies, *The Industrialization of Soviet Russia 3: The Soviet Economy in Turmoil, 1929–1930* (Cambridge, MA, 1989), 155.
3. B. Berkovskii, "K voprosu o kharakteristike denezhnoi sistemy SSSR," *PE* 7–8 (1929): 158.
4. Oleg Khlevniuk and R. W. Davies, "The End of Rationing in the Soviet Union, 1934–1935," *Europe-Asia Studies* 51: 4 (1999): 559.
5. Davies, *Soviet Economy in Turmoil,* 167–71, 296.
6. Iu. Mitlianskii, "Normirovanie potrebleniia i problema tovarnykh rezervov," *PK* 2 (1930): 105–17; L. Gatovskii, "O prirode menovykh sviazei na novom

etape," *PK* 5 (1930): 147; K. Butaev, "Ot novom etape nepa," *Bol'shevik* 9 (1930): 83–98.

7. Davies, *Soviet Economy in Turmoil*, 418.
8. Wendy Z. Goldman, *Women at the Gates: Gender and Industry in Stalin's Russia* (Cambridge, 2002), 84.
9. M. D., "Vneocherednye aktivistki," *Rabotnitsa* 33 (1930): 17.
10. Jeffrey Rossmann, *Worker Resistance under Stalin: Class and Revolution on the Shop Floor* (Cambridge, MA, 2005), 119.
11. In principle the party-state planned to compensate the peasantry by establishing a supply system for villages that would allow peasants to purchase vital commodities. In practice this system functioned extremely poorly.
12. E. A. Osokina, *Za fasadom "Stalinskogo izobiliia": Raspredelenie i rynok v snabzhenii naseleniia v gody industrializatsii, 1927–1941* (Moscow, 1998), 97–8, 121; R. W. Davies, *The Industrialization of Soviet Russia 4: Crisis and Progress in the Soviet Economy, 1931–33* (London, 1996), 206–7; Julie Hessler, *A Social History of Soviet Trade: Trade Policy, Retail Practices, and Consumption, 1917–1953* (Princeton, 2004), 169.
13. *Pravda*, February 14 1930, 4.
14. *XVI s"ezd VKP (b): Stenograficheskii otchet* (Moscow, 1935), 427; Hiroaki Kuromiya, *Stalin's Industrial Revolution: Politics and Workers, 1928–1932* (Cambridge, 1988), 257–8; Davies, *Soviet Economy in Turmoil*, 408.
15. Although criticism of consumer cooperatives was not new, it intensified in 1930.
16. "O rabote potrebkooperatsii," *Pravda*, May 17 1930, 2.
17. *XVI S"ezd VKP (b)*, 71. For similar statements, see "Litsom k potrebiteliu," July 21 1930, 1; "Vsiu rabotu potrebitel'skoi kooperatsii – pod ogon' rabochei samokritiki," July 22 1930, 3, both in *Izvestiia*.
18. *XVI S"ezd VKP (b)*, 427; "Doklad predsedatel'ia Tsentrosoiuza Tov. Badaeva," *Pravda*, 25 July 1930, 7; *KPSS v resoliutsiiakh i resheniiakh s"ezdov, konferentsii i plenumov TsK*, vol. 5 (Moscow, 1984), 237–44.
19. Zelenskii as quoted in G. Neiman, *Puti razvitiia sovetskoi torgovli* (Moscow, 1934), 342.
20. "O rabote potrebitel'skoi kooperatsii," *Pravda*, February 19 1931, 1.
21. *S"ezdy sovetov RSFSR v postanovleniiakh i rezoliutsiiakh* (Moscow, 1939), 435–6.
22. My emphases. *Direktivy KPSS i sovetskogo pravitelstva po khoziaistvennym voprosam, vol. 2, 1929–1945* (Moscow, 1957), 273.
23. RGASPI 511/11/1115: 28, 30–1. For press coverage, see: September 25 1931, 3; October 31 1931, 1; November 1 1931, 1; November 11 1931, 3, all in *Pravda*.
24. *Industrializatsiia Sovetskogo Soiuza: Novye dokumenty, novye fakty, novye podkhody, vol. 2* (Moscow, 1999), 87–99. Oblomovism (*oblomovshchina*) refers to the central character of Ivan Goncharov's nineteenth-century novel, *Oblomov*, who lounges apathetically in bed and does not pursue life actively.
25. *KPSS v resoliutsiiakh*, 366–7.
26. V. Nosov, "K voprosu o prirode sovetskoi torgovli i zadachakh snabzheniia rabochikh," *PE* 10–12 (1931): 58.

27. "Potrebkooperatsiia – vazhneiushii rychag," *Izvestiia*, March 7 1931, 1; V. I. Lenin, *Polnoe sobranie sochinenii* (Moscow, 1976–1982), vol. 45, 373. For more on prerevolutionary conceptualizations of "Asiatic" retailing, see Robert Gohstand, "The Internal Geography of Trade in Moscow from the Mid-Nineteenth Century to the First World War," Ph.D. diss., University of California, Berkeley, 1973; Christine Ruane, "Clothes Shopping in Imperial Russia," *Journal of Social History* (Summer 1995): especially 766–7.
28. Nosov, 51; L. Gatovskii, *O prirode sovetskoi torgovli na sovremennom etape* (Moscow, 1931), 87, 142.
29. I. V. Stalin, *Sochineniia* 13 (Moscow, 1951), 203–4.
30. *XVII s"ezd VKP (b): Stenograficheskii otchet* (Moscow, 1934), 26.
31. L. Kaganovich quoted Lenin in January 1932. See E. S. Fain, *Bor'ba za sotsializm i sovetskaia torgovlia* (Moscow, 1932), 20. For other references to this dictum, see Nosov, 60; L. Gatovskii, "O kharaktere sovetskoi torgovli na sovremennom etape," *PE* 7 (1931): 155; V. Stushkov, "Sovetskaia torgovlia vo vtoroi piatiletke," *ST* 2 (1934): 30; "Litsom k sovetskoi torgovle," *Pravda*, September 25 1931, 3.
32. For example, Lenin talked about how "the smart communist" should not be afraid of learning from capitalists, even when it came to trade (Lenin, vol. 43, 242–4). He also noted that "to learn to understand commercial relations and trade – this is our duty"; and "The proletarian government can master trade, give it direction, and place it within a certain framework" (Vol. 44, 218 and 227. In 1922 Lenin said that the "responsible communist" did not know how to carry out trade and did not "understand that it is necessary to learn from the ABCs" (vol. 45, 82).
33. Fain, 20. Zelenskii made a similar point about Lenin's instructions in "O tekushchikh zadachakh potrebkooperatsii," *Problemy marksizma* 5–6 (1931): 4–5.
34. *KPSS v resoliutsiiakh*, 396–7.
35. Neiman, *Puti razvitiia*, 70–1; Gatovskii, "O kharaktere sovetskoi torgovli," 152; Stalin, *Sochineniia* 13, 58–9, 202.
36. Gatovskii, "O kharaktere sovetskoi torgovli," 145–96.
37. *KPSS v resoliutsiiakh*, 397; *XVII s"ezd*, 26.
38. Khlevniuk and Davies, 557, 561.
39. Ibid., 561.
40. Davies, *Crisis and Progress*, 62, 206–7.
41. RGASPI 511/11/1115: 25, 37–8.
42. Ibid., 28–9.
43. RGASPI 17/2/477: 239–40.
44. Z. S. Bolotin, *Bez kartochek* (Moscow, 1935), 6; G. Neiman, "Otmena kartochek, razvertyvanie tovarooborota i ukruplenia rubliia," *PE* 1 (1935): 60.
45. Quoted in Khlevniuk and Davies, 575. Stalin made this comment in an unpublished speech in 1934.
46. RGASPI 511/11/1115: 37–8.
47. Molotov quoted in Neiman, "Otmena kartochek," 56.
48. Kaganovich quoted in G. Ia. Neiman, *Vnutrennaia torgovlia SSSR* (Moscow, 1935), 279; Osokina, 175; Bolotin, *Bez kartochek*, 6, 22; Neiman, "Otmena kartochek," 59–60.

49. Torgsin stores, which allowed customers to purchase items in exchange for valuables (such as gold, diamonds, and so on) but not ordinary Soviet rubles, were another important venue for retailing in the 1930s. But authorities never championed them as part of "Soviet trade," partly because of the shameful way in which they functioned, encouraging people to part with precious family heirlooms (and the like) to procure basic foodstuffs. Torgsin stores were closed in early 1936. Osokina, 161–9.
50. *KPSS v rezoliutsiiakh*, 205–6, 242; G. L. Rubinshtein, *Razvitie vnutrennei torgovli v SSSR* (Leningrad, 1964), 290.
51. Sheila Fitzpatrick, *Everyday Stalinism: Ordinary Life in Extraordinary Times: Soviet Russia in the 1930s* (Oxford, 1999), 55–6, 97; Hessler, 171.
52. By January 1934, workers' supply departments (a form of closed trade) served almost 16.5 million workers and their family members. Eds. L. Gatovskii, G. Neiman, and V. Nodel, *Ekonomika sovetskoi torgovli* (Moscow, 1934), 255.
53. Nosov, 56.
54. Z. Bolotin, "Itogi i perspektivy razvitiia sovetskoi torgovli," *PK* 1 (1935): 152.
55. *XVII s"ezd*, 184.
56. Rubinshtein, 331; G. A. Dikhtiar, *Sovetskaia torgovlia v period postroeniia sotsializma* (Moscow, 1961), 401.
57. Davies, *Soviet Economy in Turmoil*, 302; Rubinshtein, 294–6; V. Nodel', "O zakrytoi i otkrytoi torgovle," *ST* 6 (1933): 23. Narkomsnab and its successor, Narkomvnutorg, were officially in charge of most of these stores, although various industries also administered a small but not insignificant network of stores.
58. Nodel', 23; G. Neiman, "O sovetskoi torgovli," *PE* 2 (1934): 13; Iu. Shnirlin, "Roznichnaia torgovlia vo vtoroi piateletke," *PK* 4 (1934): 115–16.
59. Nodel', 23; *XVII s"ezd*, 27, 181; Bolotin, *Bez kartochek*, 15.
60. *KPSS v resoliutsiiakh i resheniiakh s"ezdov, konferentsii i plenumov TsK*, vol. 6 (1985), 274–8. For some positive results of reorganization, see Dikhtiar, 400–1, 424–7.
61. Dikhtiar, 399, 401.
62. Hessler, 208–9; Dikhtiar, 404, 406. For example, in 1937 the number of cameras distributed to the countryside for sale was 10.5 times higher than the number distributed in 1932. But in 1937 the percentage of cameras sold in the countryside still constituted a negligible percentage of the total for sale in the Soviet Union, a mere 5.9 percent.
63. Davies, *Soviet Economy in Turmoil*, 284, 303; *Crisis and Progress*, 213. Government regulation was not very effective. But it did exist. For example, the government required sellers to purchase licenses.
64. Policy changes in 1932, particularly regarding *kolkhoz* trade, fueled talk about a new "neo-NEP" stage in the economy. For more on the reforms, see Davies, *Crisis and Progress*, 209–19. For the idea of a "Neo-NEP," see Vadim Rogovin, *Stalinskii neonep* (Moscow, 1992), 21–9.
65. Stalin and Molotov quoted in Neiman, *Puti razvitiia*, 85–6.
66. Osokina, *Ierarkhiia potrebleniia: o zhizni liudei v usloviiakh stalinskogo snabzheniia, 1928–1935 gg.* (Moscow, 1993), 108.
67. Hessler, 256–7.
68. Stalin, *Sochineniia* 13, 58–9.

69. *XVII s''ezd*, 26.
70. Stalin, *Sochineniia* 13, 59.
71. *KPSS v resoliutsiiakh*, vol 5, 393.
72. Davies, *Crisis and Progress*, 203–6, 222–3.
73. Jeffrey Rossmann, *Worker Resistance under Stalin: Class and Revolution on the Shop Floor* (Cambridge, MA, 2005).
74. *Direktivy KPSS*, 352–7.
75. S. M. Kirov, *Ob itogakh sentiabrskogo plenuma TsK VKP(b)* (Moscow, 1932), 27–32.
76. When the Second FYP was finally approved, extremely ambitious target goals from early on in the planning process had been revised and reduced.
77. For example, Dikhtiar claims there were 982 millions of canned goods in 1937 vs. 95 million in 1913. Dikhtiar, 365–7, 404; P. S. Zhemchuzhina, *The Food Industry of the U.S.S.R.* (Moscow, 1939), 20–6.
78. While there was some improvement in the general standard of living between 1934 and 1936, scarcity and material deprivation persisted. R. W. Davies, Mark Harrison, and S. G. Wheatcroft, eds., *The Economic Transformation of the Soviet Union, 1913–1945* (Cambridge, 1994), 17, 54, 102–3, 302.
79. Quoted in Naum Jasny, *Soviet Industrialization, 1928–1952* (Chicago, 1961), 76.
80. I. V. Stalin, *Sochineniia* I [XIV], 1934–1940 (Stanford, 1967), 81.
81. *XVIII S''ezd VKP (b): Stenograficheskii otchet* (Moscow, 1939), 18. By the West, I mean the United States and Western Europe.
82. F. G. Shumakov, "Potrebitel'skii spros kolkhoznoi derevni na sovremennom etape," in *Potreblenie i spros v SSSR*, ed., A. I. Malkis (Leningrad, 1935), 157.
83. I. Plotnikov, "Stakhanovskoe dvizhenie i bor'ba za kul'turu torgovogo obsluzhivaniia," in *Za stakhanovskoe dvizhenie v sovetskoi torgovle*, ed., G. Ia. Neiman (Moscow, 1936), 102.
84. Authorities adopted plans, for example, for the mass production of champagne, establishing targets of 500,000 bottles in 1937 and 800,000 in 1938, and in 1937 and 1938 "new factories, vineyards, and warehouses opened to satisfy the plans of the Party and the central government." For more on the creation of a "luxury goods" economy in the 1930s, see Jukka Gronow, *Caviar with Champagne: Common Luxury and the Ideals of the Good Life in Stalin's Russia* (Oxford and New York, 2003), 24.
85. The mass production of records was particularly successful, and in 1939 an extraordinary 60 million records were sold. Zhemchuzhina, 26; Dikhtiar, 404; Gronow, 63.
86. Sheila Fitzpatrick also points out how authorities depicted some items as symbols of modernity in *Everyday Stalinism*, 90–1.
87. Eugene Gordon, *Pancakes and Caviar: The Food Industry in the U.S.S.R.* (Moscow, 1936), 30; A. Mikoian, "Dva mesiatsa v SShA," *SShA, ekonomika, politika, ideologiia* 11 (1971): 76.
88. "Bul'on v kubikakh," *VM*, September 19 1937, 2; "Obed iz polufabrikatov," *Trud*, July 17 1936, 3.
89. Z. Bolotin, *Sovetskaia torgovlia v stakhanovskom godu* (Moscow, 1937), 39. Semi-prepared food products were also depicted as important conveniences for young housewives, unfamiliar with "the subtleties of culinary affairs," and for bachelors.

90. A. I. Malkis, "Potreblenie i spros v stranakh kapitala i v SSSR," and G. A. Zhukovskii, "Sdvigi potrebitel'skom sprose gorodskogo naseleniia SSSR," in *Potreblenie i spros v SSSR*, 49 and 74; A. Leon'tev, "Zamechatel'naia vystavka," *Pravda*, July 21 1935, 4.
91. Russian State Library, Poster Collection, P5 II.9d/2.D.
92. "Voprosy nashego byta," *Trud*, August 3 1936, 3. A.V. Artiukhina was head of the *Zhenotdel* from 1925 to 1930. For more on Artiukhina, see Barbara Clements, *Bolshevik Women* (1997), 267; and Wendy Z. Goldman, "The Death of the Proletarian Women's Movement," *Slavic Review* 55: 1 (1996): 54–62. In a 1930 discussion about *byt'*, Artiukhina advocated the growth of collective institutions and resources for women and children in place of an increase in individual "mops, irons, and frying pans." See her "Za sotsialisticheskuiu peredelku byta," *Rabotnitsa* 4 (1930): 3. But because of the slow growth of such collective facilities, by 1936 Artiukhina also emphasized the importance of consumer items that would improve women's daily lives on a more individual basis. Thanks to Barbara Clements for pointing out Artiukhina's earlier position.
93. O. Ershova, "O torgovle tekhnicheskoi igrushkoi," *Sovetskaia igrushka* 3 (1936): 29; and Zavriev, "Vystavka igrushek v Tbilisi," *Igrushka* 5 (1938): 16.
94. S. Likhov, "Uluchshit' kachestvo tekhnicheskoi igrushki," *ST*, 5 June 1935, 4; G. Svistunov, "V 'zakoldovannom krugu'," *Igrushka* 8 (1937): 28; TsAGM 2458/1/122: 6.
95. A. T. Kovaleva, "Bol'she zaboty ob assortimente," *Sovetskaia igrushka* 6 (1935): 29. Another sign of the recasting of trade as a socialist affair was an article that applauded the value of children pretending to be salespeople and customers in their play games. V. Nikonov, "Nash magazin," *Igrushka* 7 (1938): 24.
96. RGAE 7971/1/250: 46, 35, respectively.
97. For toys and Soviet socialization, see Catriona Kelly, "Shaping the 'Future Race': Regulating the Daily Life of Children in Early Soviet Russia," in *Everyday Life in Early Soviet Russia: Taking the Revolution Inside* (Bloomington, 2006), especially 267–70.
98. My emphasis. *XVII s"ezd*, 30–1.
99. David Hoffmann points out that the "purported attainment of socialism" in the mid-1930s allowed Party leaders to embrace "material well-being" as "central to the vision of life under socialism." See *Stalinist Values: The Cultural Norms of Soviet Modernity* (Cornell, 2003), 125.
100. Stalin, *Sochineniia* I [XIV], 89–90. The *oprichniki* were members of a private guard assembled by Ivan the Terrible in the sixteenth century to terrorize and subdue the general population.
101. "Bol'she tovarov shirpotreba!" *Rabotnitsa* 23 (1938), 2.
102. "Chto my pokupaem ran'she, chto pokupaem teper'," *ST*, October 29 1937, 3.
103. Karen Petrone, *Life has Become More Joyous, Comrades: Celebrations in the Time of Stalin* (Bloomington, 2000), 6.
104. Quotation from Sarah Davies, *Popular Opinion in Stalin's Russia: Terror, Propaganda, and Dissent, 1934–1941* (Cambridge, 1997), 35.
105. Eds. Sheila Fitzpatrick and Yuri Slezkine, *In the Shadow of Revolution: Life Stories of Russian Women from 1917 to the Second World War* (Princeton, 2000), 399–400.

106. Vadim Volkov, "The Concept of *Kul'turnost'*: Notes on the Stalinist Civilizing Process," in *Stalinism: New Directions*, ed., Sheila Fitzpatrick (London and New York, 2000), 210–30. For a similar argument, see Marina Vitukhnovskaia, "'Starye' i 'novye' gorozhane: migranty v Leningrade 1930-x godov," in *Normy i tsennosti povsednevnoi zhizni: stanovlenie sotsialisticheskogo obraza zhizni v Rossii, 1920–1930-e gody* (Saint Petersburg, 2000), 99–150. For more on *kul'turnost'*, see Catriona Kelly and Vadim Volkov, "Directed Desires: *Kul'turnost'* and Consumption," in *Constructing Russian Culture in the Age of Revolution, 1881–1940* (Oxford, 1998), 291–313; Julie Hessler, "Cultured Trade: the Stalinist Turn to Consumerism," in *Stalinism: New Directions*, 182–209; Sheila Fitzpatrick, "Becoming Cultured: Socialist Realism and the Representation of Privilege and Taste," in *The Cultural Front: Power and Culture in Revolutionary Russia* (Ithaca, 1992); Vera Dunham, *In Stalin's Time* (London, 1976; Durham, 1990). For the ruralization of cities, see Moshe Lewin, *The Making of the Soviet System: Essays in the Social History of Interwar Russia* (New York, 1985), 220.
107. Quoted in Khlevniuk and Davies, 576.
108. Bolotin, *Bez kartochek*, 27.
109. For example, see *Za industrializatsiiu*, "Pokupatel' idet tuda, gde luchshe torguiut,' January 2 1935, 1; "Pokupatel' beret tol'ko khoroshii khleb," January 9 1935, 3; "Uvelichivaetsia torgovyi oborot – plokhie magaziny teriaiut pokupatelei," *Pravda*, October 10 1935, 3; Bolotin, *Bez kartochek*, 25.
110. Z. Bolotin, "Kul'turno torgovat' i zabotit'sia o potrebitele," *Bol'shevik* 3 (1935): 36.
111. V. Stushkov, "O sovetskoi torgovle v svete zadachi vtoroi piatiletki," *PE* 6 (1932): 62–80, esp. 69.
112. For example, Molotov claimed that Soviet trade could help to introduce a new culture in the daily life of the populace. *Pravda*, January 17 1936, 1. For more on how Soviet trade could contribute to acculturation, see Chapter 4.
113. Bolotin, "Kul'turno torgovat'," 36; "Rech' tov. I. Ia. Veitsera," January 14 1936, 3; and "Luchshe torgovat'," July 29 1936, 2, both in *Pravda*.
114. TsAGM 489/1/93: 164ob.
115. Mikoian cited in Gordon, 41.
116. Plotnikov, 92; V. M. Molotov, "Plan i nashi zadachi," *Pravda*, January 11 1936, 1–3.
117. A. Pavlovich, "Novoe v kolkhoznom sprose i nashi zadachi," *ST* 4 (1935): 17. Economist Shnirlin similarly applauded collective farm workers who no longer limited their consumer demands to simple items of mass consumption, such as shoes or cloth, but instead asked for "iron beds, enamel-ware dishes, silk articles, and a fine quality of ready-made clothes, cultured goods, and haberdashery" (Shnirlin, 123).
118. I. Ia. Veitser, "Voprosy sovetskoi torgovli," *Bol'shevik* 8 (1936): 13.
119. Lewis Siegelbaum, *Stakhanovism and the Politics of Productivity in the USSR, 1935–1941* (Cambridge, 1988), 228.
120. As the head of an Uzbek state trade organization explained, "Last year the opinion that European good[s] were not in demand in villages [in Central Asia] was dispelled." Among other things, he noted, the demand for

European shoes exceeded the supply. "Respublikanskii slet otlichnikov torgovli," *Pravda Vostoka*, January 18 1936, 1.
121. "Bibliografiia," *ST* 9 (1936): 79.
122. "Respublikanskii slet otlichnikov torgovli," 1.
123. A. I. Mikoian, "Pishchevaia industriia Sovetskogo Soiuza," *Rabochaia Moskva*, January 24 1936, 3.

2 The *"Perestroika"* of Retail Trade: Visionary Planning for Revolutionary Retailing

1. RGASPI 17/3/974: 21; M. Epshtein, *Osnovnye zadachi Moskovskoi torgovli* (Moscow, 1936), 22.
2. When the store initially opened it offered 6 fixed prices. Later the store adopted 11 prices. RGASPI 17/21/3051: 15; RGAE 7971/1/233: 255.
3. I. Saffo, "Torgovlia po standartnymi tsenam," June 10 1937, 3; "Novye tovary univermaga standartnykh tsen,' August 29 1937, 4, both in *ST*; L. Zholkovskii, "Magazin standartnykh tsen," *VST* 4–5 (1938): 64–83.
4. "Otchet pered pokupateliami," *ST*, October 10 1937, 1.
5. *Direktivy KPSS i sovetskogo pravitelstva po khoziaistvennym voprosam, vol. 2, 1929–1945* (Moscow, 1957), 327, 330; *KPSS v resoliutsiiakh i resheniiakh s''ezdov, konferentsii i plenumov TsK*, vol. 5 (Moscow, 1984), 397.
6. When I refer to trade authorities, I mean top- and low-level state officials, planners, administrators, and economists.
7. Z. Bolotin, a deputy commissar of trade, entitled a section of his book, "The Organized *Perestroika* of Trade." Z. Bolotin, *Reshaiushchii god v razvertyvanii sovetskoi torgovli* (Moscow, 1936), 26. Other trade authorities also used this term. See G. Ia. Neiman, *Vnutrenniaia torgovlia SSSR* (Moscow, 1935), 348; Epshtein, 16.
8. I. Zelenskii, "O tekhushchikh zadachakh potrebkooperatsii v sviazi s resheniem TsK VKP(b) i SNK SSSR ot maia 12 1931," *Problemy marksizma* 5–6 (1931), 13–14.
9. GARF 5452/28/428: 349.
10. RGAE 7971/1/246: 19–20, 40; GARF 5452/28/48: 60ob; L. Berlinraut, "Posylochnaia torgovlia v SShA," *ST* 3 (1936): 78; I. Isaev, "Torgovlia v Amerike," *Izvestiia*, November 1 1936, 4; idem, "Kak torguiut prodovol'stviem v Amerike," *Za pishchevuiu industriiu*, November 2 1936, 3.
11. RGASPI 17/3/975: 6; 17/3/977: 7; 17/114/615: 4; RGAE 7971/1/246 and 371a; 7971/16/24: 132; 7971/16/25: 26–32, 42–4, 61–5, 70–2, 80–2, 158, 266–70. For a brief discussion of how trade leaders traveled to the West in search of new "commercial techniques," see Julie Hessler, "Cultured Trade: The Stalinist Turn to Consumerism," in *Stalinism: New Directions*, ed., Sheila Fitzpatrick (London and New York, 2000), 191. According to Osokina, the Soviet leadership's interest in reproducing the "abundance" they saw in capitalist retailing – both in terms of consumer goods as well as trade equipment – "appeared genuine." Elena Osokina, *Za fasadom, "Stalinskogo izobiliia": Raspredelenie i rynok v snabzhenii naseleniia v gody industrializatsii, 1927–1941* (Moscow, 1997), 176.

12. Many household items, for example, were brought back and displayed at an exhibit organized by the All-Union Chamber of Commerce. Specialists then selected goods for mass production that were not yet produced in the U.S.S.R. "Bytovoi shirpotreb," *VM*, August 11 1937, 2. For more on the borrowing of goods and machinery, see Jukka Gronow, *Caviar with Champagne: Common Luxury and the Ideals of the Good Life in Stalin's Russia* (Berg, 2003), 74–5, 116.

13. GARF 5446/18a/272: 126; RGAE 7971/1/234: 116–18.

14. RGASPI 17/3/975: 6.

15. Epshtein, 20, 22; Iu. Berkovich, "Stakhanovskoe dvizhenie v torgovle," *ST* 12 (1935): 23.

16. "Dvizhushchaiasia vitrina," and "Stend s podstavkoi dlia gotovogo plat'ia," *ZKU* 2 (1937), 18–19, 22; "Okonnye vitriny," *ZKU* 3 (1937): 20–2. For Selfridge, see Victoria de Grazia, *Irresistible Empire: America's Advance through 20th-Century Europe* (Cambridge, MA, 2005), 138–9; Erika Diane Rappaport, *Shopping for Pleasure: Women in the Making of London's West End* (Princeton, 2000), 144–70.

17. Quoted in Hessler, 191.

18. Emile Zola, *The Ladies' Paradise* (1883), trans. Brian Nelson (Berkeley, 1992). For France's association with a bourgeois regime of consumption, see Michael B. Miller, *The Bon Marché: Bourgeois Culture and the Department Store, 1869–1920* (Princeton, 1981); De Grazia, *Irresistible Empire*, 154–9; Leora Auslunder, *Taste and Power: Furnishing Modern France* (Berkeley, 1996); Lisa Tiersten, *Marianne in the Market: Envisioning Consumer Society in Fin-de-Siècle France* (Berkeley, 2001).

19. See Gronow.

20. "Iz praktiki zagranichnykh universal'nykh magazinov," *ZKU* 6 (1936): 11–19; I. Tsitron, "Bor'ba za pokupatelia," *ST* 3 (1936): 58–64; RGAE 7971/1/371a: 1–7. For Tsarist Russia's interest in German technologies and practices, see Kendall Bailes, "The American Connection: Ideology and the Transfer of American Technology to the Soviet Union, 1917–1941," *Comparative Studies in Society and History* 23: 3 (1981): 425–48.

21. T. Gumnitskii, "Kak zavoevyvaiut pokupatelia," *ST* 1 (1937): 64.

22. The monthly journal *Sovetskaia torgovlia* (renamed *VST* in 1938) provided readers with sections entitled, "Techniques of trade," "The organization and techniques of capitalist trade," and "Trade technology from abroad" in which new retail technologies and methods from capitalist countries, especially the United States, were often discussed. The journal *ZKU* referred specifically to articles published in American retail journals in 1936 and 1937.

23. M. P. Smirnov, "Prodovol'stvennaia torgovlia," February 27 1937, 2; M. Tupitsyn, "Promtovaryne magaziny v SShA," October 27 1936, 2, both in *ST*; "Amerikanskie produktovye sverkhrynki," *VST* 4–5 (1938): 106–10.

24. Joseph Bradley, *Guns for the Tsar: American Technology and the Small Arms Industry in Nineteenth-Century Russia* (DeKalb, 1990); Bailes, 428–9.

25. Quoted in Bailes, 428.

26. Hans Rogger, "Amerikanizm and the Economic Development of Russia," *Comparative Studies in Society and History* 23: 3 (1981); Alan Ball, *Imagining America: Influence and Images in Twentieth-Century Russia* (New York and

Oxford, 2003). This interest was not one-sided. Many Americans were similarly fascinated with the Soviet Union's economic experimentation as a possible model for emulation. David Engerman, *Modernization from the Other Shore: American Intellectuals and the Romance of Russian Development* (Cambridge, MA, 2004).

27. De Grazia, *Irresistible Empire*, 171 and chapter 3. For German fascination with and anxiety about the U.S., see Mary Nolan, *Visions of Modernity: American Business and the Modernization of Germany* (Oxford, 1994). For general European interest and ambivalence, see Victoria de Grazia, "Changing Consumption Regimes in Europe," in *Getting and Spending: European and American Consumer Societies in the Twentieth Century* (Cambridge, 1998), 59–83.

28. For these efforts, see Chapter 5.

29. RGAE 7971/1/105: 70.

30. Bolotin, *Reshaiushchii*, 56.

31. Zelenskii, 13; GARF 5446/18a/281: 21–2; 5452/28/119: 320.

32. G. Neiman, "Za razvernutuiu sovetskuiu torgovliu," *PK* 2 (1932): 77–8.

33. GARF 5452/28/119: 318–19; RGAE 7971/1/195: 71, 73.

34. A. Koniaev, "O vesoizmeritel'nom khoziaistve," *ST* 10–11 (1935): 141. To improve manufacturing, Communist authorities ordered the standardization of weighing and measuring devices. K. Grichik and V. Pirkovskii, eds., *Organizatsiia i pravila roznichnoi torgovli* (Moscow, 1936), 213.

35. Koniaev, 141; I. Aizenshtein, "Za kul'turnoe vesovoe khoziaistvo," *ST* 5 (1934): 74; GARF 5446/18a/281: 6, 24; RGAE 7971/1/105: 73.

36. By 1911 the National Cash Register (NCR) Company had produced one million cash registers. *Cash Registers to Computers* (Dayton, 1984), 7. The NCR introduced the mechanized cash register to Europe in the 1880s, and by the interwar era had established European subsidiaries for mass production. See de Grazia, *Irresistible Empire*, 163.

37. GARF 5446/18a/281: 23. To remedy the situation, Narkomvnutorg sent specialists abroad to bring back sample models for possible emulation and to conclude purchasing agreements with companies. Of particular interest were registers from the American company, "National Cash Register." Ultimately the trade establishment envisioned the expansion of domestically produced and standardized mechanical cash registers that would combine all the best elements of foreign models. RGAE 7971/16/25: 72; I. K. i L. P., "Sovetskie avtomaticheskie kassy," *ST* 1 (1933): 136–7; Z. Bolotin, "Kul'turno torgovat' i zabotit'sia o potrebitele," *Bol'shevik* 3 (1935): 40; I. Kaganov, "Rekonstruktsiia material'no-tekhnicheskoi bazy torgovli," *ST* 1 (1934): 138.

38. Bolotin, "Kul'turno," 40; P. Savostikov, "Mekhanizatsiia i khladofikiatsiia v sovetskoi torgovle," *VST* 5 (1939): 20; Kaganov, 138.

39. RGAE 7971/1/275: 156.

40. TsAGM 2458/1/47: 6ob.

41. N. Shinkarevskii, "Chto my videli v SShA," *VM*, March 13 1937, 2. Trade delegate Breidov also reported on the prominence of refrigeration in the United States in RGAE 7971/1/246: 43.

42. RGAE 7971/1/246: 55; Isaev, "Torgovlia v Amerike," 4; S. Chizhevskii, "Novoe v oborudovanii plodoovshchnykh magazinov," *ST* 10–11 (1935): 129–30.

43. Chizhevskii, 129–30.
44. *Potrebitel'skaia kooperatsiia ot VI k VII s"ezdu sovetov soiuza SSR* (Moscow, 1935), 25; TsAGM 346/1/57: 4a; Epshtein, 21; I. Tsitron, "O rekonstruktsii torgovoi seti Moskvy," *ST*, November 24 1937, 3; GARF 5452/28/119: 319.
45. E. P. Golovina, "Bor'ba partii za razvitie torgovli v period pobedi uprocheniia sotsializma, 1933–1941," in *Sbornik trudov*, vol. 34 (Leningrad, 1969), 256–308; *Potrebitel'skaia kooperatsiia*, 26–7.
46. GARF 5446/18a/281: 22; N. B. Perepelitskii, "Novoe v obsluzhivanii pokupatelei," *ST*, June 3 1936, 2. Trade authorities claimed that prepackaging was good for food and nonfood items. RGAE 7971/1/246: 37; T. Gumnitskii, "Priemka, khranenie i kontrol' v univermage firmy Meisi," *ST* 2 (1937): 66.
47. GARF 5452/28/119: 318; I. Tsitron, "Kul'tura torgovli," *VM*, June 3 1937, 2; Smirnov, "Prodovol'stvennaia," 2.
48. Tsitron, "Kul'tura torgovli," 2; M. P. Smirnov, "Iz opyta Amerikanskoi prodovol'stvennoi torgovli," *ST* 5 (1937): 55; RGAE 7971/1/275: 155–6.
49. K. M., *VM*, September 16 1937, 3. For dirty paper, also see GARF 5452/28/70: 16.
50. Narkomvnutorg issued a 1936 decree forbidding the use of such paper. RGAE 7971/1/228: 74–7.
51. GARF 5446/18a/278: 1–5; G. Neiman, "Sovetskaia torgovlia na pod"eme," *ST* 4–5 (1936): 20.
52. GARF 5452/28/428: 500, 508–9. For similar views, see idem., 5452/28/435: 178, 181.
53. GARF 5452/28/9: 13.
54. GARF 5452/28/435: 180.
55. M. Ostroumov and I. Tsitron, "Tekhnicheskoe oborudovanie krupnogo univermaga," *ST* 1 (1936): 67; "Protivopozharnye meropriatiia," *ZKU* 1 (1937): 21–2.
56. RGAE 7971/1/246: 19–20, 40.
57. Epshtein, 16–24.
58. Christine Ruane, "Clothes Shopping in Imperial Russia: The Development of a Consumer Culture," *Journal of Social History* 28 (1995): 767.
59. GARF 5452/28/9: 12.
60. Bolotin, *Reshaiushchii*, 61.
61. Epshtein, 16–24. For similar negative commentary, see "Zadachi stakhanovskogo goda v torgovle," *ST* 1 (1936): 9; Bolotin, "Kul'turno," 39. For more on the planning for rural stores and their architectural design, see A. Zhivotovskii i V. Makhov, "Rol' i zadachi raimagov v sele," *ST* 2 (1934): 74–84; M. Ostroumov i I. Tsitron, "Tipovye proekty raimagov i sel'magov Tsentrosoiuza," *ST* 4–5 (1936): 117–24.
62. RGAE 484/1/2725: 75.
63. RGAE 7971/1/246: 32–3.
64. T. L. Gumnitskii, "Proektirovanie krupnykh univermagov," *ST*, June 10 1937, 3.
65. Bolotin, *Reshaiushchii*, 60.
66. D. Frenkel', "Torgovoe oborudovanie dolzhno byt' standartnym," *ST*, August 3 1936, 3. The one Soviet factory that produced trade equipment did not make standardized furniture and was "completely underutilized."

67. Bolotin, "Kul'turno," 39; RGAE 7971/1/246: 3, 24, 38, 56; Isaev, "Torgovlia v Amerike," 4.
68. Smirnov, "Iz opyta," 54.
69. RGAE 7971/1/246: 4; Kaganov, 127; Smirnov, "Iz opyta," 54.
70. For Bolotin's various statements about uniform layout, see GARF 5452/28/48: 58–58ob; Bolotin, *Reshaiushchii*, 56; idem, "Kul'turno," 39. Others also praised the standardized layout of American stores, such as Epshtein, 20.
71. TsAODM 69/1/944: 39.
72. RGAE 7971/1/246: 3–4.
73. William Leach, *Land of Desire: Merchants, Power, and the Rise of a New American Culture* (New York, 1993), 317–18.
74. "Iz praktiki zagranichnykh universal'nykh magazinov," *ZKU* 6 (1936): 13.
75. V. Lysykh, "Kak torgovat' galantereei," April 3 1936, 2; N. Strogov, "Vitrina trikotazhnykh i bel'evykh tovarov," March 10 1936, 3, both in *ST*; "Kak luchshe organizovat' prodazhu tualetnykh prinadlezhnostei," *ZKU* 4 (1936): 14.
76. M. Shereshevskii, "Zadachi sovetskoi torgovoi reklamy," *VST* 8 (1939): 32.
77. RGAE 7971/1/246: 5–6.
78. Tsitron, "Bor'ba," 59. Soviet advertising has been explored in great detail elsewhere. See R. Barnz, "Obshchestvennaia psikhologiia v SShA i SSSR 20-30-x godov v svete teorii potrebleniia," *Voprosy istorii* 2 (1995): 133–7; Randi Cox, "All This Can Be Yours! Soviet Commercial Advertising and the Social Construction of Space, 1928–1956," in *The Landscape of Stalinism: The Art and Ideology of Soviet Space*, eds. Evgeny Dobrenko and Eric Naiman (Seattle, 2003): 125–62; "NEP Without Nepmen! Soviet Advertising and the Transition to Socialism in the 1920s" in *Everyday Life in Early Soviet Russia: Taking the Revolution Inside*, eds. Christina Kiaer and Eric Naiman (Bloomington, 2006), 119–51; Christina Kiaer, *Imagine No Possessions: The Socialist Objects of Russian Constructivism* (Cambridge, MA, 2005), 143–97.
79. Bolotin, *Reshaiushchii*, 66; Lermakhovskii, "Bol'she vnimaniia vitrine," *ST* 6 (1935): 76. Poor displays were also the result of goods shortages.
80. "Torgovaia tekhnika za granitsei," *VST* 7 (1938): 67.
81. Shereshevskii, 32.
82. V. Morozov and M. Shereshevskii, "O dvizhushcheisia reklame," *ST*, February 24 1936, 3; Bolotin, *Reshaiushchii*, 67.
83. Tsitron, "Bor'ba," 59–63; V. Vinogradov i T. Gunina, "Organizatsiia vitrinnoi reklamy," *ST* 5 (1937): 46–7; "Iz zagranichnoi pechati," *ZKU* 6 (1936): 8; B. Il'in, "O vitrine i inventare dlia nee," *ZKU* 2 (1937): 7–9; T. L. Gumnitskii, "Vitrina, osveshchenie," *ZKU* 3 (1937): 2–3.
84. RGAE 7971/1/246: 3–4.
85. "Pigli-Uigli," *ST*, No. 11 (2651) January 1935, 4. Piggly Wiggly stores were the first self-service groceries in the United States. For similar statements about the cost effectiveness of self-service shopping, see "Amerikanskie produktovye sverkhrynki," 107.
86. "Dva chasa v ocheredi," *VM*, January 13 1936, 3.
87. Chizhevskii, 123.
88. "V ocheredi za mandarinom," *VM*, January 25 1936, 2; "O prostykh vesh-chakkh," *ST*, August 30 1937, 4; Alexander Wicksteed, *Life under the Soviets*

(London, 1928), 6–7; Nauchno-issledovatel'skii Institut Potrebkooperatsii, *Organizatsiia i tekhnika sovetskoi roznichnoi torgovli* (Leningrad, 1933), 129.

89. GARF 5452/23/112: 137.
90. L. Darinskaia i I. Strogov, "Novye metody i formy obsluzhivaniia pokupatelia," *ST* 7–8 (1936): 95–100.
91. Epshtein, 22–3.
92. N. Shinkarevskii, "Torgovlia shtuchnymi tovarami," *ST* 4 (1937): 55.
93. Isaev, "Torgovlia v Amerike," 4.
94. G. Ravdin, "Novye formy torgovli," *ST* 2–3 (1932): 192–9.
95. V. Utrobin, "Dostavka tovarov na dom," *ST* 10–11 (1935): 137–40; Perepelitskii, 2; RGAE 7971/1/246: 44, 56.
96. "Palatki-peredvizhki," *Stakhanovets torgovli* 1 (1936): 2; RGAE 7971/1/238: 79–80, 99–101; 7971/1/270: 378; F. Kilevits, "Peredovoe tekhnicheskoe oborudovanie – na sluzhbu kul'turnoi sovetskoi torgovle," *ST* 6 (1936): 60; "Avtolavka v raione," *ST*, May 16 1936, 2; "Informatsiia," *ST* 3 (1936): 80; "Informatsiia," *ST* 4–5 (1936): 149; Epshtein, 23.
97. RGAE 484/1/2455: 6–7.
98. These stores were initially sanctioned by the Soviet regime in 1929 and then again in 1931. *Direktivy KPSS i Sovetskogo pravitel'stva po khoziaistvennym voprosam* (Moscow, 1957), 328–9; Z. Molochnikov, "O spetsializatii gosroznitsy," *ST* 2 (1934): 85; Kaganov, 118–20.
99. V. Stushkov, "O sovetskoi torgovle v svete zadach vtoroi piatiletki," *PE* 6 (1932): 73–4.
100. Epshtein, 19–21. For a similar perspective see GARF 5452/28/119: 332.
101. Kaganov, 120–1.
102. Neiman, *Vnutrenniaia*, 273–5.
103. Gronow, 103.
104. Sheila Fitzpatrick, "Becoming Cultured: Socialist Realism and the Representation of Privilege and Taste," in *The Cultural Front: Power and Culture in Revolutionary Russia* (Ithaca, 1992), 224; A. Gnedysh, "'Gastronom' No 1," *ST*, November 4 1937, 3.
105. Elena Osokina, *Ierarkhiia potrebleniia: o zhizni liudei v usloviiakh stalinskogo snabzheniia, 1928–1935 g.g.* (Moscow, 1993).
106. G. Neiman, "Otmena kartochek, razvertyvanie tovarooborota i ukreplenia rublia," *PE* 1 (1935): 72–3; N. Shinkarevskii, "Sostoianie i zadachi spetsializirovannoi seti 'Gastronom' i 'Bakaleia,'" *ST* 3 (1936): 37.
107. Shinkarevskii, "Sostoianie," 38.
108. Both organs also reported successes in increasing their number of *oblast'* wholesale depots and interregional trading bases. *Itogi plenuma TsK VKP (b) – O razvitii sovetskoi torgovli* (Moscow, 1932), 50.
109. *Tsentral'noe statisticheskoe upravlenie, ST – statisticheskii sbornik* (Moscow, 1956), 7, 137, 140–1.
110. RGAE 7971/1/367: 9; I. Serebrennikov, "Peredvizhnye formy torgovli v Moskve," *ST* 3 (1937): 48–50.
111. G. A. Dikhtiar, *Sovetskaia torgovlia v period postroeniia sotsializma* (Moscow, 1961), 427.
112. Leonard Hubbard, *Soviet Trade and Distribution* (London, 1938), 89; V. Dekanozov, "'Gastronom' i 'Bakaleia' v Tiflise," *ST*, May 22 1936, 2; RGASPI 17/3/975: 40–1.

113. "Khrustal'," *ST*, February 1 1936, 1; "Pervyi magazin khrustalia," February 1 1936, 2; "Magazin dieticheskikh produktov," January 8 1937, 1, both in *VM*.
114. "O kioskakh standartnykh tovarov," *ZKU* 6 (1936): 4–7; "Produkty po standartnym tsenam," *VST* 4–5 (1938): 102–3.
115. Koniaev, 141; "Informatsiia," *ST* 5 (1934): 82.
116. GARF 5446/18a/281: 3, 24; RGAE 7971/1/377: 166–71; 7971/1/234: 207–8; Neiman, "Sovetskaia torgovlia na pod"eme," 19; Iur. Zolotarev, "Kul'tura prilavka," *VM*, October 8 1934, 2.
117. Chizhevskii, 127; Koniaev, 140; GARF 5452/28/119: 140.
118. RGAE 7971/1/487: 195.
119. "Uvazhenie k sovetsomu potrebiteliu," *Pravda*, February 6 1936, 1; Shereshevskii, 31.
120. It is important to point out that despite abundant scapegoating, many workers did actually engage in stealing.
121. V. A. Arkhipov and L. F. Morozov, *Bor'ba protiv kapitalisticheskikh elementov v promyshlennosti i torgovle: dvadtsatye–nachalo tridtsatykh godov* (Moscow, 1978), 218–20.
122. RGAE 7971/1/105: 71.
123. Quotes from Savostikov, 19–20.
124. TsAOPIM 69/1/944: 35; 78/1/189: 37.
125. Ibid., 78/1/189: 31.
126. Peredovaia, "Vyshe massovuiu politiko-vospitatel'nuiu rabotu," *ST* 2 (1937): 9.

3 Legitimizing Soviet Trade: Gender and the Feminization of the Retail Workforce

1. Quoted in A. M. Gudvan, "Essays on the History of the Movement of Sales-Clerical Workers in Russia," in *The Russian Worker: Life and Labor under the Tsarist Regime*, ed., Victoria Bonnell (Berkeley, 1983), 195–6. These quotations were reprinted in a Soviet article, "Torgovye kadry USSR," *ST* 7–8 (1936): 66.
2. Gudvan, 194.
3. "Zhenshchina v torgovle nashei strany," October 18 1937, 1; "Kommentarii k rasskazu," August 4 1936, 3, both in *ST*; "Torgovye kadry USSR," 66.
4. B. Kafengauz, "Ekspluatatsiia torgovykh sluzhashchikh v kapitalis-ticheskikh stranakh," *ST* 9 (1935): 47, 50; "Zhenshchina v torgovle," 1.
5. "Zhenshchina v kooperatsii – bol'shaia sila," May 16 1936, 1; Iu. Berkovich, "Zhenshchina v sovetskoi torgovle," March 8 1936, 2, both in *ST*; V. Nodel', "Torgovye kadry i problemy rukovodstva," *ST* 1 (1934): 90; RGAE 484/1/2725: 21. In calling women trade workers a "great force," the press and others echoed Stalin's comments about the great value of women in collective farms. There is some irony in Stalin's dictum, given many women peasants' resistance to collectivization. See Lynne Viola, "*Bab'i Bunty* and Peasant Women's Protest during Collectivization," *The Russian Review* 45: 1 (1986): 23–42.
6. "1,400 zhenshchin-ordenonosok" and "Desiat' biografii," *ST*, March 8 1937, 2–3; GARF 5452/28/100: 5, 11; RGAE 484/1/2725: 69–71.

7. RGAE 484/1/2667: 66–71; 484/3/625: 24, 98–9; 7971/1/245: 147, 205–11.
8. Arustamian, "Ot chadry k udarnichestvu," *Revoliutsiia i natsional'nosti* 10–11 (1932): 110.
9. GARF 5452/23/68: 65; 5452/23/234: 148; Benedikt Mart, "Zhenskii magazin – luchshii v Kieve," *Rabotnitsa* 43 (1931); 9; Brigada "SKT," "Zhenskomu magazinu No. 31 Moskoopprodukta," and "Kak idet podgotovka k 8 March v raionakh Moskvy," *SKT* 53 (1932), 3; 53 (1932), 3; "Zhenskii, udarnyi," *ST*, March 8 1935, 1; V. N. Plost, "Nashi izdeliia poluchili vysokuiu otsenku," *ST*, February 16 1937, 3.
10. Susan Porter Benson, *Counter Cultures: Saleswomen, Managers, and Customers in American Department Stores, 1890–1940* (Urbana, 1986); Sarah Malino, "Behind the Scenes in the Big Store: Reassessing Women's Employment in American Department Stores, 1870–1920," in *Work, Recreation, and Culture: Essays in American Labor History*, eds., Martin Blatt and Martha Norkunas (New York, 1996), 17–38; William Leach, "Transformations in a Culture of Consumption: Women and Department Stores, 1890–1925," *Journal of American History* 71: 2 (1984): 331–2; Theresa McBride, "A Woman's World: Department Stores and the Evolution of Women's Employment, 1870–1920," *French Historical Studies* 10 (Fall 1978): 664–83; Ellen Furlough, *Consumer Cooperation in France: The Politics of Consumption 1834–1930* (Ithaca, 1991); Bill Lancaster, *The Department Store: A Social History* (London and New York, 1995), chapter 10; Carole Elizabeth Adams, *Women Clerks in Wilhelmine Germany: Issues of Class and Gender* (New York, 1998); Geoffrey Crossick and Serge Jaumain, "The World of the Department Store: Distribution, Culture, and Social Change," in *Cathedrals of Consumption: The European Deparment Store, 1850–1939* (Aldershot, 1999), 1–45.
11. Many Communists as well as nonparty supporters saw non-wage earning women, particularly housewives, as "politically unconscious," or worse, as "philistine women hostile to communism." For these views and more on suspicion toward women, see Elizabeth Wood, *The Baba and the Comrade: Gender and Politics in Revolutionary Russia* (Bloomington, 1997), 203–12.
12. Anne Gorsuch, *Youth in Revolutionary Russia: Enthusiasts, Bohemians, Delinquents* (Bloomington, 2000), 102.
13. Wood; Barbara Evans Clements, "The Birth of the New Soviet Woman," in *Bolshevik Culture: Experiment and Order in the Russian Revolution*, eds., A. Gleason, P. Kenez, and R. Stites (Bloomington, 1985), 220–37.
14. See Tsentral'nyi Komitet Profsoiuza Sovetskikh i Torgovykh Sluzhashchikh, *Rabota sredi zhenshchin chlenov nashego soiuza* (Moscow, 1926), 13–14; Norton Dodge, *Women in the Soviet Economy* (Baltimore, 1966), 178. A 1926 survey that included all sectors of the economy, including the private sector, details a higher percentage of women employees, 23 percent. Because this figure deviates from the other figure given for 1926 and the figure given for 1929, this survey suggests that more women were employed in the private retail sector than the cooperative and state sector. See *Vsesoiuznaia perepis' naseleniia 1926 goda*, vol. 34 (Moscow, 1928–1931), 2.
15. RGAE 484/3/399; N. Ostrovskaia, "Vovlechenie rabotnits i krest'ianok v kooperatsiiu," *Kommunistka* 3 (1924): 33–6. Women could shop in cooperative stores via their husband's membership. But government leaders wanted women to become full-fledged members so that women could strengthen

the economic power of cooperatives and participate in cooperative affairs (e.g., members' meetings).

16. N. Makerova, "Kooperatsiia i byt'," 3–4 (1923): 16–17; E. Butuzova, "Rabota kooperatsii v oblasti raskreposhcheniia byta trudiashchikhsia zhenshchin," 3 (1927): 38–9, both in *Kommunistka*; S. Zhukova, *Rabotnitsa, v riady kooperatsii* (Moscow, 1927), 23–7.

17. Zhukova, 9; TsGARUz 217/1/120: 14.

18. TsGARUz 217/1/115: 19; E. V. Butuzova, "Zhenshchina v kooperatsii," in *Uchastnitsy velikogo sozidaniia* (Moscow, 1962), 320–1.

19. TsGARUz 217/1/121: 6–8, 97.

20. TsGARUz 217/1/119: 31; D. A. Abidova, "V aulakh i kishlakakh," and Butuzova, "Zhenshchina v kooperatsii," 303 and 320, respectively. *Zhenotdel* activists refer to activists from the women's section of the Communist Party.

21. GARF 5468/9/317: 10; 5468/11/300: 107–107ob; 5468/12/251: 2, 6–6ob, 12ob, 16, 18, 27ob, 35ob, 42; 5468/12/416: 46ob. Many but not all trade administrators and workers linked men with retail work and evaluated women retail workers negatively. But some individuals argued that women's inexperience could be remedied by training programs and that women's physical weakness did not have to be an impediment, so long as conditions were adapted for women workers. Some even praised women workers for their commendable qualities: sobriety, politeness, honesty. Idem, 5468/12/251: 16ob, 28ob–29, 31.

22. RGAE 484/3/527: 70.

23. GARF 5468/13/163: 26. For similar comments, see 5468/13/162: 46, 137. Some men also suggested that women could not handle the grime of retail work. RGAE 484/1/2725: 68.

24. Mary Buckley, *Women and Ideology in the Soviet Union* (Ann Arbor, 1989), 113.

25. Wendy Z. Goldman, *Women at the Gates: Gender and Industry in Stalin's Russia* (Cambridge, 2002), 169–73; Dodge, 64–7, 175–6; Melanie Ilič, *Women Workers in the Soviet Interwar Economy: From 'Protection' to 'Equality'* (London, 1999), 216–17. Planners originally forecast a modest 5.5 percent increase in women's labor (over 5 years) at the outset of the First FYP. Gail Warshofsky Lapidus, *Women in Soviet Society: Equality, Development, and Social Change* (Berkeley, 1978), 98.

26. Goldman, 144.

27. Wood, 158–9.

28. B. Marsheva, "Poltora milliona zhenshchin vovlechem v stroitel'stvo sotsializma," *Trud*, March 6 1931, 4; idem, "Zhenskii trud v 1931 godu," *Voprosy truda* 1 (1931): 32–41. Research data apparently backed up these claims, confirming women's dependability and productivity. Data also showed that women had fewer absences than men, even including pregnancy-related absences.

29. For the wife-activists' movement, see Mary Buckley, "The Untold Story of *Obshchestvennitsa* in the 1930s," *Europe-Asia Studies* 48: 4 (1996): 569–86; idem, "The Soviet 'Wife-Activist' Down on the Farm," *Social History* 26: 3 (2001): 282–98; Rebecca Balmas Neary, "Mothering Socialist Society: The Wife-Activists' Movement and the Soviet Culture of Daily Life, 1934–1941," *The Russian Review* 58 (July 1999): 396–412; Thomas Schrand, "Soviet

'Civic-Minded Women' in the 1930s: Gender, Class, and Industrialization in a Socialist Society," *Journal of Women's History* 11: 3 (1999): 126–50; Sheila Fitzpatrick, *Everyday Stalinism: Ordinary Life in Extraordinary Times: Soviet Russia in the 1930s* (Oxford, 1999): 156–63.

30. TsAGM 2458/1/34: 121; TsGARUz 816/1/5: 97.
31. *Vsesoiuznaia perepis' naseleniia 1939 goda: Osnovnye itogi – Rossiia* (Moscow, 1939), 178; Dodge, 179. By 1935, approximately 31 percent of all trade workers and 45 percent of salesclerks were women. *Kadry sovetskoi torgovli* (Moscow, 1935), 11. After the Second World War the feminization of retail trade continued.
32. I. M. Novikov, *Novyi etap v rabote potrebitelskoi kooperatsii* (Moscow, 1931), 47; N. Riauzov, "Za bol'shevistskie kadry sovetskoi torgovli," *ST* 5 (1933): 73–4.
33. Goldman, 152–3.
34. L. Gatovskii, et al., "Voprosy razvertyvaniia sovetskoi torgovli," *PE* 1 (1932): 58; G. Neiman, "Za razvernutuiu sovetskuiu torgovliu," *PK* 2 (1932): 78; Nauchno-issledovatel'skii Institut Potrebkooperatsii, *Organizatsiia i tekhnika sovetskoi roznichnoi torgovli* (Leningrad, 1933), 250; GARF 5452/23/68: 64, 67; 5452/28/119: 318.
35. Significantly, most of the qualities applauded in the 1930s were not the same ones highlighted in the 1920s. For example, women's reliability and civilized behavior were promoted as feminine virtues in the 1930s, whereas women's tendency to get ill and shyness were promoted as feminine shortcomings in the 1920s.
36. RGAE 484/3/661: 13, 27; 484/3/660: 4.
37. *S''ezdy sovetov RSFSR v postanovleniiakh i rezoliutsiiakh* (1939), 436, 439; Novikov, 46. SR refers to the Socialist Revolutionaries, discredited by the Bolsheviks in the early years of Soviet rule.
38. "Rech' sekretaria VTsSPS tov. Shvernika," *Izvestiia*, July 27 1930, 4.
39. "Preniia po dokladu T. Zelenskogo," *Izvestiia*, March 5 1931, 2; and "Potrebkooperatsiia-vazhneishii rychag bol'shevistskogo nastupleniia," *Pravda*, March 6 1931, 6.
40. GARF 5452/23/68: 66.
41. Despite this discourse, many women were still prosecuted for criminal activities in trade.
42. Nodel', 91; Berkovich, 2; GARF 5452/23/68: 67; RGAE 484/3/660: 4–5; 484/3/662: 16; 484/1/2725: 15, 67.
43. RGAE 484/1/2725: 21.
44. RGAE 484/3/660: 3. For similar sentiments, see GARF 5452/23/414: 124; RGAE 484/3/661: 36.
45. RGAE 484/1/2455: 14.
46. RGAE 484/1/2667: 96–115; 484/3/629: 18; "Budem podlinnymi khoziaevami svoikh kooperativov," *SKT* 55 (1934), 1; Gin, "Initsiative rabotnits," *SKT* 47 (1932), 3; G. Nikolaev, "O nas malo zabotiatsia," *ST*, May 11 1935, 1.
47. RGAE 484/3/661: 27, 36; GARF 5452/23/68: 65–7.
48. For insobriety and theft, see *Postanovleniia VIII s''ezda soiuza sovtorgsluzhashchikh* (Moscow, 1929), 86. Drunkenness appears to have been an issue primarily among male trade workers. There were very few accounts of women's insobriety in primary sources from the 1930s, while there were countless accounts of and much discussion about men's drunkenness.

49. RGAE 484/3/629: 17–18; GARF 5452/23/68: 65; 5452/28/119: 213ob.
50. "Rech' tov. Toiba," *Pravda Vostoka*, January 22 1936, 3.
51. Berkovich, 2.
52. Nodel', 91.
53. Cited in Sheila Fitzpatrick, "After NEP: The Fate of NEP Entrepreneurs, Small Traders, and Artisans in the 'Socialist Russia' of the 1930s," *Russian History/ Histoire Russe* 13: 2–3 (1986): 208; G. Kalish'ian, "Za kul'turnuiu torgovliu khlebom," *Rabotnitsa* 1 (1935): 14, respectively.
54. Gin, 3.
55. RGAE 484/3/662: 17.
56. GARF 5452/23/68: 65; RGAE 484/3/631: 102; 484/3/661: 13; 484/1/2667: 69.
57. RGAE 484/1/2667: 69, 101, 105, 107–8.
58. RGAE 7971/1/245: 212.
59. RGAE 484/3/662: 16.
60. "Zadachi stakhanovskogo goda v torgovle," *ST* 1 (1936): 10.
61. In the 1920s, women's association with the domestic was usually (although not always) assumed to be a negative.
62. RGAE 484/1/2725: 21. Presumably women were thrifty because of their experience as managers of the household economy.
63. Riauzov, 73; Gin, 3, respectively.
64. S. Smidovich, "Beseda s delegatkami o kooperatsii," *Krest'ianka* 4 (1929): 1; Gik, "Rabochee snabzhenie – v ruki rabochikh," *Rabotnitsa* 38 (1930): 3. This logic about the value of recruiting women as retail activists, particularly as controllers, continued to be used in the 1930s. See *Tri goda bor'by za sovetskuiu kul'turnuiu torgovliu* (Moscow, 1934), 35; E. V. Butuzova, "My za rubezhom," in *Bez nykh my ne pobedili by* (Moscow, 1975), 407; F. U. Lobachev, "Luchshe ispol'zovat' tsennuiu pomoshch'," *ST*, 10 May 1936, 3. Party officials utilized a similar rhetoric about the value of the "housewife's eye" during the Civil War and in the immediate postwar period. See Wood, 66, 143.
65. Z. Bolotin, "Stakhanovskie metody v sovetskoi torgovle," *ST* 2 (1936): 4.
66. For example, "Liubliu svoe delo i gorzhus' svoei rabote," *ST* 1 (1936): 52.
67. RGAE 484/1/2725: 21; GARF 5452/23/234: 148.
68. I. A. Zelenskii, "Bol'she zhenshchin na rukovodiashchuiu rabotu," *ST*, March 10 1936, 2.
69. Novikov, 48.
70. "Kak idet podgotovka k 8 marta," 3; RGAE 7971/1/370: 75; N. N. Burnova, "Kak my rabotaem," *ST*, March 8 1936, 2.
71. For example, in 1933 women made up 28.3 percent of all trade workers in the SU, but only 14.5 percent of the total in Kirghizia. Nodel', 91; Novikov, 47.
72. Dodge makes some of these points when discussing the overall percentage of women wage earners (in all fields) in different Soviet republics. Dodge, 239.
73. GARF 6983/1/159: 18.
74. GARF 5452/23/68: 66.
75. Mart, 9.
76. Kaminskii, "O podgotovke rabotnikov prilavka," *ST* 7–8 (1936): 88.
77. GARF 5452/28/119: 213–213ob.

78. GARF 5452/23/69: 60. This pattern was not unique to the retail sector. Notwithstanding the significant increase in Soviet women's labor throughout the 1930s, the majority of women remained in low paying and low status jobs. See Goldman, esp. 212–19; Buckley, *Women and Ideology*, 117–18; David Hoffmann, *Peasant Metropolis: Social Identities in Moscow, 1929–1941* (Ithaca, 1994): 121. Even in predominately female professions, such as elementary school teaching, women workers faced a gender hierarchy that did not privilege them. Larry Holmes, *The Kremlin and the Schoolhouse: Reforming Education in Soviet Russia, 1917–1931* (Bloomington, 1991), 50.
79. Nodel', 90.
80. *Kadry sovetskoi torgovli*, 11, 94.
81. *Vsesoiuznaia perepis' naseleniia 1939 goda*, 176, 178. The numbers for 1935 and 1939 are not entirely comparable. The percentage for 1939 includes heads of store sections along with salesclerks in stores and stalls.
82. RGAE 484/1/2667: 66–8.
83. I. Zelenskii, "Bol'she zhenshchin na rukovodiashchuiu rabotu," *ST*, March 10 1936, 2.
84. RGAE 7971/1/233: 111; D. Zenin, "Podrugi," *ST*, May 1 1936, 3; "Informatsiia," 3 (1936): 80; "Informatsiia," 4–5 (1936): 156; "Informatsiia," 4 (1937): 70–1, all in *ST*.
85. *Kadry sovetskoi torgovli*, 11, 94.
86. GARF 5452/23/68: 67; 5452/23/234: 135, 149; RGAE 484/3/660: 1–6.
87. TsAGM 2458/1/34: 79; GARF 5452/23/68: 65, 67; 5452/23/69: 31.
88. GARF 5452/23/234: 143.
89. GARF 5452/23/69: 44, 72–3; 5452/23/234: 149.
90. Hostility to women in leadership positions was not specific to the retail sector. See Mary Buckley, "Complex 'Realities' of the 'New' Women of the 1930s: Assertive, Superior, Belittled and Beaten," in *Gender and Russian History and Culture*, ed., Linda Edmondson (New York, 2001), 181–4; Goldman, chapter 7.
91. Berkovich, 2.
92. V. F. Polozhenskaia, "Ia s rabotoi spravilas'," *ST*, March 8 1936, 3. For additional examples of men who were unhappy with the promotion and authority of women, see Antonova Ekaterina Vasil'evna, "Piat' let v odnom sel'po," March 8 1936, 3; G. Nikolaev, "Vydvizhenka," August 16 1937, 2, both in *ST*.
93. For opposition to female Stakhanovite instructors, see Chapter 4.
94. RGAE 484/3/629: 101.
95. Other industries and state agencies grappled with this problem. Wendy Z. Goldman, *Women, the State and Revolution – Soviet Family Policy and Social Life, 1917–1936* (Cambridge, 1993), 314.
96. For efforts to expand options, see TsAGM 2458/1/50: 87; TsGAMO 747/1/625: 9, 16, 20; GARF 5452/23/69: 28; 5452/28/208: 7, 42. For the failure to address needs, see GARF 5452/23/69: 64; 5452/23/234: 138, 149, 151.
97. "V tsentral'nom univermage," *ST*, May 28 1936, 1.
98. GARF 5452/28/365: 51. *Glavtorg* RSFSR supervised 57 torgs (trade organizations).
99. *Otchet tsentral'nogo komiteta*, 49.

100. GARF 5452/28/208: 2–5; 5452/28/382: 43; RGAE 7971/1/487: 3.
101. GARF 5452/28/126: 1, 1ob.
102. RGAE 7971/1/488: 359–60.
103. GARF 5452/28/365: 51.
104. Brigada "SKT," 3.
105. GARF 5452/23/69: 30, 55.
106. TsAGM 2458/1/45: 18.
107. V. A. Karakhin, "Chutko podkhodim k kazhdomu prodavtsu," *ST* 1 (1936): 56. For a store director's similar evaluation of the importance of child care for women workers, see GARF 5442/28/428: 497–8.
108. GARF 5452/23/234: 150; 5452/28/296: 113; RGAE 484/3/631: 30; Shakhbaz'ian, "Povysit' kul'tury sovetskoi torgovli," *Rabotnitsa* 32 (1938): 15. Usually women workers did not have access to facilities (such as breastfeeding rooms) with which to make their mothering easier. See GARF 5452/28/428: 512.
109. Victoria Bonnell, *Iconography of Power: Soviet Political Posters Under Lenin and Stalin* (Berkeley, 1997); Choi Chatterjee, "Soviet Heroines and the Language of Modernity, 1930–1939," in *Women in the Stalin Era*, ed. Melanie Ilič (Houndmills, Basingstoke, 1999); Elizabeth Waters, "The Female Form in Soviet Political Iconography," in *Russia's Women: Accommodation, Resistance, Transformation*, eds., Barbara Evans Clements, Barbara Alpern Engel, and Christine Worobec (Berkeley, 1991), 238.
110. For the glorification of women in agriculture, see Matt Oja, "From Krestianka to Udarnitsa: Rural Women and the Vydvizhenie Campaign, 1933–1941," in *The Carl Beck Papers in Russian and East European Studies* (Pittsburgh, 1996); Buckley, "The Soviet 'Wife-Activist'"; Roberta Manning, "Women in the Soviet Countryside on the Eve of World War II, 1935–1940," in *Russian Peasant Women*, eds., Beatrice Farnsworth and Lynne Viola (Oxford, 1992), 206–35.
111. Chatterjee, 49.
112. Retail labor heroes were never as celebrated as those who won recognition in coal mining or metallurgy. The feminized retail sector continued to have a secondary status vis-à-vis the masculinized industrial sector. For similar arguments about labor and economic hierarchies, and the subordination of agriculture to industry, see Bonnell, *Iconography of Power*, 122; Susan Reid, "All Stalin's Women: Gender and Power in Soviet Art of the 1930s," *Slavic Review* 57: 1 (Spring 1998): 147; Waters, 240–1.
113. This essentialized view of women affected the hiring, retention, advancement, and acceptance of women workers in the 1920s. See Diane Koenker, "Men Against Women on the Shop Floor in Early Soviet Russia: Gender and Class in the Socialist Workplace," *American Historical Review* 100: 5 (December 1995): 1442; Goldman, *Women, the State and Revolution*, 109–18; Wood, 157–60. Such a perspective appears to have adversely affected women's employment and promotion in the trade sector in the 1930s. For example, some store managers opposed women's promotion by arguing that women's family obligations would hinder their dependability. Tov. Moroz, "Podgotovit' novye kadry prodavtsov," *Trud*, January 1 1935, 2; Vasil'evna, 3.

4   "Revolutionary Bolshevik Work":
Stakhanovite Retail Labor Heroes

1. RGAE 7971/1/245: 147, 205–11; GARF 5452/28/39: 5–8.
2. For more on Stakhanovism see Lewis Siegelbaum, *Stakhanovism and the Politics of Productivity in the USSR, 1935–1941* (Cambridge, 1988); Donald Filtzer, *Soviet Workers and Stalinist Industrialization: The Formation of Modern Soviet Production Relations, 1928–1941* (Armonk, 1986); R. W. Davies and Oleg Khlevnyuk, "Stakhanovism and the Soviet Economy," *Europe-Asia Studies* 54: 6 (September 2002): 867–904; Mary Buckley, "Krest'yanskaya gazeta and Rural Stakhanovism," *Europe-Asia Studies* 46: 8 (1994): 1387–1407; idem, "Why be a Shock Worker or a Stakhanovite?" in *Women in Russia and Ukraine*, ed., Rosalind Marsh (Cambridge, 1996), 199–213; idem, *Mobilizing Soviet Peasants: Heroines and Heroes of Stalin's Fields* (Lanham, 2006).
3. Despite its significant presence in retailing, scholars have largely ignored or misunderstood Stakhanovism in the retail sector. Julie Hessler briefly discusses it in "Culture of Shortages: A Social History of Soviet Trade, 1917–1953," Ph.D. diss., University of Chicago, 1996, 273–4. Her book, *A Social History of Soviet Trade: Trade Policy, Retail Practices, and Consumption, 1917–1953* (Princeton, 2004), does not provide any further examination of Stakhanovism. Leonard Hubbard devotes 2 sentences to Stakhanovism in *Soviet Trade and Distribution* (London, 1938), 256. He argues, incorrectly, that "the term Stakhanovite, strictly speaking, [was] not applied to shop assistants."
4. *XVII S"ezd vsesoiuznoi kommunisticheskoi partii (b): Stenograficheskii otchet* (Moscow, 1934), 26 and 184, respectively.
5. Ibid., 502.
6. Ibid., 26.
7. "Pis'mo tovarishu Stalinu ot otlichnikov sovetskoi torgovli," *ST*, November 29 1935, 1.
8. In the 1920s, as opposed to the 1930s, those who worked in the retail sector were usually referred to as employees rather than workers. This categorization was reflected in the name of their trade union. From 1918–1931 the union was called the Trade Union of Soviet and Trade Employees. In 1931 it became the Trade Union of Cooperative and State Trade *Workers*.
9. The Stakhanovite movement was an important addition to efforts to educate retail workers in the 1930s, particularly since these efforts were not expansive or successful enough to reach most employees, nor did they guarantee better work practices. It was also an extension of earlier shock worker and socialist competition initiatives that similarly sought to improve work performance. Shock work usually involved brigades of workers who successfully set out to achieve specific tasks, and socialist competition "represented the expansion and systematization of such efforts." (Siegelbaum, 40–53).
10. For more on the campaign for *kul'turnost'* and consumption, see Chapter 1, especially note 106.
11. I. Ia. Veitser, "Stakhanovskie metody – v torgovliu," *ST* 12 (1935): 12.
12. Veitser quoted in M. Zernov and I. Dimant, "Stakhanovskie metody v rabote prodmagov," *ST* 2 (1936): 52.

13. RGAE 7971/1/245: 213.
14. RGAE 7971/1/100: 1-3.
15. RGAE 7971/1/245: 147-50. Veitser emphasized these points repeatedly.
16. Zernov and Dimant, 54; RGAE 7971/1/100: 2, 5-6, 17, 21, 23; 7971/1/360: 247; 7971/1/370: 218.
17. RGAE 7971/1/245: 148-9.
18. Z. Bolotin, "Stakhanovskie metody v sovetskoi torgovle," *ST* 2 (1936): 8-9.
19. In the process of outperforming norms, workers often exerted excessive stress on machinery and broke it. For this and the criteria for determining an industrial Stakhanovite, see Siegelbaum, 154-5, 163. For attributes and techniques of agricultural Stakhanovites, see Mary Buckley, "*Krest'yanskaya Gazeta* and Rural Stakhanovism," 1391.
20. "Byt' provodnikami bol'shevistskogo dela," *Pravda*, September 26 1936, 1.
21. Personnel reports of Stakhanovites underscored their excellent customer service. RGAE 7971/1/362: 82-3.
22. For more on how Stakhanovism was not merely defined from above, see Siegelbaum, 297-8.
23. N. Strogov and D. Frenkel', "Stakhanovskaia tekhnika torgovli tkaniami," *VST* 6 (1938): 62-3; GASO 2108/1/20: 33-4; "Ratsionalizatorskie predlozheniia v univermagakh," *ZKU* 6 (1936): 1. Apparently Stakhanovites offered almost 700 additional proposals, but these proposals were more localized.
24. GASO 2108/1/20: 24.
25. Zernov and Dimant, 51.
26. RGAE 7971/1/365: 43.
27. N. Strogov, "Izuchenie pokupatel'skogo sprosa v pokazatel'nykh univermagakh," *ST* 9 (1936): 56-62; Iu. Berkovich, "Rastit' podlinnykh stakhanovtsev torgovli," *ST* 10 (1936): 19.
28. Veitser, 4-5.
29. Bolotin, 4; GARF 5452/28/9: 14; Zernov and Dimant, 51.
30. RGAE 7971/1/112: 10, 32.
31. "Zadachi stakhanovskogo goda v torgovle," *ST* 1 (1936): 10.
32. Bolotin, 4.
33. RGAE 7971/1/365: 39.
34. "Za kul'turnuiu sovetskuiu torgovliu," *Pravda vostoka*, January 28 1936, 4.
35. RGAE 7971/1/370: 211.
36. GARF 5452/28/9: 15
37. I. V. Stalin, "Rech' na pervom vsesoiuznom soveshchanii stakhanovtsev," *Sochineniia* I [XIV], 1934-1940 (Stanford, 1967), 89-90.
38. GARF 5452/28/9: 14-15.
39. For more on the promotion of mass-produced novelty goods in the 1930s, see Jukka Gronow, *Caviar with Champagne: Common Luxury and the Ideals of the Good Life in Stalin's Russia* (Oxford and New York, 2003).
40. Moroz quoted in "TsK Soiuza rabotnikov gostorgovli," *Trud*, January 14 1936, 2.
41. Iu. Berkovich, "Stakhanovskoe dvizhenie v torgovle," *ST* 12 (1935): 18; G. Nikolaev, "Zdes' sorevnuiutsia po-nastoiashchemu," *ST*, July 29 1937, 2.
42. "Ee uvazhaet pokupatel'," *VM*, August 29 1937, 2; RGAE 7971/1/370: 215.
43. RGAE 7971/1/245: 150.
44. L. Okun, "Stakhanovskoe dvizhenie v sel'skoi torgovle," *ST* 7-8 (1936): 75.

45. GARF 5452/28/39: 5–6.
46. RGAE 7971/1/245: 83.
47. GARF 5452/28/9: 20, 22. Note: opis' 28 incorrectly states that delo 9 contains materials only from 1935.
48. RGAE 7971/1/365: 47, 44; G. Nikolaev, "Dve Stakhanovki," *ST*, August 10 1937, 2; I. Semenychev, "Kak ia rabotaiu," *ST*, August 30 1937, 3.
49. Bolotin, 6. Other trade officials similarly emphasized the importance of Stakhanovites fighting for goods. See RGAE 7971/1/245: 143; 7971/1/370: 204, 216.
50. I. Strogov, "Stakhanovskaia tekhnika torgovli galantereei," *VST* 8–9 (1938): 57–9.
51. RGAE 7971/1/365: 46.
52. GARF 5452/28/185: 31–2.
53. E. P. Golovina, "Borba partii za razvitie torgovli v period pobedi uprocheniia sotsializma, 1933–1941," in *Sbornik trudov, vol. 34*, ed., Ministerstvo torgovli RSFSR (Leningrad, 1969), 277.
54. Narkomvnutorg and other government organs organized receptions for Stakhanovites in retail trade. For example, RGAE 7971/1/365: 101–9; "Stakhanovtsy gostorgovli Buriat-Mongolii u Tov. I. Ia. Veitsera," *ST*, June 29 1936, 2; "Delegatsiia rabotnikov 'Gastronoma' i 'Bakalei' na prieme v Kremle y tov. V. Ia. Chubariia," *Trud*, January 22 1936, 4.
55. For the Stakhanovite movement among retail workers in stores and depots under the aegis of the People's Commissariat of Food Industries, see *Stakhanovtsy magazinov i baz narkompishcheproma SSSR: Rechi na soveshchanii v marte 1936 g i soobshcheniia stakhanovtsev o svoei rabote* (Moscow, 1936).
56. Iakovleva, "My sderzhali svoe obiazatel'stvo," "S napriazhennym vnimaniem my sledili za khodom istoricheskogo soveshchaniia," and Ivanova, "Stakhanovtsev obsluzhivat' po-stakhanovski," *ST*, November 21 1935, 3; "Pis'mo tovarishu Stalinu," 1.
57. "Shire razvertyvat' stakhanovskoe dvizhenie v torgovle," *ST*, December 31 1937, 2.
58. RGAE 7971/1/245: 211, 214.
59. "Mnozhit' riady stakhanovtsev torgovli," *ST*, January 24 1936, 3.
60. GARF 5452/28/9: 18.
61. For example, "Stakhanovki sel'skoi kooperativnoi torgovli," *Pravda*, March 8 1936, 6.
62. "Zadachi stakhanovskogo goda v torgovle," 11.
63. This editorial also listed a group of supposedly well-known Stakhanovites. "Mnozhit' riady stakhanovtsev," *Stakhanovets torgovli* 2 (1936): 1.
64. "Zadachi stakhanovskogo goda v torgovle," 11.
65. GARF 5452/28/119: 320; RGAE 7971/1/24: 138.
66. GARF 5452/28/46: 5.
67. Berkovich, "Stakhanovskoe dvizhenie," 24.
68. RGAE 7971/1/233: 162; 7971/1/237: 2, 13; 7971/1/239: 46–7; GARF 5452/28/125: 190; 5452/28/168: 9, 171–2; "Obraztsovo organizuem stakhanovskii mesiachnik," February 16 1936, 1; "Za pravo raporta istoricheskomy s''ezdu sovetov," September 30 1936, 1; "Khronika sorevnovaniia," July 28 1937, 1; "Privetstvuem prizyv stakhanovtsev magazinov Mosgorbakalei," December 17 1937: 2, all in *ST*. Retail workers from major

urban centers in republics other than the RSFSR also became involved. For example, approximately 40 stores in Tashkent joined in the first Stakhanovite five-day period. See *Pravda Vostoka*, January 27 1936, 4. Rural consumer cooperative stores arranged similar campaigns. "Chto dal stakhanovskii dvykhnedel'nik v sel'skoi torgovle," *ST* 4–5 (1936): 103–5.

69. GARF 5452/28/176: 3–5; RGAE 7971/1/271: 26, 28–9; S. Likhov, "Molodye stakhanovtsy torgovli," *ST* 3 (1936): 53–4.
70. "Nauchites' postoiano perevypolniat' plan – telegramma narkoma vnutrennei torgovli SSSR t. Veitsera," *ST*, April 4 1936, 1.
71. I. Dimant and M. Zernov, "Ot stakhanovskogo mesiachnika – k povsednevnoi rabote po-stakhanovski," *ST* 4–5 (1936): 42–9; GARF 5452/28/125: 64.
72. Dimant and Zernov, "Ot stakhanovskogo," 43–5; GARF 5452/28/125: 85; RGAE 7971/1/233: 162; 7971/1/237: 2; 7971/1/367: 23. The Stakhanovite month involved many retail workers from big cities, but far fewer elsewhere.
73. Dimant and Zernov, "Ot stakhanovskogo," 45.
74. RGAE 7971/1/370: 171; 7971/1/365: 45, 56–7, 75; GARF 5452/28/47: 19, 27; 5452/28/119: 22. For radio coverage, see RGAE 7971/1/365: 28–33; GARF 5452/28/41: 1–77.
75. Berkovich, "Rastit' podlinnykh stakhanovtsev," 20.
76. GARF 5452/28/251: 4ob–5, 10, 25–6. This survey was not comprehensive. It only included data from 23 regions, and it did not account for all retail establishments or workers. Approximately 21 percent of trade workers employed in the Tsentrovoentorg system and 17 percent of those in the Soiuzprodmag system were listed as Stakhanovites in January 1937. RGAE 7971/1/362: 81, 89. For the percentage of Stakhanovite industrial workers, see Siegelbaum, 161.
77. Some workers were more likely than others to become Stakhanovites even within the same store. Primary sources suggest that store managers and salespeople were more likely than cashier workers to become Stakhanovites.
78. RGAE 7971/1/362: 80.
79. Pashkovskaia, "Budem po-stakhanovski obsluzhivat' pokupatelia," *Rabotnitsa i krest'ianka* 17 (1936): 12. Since women constituted 80 percent of the stores' employees, many Stakhanovites were female.
80. GASO 6140/1/35: 1.
81. "Informatsiia," *ST* 6 (1936): 75.
82. M. P. Smirnov, "Ne prevrashchat' instruktorov-stakhanovtsev v inspektorov," July 4 1936, 3; "Uchit' i pomogat'," October 20 1936, 1; "Kak ia rabotaiu," August 30 1937, 3, all in *ST*.
83. A. A. Bakei, "Nas nikto ne uchit," *ST*, July 4 1936, 3.
84. P. Belorussov, "Shkola stakhanovtsev torgovli," *ST*, August 30 1937, 3.
85. Gol'dman, "Stakhanovskie shkoly v torgovle," *ST* 11 (1939): 41–7. Shvernik's quote is on pp. 41–2.
86. Siegelbaum, 197.
87. Mary Buckley, "Categorizing Resistance to Rural Stakhanovism," in *Politics and Society under the Bolsheviks*, eds., Kevin McDermott and John Morison (New York, 1999), 162, 172.
88. Siegelbaum, 199. For a similar statement see Buckley, ibid., 185.

89. Siegelbaum, 198, 299; Filtzer, *Soviet Workers*, 179, 205; Leon Trotsky, *The Revolution Betrayed* (New York, 1972), 124; Buckley, "Why be a Shock Worker or Stakhanovite?" 205.
90. Buckley, "Categorizing Resistance," 185; idem, "Krest'yanskaya gazeta and Rural Stakhanovism," 1390; Roberta Manning, "Women in the Soviet Countryside on the Eve of World War II, 1935–1940," in *Russian Peasant Women*, eds., Beatrice Farnsworth and Lynne Viola (Oxford, 1992), 221–2.
91. RGAE 7971/1/370: 168, 173, 180, 187, 191.
92. GARF 5452/28/125: 111ob–112.
93. RGAE 7971/1/245: 140–1. For similar comments see "Znatye liudi sovetskoi torgovli Kievshchiny," *ST*, February 14 1936, 4.
94. GARF 5452/28/9: 49; RGAE 7971/1/366: 61–4; GASO 2108/1/20: 23–23ob; TsDNISO 30/6/177: 68–9; TsGARUz 91/8/156: 1, 7, 14–15, 26–7, 35; 91/8/157: 2–3, 5; Ekel'chik, "Direktor otorvavshiisia ot massy," *ST*, March 26 1937, 2; E. Sadal'skaia, "Direktor Panteleiimov ne liubit kritiki," *Rabotnitsa* 11 (1937): 12; L. Mirkina, "Istoriia odnogo ratsionalizatskogo predlozhenia," *Stakhanovets torgovli* 2 (1936): 2.
95. GASO 2108/1/20: 23.
96. TsGARUz 91/8/156: 15.
97. A. Osipov, "Krugovaia poruka," *Stakhanovets torgovli* 2 (1936): 3; Sadal'skaia, 12; Ekel'chik, 2; M. Zernov, "Opyt raboty instrukturov po vnedreniiu stakhanovskikh metodov raboty," *ST* 7–8 (1936): 81.
98. RGAE 7971/1/366: 63–4.
99. Semenychev, 3. Also see Berkovich, "Rastit' podlinnykh stakhanovtsev," 23; GARF 5452/28/365: 65; V. V. Egorova, "Kak ia rabotaiu," *ST*, August 1 1936, 2.
100. Smirnov, 3.
101. "Uchit' i pomogat'," October 20 1936, 1; "Prislushivat'sia k golosu 'malen'kikh liudei,'" April 20 1937, 2, both in *ST*; Ekel'chik, 2; Zernov, 81.
102. "Ratsionalizatorskie meropriiatiia instruktorov-stakhanovtsev pokazatel'nykh univermagov," *ZKU* 1 (1937): 9.
103. TsAOPIM 69/1/944: 44.
104. TsGARUz 91/8/157: 5; A. Vasil'ev, "Skuchaiu po takoi rabote," *ST*, March 26 1937, 2.
105. TsAOPIM 69/1/944: 44, 51.
106. Zernov, 81.
107. RGAE 7971/1/245: 137.
108. GASO 2108/1/20: 117a–118; RGAE 7971/1/366: 61, 86, 124; TDNISO 30/6/177: 68–9; Vasil'ev, 2.
109. "Shire razvertyvat' stakhanovskoe dvizhenie v torgovle," 2.
110. Dimant and Zernov, "Za novyi pod"em stakhanovskogo dvizheniia v torgovle," *VST* 1–2 (1938): 35.
111. See Siegelbaum, chapter 3.
112. "Prazdnye obeshchaniia," "Administratsiia glukha k moim zaiavleniiam," and "Nashi trebovaniia," April 11 1936, 3; "Osvobodite nas ot podsobnykh rabot," and "Chto nam meshaet stat' stakhanovstami," May 24 1936, 1, all in *ST*; GASO 2108/1/20: 23–23ob; TDNISO 30/6/177: 68–9.
113. RGAE 7971/1/366: 63.
114. RGAE 7971/1/371: 2, 4, 35; S. Braginskaia, *Stakhanovets torgovli* 1 (1937): 1.

115. Marusia Soldatova, "Kak ia stala stakhanovkoi," *ST,* April 11 1936, 2. For other promotions, see GASO 2108/1/20: 25–6, 33, 55ob.
116. RGAE 7971/1/371: 21, 31. For other benefits see 7971/1/370: 202–3, 206–206ob, 209, 211; GARF 5452/28/48: 25.
117. "Desiat' biografii," March 8 1937, 3; "Samyi schastlivyi god moei zhizni," August 12 1936, 2, both in *ST.*
118. For more on the education of Stakhanovites, see RGAE 7971/4/57: 1–6; 7971/1/371: 32, 15; GARF 5452/28/125: 66, 246; GASO 2108/1/20: 25.
119. RGAE 7971/1/371: 13.
120. "Sizhu za partoi," *ST,* April 11 1936, 2.
121. RGAE 7971/4/57: 1.
122. GARF 5452/28/125: 189ob.
123. V. Sheinman, "Ne umeiushchie schitat'," *ST,* May 24 1936, 3.
124. For more on Stakhanovite "celebrities" in industry see Siegelbaum, 181; Stephen Kotkin, *Magnetic Mountain: Stalinism as Civilization* (Berkeley, 1995), 210–11.
125. For Borisova, see Berkovich, "Stakhanovskoe dvizhenie," 20; and "Stakhanovtsy o svoei rabote," *ST* 1 (1936): 52–4.
126. "Knizhnaia polka," *ST* 11–12 (1936), 125–7. For other examples, see "Znatye liudi sovetskoi torgovli Kievshchiny," 4; GARF 5452/28/125: 137–9.
127. "Anna Iakovlevna Parchevskaia i ee kniga," *ST,* August 22 1937, 3; F. Parfenov, *Kak my uchimsia torgovat',* and S. A. Guk, *Sovetskaia torgovlia – rodnoe delo,* mentioned in listings of publications on the Stakhanovite experience in trade in "Knizhnaia polka," *VST* 6 (1939) and 7 (1939) respectively.
128. RGAE 7971/1/365: 52, 55, 72, 75, 77.
129. S. Levin and M. Gurovich, "Desiat' biografii," *ST,* May 1 1936, 3.
130. Soldatova, 2.
131. RGAE 7971/1/365: 46.
132. "Kak ia dobilas' vysokoi proizvoditel'nosti truda," *ST* 1 (1936): 55.
133. RGAE 7971/1/365: 70. For similar statements from Stakhanovites about how customers knew and valued them, see I. F. Krestov, *Stakhanovets torgovli* 2 (1936): 1; GASO 2108/1/20: 24.
134. RGAE 7971/1/245: 84, 7971/1/362: 82–3; GARF 5452/28/168: 144.
135. "Liubliu svoe delo i gorzhus' svoei rabote," *ST* 1 (1936): 52.
136. RGAE 7971/1/245: 86, 205–11; GARF 5452/28/39: 7.
137. Choi Chatterjee, "Soviet Heroines and the Language of Modernity, 1930–1939," in *Women in the Stalin Era,* ed., Melanie Ilic (Basingstoke, 1999), 49.
138. *ST* 1 (1936): 54.

5 The *Kontrol'* of Soviet Trade from Above and from Below

1. M. Epshtein, "Likvidirovat' posledstviia vreditel'stva," *ST* 6 (1937): 16.
2. E. A. Rees, *State Control in Soviet Russia: The Rise and Fall of the Workers' and Peasants' Inspectorate, 1920–1934* (London, 1987), 14–15; Jan Adams, *Citizen*

Inspectors in the Soviet Union: The People's Control Committee (New York and London, 1977), 5.

3. Sheila Fitzpatrick, "Ascribing Class: The Construction of Social Identity in Soviet Russia," in *Stalinism: New Directions*, ed., Sheila Fitzpatrick (London and New York, 2000), 20–46; Amir Weiner, "Nature, Nurture, and Memory in a Socialist Utopia: Delineating the Soviet Socio-Ethnic Body in the Age of Socialism," *American Historical Review* 104: 4 (1999): 1114–55; Jeffrey Brooks, *Thank You, Comrade Stalin!* (Princeton, 2000), 130–5, 142–50. From the early 1920s, the secret police organized ordinary people as covert police informants to monitor fellow citizens. Vladlen Izmozik, *Glaza i ushi rezhima* (St. Petersburg, 1995), 141.

4. Surveillance functioned differently under the Tsarist and Communist regimes. For more on these differences, and the use of surveillance by various governments as a modern political practice for governing populations, see Peter Holquist, "Information is the Alpha and the Omega of Our Work: Bolshevik Surveillance in its Pan-European Context," *Journal of Modern History* 69: 3 (1997): 415–50.

5. For more on the different forms of *kontrol'* in the SU, see Rees, 6–7; Adams, chapter 2; Izmozik, especially part 2; L. F. Morozov and V. P. Portnov, *Sotsialisticheskii kontrol' v SSSR: istoricheskii ocherk* (Moscow, 1984); Thomas Remington, "The Rationalization of State *Kontrol'*," in *Party, State, and Society in the Russian Civil War: Explorations in Social History*, eds., Diane Koenker, William Rosenberg, and Ronald Grigor Suny (Bloomington, 1989), 210–31; idem, "Institution Building in Bolshevik Russia: The Case of 'State *Kontrol'*,'" *Slavic Review* 41: 1 (1982): 91–103; Grey Hodnett, "Khrushchev and Party-State Control," in *Politics in the Soviet Union*, eds., Alexander Dallin and Alan Westin (New York, 1966), 113–63; V. I. Turovtsev, *Narodnyi kontrol' v sotsialisticheskom obshchestve* (Moscow, 1974); V. I. Turovtsev, ed., *Gosudarstvennyi i obshchestvennyi kontrol' v SSSR* (Moskva, 1970); S. N. Ikonnikov, *Sozdanie i deiatel'nost' ob"edinennykh organov TsKK-RKI v 1923–1934 gg* (Moscow, 1971); A. I. Chugunov, *Organy sotsialisticheskogo kontrolia RSFSR, 1923–1934 gg* (Moscow, 1972).

6. GARF 5452/23/415: 52; 5452/23/414: 97–9; 5452/23/427: 56–91; *Profsoiuzy SSSR i narodnyi kontrol', 1917–1965* (Moscow, 1965), 137–9.

7. Individual "criticism from below," also a form of public *kontrol'*, is discussed in Chapter 6.

8. Local and federal regulations aimed at protecting consumers were also introduced in the 1920s. Julie Hessler, *A Social History of Soviet Trade* (Princeton, 2004), 117–18.

9. K. Grichik and V. Pirkovskii, *Organizatsiia i pravila roznichnoi torgovli* (Moscow, 1936), 240.

10. Ibid., 121–5.

11. Ibid., 340–1, 352–3; "O bor'be so spekuliatsiei," *Pravda*, August 23 1932, 1.

12. Grichik and Pirkovskii, 212–13.

13. Rees, 7; Adams, 4–5.

14. Morozov and Portnov, 24–8; Remington, "The Rationalization," 223–4.

15. Remington, "The Rationalization," 224–6. Remington proposes that by founding Rabkrin Communist leaders sought to end "the implicit war over turf between the state controllers and trade unions."

16. As Rees notes, "the scale of popular involvement" in TsKK-Rabkrin remains unclear. Even contemporaries disputed TsKK-Rabkrin's claims about its large number of volunteers. Rees, 215; Adams, 35.
17. TsKK-Rabkrin was replaced with two new control bodies: the Party Control Commission (KPK) and the Soviet Control Commission (KSK). Because these bodies did not organize public *kontrol'* on a mass scale, TsKK-Rabkrin's abolition has been interpreted as proof that the Soviet regime abandoned its "commitment to popular control." Adams argues that "from the time of the Seventeenth Party Congress, public participation in state control was gradually suppressed." Soviet leader Nikita Khrushchev and some scholars have also suggested that TsKK-Rabkrin's abolition was due to "distrust of the public." Rees, 221, 231–2; Adams, 2, 38; Hodnett, 115, 117. Interestingly, the KSK continued Rabkrin's policy of trying to involve "workers in control-revision work," and sought to engage various public organizations in the KSK's control activities. Morozov and Portnov, 128, 130.
18. *XVII S"ezd VKP (b): Stenograficheskii otchet* (Moscow, 1934), 35, 562, 673–4.
19. The abolition did, however, affect the organization of public *kontrol'*.
20. During the Second Five-Year Plan (1933–1937), for example, reportedly more than 450,000 trade-union activists assisted the Commission for the Protection of Labor by investigating adherence to labor laws and rules for governing workplace safety. Turovtsev, *Gosudarstvennyi*, 102.
21. Literature on this topic is extensive. For a partial list, see citations in Chapter 6. Many people also continued to act as covert informants for the secret police.
22. For the popular *kontrol'* that the trade-union campaign for democracy encouraged, and its implications, see Wendy Z. Goldman, "Stalinist Terror and Democracy: The 1937 Union Campaign," *American Historical Review* 110: 5 (2005): 1427–53. For how mass *"kontrol' from below"* advanced the Terror of the 1930s, see Cynthia Hooper, "Terror from Within: Participation and Coercion in Soviet Power, 1924–1964," Ph.D. dissertation, Princeton University, 2003.
23. Turovtsev, *Narodnyi*, 18–43, 68.
24. Turovtsev, *Gosudarstvennyi*, 15.
25. GARF 5452/23/415: 52.
26. V. I. Lenin, *Polnoe sobranie sochinenii*, vol. 40 (Moscow, 1964), 201.
27. GARF 5452/23/427: 5.
28. For example, Jochen Hellbeck has argued that Communist authorities sought to foster new forms of self-identification among the general populace to produce new revolutionary selves. Jochen Hellbeck, "Working, Struggling, Becoming: Stalin-Era Autobiographical Texts," *The Russian Review* 60: 3 (2001): 340–59.
29. Lenin, vol. 33, 116.
30. RGAE 484/1/2455: 13.
31. RGAE 7971/1/100: 49.
32. Veitser quoted in "Prislushivat'sia k golosu 'malen'kikh liudei," *ST*, April 20 1937, 2. For a similar statement by an inspectorate functionary, see GARF 5452/28/549: 47ob.
33. RGAE 484/3/597: 1; GARF 5452/28/249: 17, 34.

34. GARF 5452/23/427: 8ob–9. For a similar statement see RGAE 5452/23/415: 52.
35. GARF 5452/23/427: 5. For participation in *kontrol'* as a "form of political education," also see "Rabota Komsomola v torgovom apparate," *ST* 5 (1937): 15.
36. GARF 5452/23/415: 52; 5452/23/414: 97–9; 5452/23/427: 56–91; *Profsoiuzy SSSR i narodnyi kontrol'*, 137–9.
37. The State Sanitation Inspectorate and the State Milk Inspectorate monitored trade. For examples of the *kontrol'* of trade by the Party Control Commission and Soviet Control Commission, see "Pochemu v magazinakh pustuiut polki?" *Trud*, April 10 1934, 2; "O biurokraticheski-prenebrezhitel'nom otnoshenii k nuzhdam potrebitelia," *Pravda*, September 5 1936, 4; "Mezhdunarodnyi den' kooperatsii," *Vlast' sovetov* 12 (1936): 31. In addition to carrying out criminal investigations and prosecutions, the procuracy was responsible for monitoring other governmental agencies (such as the secret police).
38. For assistance groups aiding the procuracy, see GARF 5452/23/414: 99; TsAGM 2458/1/313: 7. Although state trade organizations depended on the GTI for *kontrol'* work, they also established their own internal inspectorates, which mobilized volunteer activists as controllers, although on a small scale. For example, in Minsk approximately 45 individuals served as volunteer controllers for the internal trade inspectorate in 1935. Grichik, 53; RGAE 7971/1/85: 1–18. Rabkrin organized assistance groups (aka cells) in government enterprises and institutions. Turovtsev, *Narodnyi kontrol'*, 40, 45; *Profsoiuzy SSSR i narodnyi kontrol'*, 55–6; Rees, 213–15.
39. "Legkaia kavaleriia v bor'be za rabochee snabzhenie," *ZTKP* 9–10 (1933): 46–7; Ikonnikov, 143.
40. Ia. Lekhovitser, "S pomoshch'iu mass," *ZTKP* 22 (1933): 24–5; L. F. Morozov and V. P. Portnov, *Organy TsKK-NK RKI v bor'be za sovershentsvovanie sovestkogo gosudarstvennogo apparata (1923–1934 gg.)* (Moscow, 1964), 213; Ikonnikov, 397. The State Inspectorate of Prices was established in 1931. During its first 2 years, it reportedly inspected over 100,000 trade organs. "Dva goda inspektsii tsen," *ZTKP* 22 (1933): 21.
41. Grichik, 43, 54; GARF 5452/28/71: 13–14. Among other things, the GTI was an example of the more specialized forms of departmental state control that developed in the 1930s. For other forms, such as the All-Union State Veterinarian Inspectorate, see Turovtsev, *Gosudarstvennyi*, 93. The GTI inspected the entire retail system, including the cooperative sector. RGAE 7971/1/275: 154–9.
42. GARF 5452/28/71: 14; 5452/28/188: 34ob.
43. "Torgovaia sektsiia Mossoveta," March 29 1936, 2; "Kak my rabotaem," "Domashnie khoziaiki v torgovykh sektsiiakh," and "Rabotaiu brigadirom," April 18 1936, 3, all in *ST*; M. Lavrova-Sokolova, "Kul'turno torgovat'," *Rabotnitsa* 34 (1938): 13; GARF 5452/28/428: 109; 5452/28/548: 160; 5452/28/549: 24.
44. Turovtsev, *Narodnyi kontrol'*, 31. As scholars have noted, workers' control did *not* grant workers the right to make executive or macroeconomic decisions regarding enterprises. Paul Avrich, "The Bolshevik Revolution and Workers' Control in Russian Industry," *Slavic Review*, 22 (March 1963): 47–63; William

Rosenberg, "Workers and Workers' Control in the Russian Revolution," *History Workshop* 5 (1978): 89–97.

45. For unions' "temporary *kontrol'* commissions" see *Profsoiuzy SSSR i narodnyi kontrol'*, 61; Turovtsev, *Gosudarstvennyi*, 98–9. For their *shefstvo* (oversight) movement, see Adams, 42; Morozov and Portnov, *Sotsialisticheskii kontrol'*, 118–22.

46. *Profsoiuzy SSSR i narodnyi kontrol'*, 358; *KPSS o profsoiuzakh* (Moscow, 1957), 443–6; *KPSS v resoliutsiiakh i resheniiakh s"ezdov, konferentsii i plenumov TsK*, vol. 5 (Moscow, 1984), 244; *S"ezdy sovetov RSFSR v postanovleniiakh i rezoliutsiiakh* (Moscow, 1939), 440.

47. *Profsoiuzy SSSR i narodnyi kontrol'*, 359.

48. Turovstev, *Gosudarstvennyi*, 101.

49. *XVII S"ezd*, 673; Rees, 223.

50. *Profsoiuzy SSSR – dokumenty i materialy v chetyrekh tomakh* (Moscow, 1963), 756; "Khlebom torgovat' kul'turno, Postanovlenie prezidiuma VTsSPS," *Trud*, May 22 1935, 4; Shakhbaz'ian, "Povysit' kul'tury sovetskoi torgovli," *Rabotnitsa* 32 (1938): 15; *Postanovleniia plenumov VTsSPS* (Moscow, 1949), 142–3; *Postanovleniia VIII Plenuma VTsSPS* (Moscow, 1939), 16.

51. Trade unions for different industries organized workers to inspect Soviet trade. Some industrial unions dragged their feet. For workers' brigades sent out by various trade unions, see GARF 5452/23/427: 82, 112; "Po gorodam Soiuza," *Trud*, October 3 1935, 1; *Profsoiuzy SSSR i narodnyi kontrol'*, 123–5, 127–31, 143. For resistance on the part of some industrial trade unions, see V. Zheleznogorskii, "Massovy *kontrol'* – vazhneishee zveno rabotu profsoiuzov," *Voprosy profdvizheniia* 7 (1936): 11–15. As part of a massive restructuring of all trade unions in September 1934, the PRKGT split into eight unions. The two largest unions to emerge from this restructuring were the Trade Union of Cooperative Workers of Central Districts and the Trade Union of State Trade Workers. They pursued the same general *kontrol'* activities as the PRKGT (and it is likely that the other six unions carried out many similar initiatives). For the restructuring of 47 trade unions into 154, see N. Shvernik, *O perestroike profoiuzov* (Moscow, 1934).

52. *Profsoiuzy SSSR i narodnyi kontrol'*, 140. Also see GARF 5452/23/426: 100–1.

53. GARF 5452/23/152: 12; 5452/23/303: 1, 9. Signal posts additionally had a specific mandate to shed light on internal trade-union issues, to "signal," for example, a "negligent attitude" by local trade-union committees toward the "needs of trade-union members."

54. TsAGM 2458/1/313: 7–8; GARF 5452/23/152: 2; 5452/23/415: 8ob, 57.

55. Consumer cooperative societies were officially "public" economic organizations composed of members who voluntarily joined them. Although they had some limited autonomy, they were not independent from but subject to the party-state.

56. In some primary sources *koopaktiv* refers to all cooperative activists, including those in revision commissions, shop commissions, and cooperative bureaus. But *koopaktiv* often refers to a more general group of cooperative activists who were not a part of these other bodies. Here I am referring to the more general groups.

57. GARF 5446/18a/273: 96; 5452/23/234: 143; RGAE 484/1/2725: 18; 484/3/532: 44; 484/3/598: 3–4; "Informatsiia," *ST* 9 (1936): 71–2. Unlike other public

controllers, leaders of revision commissions appear to have been rewarded a small sum for their efforts.

58. Nauchno-issledovatel'skii Institut Potrebkooperatsii, *Organizatsiia i tekhnika sovetskoi roznichnoi torgovli* (Leningrad, 1933), 130–2; GARF 5452/23/426: 78–80; 484/1/2725: 18, 39; *Tri goda*, 37–8. In addition to engaging in surveillance, many shop commissions actively participated in practical retail work – for example, helping to wrap goods.
59. TGA 195/1/17: 117.
60. RGAE 484/1/2845: 67ob; P. Aleksandrovich, "Peredoviki kooperativnoi torgovli," *VST* 11–12 (1938): 50.
61. Shakhbaz'ian, 15.
62. When Rabkrin was formally established, its mandate included Lenin's proposition that "special attention should be paid to attracting women." Authorities justified women's involvement by arguing that they had particular attributes that made them good candidates for *kontrol'* work: "tender hearts, caring hands, sharp eyes." Elizabeth Wood, *The Baba and the Comrade: Gender and Politics in Revolutionary Russia* (Bloomington, 1997), 61–7, 211; Turovtsev, *Narodnyi*, 35; Morozov and Portnov, *Sotsialisticheskii kontrol'*, 102.
63. P. Morenov and M. Gribanov, "Rol' zhenshchiny v perestroike rabochego snabzheniia," *Rabotnitsa* 1 (1933): 7.
64. *Profsoiuzy SSSR i narodnyi kontrol'*, 117; *S"ezdy sovetov*, 437–40; RGAE 484/3/601: 37; Shakhbaz'ian, 15; *Presidium Moskovskogo Soveta R. K. i K. D., Protokol No. 40 prilozhenie* (Moscow, 1936), 8.
65. "Zhenshchina v kooperatsii bol'shaia sila," *ST*, May 16 1936, 1. Also see "Zhenshchina – velikaia sila," *ST*, March 8 1935, 1.
66. *Tri goda bor'by za sovetskuiu kul'turnuiu torgovliu* (Moscow, 1934), 35–6.
67. M. Shaburova, "Sovety i organizatsiia zhenskikh trudiashchikhsia mass," *Rabotnitsa* 19 (1934): 2–3.
68. "Domokhoziaika pomogaet fabzavkomu," *Trud*, March 11 1935, 3.
69. *Tri goda*, 35. For a similar comment, see G. Kalish'ian, "Za kul'turnuiu torgovliu khlebom," *Rabotnitsa* 1 (1935): 14.
70. F. U. Lobachev, "Luchshe ispol'zovat' tsennuiu pomoshch'," *ST*, May 10 1936, 3. The argument that women's domestic duties contributed to their talent for participating in consumer cooperatives was not unique to the SU. See Ellen Furlough, *Consumer Cooperation in France: The Politics of Consumption* (Ithaca, 1991), 210, 279.
71. Gin-ev, "Vozglavit's aktivnost' rabotnits prilavka i zhenskogo koopaktiva," *SKT* 46 (1932): 2; *Tri goda*, 35; E. Kukhareva, "Boremsia s obveshivaniem rabochikh," *Rabotnitsa* 26 (1934): 16; Lobachev, 3; "Prevratim magazine v obraztsovyi," *Stakhanovets torgovli* 7 (1936): 2.
72. RGAE 7971/1/362: 20; GARF 5452/28/543: 22–3; Lobachev, 3.
73. GARF 5452/28/543: 24, 49; K. A. Tochilina, "Naveli poriadok," May 10 1936, 3; A. Volkova, "My pomogaem nashimi," October 24 1936, 2; "Nash opyt," March 8 1937, 2, all in *ST*.
74. "Sleduiute nashemu primeru," *SKT* 62 (1934): 3.
75. "Nash opyt," 2. At a meeting among wife-activists, participants discussed how it was important to be proactive in addressing the insufficiencies of

Soviet trade. RGAE 7971/4/77: 1, 44. For wife-activists' actual practical work, see GARF 5452/28/543: 22; "V nogu s muzh'iami," *ST,* March 8 1937, 2. Wife-activists also investigated available resources for workers, particularly women workers (such as kindergartens). GARF 5452/28/208: 42, 141; Volkova, 2.

76. An editorial claimed that tens of thousands of women were involved in the *kontrol'* of cooperatives. See "Zhenshchina – velikaia sila," *ST,* March 8 1935, 1. This figure by no means includes all women controllers in the retail sector.

77. *Tri goda,* 37.

78. This survey was not comprehensive. "Zhenshchina na kooperativnoi rabote," *ST,* March 8 1935, 2.

79. "Domashnie khoziaiki," 3.

80. "Zhenshchina na kooperativnoi rabote," 2.

81. In Kazakhstan there was little development of the wife-activists' movement in trade as of June 1938. Although there was more activity in Uzbekistan, as of February 1938 only about 130 wives of trade workers in the entire republic were reported as involved in public activism. Presumably only a select number of these activists were involved in *kontrol'.* GARF 5452/28/543: 20, 50–1.

82. A. Tolokonnikova, "Nashi magaziny dolzhny byt' obraztsovymi," *ST,* August 6 1938, 3.

83. Volkova, 2.

84. "Domashniaia khoziaika," *Pravda,* October 25 1936, 3.

85. *Tri goda,* 37–8.

86. GARF 5452/23/427: 80.

87. For example, P. Aleksandrovich, "Peredoviki kooperativnoi torgovli," *VST* 11–12 (1938): 45.

88. MGA 2458/1/342: 76; GARF 5452/23/345: 113–14; 5452/28/549: 24; RGAE 484/3/629: 19; S. Krylov, "Pokonchit' s raskhishcheniem kooperativnoi sobstvennosti," *VST* 10 (1938): 23.

89. GARF 5452/23/428: 41.

90. GARF 5452/23/414: 110; 5452/23/427: 7ob; RGAE 484/3/532: 7; 484/3/601: 3, 23.

91. GARF 5452/28/549: 24.

92. Both quotes from GARF 5452/23/414: 120.

93. GARF 5446/16a/329: 55; 5446/18a/273: 71; 5452/23/345: 79–80; 5452/23/428: 54–60.

94. RGAE 484/3/601: 18–19.

95. GARF 5446/18a/309: 301; 5452/28/549: 28; RGAE 484/3/598: 3. During the 1930s, judges "regularly avoided" giving harsh sentences to trade employees for offenses they deemed minor. Peter Solomon, Jr., "Criminal Justice and the Industrial Front," in *Social Dimensions of Soviet Industrialization* (Bloomington, 1993), 235.

96. GARF 5452/28/188: 69.

97. GARF 5452/28/549: 21–2, 36ob–38.

98. GARF 5452/23/428: 36; 5452/23/427: 66.

99. GARF 5452/23/428: 36–7.

100. GARF 5452/23/345: 128; 5452/23/414: 111ob; "Kak my dobivalis' pere-stroika raboty v univermage No 22," *SKT* 234 (1933): 3; Tochilina, 3.
101. Their work disrupted a longstanding gender-based division of labor in inspection work. Under the Tsarist regime, women did not work as inspectors in the workplace. Nor had a female work inspectorate formed at the end of the nineteenth or beginning of the twentieth centuries (unlike some other industrializing countries in Europe). In 1914 the Duma passed legislation to organize one, which was never realized. Rose Glickman, *Russian Factory Women: Workplace and Society, 1880–1914* (Berkeley, 1984), 266–72. What is interesting is that Soviet men persisted in being the main inspectors when it came to the *production* of goods, even in industries dominated by women. This suggests that a stereotypical gender division of inspection may have prevailed, with men inspecting the sphere of production and women inspecting the sphere of service and consumption. Susan Reid, "All Stalin's Women: Gender and Power in Soviet Art of the 1930s," *Slavic Review* 57: 1 (1998): 144.
102. Epshtein, 13; GARF 5452/23/427: 5ob; 5452/23/428: 121; 5452/28/549: 30–30ob, 55; Zheleznogorskii, 12.
103. GARF 5452/23/428: 121; 5452/23/427: 5ob.
104. GARF 5452/28/70: 2–4, 5–13, 14–21, 30–1, 75–9.
105. GARF 5452/23/345: 77, 80–1; 5452/28/366: 17.
106. In 1934 Sovnarkom RSFSF passed a resolution requiring the state trade system to hire workers only after reviewing them via attestation committees. See GARF 5452/28/70: 79. Reports suggest that this requirement was largely neglected. RGAE 484/3/598; 484/3/601: 23; GARF 5452/23/426: 101.
107. RGAE 7971/1/465: 55ob; GARF 5452/23/342: 92; 5452/28/70: 79; 5452/28/367: 14–15.
108. GARF 5452/23/427: 78, 82, 88.
109. GARF 5452/23/427: 90; 5452/23/415: 58ob.
110. GARF 5452/23/426: 100. Lack of employee awareness was also uncovered by state controllers. RGAE 7971/1/57: 129–30.
111. GARF 5452/28/549: 36ob; 5446/16a/404: 15–16.
112. GARF 5452/28/188: 12ob–13, 14–15ob.
113. GARF 5452/23/427: 11ob; 5452/23/428: 111; 5452/28/70: 22.
114. GARF 5452/23/427: 5ob.
115. GARF 5452/23/414: 41; 5452/23/415: 50–9; 5452/23/427: 3–13; 5452/23/428: 118–19. Courses and seminars were made available for PRKGT members as well as others.
116. RGAE 484/3/598: 3.
117. RGAE 7971/1/465: 57ob–59.
118. "Prislushivat'sia k golosu," 2.
119. GARF 5452/23/427: 56, 62, 64, 118.
120. For the term "speaking Bolshevik," see Stephen Kotkin, *Magnetic Mountain: Stalinism as Civilization* (Berkeley, 1995).
121. For a good example of what appears to have been a standard report format that many controllers followed, see GARF 5452/28/70: 36–7.
122. This attention may have contributed to what Oleg Kharkordin terms the Stalinist "individuation drive" of the mid-1930s, in which individuals came to know themselves through an awareness of how their deeds were evaluated

by the collective. Oleg Kharkhordin, *The Collective and the Individual in Russia: A Study of Practices* (Berkeley, 1999), especially chapter 5.

123. For radio shows, see GARF 5452/23/427: 56–91; 5452/23/414: 99. The government repeatedly directed the all-union Procuracy as well as republican and local procuratorial organs to organize show trials about problems in the retail sector. GARF 5446/18a/273: 71; 5446/18a/309: 101 (secret decree). The TsKK-Rabkrin organized similar trials. Show trials gave individuals opportunities to act as volunteer public prosecutors and lay assessors. For example, in 1934 two of the "best salesclerks" in the Azovo-Chernomorskii *krai* performed as public prosecutors in a show trial of the "biggest culprits" recently uncovered by public controllers. See idem, 5452/23/427: 116.

124. In discussing the "collectivization of life" in the Soviet Union, Oleg Kharkhordin argues that such a society of mutual surveillance was consolidated during the Khrushchev era, particularly when Khrushchev resurrected the party-state's previous emphasis on public *kontrol'*. See 292–3. Mass participation in *kontrol'* in the 1930s, in combination with mass participation in clandestine surveillance, suggests that this society of mutual surveillance took root earlier than Kharkhordin suggests.

6 The Making of the New Soviet Consumer

1. RGAE 7971/1/250: 22.
2. Literature on this topic is too extensive to cite in full. In addition to sources cited in this chapter, see Sheila Fitzpatrick, "Signals from Below: Soviet Letters of Denunciation of the 1930s," *The Journal of Modern History* 68 (December 1996): 831–66; Robert Thurston, "Reassessing the History of Soviet Workers: Opportunities to Criticize and Participate in Decision-Making, 1935–1941," in *New Directions in Soviet History* (Cambridge, 1992), 160–88; Golfo Alexopoulis, "Exposing Illegality and Oneself: Complaint and Risk in Stalin's Russia," in *Reforming Justice in Russia, 1864–1996* (Armonk and London, 1997): 168–89; Youngok Kang-Bohr, "Appeals and Complaints: Popular Reactions to the Party Purges and the Great Terror in the Voronezh Region, 1935–1939," *Europe-Asia Studies* 57: 1 (2005): 135–54.
3. Alex Inkeles and Kent Geiger, "Critical Letters to the Editors of the Soviet Press: Areas and Modes of Complaint," 17: 6 (1952): 703; idem, "Critical Letters to the Editors of the Soviet Press: Social Characteristics and Interrelations of Critics and the Criticized," 18: 1 (1953): 21–2, both in *American Sociological Review*; Merle Fainsod, *Smolensk Under Soviet Rule* (London: 1958, 1989), 408.
4. Stephen Kotkin, *Magnetic Mountain: Stalinism as Civilization* (Berkeley, 1995), 263.
5. Sheila Fitzpatrick, *Everyday Stalinism: Ordinary Life in Extraordinary Times: Soviet Russia in the 1930s* (Oxford: 1999), 165; idem, "Suppliants and Citizens: Public Letter-Writing in Soviet Russia in the 1930s," *Slavic Review* 55: 1 (1996): 85–7; Fainsod, 378.
6. There is an extensive literature that talks about these efforts. For an overview of many efforts, see David Hoffmann, *Stalinist Values: The Cultural Norms of Soviet Modernity, 1917–1941* (Ithaca, 2003).

7. "Uvazhenie k sovetskomy potrebiteliu," *Pravda*, February 6 1936, 1.
8. Z. Bolotin, "Kul'turno torgovat' i zabotit'sia o potrebitele," *Bol'shevik* 3 (1935): 36.
9. "Veskoe slovo pokupatelia," *ST*, April 8 1937, 1.
10. "Rabotat' po-bol'shevistski," *VST* 3 (1938): 23; "Za vysokoe kachestvo tovarov, za kul'turnuiu torgovliu," *ST* 9 (1936): 9; "Bol'she zaboty o potrebitele!" *Za pishchevuiu industriiu*, July 6 1937, 1.
11. RGAE 7971/1/364: 73–4.
12. Gosudarstvennyi arkhiv Sverdlovskoi oblasti A-37/56 and A-137/28 and 108. Thanks to Aleksei Kilin for bringing these photos to my attention.
13. N. Shinkarevskii, "Konferentsii pokupatelei," *ST*, May 18 1936, 3.
14. RGAE 7971/1/250: 1.
15. The Central Committee plenum endorsed these conferences in a draft resolution, October 25 1931. (RGASPI 82/2/690: 44). Although the CC did not speak explicitly about such conferences in resolutions adopted a few days later, it did identify improving the quality of consumer goods as an urgent task, and instructed various organizations to include consumers in the process. *KPSS v resoliutsiiakh i resheniiakh s''ezdov, konferentsii i plenumov TsK*, vol. 5 (Moscow, 1984), 368. For "three-sided" conferences and meetings from 1931–1933, see GARF 5452/23/33: 1–45; 5452/23/114: 195–6, 247ob; 5452/23/195: 1–74; 5452/23/330: 105.
16. GARF 5452/23/33: 37, 39.
17. GARF 5452/23/195: 75–9. Sometimes a select group of consumers with particular interests was invited to participate in these meetings. For example, in 1936 artists, dancers, and stage make-up employees met with the Deputy Commissar of Food Industries, the head of the perfume-cosmetics industry, and a factory director to discuss perfume, cosmetics, etc. "Vstrecha s potrebiteliami," *VM*, September 14 1936, 2.
18. "Dom Modelei," *ST*, January 9 1936, 4. In 1936 garment factories in Tashkent organized similar conferences "on fashion" with consumers. "Odevat'sia krasivo – konferentsii potrebitelei," *Pravda vostoka*, March 20 1936, 4.
19. *VM*, 19 and 26 June 1936, 4. Apparently many stores held these meetings in 1936. "Uvazhat' potrebitelia," *ST*, November 20 1937, 3.
20. "Uroki vystavki," *Igrushka* 2 (1937): 26. For more exhibits see "Vystavka 'Mosbel'e'," *VM*, 9 March 1934, 2; I. Tsitron, "Obraztsovye raiunivermagi potrebkooperatsii," *ST* 10–11 (1935): 96.
21. Julie Hessler, "Cultured Trade: The Stalinist Turn to Consumerism," in *Stalinism: New Directions*, ed., Sheila Fitzpatrick (London and New York, 2000), 196. For more on the Soviet pursuit of a dream world of industrial modernity and mass utopia, see Susan Buck-Morss, *Dreamworld and Catastrophe: The Passing of Mass Utopia in East and West* (Cambridge, MA, 2000).
22. Rosalind Williams discusses the role of the commodity exhibition in fostering this dream world in the capitalist West. See Williams, *Dream Worlds: Mass Consumption in Late Nineteenth-Century France* (Berkeley, 1982), especially 58–66.
23. Z. Medvedovskaia, "Kukla chitaet stikhi," *VM*, February 28 1937, 2; "Kritikuiut deti," *Igrushka* 6–7 (1937): 11.

24. Some exhibits concluded with a final conference with consumers, providing yet another forum for feedback. "Konferentsiia po assortimentu destkikh tovarov na Trekhgorke," *Trud*, October 27 1936, 4; RGAE 7971/1/250.
25. TsGARUz 91/8/27: 13.
26. Ibid., 17, 18ob, 60.
27. Ibid., 1–6, 88.
28. "Uvazhat' potrebitelia," 3.
29. G. A. Zhukovskii, "Sdvigi potrebitel'skom sprose gorodskogo naseleniia SSSR," in *Potreblenie i spros v SSSR*, ed., A. I. Malkis (Leningrad, 1935), 121; TsGARUz 91/8/27: 66. For other examples of supposed influence, see "Odevat'sia krasivo," 4; Tsitron, 96; "Modeli idut v proizvodstvo," *ST*, February 18 1936, 3.
30. TsAGM 2458/1/342: 53–8, 88, 144–9, 168; 2458/1/368: 1–5, 11; TsGARUz 91/8/113: 30–6; RGAE 7971/1/272: 5–13, 54; GARF 5452/28/555: 4–5, 11–16; "Torgovtsy brakom," and "O stat'e 'Pravdy' 'torgovtsy brakom'," *Pravda*, August 28 and 30 1936.
31. GARF 5452/28/125: 66ob–67, 88.
32. "Signaly priniaty," *VM*, January 27 1937, 3.
33. "Vopros Narkomvnutorgu" and "Otvet Narkomvnutorga," *Rabotnitsa* 18 (1937): 11.
34. TsGARUz 91/8/113: 36.
35. TsAOPIM 2855/1/41: 59.
36. TsGARUz 91/8/113: 69.
37. Some stores had complaint books in the 1920s. The origin of complaint books is not clear. As best as I can tell, complaint books appear to have originated in the late nineteenth century in the Russian railroad system, and then spread to other service industries. In 1884 Anton Chekhov published a short story entitled "Complaint Book" in a literary journal. A. P. Chekhov, *Sobranie Sochineneii*, vol. 2 (Moscow, 1960), 199–200, 566.
38. " 'Pravdy' i proletarskogo raikoma VKP(b) pereshli v pokhod za povyshenie," *Pravda*, July 25 1930.
39. Ia. Volevich, "O chem govoriat zhalobnye knigi," *SKT* 104 (1933), 3. For other articles critical of responses, see "Obmanivaiut pokupatelia," *Trud*, July 4 1934, 4; "Za deistvennost' zhalob potrebitelia," and "Zhaloby 'neobosnovannye' i 'sluchainye'," *Rabotnik prilavka*, July 22 1934.
40. "Za zakonnuiu zhalobu...otpravliaiut v militsiiu," *Rabotnik prilavka*, July 22 1934.
41. K. Grichik and V. Pirkovskii, *Organizatsiia i pravila roznichnoi torgovli* (Moscow, 1936), 228–9.
42. RGAE 7971/1/57: 127–8; 7971/1/226: 101; Grichik and Pirkovskii, 229–30; "Uluchshit' obsluzhivanie pokupatelei," *ST*, August 5 1936, 1.
43. "Prisluchivat'sia k golosu 'malen'kikh liudei'," *ST*, April 20 1937, 2.
44. "Ser'eznoe preduprezhdenie," *ST*, January 14 1936, 2.
45. RGAE 7971/1/364: 62.
46. TsAOPIM 78/1/189: 49.
47. RGAE 7971/1/364: 103; S. Pavlov, "Khoziaika magazina," *VM*, January 9 1933, 2.
48. RGAE 7971/1/360: 124–6; 7971/1/363: 56; 7971/1/365: 42, 71, 101–2; GASO 2108/1/20: 21ob–22, 29.

49. RGAE 7971/1/245: 163.
50. GARF 5452/28/167: 300–2.
51. RGAE 7971/1/57: 129–30. The inspectors discovered that many store workers did not even know about Narkomvnutorg's decree.
52. TsAOPIM 69/1/944: 32; 78/1/189: 32–3, 48.
53. "Prisluchivat'sia k golosu," 2; "Zhaloby pokupatelei," *Pravda Vostoka*, March 21 1937, 4.
54. "Ser'eznoe preduprezhdenie," *ST*, January 14 1936, 2; "Za sem'iu zamkami," March 21 1936, 3; A. Belov, "Inspektor Savenkov," September 13 1937, 3, both in *VM*; D. Iazev, "Kniga zhalob," *Trud*, July 10 1936, 2.
55. TsDNISO 30/6/177: 64.
56. RGAE 7971/1/270: 37–9; GASO 2108/1/69: 17–17ob. Archival and other primary sources underscore that there was some flexibility in how customer conferences were subsequently organized. For example, representatives from local trade departments and the trade inspectorate did not always attend the conferences. In addition, some conferences were organized in trade-union clubs, and some focused on not just one store but a series of stores.
57. V. Vinogradov, "Konferentsii pokupatelei," *ST* 10 (1936): 63; "Konferentsii pokupatelei," *ST*, February 5 1936, 1; Shinkarevskii, 3; "Veskoe slovo," 1.
58. RGAE 7971/1/364: 41, 57, 62, 69, 183–4; 7971/1/363: 43, 50, 66, 70.
59. "Veskoe slovo," 1.
60. RGAE 7971/1/396: 13; GARF 5452/28/549: 8. For more on the importance of mobilizing women in the conferences, see Shinkarevskii, 3.
61. RGAE 7971/1/363: 83; 7971/1/364: 101.
62. This recharacterization of women's domestic roles and experiences was part of a broader rehabilitation of the domestic and the feminine in the 1930s. For more on this, see in particular the scholarly literature on the wife-activists movement cited in Chapter 3, note 29.
63. "Konferentsii pokupatelei," 1; Shinkarevskii, 3; RGAE 7971/1/396: 13.
64. "Konferentsii pokupatelei," 1.
65. Shinkarevskii, 3.
66. RGAE 7971/1/363: 81; 7971/1/364: 112.
67. RGAE 7971/1/363: 59; Shinkarevskii, 3.
68. RGAE 7971/1/362: 40; 7971/1/363: 24; "Slovo pokupatelia," *ST*, February 8 1936, 1; A. Vladimirov, "Kak my obsluzhivaem detei," *ST*, December 12 1937, 4.
69. RGAE 7971/1/363: 34–5, 44, 54, 88; 7971/1/364: 112; "Pokupatel' trebuet," *ST*, September 24 1937, 2.
70. RGAE 7971/1/364: 16, 32–6.
71. "Veskoe slovo," 1.
72. "Konferentsiia pokupatelei v malakhovke," *VM*, July 16 1937, 2 (approximately 200 attended); Shinkarevskii, 3 (*Gastronom* and *Bakaleia* chains organized over 100 conferences in four months in early 1936, with 100 to 500 participants at each); RGAE 7971/1/363 and 364 (approximately 80 to 200 consumers attended the many conferences discussed in these files).
73. David Hoffmann, *Peasant Metropolis: Social Identities in Moscow, 1929–1941* (Ithaca, 1994), 201.

74. Sheila Fitzpatrick, *Stalin's Peasants: Resistance and Survival in the Russian Village after Collectivization* (Oxford, 1994), 269.
75. A. Shtylko, "Posle vystavki," *ST*, August 26 1937, 3.
76. TsAGM 2458/1/368: 11. For repeat or multiple uses of forums, see RGAE 7971/1/363: 64; A. Tsarev, under "Korotkie signaly," *VM*, July 29 1937, 3.
77. "Po retseptam domokhoziaek;" "Po retseptu domashnikh khoziaek;" L. Litli, "Po retseptu domashnikh khoziaek," all in *VM*, January 17, 20, and 26, 1937, 2, 4, and 3, respectively. For another example of housewives helping with the production of foodstuffs, see "Ispol'zuem opyt domashnikh khoziaek," *VM*, December 29 1936, 3.
78. "Dovol'nye pokupateli," *ST*, January 30 1936, 3; E. R., "Plokhoi vybor igrushek," *VM*, December 21 1936, 3, and "Chto my pokupaem ran'she, chto pokupaem teper'," *ST*, October 29 1937, 3; GARF 5452/28/185: 60.
79. "Znatye liudi strany o sovetskoi torgovle," *ST*, November 7 1937, 4.
80. "Konferentsii pokupatelei," 1; RGAE 7971/1/364: 2
81. RGAE 7971/1/360: 125.
82. RGAE 7971/1/364: 13.
83. S. Kaplan, "Konferentsii pokupatelei," *ST*, October 9 1937, 1.
84. S. L., "Pokupatel' trebuet," *ST*, March 12 1936, 3.
85. Vinogradov, 64.
86. Strel'nikov, under "Korotkie signaly," *VM*, October 11 1937, 3.
87. RGAE 7971/1/363: 50, 77.
88. "Izdevatel'stvo nad pokupateliami," *Pravda vostoka*, June 6 1937, 4.
89. A. Nalatova, "Pora odevat'sia v sovetskom stile," *Rabotnitsa* 26 (1934): 16. For similar comments by working women about the need for comfortable and practical clothing, see "Dom modelei," 4.
90. "Predlozheniia delegatov," *Trud*, August 3 1936, 4. Some women linked their consumer interests more directly to women's emancipation as a goal. A. K. Trifonova, for example, expressed frustration in a newspaper letter about the lack of appropriate books for young girls. The problem? Books featured boy-heroes but not girl-heroines, an obvious injustice. See *Komsomol'skaia pravda*, December 27 1936, 3.
91. P. V. Artemova, "Domashnie voprosy," *Trud*, July 15 1936, 3.
92. "Pis'mo domokhoziaek," *VM*, February 16 1937, 2. See the letter from a metalworker and a teacher complaining about similar problems in a worker's area 10 kilometers from Moscow, *ST*, July 20 1937, 3.
93. RGAE 7971/1/364: 20.
94. GARF 5452/28/548: 181.
95. For more on the regime's pronatalist policies see Wendy Goldman, *Women, the State and Revolution – Soviet Family Policy and Social Life, 1917–1936* (Cambridge, 1993); David Hoffmann, "Mothers in the Motherland: Stalinist Pronatalism in Its Pan-European Context," *Journal of Social History* 34: 1 (2000): 35–54.
96. Kaplan, 1.
97. T. Andreev, "Govoriat pokupateli," *ST*, December 2 1937, 3.
98. Inzhener Gavrilov, "Kak kupit' knigu," *VM*, November 28 1937, 3.
99. RGAE 7971/1/250: 16.
100. *VM*, October 26 1936, 3.

101. M. P. Klimova, "O kukhonnykh priborakh i servirovke," *Trud*, July 9 1936, 3. For similar complaints by housewives, see V. B., "Predlozhenie domokhoziaiki," *VM*, November 21 1936, 3.
102. Ivanov, *VM*, November 23 1937, 3; Ians, *VM*, October 2 1937, 3.
103. RGAE 7971/1/364: 194. For another example of a woman representing all housewives, see idem., 105–6.
104. M. Makarova, "Kulinaria i arifmetika," *VM*, February 26 1937, 3.
105. Quoted in "Oblegchite trud domashnei khoziaiki!" *Rabotnitsa* 28 (1937): 13. For similar examples of housewives speaking on behalf of the larger group, see "Khotim, chtoby stol byl vkusnym i pitatel'nym," *Za pishchevuiu industriiu*, January 14 1936.
106. S. I., "Pochemu zdes' net obinona," *Qzil Qzbekistan*, January 14 1935, 4.
107. RGAE 7971/1/363: 30.
108. Fekla Zubkina et al., "Obsluzhit's nuzhdy detei," *ST*, August 17 1935, 1.
109. For a comparative discussion of the citizen-consumer, see Chapter 7.
110. V. Tez., "Stoly zakazov v prodmagakh," *VM*, January 25 1936, 2. For a store director's use of "citizen-customer," see RGAE 7971/1/364: 103. For an editorial's use of the term, see "Rabotat' po-bol'shevistski," 23.
111. James Scott, *Weapons of the Weak: Everyday Forms of Peasant Resistance* (New Haven, 1987).

7 Soviet Retailing and Consumer Culture in Comparative Perspective

1. Victoria de Grazia, "Changing Consumption Regimes in Europe, 1930–1970: Comparative Perspectives on the Distribution Problem," in *Getting and Spending: European and American Consumer Societies in the Twentieth Century*, eds., Susan Strasser, Charles McGovern, and Matthias Judt (Cambridge, 1998), 61. For recent scholarship that focuses more explicitly on the role of the state in the making of retail sectors, consumer cultures, and the consumer, see *Getting and Spending*; Martin Daunton and Matthew Hilton, eds., *The Politics of Consumption: Material Culture and Citizenship in Europe and America* (Oxford, 2001); Frank Trentmann, ed., *The Making of the Consumer: Knowledge, Power and Identity in the Modern World* (Oxford, 2006).
2. For a useful overview of this new age, see Stephen Kotkin, "Modern Times: The Soviet Union and the Interwar Conjuncture," *Kritika* 2: 1 (2001): 111–64.
3. For how the fascist government in Italy appealed to consumers to pursue certain consumption patterns in an effort to combat Americanization, encourage national autarkic economic growth, and nationalize women, see Victoria de Grazia "Nationalizing Women: The Competition Between Fascist and Commercial Cultural Models in Mussolini's Italy," in *The Sex of Things: Gender and Consumption in Historical Perspective*, eds., Victoria de Grazia and Ellen Furlough (Berkeley, 1996), 337–58; Alexander Nützenadel, "Dictating Food: Autarchy, Food Provision, and Consumer Politics in Fascist Italy, 1922–1943," in *Food and Conflict in the Age of the Two World Wars*, eds., Frank Trentmann and Flemming Just (Houndmills, Basingstoke,

2006), 88–108; Eugenia Paulicelli, *Fashion under Fascism: Beyond the Black Shirt* (Oxford, 2004). Karl Gerth shows how the National Products Movement, and to some extent the Nationalist Government in China (after its elevation to power in 1928), encouraged consumers "to practice nationalism and anti-imperialism" through specific acts of consumption and nonconsumption. Karl Gerth, *China Made: Consumer Culture and the Creation of the Nation* (Cambridge, MA, 2003).

4. Of course sumptuary laws regulating dress had long been in existence. In addition, local ordinances (municipal or state-level) that affected commercial activities and/or the production of foodstuffs had already been adopted in some places. For example, in the late nineteenth century some larger German cities passed laws against the adulteration of milk. See Hans J. Teuteberg, "Food Adulteration and the Beginnings of Uniform Food Legislation in Late Nineteenth-Century Germany," in *The Origins and Development of Food Policies in Europe*, eds., J. Burnett and D. Oddy (London, 1994), 146–60. In the United States, many states adopted "Blue Laws" that restricted retail sales and other commercial activities on Sunday (the Christian Sabbath). Some governments also resorted to protectionist trade policies, such as tariffs on imported goods, to protect domestic economies during times of perceived or actual economic crisis.

5. Jim Phillips and Michael French, "Adulteration and Food Law, 1899–1939," *Twentieth-Century British History* 9: 3 (1998): 360; idem, "State Regulation and the Hazards of Milk, 1900–1939," *The Society for the Social History of Medicine* 12: 3 (1999): 376–7; Frank Trentmann, "Bread, Milk and Democracy: Consumption and Citizenship in Twentieth-Century Britain," in *The Politics of Consumption* (Oxford, 2001), 138–9.

6. Lizabeth Cohen, *A Consumers' Republic: The Politics of Mass Consumption in Postwar America* (New York, 2003), 21.

7. Trentmann, "Bread, Milk and Democracy," 141–3; Matthew Hilton, *Consumerism in 20th-Century Britain* (Cambridge, 2003), 61–74; Jonathan Manning, "The War and Civil Consumption in London," *Guerres Mondiales et Conflits Contemporains* 46 (1996): 29–45. Because free trade was such a popular ideology and movement in Britain in the late nineteenth century, many people resisted the idea of state regulations. However, popular opinion began to shift during the First World War, and in the interwar era many who had previously opposed state intervention in the retail sector began to rethink their positions. For more on this change see Trentmann, op. cit., and "Civil Society, Commerce, and the 'Citizen-Consumer'," in *Paradoxes of Civil Society: New Perspectives on Modern German and British History*, ed., Frank Trentmann (Oxford and New York, 2000), 307–31.

8. Belinda Davis, *Home Fires Burning: Food, Politics, and Everyday Life in World War I Berlin* (Chapel Hill, 2000), chapter 6.

9. Cohen, *A Consumers' Republic*, 31; Trentmann, "Bread, Milk and Democracy," and Hartmut Berghoff, "Enticement and Deprivation: The Regulation of Consumption in Pre-War Germany," both in *The Politics of Consumption*, 155 and 171, 179, respectively; Nützenadel, 99. Apparently by the late 1920s the Weimar Government in Germany had already moved to regulate prices for many goods, either at the national or local level. See Uwe Spiekermann, "From Neighbour to Consumer: The Transformation of Retailer-Consumer

Relationships in Twentieth-Century Germany," in *The Making of the Consumer*, 155.

10. Jonathan Morris, "The Fascist 'Disciplining' of the Italian Retail Sector, 1922–40," *Business History* 40: 4 (1998): 151.

11. Victoria de Grazia, *Getting and Spending*, 72–3; idem, *Irresistible Empire: America's Advance Through Twentieth-Century Europe* (Cambridge, MA, 2005), 125, 167.

12. Walter Froelich, "European Experiments in Protecting Small Competitors," *Harvard Business Review* 17: 4 (Summer 1939): 449.

13. Irene Guenther, *Nazi Chic: Fashioning Women in the Third Reich* (Oxford and New York, 2004): 162–3.

14. For more on the role of scientists and medical experts as controllers for food manufacturers, see Sally M. Horrocks, "Quality Control and Research: the Role of Scientists in the British Food Industry, 1870–1939," in *The Origins and Development of Food Policies in Europe*, 130–45; and Phillips and French, "Adulteration and Food Law," 353, 364–5.

15. M. French and J. Phillips, *Cheated not Poisoned: Food Regulation in the United Kingdom, 1875–1938* (Manchester, 2000), 11–12, 186.

16. Philips and French "Adulteration and Food Law," 354.

17. Cohen, *A Consumers' Republic*, 21, 33–35; Gwen Kay, "Healthy Public Relations: The FDA's 1930s Legislative Campaign," *Bulletin of the History of Medicine* 75 (2001): 471. Before the Great Depression, Cohen points out, consumers' associations focused primarily on using their purchasing power to support workers. In the 1930s, however, these associations and women's groups began to focus more on protecting consumers' interests.

18. Davis, especially chapter 3; idem, "Food Scarcity and the Empowerment of the Female Consumer in World War I Berlin," in *The Sex of Things*, 287–310.

19. Phillips and French, "State Regulation," 386.

20. In practice the act appears to have been an ineffectual piece of legislation that did little to restrain profiteering. Rather, its purpose and outcome appear to have been to "check social criticism" and "educate the public" about "the inevitability and rightness of trusts, high prices and profits." Hilton, *Consumerism*, 72–5.

21. In the United States in the 1930s, for example, some ordinary consumers joined county councils to monitor retail prices. Meg Jacobs, "The Politics of Plenty in the Twentieth-Century United States," in *The Politics of Consumption*, 233. The involvement of the public in the monitoring of retailing has grown in western capitalist countries since the interwar era. During the Second World War, consumers temporarily became much more involved in the official regulation of the retail sector. Meg Jacobs, " 'How About Some Meat?': The Office of Price Administration, Consumption Politics, and State Building from the Bottom Up, 1941–1946," *Journal of American History* 84:3 (Dec., 1997): 910–41.

22. For more on state intervention in the economy during the First World War, see Hilton, *Consumerism*, chapter 2; Trentmann, "Bread, Milk and Democracy," 129–62; Manning, 29–45.

23. Davis, *Home Fires*, 116.

24. E. P. Thompson, "The Moral Economy of the English Crowd in the Eighteenth Century," *Past and Present* 50 (1971): 76–136.
25. Frank Trentmann, "The Evolution of the Consumer: Meanings, Identities, and Political Synapses Before the Age of Influence," in *The Ambivalent Consumer: Questioning Consumption in East Asia and the West*, eds., Sheldon Garon and Patricia L. Machlachlan (Ithaca, 2006), 32; Davis, *Home Fires*, 3.
26. The phrase "the point of consumption" is borrowed from Jacobs, "The Politics of Plenty," 226.
27. Meg Jacobs, "'Democracy's Third Estate': New Deal Politics and the Construction of a 'Consuming Public,'" *International Labor and Working-Class History* 55 (1999): 38; Charles McGovern, "Consumption and Citizenship in the United States, 1900–1940," and Lizabeth Cohen, "The New Deal State and the Making of the Citizen Consumer," both in *Getting and Spending*, 37–83, esp. 55, and 111–25, esp. 117–22. Roosevelt's quote is from idem, 121. For more on the changing relationship between American consumers and the state in the 1930s, also see Jacobs, "The Politics of Plenty," especially 232–7; and Cohen, *A Consumers' Republic*.
28. Hilton, *Consumerism*, 117–35, especially 135.
29. Trentmann, "Bread, Milk, and Democracy," 134.
30. Trentmann, "Civil Society, Commerce, and the 'Citizen-Consumer,'" esp. 321–3.
31. Shelley Baranowski, *Strength Through Joy: Consumerism and Mass Tourism in the Third Reich* (Cambridge, 2004), 31.
32. Berghoff, 173, 175–7.
33. De Grazia, *Irresistible Empire*, 125; Baranowski, 35–6; Berghoff, 178.
34. Baranowski, 35, 55, 60.
35. Jacobs, "Democracy's Third Estate," 36–7, 41.
36. Ibid., 34. According to Cohen, this increased emphasis on consumers as purchasers began to displace the idea of consumers as citizens who had the "right to be protected in the marketplace or to be heard in government chambers." See Cohen, *A Consumers' Republic*, 54. While this may be true, the conceptualization of consumers as purchasers who were central to American economic health nonetheless cast consumers as citizens with a national role.
37. Lizabeth Cohen, "Citizens and Consumers in the US in the Century of Mass Consumption," in *The Politics of Consumption*, 220.
38. Stephen Constantine, "The Buy British Campaign of 1931," *Journal of Advertising History* 10: 1 (1981): 44–59. Quotes from pp. 46 and 55.
39. Kate Lacey, *Feminine Frequencies, Gender, German Radio, and the Public Sphere, 1923–1945* (Ann Arbor, 1997), 179.
40. Nancy Reagin, "Comparing Apples and Oranges: Housewives and the Politics of Consumption in Interwar Germany," in *Getting and Spending*, 260; idem, "Marktordnung and Autarkic Housekeeping: Housewives and Private Consumption under the Four-Year Plan, 1936–1939," *German History* 19: 2 (2001): 162–83; Lacey, 179–81.
41. Uwe Spiekermann, "Brown Bread for Victory" in *Food and Conflict*, 149.
42. Berghoff, 180–3.
43. Jacobs, "'Democracy's Third Estate,'" 36–7, 41.
44. Constantine, 51.

45. Berghoff, 180; Reagin, "Comparing Apples and Oranges," 256.
46. Reagin, "Marktordnung," 169.
47. Reagin, "Comparing Apples and Oranges," 256–7; idem, "Marktordnung," 169–77. Goering's quote is from Lacey, 175.
48. Cohen, *A Consumers' Republic*, 34; idem, "Citizens and Consumers in the US," 208.
49. Cohen, *A Consumers' Republic*, 33–6. Quote from p. 36.
50. Cohen, "Citizens and Consumers in the US," 209.
51. To some extent, of course, women consumer activists had also promoted this identity earlier, when they had spoken on behalf of the wider public and tried to use consumption to influence politics. For a brief summary of these efforts, see Matthew Hilton, "The Female Consumer and the Politics of Consumption in Twentieth-Century Britain," *The Historical Journal* 45: 1 (2002), 108–11.
52. Trentmann, "Bread, Milk, and Democracy," 155.
53. N. Shinkarevskii, "Konferentsii pokupatelei," *ST*, May 18 1936, 3.
54. See Chapter 6.
55. RGAE 7971/1/364: 62.
56. RGAE 484/3/629: 77, 97.
57. Don Slater, *Consumer Culture and Modernity* (Cambridge, 1997), 35.
58. Julie Hessler, *A Social History of Soviet Trade: Trade Policy, Retail Practices, and Consumption, 1917–1953* (Princeton, 2004), 229.

Conclusion

1. GARF 5452/28/48: 14–15.
2. GARF 5452/28/122: 54.

Bibliography

Archival sources

Rossisskii gosudarstvennyi arkhiv sotsial'no-politicheskoi istorii (RGASPI)
Rossiiski gosudarstvennyi arkhiv po ekonomiki (RGAE)
Gosudarstvennyi arkhiv Rossiiskoi Federatsii (GARF)
Tsentral'nyi arkhiv goroda Moskvy (TsAGM)
Tsentral'nyi arkhiv obshchestvenno-politicheskoi istorii Moskvy (TsAOPIM)
Tsentral'nyi gosudarstvennyi arkhiv Moskovskoi oblasti (TsGAMO)
Gosudarstvennyi arkhiv Saratovskoi oblasti (GASO)
Tsentr dokumentatsii noveishei istorii Saratovskoi oblasti (TsDNISO)
Tashkentskii gorodskoi arkhiv (TGA)
Tsentral'nyi Gosudarstvennyi Arkhiv Respubliki Uzbekistan (TsGARUz)
Tsentral'nyi Gosudarstvennyi Arkhiv Respubliki Uzbekistan Kino, Foto, i Fono
  Dokumentov

Selected published primary sources

Journals and Newspapers
Biulleten' pravdy
Bol'shevik
Igrushka/Sovetskaia igrushka
Izvestiia
Kommunistka
Komsomol'skaia pravda
Krest'ianka
Planovoe khoziaistvo
Pravda
Pravda Vostoka
Rabochaia Moskva
Rabotnitsa
Rabotnitsa i krest'ianka
Revoliutsiia i natsional'nosti
Problemy ekonomiki
Snabzhenie, kooperatsiia, torgovlia/ Sovetskaia torgovlia
Soiuz potrebitelei
Sovetskaia torgovlia/Voprosy sovetskoi torgovli
Stakhanovets torgovli
Trud
Vechernaia Moskva
Voprosy truda/Voprosy profdvizheniia

Za kul'turnyi univermag
Za pishchevuiu industriiu/Pishchevaia industriia
Za tempy, kachestvo, proverku

Books, stenographic reports, document collections, statistical sources

Bolotin, Z. S. *Bez kartochek.* Moscow, 1935.
———. *Reshaiushchii god v razvertyvanii sovetskoi torgovli.* Moscow, 1936.
———. *Sovetskaia torgovlia v stakhanovskom godu.* Moscow, 1937.
Direktivy KPSS i Sovetskogo pravitel'stva po khoziaistvennym voprosam, 1917–1957. Sbornik dokumentov. 4 vols. Moscow, 1957.
Epshtein, M. *Osnovnye zadachi Moskovskoi torgovli.* Moscow, 1936.
Fain, E. S. *Bor'ba za sotsializm i sovetskaia torgovlia.* Moscow, 1932.
Gatovskii, L. *O prirode sovetskoi torgovli na sovremennom etape.* Moscow, 1931.
Grichik, K. and V. Pirkovskii. *Organizatsiia i pravila roznichnoi torgovli.* Moscow, 1936.
Industrializatsiia SSSR, 1933–1937 gg.: Dokumenty i materialy. Moscow, 1971.
Industrializatsiia Sovetskogo Soiuza: Novye dokumenty, novye fakty, novye podkhody, vol. 2. Moscow, 1999.
Itogi plenuma TsK VKP (b) 28 Sent-2 Okt 1932 – O razvitii sovetskoi torgovli. Moscow, 1932.
Itogi razvitiia sovetskoi torgovli ot VI k VII S"ezdu sovetov SSSR. Moscow, 1935.
Kirov, S. M. *Ob itogakh sentiabrskogo plenuma TsK VKP(b).* Moscow, 1932.
KPSS o profsoiuzakh, 3rd edn. Moscow, 1957.
KPSS v resoliutsiiakh i resheniiakh s"ezdov, konferentsii i plenumov TsK, vols 5 & 6. Moscow, 1984–1985.
Kontrol' za rabochim snabzheniemi: sbornik ofitsial'nykh dokumentov – iuridicheskoe izdatel'stvo NKIU SSSR. Moscow, 1943.
Lenin, V. I. *Polnoe sobranie sochinenii,* 5th edn. Moscow, 1976–1982.
Malkis, A. I., ed. *Potreblenie i spros v SSSR.* Leningrad, 1935.
Mikoian, A. "Dva mesiatsa v SShA." *SShA, ekonomika, politika, ideologiia* 10 and 11 (1971): 66–77; and 73–84, respectively.
Nauchno-issledovatel'skii Institut Potrebkooperatsii, *Organizatsiia i tekhnika sovetskoi roznichnoi torgovli.* Leningrad, 1933.
Neiman, G. Ia. *Puti razvitiia sovetskoi torgovli.* Moscow, 1934.
———. *Vnutrenniaia torgovlia SSSR.* Moscow, 1935.
———, ed. *Za stakhanovskoe dvizhenie v sovetskoi torgovle.* Moscow, 1936.
Novikov, I. M. *Novyi etap v rabote potrebitel'skoi kooperatsii.* Moscow, 1931.
Otchet tsentral'nogo komiteta professional'nogo Soiuza rabotnikov gostorgovli (1934–1937 gg). Moscow, 1937.
Plotnikov, I. "Stakhanovskoe dvizhenie i bor'ba za kul'turu torgovogo obsluzhivaniia." In *Za stakhanovskoe dvizhenie v sovetskoi torgovle,* ed. G. Ia. Neiman. Moscow, 1936.
Postanovleniia plenumov VTsSPS. Moscow, 1949.
Postanovleniia VIII Plenuma VTsSPS. Moscow, 1939.
Potrebitel'skaia kooperatsiia ot VI k VII s"ezdu sovetov soiuza SSR. Moscow, 1935.
Presidium Moskovskogo Soveta R.K. i K. D., Protokol no. 40 prilozhenie. Moscow, 1936.

Profsouzy SSSR – dokumenty: materialy v chetyrekh tomakh. Moscow, 1963.
Profsoiuzy SSSR i narodnyi kontrol', 1917–1965: Dokumenty i materialy. Moscow, 1965.
Sedmoi s''ezd sovetov soiuza SSR: Stenograficheskii otchet. Moscow, 1935.
Semnadtsataia konferentsiia VKP (b): Stenograficheskii otchet. Moscow, 1932.
S''ezdy sovetov RSFSR v postanovleniiakh i rezoliutsiiakh. Moscow, 1939.
Shvernik, N. *O perestroike profoiuzov.* Moscow, 1934.
Smirnov, M. "Boevye zadachi sovetskoi torgovli v 1938 godu." In *Rabotniki sovetskoi torgovli sluzhat narodu.* Moscow, 1938.
Sovetskaia torgovlia. Statisticheskii sbornik. Moscow, 1956.
Stalin, I. V. *Sochineniia.* 13 volumes. Moscow, 1946–1951.
———. *Sochineniia I [XIV], 1934–1940.* Stanford, 1967.
Tri goda bor'by za sovetskuiu kul'turnuiu torgovliu. Moscow, 1934.
TsUNKhU Gosplan SSSR. *Kadry sovetskoi torgovli.* Moscow, 1935.
Veitser, Ia. *Pis'mo narkoma I. Veitsera po stakhanovskomu dvizheniiu.* Moscow, 1935.
Vsesoiuznaia perepis' naseleniia 1926 goda. Moscow, 1928–1931.
Vsesoiuznaia perepis' naseleniia 1939 goda: osnovnye itogi – Rossiia. Moscow, 1939.
XVI S''ezd vsesoiuznoi kommunisticheskoi partii (b), 26 Iiunia–13 Iiulia 1930 g.: Stenograficheskii otchet. Moscow, 1935.
XVII S''ezd vsesoiuznoi kommunisticheskoi partii (b), 26 Ianvaria–10 Fevralia 1934 g.: Stenograficheskii otchet. Moscow, 1934.
XVIII S''ezd vsesouiznoi kommunisticheskoi partii (b), 10–21 Marta 1939 g.: Stenograficheskii otchet. Moscow, 1939.
Zhukova, S. *Rabotnitsa, v riady kooperatsii.* Moscow, 1927.
Zhukovskii, G. A. "Sdvigi potrebitel'skom sprose gorodskogo naseleniia SSSR." In *Potreblenie i spros v SSSR,* ed. A. I. Malkis. Leningrad, 1935.

Selected secondary sources

Abelson, Elaine. *When Ladies Go A-Thieving: Middle-Class Shoplifters in the Victorian Department Store.* New York, 1989.
Adams, Jan S. *Citizen Inspectors in the Soviet Union: The People's Control Committee.* New York and London, 1977.
Alexopoulis, Golfo. "Exposing Illegality and Oneself: Complaint and Risk in Stalin's Russia." In *Reforming Justice in Russia, 1864–1996: Power, Culture, and the Limits of Legal Order,* ed. Peter H. Solomon, Jr. Armonk and London, 1997.
Arkhipov, V. A. and L. F. Morozov. *Bor'ba protiv kapitalisticheskikh elementov v promyshlennosti i torgovle: dvadtsatye – nachalo tridtsatykh godov.* Moscow, 1978.
Avrich, Paul. "The Bolshevik Revolution and Workers' Control in Russian Industry." *Slavic Review* 22 (1963): 47–63.
Bailes, Kendall E. *Technology and Society under Lenin and Stalin: Origins of the Soviet Technical Intelligentsia, 1917–1941.* Princeton, 1978.
———. "The American Connection: Ideology and the Transfer of American Technology to the Soviet Union, 1917–1941." *Comparative Studies in Society and History* 23: 3 (1981): 421–48.

Ball, Alan. *Russia's Last Capitalists: The Nepmen, 1921–1929*. Berkeley, 1987.
————. *Imagining America: Influence and Images in Twentieth-Century Russia*. New York and Oxford, 2003.
Banerji, Arup. *Merchants and Markets in Revolutionary Russia, 1917–1930*. New York, 1997.
Baranowski, Shelley. *Strength through Joy: Consumerism and Mass Tourism in the Third Reich*. Cambridge, 2004.
Beissinger, Mark R. "Soviet Empire as 'Family Resemblance'." *Slavic Review* 65: 2 (2006): 294–303.
Benson, Susan Porter. *Counter Cultures: Saleswomen, Managers, and Customers in American Department Stores, 1890–1940*. Urbana, 1986.
Berghoff, Hartmut. "Enticement and Deprivation: The Regulation of Consumption in Pre-War Germany." In *The Politics of Consumption: Material Culture and Citizenship in Europe and America*, eds. Martin Daunton and Matthew Hilton. Oxford and New York, 2001.
Blitstein, Peter A. "Cultural Diversity and the Interwar Conjuncture: Soviet Nationality Policy in its Comparative Context." *Slavic Review* 65: 2 (2006): 273–93.
Bonnell, Victoria. *Iconography of Power: Soviet Political Posters Under Lenin and Stalin*. Berkeley, 1997.
Borrero, Mauricio. *Hungry Moscow: Scarcity and Urban Society in the Russian Civil War*. New York, 2003.
Boym, Svetlana. *Common Places: Mythologies of Everyday Life in Russia*. Cambridge, MA, 1994.
Bradley, Joseph. *Muzhik and Muscovite: Urbanization in Late Imperial Russia*. Berkeley, 1985.
————. *Guns for the Tsar: American Technology and the Small Arms Industry in Nineteenth-Century Russia*. DeKalb, 1990.
Brooks, Jeffrey. *Thank You, Comrade Stalin!: Soviet Public Culture from Revolution to Cold War*. Princeton, 2000.
Buck-Morss, Susan. *Dreamworld and Catastrophe: The Passing of Mass Utopia in East and West*. Cambridge, MA, 2000.
Buckley, Mary. *Women and Ideology in the Soviet Union*. Ann Arbor, 1989.
————. "*Krest'yanskaya gazeta* and Rural Stakhanovism." *Europe-Asia Studies* 46: 8 (1994): 1387–407.
————. "The Untold Story of *Obshchestvennitsa* in the 1930s." *Europe-Asia Studies* 48: 4 (1996): 569–86.
————. "Why Be a Shock Worker or a Stakhanovite?" In *Women in Russia and Ukraine*, ed. Rosalind Marsh. Cambridge, 1996.
————. "Categorizing Resistance to Rural Stakhanovism." In *Politics and Society under the Bolsheviks*, eds. Kevin McDermott and John Morison. New York, 1999.
————. "The Soviet Wife-Activist Down on the Farm." *Social History* 26: 3 (2001): 282–98.
————. "Complex 'Realities' of the 'New' Women of the 1930s: Assertive, Superior, Belittled and Beaten." In *Gender and Russian History and Culture*, ed. Linda Edmondson. New York, 2001.
————. *Mobilizing Soviet Peasants: Heroines and Heroes of Stalin's Fields*. Lanham, 2006.

Burds, Jeffrey. *Peasant Dreams and Market Politics: Labor Migration and the Russian Village, 1861–1905*. Pittsburgh, 1998.

Burnett J. and D. Oddy, eds. *The Origins and Development of Food Policies in Europe*. London and New York, 1994.

Chase, William J. *Workers, Society, and the Soviet State: Labor and Life in Moscow, 1918–1929*. Urbana, 1987.

Chatterjee, Choi. "Soviet Heroines and the Language of Modernity, 1930–1939." In *Women in the Stalin Era*, ed. Melanie Ilič. Houndmills, Basingstoke, 1999.

Chugunov, A. I. *Organy sotsialisticheskogo kontrolia RSFSR, 1923–1934 gg*. Moscow, 1972.

Clements, Barbara Evans. "The Birth of the New Soviet Woman." In *Bolshevik Culture: Experiment and Order in the Russian Revolution*, eds. A. Gleason, P. Kenez, and R. Stites. Bloomington, 1985.

———, *Bolshevik Women*. London and New York, 1997.

———, Barbara Alpern Engel, and Christine Worobec, eds. *Russia's Women: Accommodation, Resistance, Transformation*. Berkeley, 1991.

Cohen, Lizabeth. *Making a New Deal: Industrial Workers in Chicago, 1919–1939*. New York, 1990.

———. *A Consumers' Republic: The Politics of Mass Consumption in Postwar America*. New York, 2003.

Cox, Randi. "All This Can Be Yours!: Soviet Commercial Advertising and the Social Construction of Space, 1928–1956." In *The Landscape of Stalinism: The Art and Ideology of Soviet Space*, eds. Evgeny Dobrenko and Eric Naiman. Seattle, 2003.

———. "NEP Without Nepmen! Soviet Advertising and the Transition to Socialism in the 1920s." In *Everyday Life in Early Soviet Russia: Taking the Revolution Inside*, eds. Christina Kiaer and Eric Naiman. Bloomington, 2006.

Crossick, Geoffrey and Serge Jaumain. *Cathedrals of Consumption: The European Department Store, 1850–1939*. Aldershot, 1999.

Daunton, Martin and Matthew Hilton, eds. *The Politics of Consumption: Material Culture and Citizenship in Europe and America*. Oxford and New York, 2001.

Davies, Sarah. *Popular Opinion in Stalin's Russia: Terror, Propaganda, and Dissent, 1934–1941*. Cambridge, 1997.

Davies, R. W. *The Industrialization of Soviet Russia 3: The Soviet Economy in Turmoil, 1929–1930*. Cambridge, MA, 1989.

———. *The Industrialization of Soviet Russia 4: Crisis and Progress in the Soviet Economy, 1931–1933*. London, 1996.

———, Mark Harrison, and S. G. Wheatcroft, eds. *The Economic Transformation of the Soviet Union, 1913–1945*. Cambridge, 1994.

——— and Oleg Khlevnyuk. "Stakhanovism and the Soviet Economy." *Europe-Asia Studies* 54: 6 (2002): 867–904.

Davis, Belinda. *Home Fires Burning: Food, Politics, and Everyday Life in World War I Berlin*. Chapel Hill, 2000.

———. "Food Scarcity and the Empowerment of the Female Consumer in World War I Berlin." In *The Sex of Things: Gender and Consumption in Historical Perspective*, eds. Victoria de Grazia and Ellen Furlough. Berkeley, 1996.

De Grazia, Victoria. "Changing Consumption Regimes in Europe." In *Getting and Spending: European and American Consumer Societies in the Twentieth Century*, eds. Susan Strasser, Charles McGovern, and Matthias Judt. Cambridge, 1998.

De Grazia, Victoria. *Irresistible Empire: America's Advance through 20th-Century Europe*. Cambridge, MA, 2005.

—— and Ellen Furlough, eds. *The Sex of Things: Gender and Consumption in Historical Perspective*. Berkeley, 1996.

Dikhtiar, G. A. *Sovetskaia torgovlia v period postroeniia sotsializma*. Moscow, 1961.

Dneprovskii, S. P. *Kooperatory: 1898–1968*. Moscow, 1968.

Dodge, Norton. *Women in the Soviet Economy*. Baltimore, 1966.

Dunham, Vera. *In Stalin's Time: Middleclass Values in Soviet Fiction*. Enlarged and updated edition. Durham, 1990.

Edgar, Adrienne. "Bolshevism, Patriarchy, and the Nation: The Soviet 'Emancipation' of Muslim Women in Pan-Islamic Perspective." *Slavic Review* 65: 2 (2006): 252–72.

Engel, Barbara Alpern. "Not By Bread Alone: Subsistence Riots in Russia during World War I." *The Journal of Modern History* 69: 4 (1997): 696–721.

Engerman, David. *Modernization from the Other Shore: American Intellectuals and the Romance of Russian Development*. Cambridge, MA, 2004.

Fainsod, Merle. *Smolensk Under Soviet Rule*. London, 1958, 1989.

Farnsworth, Beatrice and Lynne Viola, eds. *Russian Peasant Women*. Oxford, 1992.

Filtzer, Donald. *Soviet Workers and Stalinist Industrialization: The Formation of Modern Soviet Production Relations, 1928–1941*. Armonk and New York, 1986.

Fitzpatrick, Sheila. *Education and Social Mobility in the Soviet Union 1921–1934*. Cambridge, 1979.

——. "After NEP: The Fate of NEP Entrepreneurs in the 1930s." *Russian History/Histoire Russe* 13: 2–3 (Summer–Fall 1986): 187–234.

——. *The Cultural Front: Power and Culture in Revolutionary Russia*. Ithaca, 1992.

——. *Stalin's Peasants: Resistance and Survival in the Russian Village after Collectivization*. Oxford, 1994.

——. "Supplicants and Citizens: Public Letter-Writing in Soviet Russia in the 1930s." *Slavic Review* 55: 1 (1996): 78–105.

——. "Signals from Below: Soviet Letters of Denunciation of the 1930s." *The Journal of Modern History* 68 (December 1996): 831–66.

——. *Everyday Stalinism: Ordinary Life in Extraordinary Times: Soviet Russia in the 1930s*. Oxford, 1999.

——. "Ascribing Class: The Construction of Social Identity in Soviet Russia." In *Stalinism: New Directions*, ed. Sheila Fitzpatrick. London and New York, 2000.

—— and Yuri Slezkine, eds. *In the Shadow of Revolution: Life Stories of Russian Women from 1917 to the Second World War*. Princeton, 2000.

Frank, Dana. *Purchasing Power: Consumer Organizing, Gender, and the Seattle Labor Movement, 1919–1929*. Cambridge, 1994.

French, Michael and Jim Phillips, *Cheated Not Poisoned: Food Regulation in the United Kingdom, 1875–1938*. Manchester, 2000.

Furlough, Ellen. *Consumer Cooperation in France: The Politics of Consumption, 1834–1930*. Ithaca, 1991.

Garros, Veronique, Natalia Korenevskaya, and Thomas Lahusen, eds. *Intimacy and Terror: Soviet Diaries of the 1930s*. New York, 1995.

Gerschenkron, Alexander. *Economic Backwardness in Historical Perspective: Collected Essays*. Cambridge, MA, 1962.

Gerth, Karl. *China Made: Consumer Culture and the Creation of the Nation*. Cambridge, MA, 2003.

Gleason, Abbott, Peter Kenez, and Richard Stites, eds. *Bolshevik Culture: Experiment and Order in the Russian Revolution.* Bloomington, 1985.

Glickman, Lawrence. *A Living Wage: American Workers and the Making of a Consumer Society.* Ithaca, 1997.

Glickman, Rose. *Russian Factory Women: Workplace and Society, 1880–1914.* Berkeley, 1984.

Gohstand, Robert. "The Internal Geography of Trade in Moscow from the Mid-Nineteenth Century to the First World War." Ph.D. diss., University of California Berkeley, 1973.

Goldman, Wendy Z. *Women, the State and Revolution – Soviet Family Policy and Social Life, 1917–1936.* Cambridge, 1993.

———. "The Death of the Proletarian Women's Movement." *Slavic Review* 55: 1 (1996): 46–77.

———. *Women at the Gates: Gender and Industry in Stalin's Russia.* Cambridge, 2002.

———. "Stalinist Terror and Democracy: The 1937 Union Campaign." *American Historical Review,* 110: 5 (2005): 1427–53.

Golovina, E. P. "Bor'ba partii za razvitie torgovli v period pobedi uprocheniia sotsializma, 1933–1941." In *Sbornik trudov,* vol. 34, ed. Ministerstvo torgovli RSFSR. Leningrad, 1969.

Gorsuch, Anne. *Youth in Revolutionary Russia: Enthusiasts, Bohemians, Delinquents.* Bloomington, 2000.

Gronow, Jukka. *Caviar with Champagne: Common Luxury and the Ideals of the Good Life in Stalin's Russia.* Oxford and New York, 2003.

Gudvan, A. M. "Essays on the History of the Movement of Sales-Clerical Workers in Russia." In *The Russian Worker: Life and Labor under the Tsarist Regime,* ed. Victoria E. Bonnell. Berkeley, 1983.

Guenther, Irene. *Nazi Chic: Fashioning Women in the Third Reich.* Oxford and New York, 2004.

Hessler, Julie. "Culture of Shortages: A Social History of Soviet Trade, 1917–1953." Ph.D. diss., University of Chicago, 1996.

———. "Cultured Trade: the Stalinist Turn to Consumerism." In *Stalinism: New Directions,* ed. Sheila Fitzpatrick. London and New York, 2000.

———. *A Social History of Soviet Trade: Trade Policy, Retail Practices, and Consumption, 1917–1953.* Princeton, 2004.

Hilton, Marjorie. "Commercial Cultures: Modernity in Russia and the Soviet Union, 1880–1930." Ph.D. diss., University of Illinois, 2002.

———. "Retailing the Revolution: the State Department Store (GUM) and Soviet Society in the 1920s." *Journal of Social History* 37: 4 (2004): 939–64.

Hilton, Matthew. "The Female Consumer and the Politics of Consumption in Twentieth-Century Britain." *The Historical Journal* 45: 1 (2002): 103–28.

———. *Consumerism in 20th-Century Britain.* Cambridge, 2003.

Hodnett, Grey. "Khrushchev and Party-State Control." In *Politics in the Soviet Union,* eds. Alexander Dallin and Alan F. Westin. New York, 1966.

Hoffmann, David L. *Peasant Metropolis: Social Identities in Moscow, 1929–1941.* Ithaca, 1994.

———. "Mothers in the Motherland: Stalinist Pronatalism in Its Pan-European Context." *Journal of Social History* 34: 1 (2000): 35–54.

———. *Stalinist Values: The Cultural Norms of Soviet Modernity, 1917–1941.* Ithaca, 2003.

Holquist, Peter. "Information is the Alpha and the Omega of Our Work: Bolshevik Surveillance in its Pan-European Context." *Journal of Modern History* 69: 3 (1997): 415–50.

Hooper, Cynthia. "Terror from Within: Participation and Coercion in Soviet Power, 1924–1964." Ph.D. diss., Princeton University, 2003.

Hubbard, Leonard. *Soviet Trade and Distribution.* London, 1938.

Ikonnikov, S. N. *Sozdanie i deiatel'nost' ob"edinennykh organov TsKK-RKI v 1923–1934 gg.* Moscow, 1971.

Ilič, Melanie. *Women Workers in the Soviet Interwar Economy: From "Protection" to "Equality."* London, 1999.

Inkeles, Alex and Kent Geiger. "Critical Letters to the Editors of the Soviet Press: Areas and Modes of Complaint." *American Sociological Review* 17: 6 (1952): 694–703.

—— and Kent Geiger. "Critical Letters to the Editors of the Soviet Press: Social Characteristics and Interrelations of Critics and the Criticized." *American Sociological Review* 18: 1 (1953): 12–22.

Izmozik, Vladlen. *Glaza i ushi rezhima: gosudarstvenyi politicheskii kontrol' za naseleniem sovetskoi Rossii v 1918–1928 godakh.* St. Petersburg, 1995.

Jacobs, Meg. "'How About Some Meat?': The Office of Price Administration, Consumption Politics, and State Building from the Bottom Up, 1941–1946." *Journal of American History* 84: 3 (1997): 910–41.

——. "'Democracy's Third Estate': New Deal Politics and the Construction of a 'Consuming Public'." *International Labor and Working-Class History* 55 (1999): 27–51.

——. "The Politics of Plenty in the Twentieth-Century United States." In *The Politics of Consumption,* eds. Martin Daunton and Matthew Hilton. New York, 2001.

Kay, Gwen. "Healthy Public Relations: The FDA's 1930s Legislative Campaign." *Bulletin of the History of Medicine* 75 (2001): 446–87.

Kelly, Catriona and Vadim Volkov. "Directed Desires: *Kul'turnost'* and Consumption." In *Constructing Russian Culture in the Age of Revolution, 1881–1940,* eds. Catriona Kelly and David Shepherd. Oxford, 1998.

Kettering, Karen. "'Ever More Cosy and Comfortable': Stalinism and the Soviet Domestic Interior, 1928–1938." *Journal of Design History* 10: 2 (1997): 119–35.

Khalid, Adeeb. "Backwardness and the Quest for Civilization: Early Soviet Central Asia in Comparative Perspective." *Slavic Review* 65: 2 (2006): 131–51.

Kharkhordin, Oleg. *The Collective and the Individual in Russia: A Study of Practices.* Berkeley, 1999.

Khlevniuk, Oleg and R. W. Davies. "The End of Rationing in the Soviet Union, 1934–1935." *Europe-Asia Studies* 51:4 (1999): 557–609.

Kiaer, Christina. *Imagine No Possessions: The Socialist Objects of Russian Constructivism.* Cambridge, MA, 2005.

Klimov, A. P. *Potrebitel'skaia kooperatsiia v sisteme razvitogo sotsializma.* Moscow, 1980.

Koenker, Diane. "Men Against Women on the Shop Floor in Early Soviet Russia: Gender and Class in the Socialist Workplace." *American Historical Review* 100: 5 (December 1995): 1438–64.

——, William G. Rosenberg, and Ronald Grigor Suny, eds. *Party, State, and Society in the Russian Civil War: Explorations in Social History.* Bloomington, 1989.

Kotkin, Stephen. *Magnetic Mountain: Stalinism as Civilization.* Berkeley, 1995.
———. "Modern Times: The Soviet Union and the Interwar Conjuncture." *Kritika* 2: 1 (2001): 111–64.
———. "The State – Is It Us? Memoirs, Archives, and Kremlinologists." *The Russian Review* 61: 1 (2002): 35–51.
Kulikov, A. G. and S. G. Rodin. "Kadry sovetskoi torgovli." In *40 let sovetskoi torgovli.* Moscow, 1957.
Kuromiya, Hiroaki. *Stalin's Industrial Revolution: Politics and Workers, 1928–1932.* Cambridge, 1988.
Lacey, Kate. *Feminine Frequencies, Gender, German Radio, and the Public Sphere, 1923–1945.* Ann Arbor, 1997.
Lancaster, Bill. *The Department Store: A Social History.* London, 1995.
Lapidus, Gail Warshofsky. *Women in Soviet Society: Equality, Development, and Social Change.* Berkeley, 1978.
Leach, William. "Transformations in a Culture of Consumption: Women and Department Stores, 1890–1925." *Journal of American History* 71: 2 (1984): 319–42.
———. *Land of Desire: Merchants, Power, and the Rise of a New American Culture.* New York, 1993.
Ledeneva, Alena V. *Russia's Economy of Favours: Blat, Networking, and Informal Exchange.* Cambridge, 1998.
Lewin, Moshe. *The Making of the Soviet System: Essays in the Social History of Interwar Russia.* New York, 1985.
Lih, Lars. *Bread and Authority in Russia, 1914–1921.* Berkeley, 1990.
Malino, Sarah. "Behind the Scenes in the Big Store: Reassessing Women's Employment in American Department Stores, 1870–1920." In *Work, Recreation, and Culture: Essays in American Labor History*, eds. Martin Blatt and Martha Norkunas. New York, 1996.
Manning, Roberta. "Women in the Soviet Countryside on the Eve of World War II, 1935–1940." In *Russian Peasant Women*, eds. Beatrice Farnsworth and Lynne Viola. Oxford, 1992.
Manning, Jonathan. "The War and Civil Consumption in London." *Guerres Mondiales et Conflits Contemporains* 46 (1996): 29–45.
Marsh, Rosalind, ed. *Women in Russia and Ukraine.* Cambridge, 1996.
McAuley, Mary. *Bread and Justice: State and Society in Petrograd, 1917–1922.* Oxford, 1991.
McBride, Theresa M. "A Woman's World: Department Stores and the Evolution of Women's Employment, 1870–1920." *French Historical Studies* 10 (Fall 1978): 664–83.
McGovern, Charles. "Consumption and Ctitzenship in the United States, 1900–1940." In *Getting and Spending: European and American Consumer Societies in the Twentieth Century*, eds. Susan Strasser, Charles McGovern, and Matthias Judt. Cambridge, 1998.
Merkel, Ina. "Consumer Culture in the GDR, or How the Struggle for Antimodernity was Lost on the Battleground of Consumer Culture." In *Getting and Spending: European and American Consumer Societies in the Twentieth Century*, eds. Susan Strasser, Charles McGovern, and Matthias Judt. Cambridge, 1998.
Miller, Michael B. *The Bon Marché: Bourgeois Culture and the Department Store, 1869–1920.* Princeton, 1981.

Morozov, L. F. *Bor'ba protiv kapitalisticheskikh elementov v promyshlennosti i torgovle: dvadtsatye – nachalo tridtsatykh godov*. Moscow, 1978.

Morozov, L. F. and V. P. Portnov. *Organy TsKK-NK RKI v bor'be za sovershentsvovanie sovestkogo gosudarstvennogo apparata (1923–1934 gg.)*. Moscow, 1964.

———. *Sotsialisticheskii kontrol" v SSSR: istoricheskii ocherk*. Moscow, 1984.

Morris, Jonathan. "The Fascist 'Disciplining' of the Italian Retail Sector, 1922–40." *Business History* 40: 4 (1998): 138–64.

Naiman, Eric. *Sex in Public: The Incarnation of Early Soviet Ideology*. Princeton, 1997.

Neary, Rebecca Balmas. "Mothering Socialist Society: The Wife-Activists' Movement and the Soviet Culture of Daily Life, 1934–1941." *The Russian Review* 58 (1999): 396–412.

Nolan, Mary. *Visions of Modernity: American Business and the Modernization of Germany*. Oxford, 1994.

Northrop, Douglas. *Veiled Empire: Gender and Power in Stalinist Central Asia*. Ithaca, 2004.

Nove, Alec. *An Economic History of the USSR*. New York, Reprint 1986.

Nützenadel, Alexander. "Dictating Food: Autarchy, Food Provision, and Consumer Politics in Fascist Italy, 1922–1943." In *Food and Conflict in the Age of the Two World Wars*, eds. Frank Trentmann and Flemming Just. Houndmills, Basingstoke, 2006.

Oja, Matt. "From Krestianka to Udarnitsa: Rural Women and the Vydvizhenie Campaign, 1933–1941." In *The Carl Beck Papers in Russian and East European Studies*, no. 1203. Pittsburgh, 1996.

Osokina, Elena A. *Ierarkhiia potrebleniia: o zhizni liudei v usloviiakh stalinskogo snabzheniia, 1928–1935 gg*. Moscow, 1993.

———. "Za zerkal'noi dver'iu Torgsina." *Otechestvennaia istoriia* 2 (April 1995): 86–104.

———. "Krizis snabzheniia 1939–1941 gg. V pis'makh sovetskikh liudei." *Voprosy istorii* 1 (1996): 3–23.

———. *Za fasadom "Stalinskogo izobiliia": Raspredelenie i rynok v snabzhenii naseleniia v gody industrializatsii, 1927–1941*. Moscow, 1998.

———. *Our Daily Bread: Socialist Distribution and the Art of Survival in Stalin"s Russia, 1927–1941*. Armonk, 2001.

Paulicelli, Eugenia. *Fashion under Fascism: Beyond the Black Shirt*. Oxford, 2004.

Pence, Katherine. "'You as a Woman Will Understand': Consumption, Gender, and the Relationship between State and Citizenry in the GDR's Crisis of June 17." *German History* 19 (2001): 218–52.

Petrone, Karen. *Life has Become More Joyous, Comrades: Celebrations in the Time of Stalin*. Bloomington, 2000.

Phillips, J. and M. French. "Adulteration and Food Law, 1899–1939." *Twentieth-Century British History* 9: 3 (1998): 350–69.

——— and M. French. "State Regulation and the Hazards of Milk, 1900–1939." *The Society for the Social History of Medicine* 12: 3 (1999): 371–88.

Raleigh, Donald J. "Languages of Power: How the Saratov Bolsheviks Imagined Their Enemies." *Slavic Review* 57: 2 (1998): 320–49.

Randall, Amy E. "'Revolutionary Bolshevik Work': Stakhanovism in Retail Trade." *The Russian Review* 59: 3 (2000): 425–41.

———. "Legitimizing Soviet Trade: Gender and the Feminization of the Retail Workforce in the Soviet 1930s." *Journal of Social History* 37: 4 (2004): 965–90.

Rappaport, Erika Diane. *Shopping for Pleasure: Women in the Making of London's West End.* Princeton, 2000.

Reagin, Nancy. "Comparing Apples and Oranges: Housewives and the Politics of Consumption in Interwar Germany." In *Getting and Spending: European and American Consumer Societies in the Twentieth Century,* eds. Susan Strasser, Charles McGovern, and Matthias Judt. Cambridge, 1998.

———. "Marktordnung and Autarkic Housekeeping: Housewives and Private Consumption under the Four-Year Plan, 1936–1939." *German History* 19: 2 (2001): 162–83.

Rees, E. A. *State Control in Soviet Russia: The Rise and Fall of the Workers' and Peasants' Inspectorate, 1920–1934.* London, 1987.

Reid, Susan E. "All Stalin's Women: Gender and Power in Soviet Art of the 1930s." *Slavic Review* 57: 1 (1998): 133–73.

———. "Cold War in the Kitchen: Gender and the De-Stalinization of Consumer Taste in the Soviet Union under Khrushchev." *Slavic Review* 61: 2 (2002): 211–52.

——— and David Crowley, eds. *Style and Socialism: Modernity and Material Culture in Postwar Eastern Europe.* Oxford, 2000.

Remington, Thomas. "Institution Building in Bolshevik Russia: The Case of "State *Kontrol'*." *Slavic Review* 41: 1 (1982): 91–103.

Rimmel, Lesley. "Another Kind of Fear: The Kirov Murder and the End of Bread Rationing in Leningrad." *Slavic Review* 56: 3 (1997): 481–99.

Roberts, Mary Louise. "Gender, Consumption, and Commodity Culture." *The American Historical Review* 103: 3 (June 1998): 817–44.

Rodin, S. G. *Kadry sovetskoi torgovli.* Moscow, 1968.

Rogger, Hans. "Amerikanizm and the Economic Development of Russia." *Comparative Studies in Society and History* 23: 3 (1981): 382–420.

Rosenberg, William. "Workers and Worker's Control in the Russian Revolution." *History Workshop* 5 (1978): 89–97.

Rossmann, Jeffrey J. *Worker Resistance under Stalin: Class and Revolution on the Shop Floor.* Cambridge, MA, 2005.

Ruane, Christine. "Clothes Shopping in Imperial Russia: The Development of a Consumer Culture." *Journal of Social History* 28: 4 (1995): 765–82.

———. "Clothes Make the Comrade: A History of the Russian Fashion Industry." *Russian History/Histoire Russe* 23 (1996): 311–43.

Rubinshtein, G. L. *Razvitie vnutrennei torgovli v SSSR.* Leningrad, 1964.

Schrand, Thomas. "Soviet 'Civic-Minded Women' in the 1930s: Gender, Class, and Industrialization in a Socialist Society." *Journal of Women's History* 11: 3 (1999): 126–50.

Scott, James C. *Weapons of the Weak: Everyday Forms of Peasant Resistance.* New Haven, 1987.

Siegelbaum, Lewis H. *Stakhanovism and the Politics of Productivity in the USSR, 1935–1941.* Cambridge, 1988.

———. " 'Dear Comrade, You Ask Us What We Need': Socialist Paternalism and Soviet Rural 'Notables' in the Mid-1930s." *Slavic Review* 57: 1 (1998): 107–32.

——— and Andrei Sokolov. *Stalinism as a Way of Life.* New Haven, 2000.

Siegelbaum, Lewis H. and Ronald Grigor Suny, eds. *Making Workers Soviet: Power, Class and Identity*. Ithaca, 1994.

Slater, Don. *Consumer Culture and Modernity*. Cambridge, 1997.

Smith, Steve. "Popular Culture and Market Development in Late-Imperial Russia." In *Reinterpreting Russia*, eds. Geoffrey Hosking and Robert Service. London, 1999.

———— and Catriona Kelly. "Commercial Culture and Consumerism." In *Constructing Russian Culture in the Age of Revolution, 1880–1940*, eds. Catriona Kelly and David Shepherd. Oxford, 1998.

Solomon, Peter H., Jr. "Criminal Justice and the Industrial Front." In *Social Dimensions of Soviet Industrialization*, eds. William G. Rosenberg and Lewis H. Siegelbaum. Bloomington, 1993.

Spiekermann, Uwe. "From Neighbour to Consumer: The Transformation of Retailer–Consumer Relationships in Twentieth-Century Germany." In *The Making of the Consumer: Knowledge, Power, and Identity in the Modern World*, ed. Frank Trentmann. Oxford, 2006.

Stearns, Peter. *Consumerism in World History: The Global Transformation of Desire*. New York, 2001.

Steiner, Andre. "Dissolution of the 'Dictatorship over Needs'? Consumer Behavior and Economic Reform in East Germany in the 1960s." In *Getting and Spending: European and American Consumer Societies in the Twentieth Century*, eds. Susan Strasser, Charles McGovern, and Matthias Judt. Cambridge, 1998.

Stitziel, Judd. *Fashioning Socialism: Clothing, Politics and Consumer Culture in East Germany*. Oxford and New York, 2005.

Teuteberg, Hans J. "Food Adulteration and the Beginnings of Uniform Food Legislation in Late Nineteenth-Century Germany." In *The Origins and Development of Food Policies in Europe*, eds. J. Burnett and D. Oddy. London, 1994.

Thurston, Robert W. "Reassessing the History of Soviet Workers: Opportunities to Criticize and Participate in Decision-Making, 1935–1941." In *New Directions in Soviet History*, ed. Stephen White. Cambridge, 1992.

————. "The Stakhanovite Movement: Background to the Great Terror in the Factories." In *Stalinist Terror: New Perspectives*, eds. J. Arch Getty and Roberta T. Manning. Cambridge, 1993.

Tiersten, Lisa. "Redefining Consumer Culture: Recent Literature on Consumption and the Bourgeoisie in Western Europe." *Radical History Review* (Fall 1993): 117–59.

————. *Marianne in the Market: Envisioning Consumer Society in Fin-de-Siècle France*. Berkeley, 2001.

Timasheff, Nicolas. *The Great Retreat: The Growth and Decline of Communism in Russia*. New York, 1946.

Trentmann, Frank. "Civil Society, Commerce, and the 'Citizen-Consumer'." In *Paradoxes of Civil Society: New Perspectives on Modern German and British History*, ed. Frank Trentmann. Oxford and New York, 2000.

————. "Bread, Milk and Democracy: Consumption and Citizenship in Twentieth-Century Britain." In *The Politics of Consumption: Material Culture and Citizenship in Europe and America*, eds. Martin Daunton and Matthew Hilton. Oxford, 2001.

————, ed. *The Making of the Consumer: Knowledge, Power, and Identity in the Modern World*. Oxford, 2006.

———— and Flemming Just, eds. *Food and Conflict in Europe in the Age of the Two World Wars*. Houndmills, Basingstoke, 2006.

Trifonov, I. Ia. *Likvidatsiia ekspluatatorskikh klassov v SSSR*. Moscow, 1975.

Trotsky, Leon. *The Revolution Betrayed: What is the Soviet Union and Where is it Going?* New York, 1937; Reprint 1972.

Turovtsev, V. *Narodnyi kontrol' v sotsialisticheskom obshchestve*. Moscow, 1974.

Turovtsev, V. I., ed. *Gosudarstvennyi i obshchestvennyi kontrol' v SSSR*. Moscow, 1970.

Viola, Lynne. "Bab'i Bunty and Peasant Women's Protest During Collectivization." *The Russian Review* 45: 1 (1986): 23–42.

————. *Peasant Rebels Under Stalin: Collectivization and the Culture of Peasant Resistance*. New York and Oxford, 1996.

Vitukhnovskaia, Marina. "'Starye' i 'novye' gorozhane: migranty v Leningrade 1930-x godov." In *Normy i tsennosti povsednevnoi zhizni: stanovlenie sotsialisticheskogo obraza zhizni v Rossii, 1920–1930-e gody*, ed. Timo Vikhavainen. Saint Petersburg, 2000.

Volkov, Vadim. "The Concept of *Kul'turnost'*: Notes on the Stalinist Civilizing Process." In *Stalinism: New Directions*, ed. Sheila Fitzpatrick. London and New York, 2000.

Weiner, Amir. "Nature, Nurture, and Memory in a Socialist Utopia: Delineating the Soviet Socio-Ethnic Body in the Age of Socialism." *The American Historical Review* 104: 4 (October 1999): 1114–55.

West, Sally. "The Material Promised Land: Advertising's Modern Agenda in Late Imperial Russia." *The Russian Review* 57: 3 (1998): 345–65.

Williams, Rosalind. *Dream Worlds: Mass Consumption in Late Nineteenth-Century France*. Berkeley, 1982.

Wood, Elizabeth A. *The Baba and the Comrade: Gender and Politics in Revolutionary Russia*. Bloomington, 1997.

Zaleski, Eugene. *Planning for Economic Growth in the Soviet Union, 1918–1932*. Trans. and eds. Marie-Christine MacAndrew and G. Warren Nutter. Chapel Hill, 1971.

Index

administrative-command economy, 7
advertising, 8–9, 33, 40, 160
  see also window displays
All-Union Central Council of Trade
  Unions (VTsSPS), 76, 98, 121
All-Union Central Union of
  Consumer Cooperative Societies
  (Tsentrosoiuz), 8, 20, 27–8, 46, 57,
  62, 83, 90, 130, 156
all-union inspectorates, 120
antimaterialist aesthetic, 8
anti-Semitism, 5, 162, 169–71
Arbat, 58, 62
artisanal manufacturing, 5, 29, 54
Artiukhina, A. V., 33, 193n.92
asceticism, 5, 6, 18, 36, 135, 175
"Asiatic" retailing, 22, 53, 54
Atlantic and Pacific Tea Company
  (A&P), 54

backwardness
  association with women, 70, 72, 76,
    78, 88, 110
  overcoming, 2, 9, 31, 42, 53
Bakaleia food shops, 61, 62, 101
"Big Deal," 10
body politic, 48, 113, 165, 169
Bogda, Valentina, 38
Bolotin, Z. S., 32, 40, 54–5, 92,
  94, 96
Bon Marché, 47
Borisova, Serafima, 89, 95, 99, 108,
  110, 111
Buckley, Mary, 102
bureaucracy, 21, 25, 27, 104, 113, 131,
  144
byt', new, 9, 193n.92

canned goods, 17, 32, 40, 94,
  135, 169
capitalist dream world, 2–3
"catch up to and overtake," 9, 31,
  46, 52

Central Asia, 42, 71, 139–40
Central Control Commission (TsKK),
  116
chain stores, 48, 62, 151, 162, 171
Chatterjee, Choi, 110
child care, 84–6
  and women's employment, 84, 85
children consumers, mobilizing, 176,
  177
children's goods, 34–5, 134, 138,
  156–7
  letters about, 141
citizen-consumer identity, 157, 166,
  168, 170, 173, 174, 177, 181, 182
Civil War, 4, 7, 10, 64, 122
class, 6, 10, 14, 20, 26, 47–8, 113
closed trade, 26–7
clothing, 6, 9, 32, 34, 39, 40, 42, 43,
  55, 60, 82, 88, 94, 107, 111, 135,
  139, 153, 154
Cohen, Lizabeth, 228n.17, 229n.36
Cold War, 16, 183
collective-farm (*kolkhoz*) trade, 27,
  28–9, 135, 164, 177
collectivization, 4, 7, 15, 29–30
Communist Youth League, *see*
  Komsomol
complaint and suggestion books,
  142–5, 223n.37
conferences, 93, 137–8, 140, 224n.56
  customer conferences, 145–9, 156,
    165, 176
constructivist artists, 9
consultations, with consumers,
  137–40
  see also conferences
consumer
  activists, 167, 168, 173
  crisis, 1–2, 17, 19–21
  criticism, 135, 141, 157, 177; letters
    in the Soviet press, 140–2
  demand, 3, 30–1, 42, 140, 148, 152;
    study of, 93, 137

consumer – *continued*
  economy, 114, 141, 154, 181; state
    intervention in, 15, 162, 163,
    165, 170
  educating, 93, 94
  needs, 19, 136, 140, 157, 159, 177,
    179
  participation and voices, 134–5,
    137–57, 176
  and party-state, relationship
    between, 157, 174, 179
  regime's emphasis on, 176, 181–2
  rights, 169–70, 180; mobilization
    of, 165–78
consumer citizenship, 137, 169, 176,
  178
consumerism, 2–3, 8–10, 18–19, 31,
  34, 36, 37, 43, 95, 111
consumption, 8, 29–31
  as bourgeois, 8
  contradictory attitudes, 9
  freedom of, 10, 172, 175
  kul'turnost' (culturedness), 39–43,
    156
  legitimization of, 9, 29, 136–7, 139
  making socialist, challenges in, 4–10
  mass, *see* mass consumption
  official discourse, 8–9
  politicization of, 9, 14–15, 16,
    152–6, 181–2
  socialist objectives, 31–8
control from below, 143
  see also complaint and suggestion
    books; *kontrol'*
corruption, 25, 64, 78, 126, 128
cultured consumption, 39–43, 80,
  156
cultured trade, 22, 27, 40, 91, 95, 96,
  97, 108, 124, 129, 132, 136, 151,
  152
  promotion, 49, 79, 164
culturedness, *see kul'turnost'*
customer conferences, 93, 137–8,
  145–9, 156, 165, 176
customer service, 23, 39, 49, 92, 177
  cultured/good, 61, 68, 79, 96, 101,
    115, 123, 136, 151
  poor, 25, 126, 128, 143, 152, 182
  Stakhanovism, 92–4, 95

de Grazia, Victoria, 158, 159
democratization, 6, 9, 19, 132
Deutsches Frauenwerk (German
  Women's Work), 174
Dikhtiar, G., 30
distribution of goods
  mechanical, 22, 26, 61, 106
  rationalization of, 59–62
Diukanov, M., 42
division of labor, 74, 107
  gender-based, 82–3, 220n.101
Drakulić, Slavenka, 1
drunkenness on the job, 77–8,
  204n.48
Dunham, Vera, 10

egalitarianism, 60, 133, 153
Epshtein, M., 53, 55, 60, 64, 65, 104,
  112
Eskimo ice cream, 95
European retailing methods, 48, 139
  adoption of, 22, 47

famines, 3, 30, 180
fascism, 106, 161, 162, 226–7n.3
Feder, Gottfried, 169
Federova, N., 84
feedback, *see* consultations, consumer
  participation and voices
female collective farmers
  (*kolkhoznitsy*), 156
First Five-Year Plan, *see under*
  Five-Year Plans
First World War, 6, 159, 161, 163, 164,
  166, 227n.7
  consumer activism during, 166–7
Five-Year Plans
  First, 2, 3, 7, 9, 18, 29, 30, 36, 72, 175
  Second, 5, 24, 29, 30, 31, 135, 175,
    181, 192n.76, 215n.20
foreign experiences, 46–7, 52, 54, 56
  retail devices, machinery and
    fixtures, 46, 49–52
  see also individual countries
foreign stores, 6, 48, 50–1, 54, 56
France, 47, 68
free trade, 22, 160, 163, 172
  in Britain, 167, 168, 227n.7
  failures of, 167

Gastronom stores, 61, 62, 151
Gatovskii, Lev, 23
Germany, 47, 68, 161, 163
   see also Nazi Germany
Goering, Hermann, 173
goods exhibits, 138–40, 148
Great Britain, 47, 160
   consumer citizenship, 178
   consumers' rights, 167–8
   free trade, 167, 168, 227n.7
   mobilization of consumers, 166,
      167, 171
   regulation of retailing, 161, 163,
      164–5, 168, 171–3
   women's role, 173–4
Great Depression, 161, 173
"Great Retreat," 10
Gronow, Jukka, 61
Gudvan, A. M., 67
Gumnitskii, T., 52, 54, 55, 56

heavy industry, 19, 51, 63, 87, 89
Hellbeck, Jochen, 215n.28
Hessler, Julie, 4, 208n.3, 230n.58
Hilton, Marjorie, 186n.17
Hilton, Matthew, 168
Hitler, Adolf, 169
Hoffmann, David, 193n.99
Holquist, Peter, 113
home delivery, 59, 153
House of Fashions, 138
housewives, 12, 34, 80, 146, 149–50,
      154, 174, 176, 202n.11
   activists and controllers, 123–4, 155–6

Iakovleva, V. Ia., 96
industrial modernity, 181
industrialization, rapid, 2, 4, 5, 7, 9, 15,
      18, 19, 36, 39, 46, 69, 72, 89, 114
interwar era, 15, 121, 147, 160
   consumer economy, 165
   consumer representation, 167–8
   economic collapse, 161
Isaev, I., 59
Italy
   regulation of retailing, 152, 161

Jews, 5, 162, 170
   see also anti-Semitism

Kaganovich, Lazar, 40, 117, 130
Kharkhordin, Oleg, 220n.122
Khinchuk, L. M., 91, 98
kolkhoz, see collective farm
kolkhoznitsy, see female collective
   farmers
Komsomol (Communist Youth
   League), 116, 118, 119, 120
kontrol' (monitoring and regulation)
   as function of state, 112–14,
      116–18, 163–4
   extension and logic of, 114–19
   from below, 113, 116–17, 143
   infrastructure, 119–22
   limits of, 126–31
   mass participation, 112, 113,
      115–16, 118, 123, 133
   official discourse, 116–19
   results of, 126, 128–33
   and social hygiene, 112–13
   and social integration, 113–14,
      131–3
   Soviet *Kontrol'* Commission, 120
   and Soviet subjectivity, 113, 125–8,
      131–3
   trade employees' reaction to, 127–9
   and trade unions, 117–18, 121, 123,
      130, 143, 217n.51
   as transformative, 113, 117–19,
      123, 125
   types of, 113–25
   wife activist groups and, 125
   women and, 122–5, 127
Kuibyshev, V., 31
kul'turnost' (culteredness), 36, 39–43,
      45, 50, 78, 88
   association with women, 78–80
   consumption, 39–43, 156
   modelling, 95–6
   promotion, 9, 73, 154, 156
   Stakhanovism, 90, 95, 96, 111

labor heroes, 68, 73, 86, 207n.112
   see also Stakhanovism
Lenin, Vladimir Ilyich, 22–3, 71, 117,
      118, 123, 125, 190n.32, 218n.62
   emphasis on drawing women into
      kontrol', 122
   on workers' inspection, 117

Liamin, V., 104
luxury goods, 8, 31–2, 47, 95

Macy's, 46
Magnitogorsk Metallurgical
　Complex, 2
Makarova, M., 155
marketing, 8, 47, 57, 161, 168,
　171
　techniques, 159
Marx, Karl, 175
mass consumer culture, 6, 179
mass consumer goods, 29–30
mass consumption, 2, 5, 6, 31, 48,
　158, 159, 167, 170, 179, 194n.117
mass culture, 159
mass motorization, 169
mass participation, 2, 86, 126, 165
　in *kontrol'*, 112, 113, 115–16, 118,
　123, 133
mass politics, 159
mass production, 3, 5, 30, 32, 153,
　158, 159, 192nn.84,85, 196n.12
material conditions
　of citizens, 9, 10, 16, 29–30, 36–7,
　42, 169, 175, 183
materialism, 2, 5, 6, 9, 68, 136, 152
Mikoian, A. I., 24, 25, 42
model stores, 61–2
　Bakaleia, 61, 62, 101
　Gastronom, 61, 62, 151
　Stakhanovite retail workers, 101
modern welfare state, 159
modernization, 32, 46, 49, 163
　of retailing, 6; via mechanization,
　51, 62–3
Molotov, V. M., 28, 42, 194n.112
monitoring and regulation, *see*
　kontrol'
Moroz, G., 52, 53, 95, 96, 98, 182
Moscow Central Department Store, 57
Moscow metro, 2, 30
Moscow–Volga Canal, 2
mother and children's corners, 39, 71
mystery shoppers, 124, 180, 181

Nalatova, A., 152–3
Narkomvnutorg, *see* People's
　Commissariat of Domestic Trade
national minorities, 42, 139

National Recovery Administration
　(NRA), 167, 170, 172
Nazi Germany, 47, 160
　consumer citizenship, 178
　mobilization of consumers, 167,
　169–70, 171–2
　racialist consumer politics, 170,
　171, 172
　regulation of retailing, 161, 162,
　163
　women's role, 173, 174
Nepmen/Nepwomen, 7, 8, 9,
　175
New Deal, 163, 170
New Economic Policy (NEP), 7, 10–11
New Soviet Person, 9, 11, 35, 78, 114,
　128, 135
new Soviet consumer, making of,
　14–15, 134, 157
newspapers
　as consumer feedback option, 140
　letters in, 151
non-wage earning women,
　mobilizing, 12, 73, 74, 122, 131,
　202n.11
Nosov, V., 26

official discourse, 9, 19, 136
　about acquisition of modern
　consumer goods, 32
　about consumption, 8–9
　about equality, 70
　about *kontrol'*, 119
　about motherhood, 154
　about Soviet consumerism, 31
　about Stakhanovism, 99
　about trade employees, 90
　about women, 73, 75, 76, 80, 82,
　86, 123
Olenev, P. A., 150
Osokina, Elena, 20, 26, 28n.66, 195n.11

Party Congresses
　Seventeenth, 22, 36, 90, 116, 119,
　121, 215n.17
　Sixteenth, 21
Pavlovich, A., 42
peasants, 6, 9, 12, 28, 31, 37, 41–2, 74,
　94, 117, 135
people's car, the *Volkswagen*, 169

People's Commissariat of Domestic
    Trade (Narkomvnutorg), 24, 27,
    50, 62, 83, 85, 91, 98, 101, 108,
    114–15, 130, 141, 143, 145
    courses for Stakhanovites, 108
People's Commissariat of Food
    Industries (Narkompishcheprom),
    24, 32
People's Commissariat of Foreign and
    Internal Trade, 18
People's Commissariat of Foreign
    Trade, 18
People's Commissariat of Internal
    Affairs (NKVD), 120
People's Commissariat of Labor,
    121
People's Commissariat of Light
    Industry, 139
People's Commissariat of Supply
    (Narkomsnab), 18, 24, 62
"perestroika" of retail trade, 44, 45, 65
    resistance to, 64
piece goods (*shtuchnye tovary*), 58–9
Piggly Wiggly, 46, 57, 199n.85
Plotnikov, I., 31, 41
political police, 112–13, 120
politicization of consumption, 9,
    14–16, 152–6, 174, 179, 182
prepackaging of goods, 51
prices, standardization of, 44
Printemps, 46
PRKGT, *see* Trade Union of
    Cooperative and State Trade
    Workers
procuracy, 113, 120, 216n.37,
    221n.123
product exchange, 18, 23, 24, 26
productivity, 91–2
    and economic growth, 23

rationalization, 61
    of display of merchandise, 55–7
    of external and internal design of
        stores, 53–5
    of organization of distribution,
        59–62
    of sales process, 57–9
rationing, 20, 24–6, 40, 50, 161,
    166
Rees, E. A., 215n.16

refrigeration, 50–1, 64
Remington, T., 214n.15
repression, 11, 12, 48, 76, 106, 116,
    133
retail modernity, 160
retail trade
    challenges in making socialist,
        4–10
    cooperative and state, 7–8, 20–2
    feminization of, 13–14, 68–88,
        105, 110
    infrastructure, 4–5, 45, 49, 51, 52, 64
    mechanization, 49–52
    modernization, 53–5
    private, 4, 18, 23, 114, 164
    rationalization, 44, 46, 49, 53–63
    reorganization, 27–8
    standardization, 44, 47, 53, 54, 57
    see also cultured trade; stores; Soviet
        trade
Revolution from Above, 159, 174
Roosevelt, Eleanor, 167
Roosevelt, Franklin, 168
Russian Federation Consumer
    Protection Act in 1992, 180
Russian intelligentsia, 6

salesclerks/retail workers, 5–6,
    12, 40, 55, 67–8, 92, 136–7,
    152, 175
    feminization of, 67–9, 86, 88, 105,
        110
    and Stakhanovism, 89–92, 95–9,
        105, 107, 109–10
sanitation, 50, 64, 124, 126,
    163, 164
    women's attention to, 78–9
scientific rationalism, 45, 55, 65
Sears and Roebuck, 54
Second Five-Year Plan, *see under*
    Five-Year Plans
self identification, 109, 125, 131–2,
    182
self-policing, 114, 117, 126
Selfridge, 46, 47
Semenychev, I., 104
semi-prepared food, 32–3, 135,
    192n.89
Seventeenth Party Conference,
    23–4, 29

Sheinman, V., 108
Shereshevskii, M., 56
Shinkarevskii, N., 50, 59, 147
shopping, 1, 8, 16, 48, 58, 60, 111
  self-service, 57–8, 199n.85
Shtange, Galina, 17–18
Siegelbaum, Lewis, 110
Sinclair, Upton, 162–3
Smirnov, M. P., 51, 54, 106
Soviet consumerism, 3, 10, 18, 19, 31,
    36, 152, 157, 175, 176
  legitimacy of, 34, 42
  official discourse, 31
  promotion, 94, 95
  see also new Soviet consumer
Soviet dream world, 2–3, 10–15, 19,
    112, 135, 181, 182, 188n.36
Soviet *Kontrol'* Commission, 120
Soviet merchandise
  accessorizing, 55, 61
  advance ordering, 59
  assortment, 17, 20, 44–5, 60, 65, 91,
    100, 107, 128, 138, 142, 151
  bundling, 44
  display of, 55–7, 79, 95–6
  ensembling, 55–6
  quality of, 1, 8, 13, 17, 31–5, 57, 80,
    94, 96, 100–1, 128, 137–8, 151
Soviet press, 37, 99, 106, 134, 137,
    140, 146
  customers' letters in, 140–2
  depiction of private traders, 7, 8, 9, 32
  emphasizing importance of
    conferences, 145
  underscoring women, 67–8, 81
Soviet trade (*sovetskaia torgovlia*)
  campaign for, 1, 3, 11, 15, 17–18,
    20–2, 43, 121, 180–1
  definition of, 22, 26–9, 45, 75, 79,
    90, 136, 164
  and increased consumption, 29–31
  and Stalinist revolution, 10–16
  see also retail trade; cultured trade
speculation, 25, 115, 129, 133, 164
Stakhanov, Aleksei, 89
Stakhanovism, 89–92
  actualization, in trade, 97–102
  benefits, 107–8
  campaigns, 99–100

  courses, 108
  cultured trade and, 91, 95–6,
    108
  hostility and, 102–5
  instructors, 101, 103–4
  labor heroes, 68, 73, 86, 207n.112
  modeling *kul'turnost'*, 95–6
  and Soviet consumerism, 93–4
  schools, 101–2
  trade unions, 98
  uses, 105–10
Stalin, Joseph, 21, 22, 24, 29, 31, 36,
    47, 90
  criticism of consumer
    cooperatives, 21
  formulation of socialism, 36
  legitimizing consumption, 29
  on rationing system, 25–6
  Revolution from Above, 159, 174
State Department Store (GUM), 8
State Inspectorate of Prices, 120,
    216n.40
State Trade Inspectorate (GTI), 118,
    120, 129, 144
state
  interventionism in consumer
    economies, 158–65, 168, 173,
    177–9
  regulation of retailing, 160–5
stores
  Bakaleia food shops, 61, 62, 101
  closed, 25–7, 40
  Gastronom stores, 61, 62, 151
  mobile, 59, 62
  number/density, 4, 6, 62
  open, 27, 60
  specialized, 60–1, 62
  Stakhanovite, 98, 100, 101
  Torgsin stores, 191n.49
  types, 26–7, 60–2
  unit-price, 44–5, 62
  women's, 71
  see also retail trade
Strength through Joy (KdF), 170
Stushkov, V., 40, 60

Thompson, E. P., 166
Timasheff, Nicholas, 10
Tolokonnikova, A., 125

toys, 35, 38, 44, 94, 138, 155
Toys Committee, 35
trade campaign
　consumers' role in, 160, 165,
　　166, 172
　shortcomings of, 63, 105, 129,
　　182
　valorization of consumers' voices,
　　140–50, 181
　women's contributions to, 74, 75,
　　79, 86, 176
trade organizations' inspectorates,
　120
trade unions, 92, 116, 119, 141
　and *kontrol'*, 117–18, 121, 123, 130,
　　143, 217n.51
Trade Union of Cooperative and State
　Trade Workers (PRKGT), 74, 84–5,
　119, 121, 130, 138, 141, 217n.51
Tsarist regime, 4, 5, 6, 30, 37, 47, 67
　political police (*Okhrana*), 112
Tsentrosoiuz, *see* All-Union Central
　Union of Consumer Cooperative
　Societies

United States, 47–8, 52, 160, 167–8
　African-American consumers,
　　174
　consumer citizenship, 178
　consumers' rights, 168, 170
　mobilization of consumers, 167,
　　170–1, 173–4
　regulation of retailing, 161, 173
　women's role, 173
unpaid activists, 73, 81, 86, 117,
　124, 176
urban workforce, 5
urbanization, 4, 159
Uzbek/Uzbekistan, 42, 71, 78, 94, 139,
　142, 156, 194n.120, 219n.81

Veitser, I. Ia., 42, 50, 51, 52, 91, 94
visionary planning, 44, 49–52
Volk, 162, 171
Volkov, Vadim, 39

wage labor force, 4
　women in, 70, 73, 84, 86, 123, 152

War Communism, 10–11
Western Europe, 2, 14, 49, 68
　legislation, 162
wife-activists, 73, 116, 123–5, 154,
　218n.75, 219n.81
Williams, Rosalind, 2
window displays, 1, 47, 56, 57, 63, 65,
　114, 124, 142
women
　activist groups (*zhenskii aktiv*) in
　　stores, 81
　association with backwardness, 70,
　　72, 76, 78, 88, 110, 203n.21
　consumers, government
　　recognition of, 178–9
　as cooperative members, 71
　cultured behavior, 78–80
　domestic skills, 80–1
　employment, 68, 69, 72;
　　limitations, 71, 209n.113
　female Stakhanovite instructors,
　　104–5
　and *kontrol'*, 122–5, 127
　in leadership positions, 83–4
　mobilization of women's labor, 72–6
　Muslim, 71
　in the 1920s, 69–72
　official discourse, 73, 75, 76, 80, 82,
　　86, 123
　participation in customer
　　conferences, 146
　prostitution, 67
　recruitment efforts and their limits,
　　82
　retail workers, in Tsarist Russia, 67
　sexual harassment, 67
　Stalinist regime's approach to, 72,
　　73–4
Woolworth's, 46, 56
Workers' and Peasants' Inspectorate
　(Rabkrin), 116, 120, 214n.15,
　215nn.16,17, 216n.38, 218n.62,
　221n.123
　dissolution of, 121

Zelenskii, I., 46, 49, 59–60, 81, 118, 156
Zemliachka, P. S., 21
Zola, Emile, 47

LaVergne, TN USA
04 October 2009

159810LV00003B/71/P